Praise for *Living Well with Hypothyroidism*

"Vital for hypothyroid patients who want to get well, and for physicians who want them to do so." —Dr. John Lowe, director of research of the Fibromyalgia Research Foundation

Praise for Mary Shomon and *Living Well with Autoimmune Disease*

"This informative self-help manual is badly needed." —*Publishers Weekly*

"The truth, the whole truth, and nothing but the truth about autoimmune diseases from Mary Shomon, the woman who taught America about thyroid disease! Her book will enlighten you about how to diagnose, treat, and possibly even prevent autoimmune disease in yourself or someone you love. Mary has my highest respect for her careful research and the way she presents both the conventional and the alternative aspects in a way that anyone can understand." —Carol Roberts, M.D., director, Wellness Works Holistic Health Center

"Patients who are struggling to get diagnosed with or understand their autoimmune conditions will find Mary Shomon's book an extremely useful, essential resource to help them find the practitioners and treatment—both conventional and alternative—that will help them truly live well." —Stephen E. Langer, M.D., author of *Solved: The Riddle of Illness*

"Mary Shomon is more knowledgeable and has provided patients with more timely and comprehensive information about these conditions than most physicians. As a result of Mary's tireless work, many patients previously undiagnosed or inadequately treated are now getting the necessary tests and treatment they need." —Marie Savard, M.D., author of *How to Save Your Own Life*

"*Living Well with Autoimmune Disease* should not only prove inspirational for those afflicted with these mysterious conditions, but also offers solid, practical advice for getting your health back on track." —*Alternative Medicine* magazine

"*Living Well with Autoimmune Disease* is a much needed book. It gives hope to those who suffer from chronic illnesses. This is a wonderful book that provides information and solutions, and I would highly recommend this book to my patients." —David Brownstein, M.D., author of *The Miracle of Natural Hormones*

"At last, a book that helps people make sense of multiple mystifying symptoms, and offers a road map to proper diagnosis and the most effective treatments . . . a brilliant empowerment manual for finding the proper practitioners and moving forward in your life." —Richard Shames, M.D., and Karilee Shames, Ph.D., R.N., H.N.C., authors of *Thyroid Power*

"A must read book." —American Autoimmune Related Disease Association

Praise for Mary Shomon and *Living Well with Chronic Fatigue Syndrome and Fibromyalgia*

"Mary Shomon is a brilliant and compassionate patient advocate who has written a thorough and balanced book that will teach you how to get well now." —Jacob Teitlebaum, M.D., author of *From Fatigued to Fantastic*

"Mary Shomon has done it again! She has provided a unique, well-written, and user-friendly guide to the diagnosis and treatment of chronic fatigue syndrome and fibromyalgia, conditions that are generally ignored or mismanaged by conventional medicine. With a wealth of the latest scientific information and a wonderful personal touch, she empowers you to take control of your conditions. At the time when you need it most, she introduces you to FMS and CFS, helps you get diagnosed, and then provides you with all the tools you need to carefully craft your own comprehensive wellness and healing plan and confidently carry it out with the aid of your practitioners." —Hyla Cass, author of *Natural Highs*

"If you're one of the millions afflicted with fibromyalgia or chronic fatigue, or think you may be, start changing your life for the better now by reading this crucial book. There are very real answers that will help you even more than you dare to hope, and Mary Shomon has done an absolutely masterful job of providing them to you here." —Dr. Joseph Mercola, author of *The No-Grain Diet*

"Fibromyalgia and chronic fatigue syndrome confuse many doctors, and in turn they have difficulty giving good explanations to patients. Mary Shomon has been able to convert this 'medicalese' into simple talk that all patients can understand." —Kenneth N. Woliner, M.D., holistic family medicine practitioner

"*Living Well with Chronic Fatigue Syndrome and Fybromyalgia* is a must-read not only for those suffering from CFS and fibromyalgia but also for those practitioners who treat these illnesses. This book provides a road map and gives hope to those struggling with chronic illness." —David Brownstein, M.D., author of *The Miracles of Natural Hormones*

LIVING WELL WITH
Hypothyroidism

LIVING WELL WITH
Hypothyroidism

What Your Doctor

Doesn't Tell You . . .

That You Need to Know

MARY J. SHOMON

HARPER

NEW YORK • LONDON • TORONTO • SYDNEY

Neither the publisher; nor the author; nor any of the medical, health, or wellness practitioners, or thyroid patients quoted in this book takes responsibility for any possible consequences from any treatment, procedure, exercise, dietary modification, action, or application of medication or preparation by any person reading or following the information in this book. The publication of this book does not constitute the practice of medicine, and this book does not attempt to replace your physician or your pharmacist. Before undertaking any course of treatment, the author and publisher advise you to consult with your physician or health practitioner regarding any prescription drugs, vitamins, minerals, and food supplements, or other treatments and therapies that would be beneficial for your particular health problems and the dosages that would be best for you.

First edition published in 2000.

LIVING WELL WITH HYPOTHYROIDISM. Copyright © 2000, 2005 by Mary J. Shomon. All rights reserved. Printed in the United States of America. No part of this book may be used or reproduced in any manner whatsoever without written permission except in the case of brief quotations embodied in critical articles and reviews. For information, address
HarperCollins Publishers Inc.,
10 East 53rd Street, New York, NY 10022.

HarperCollins books may be purchased for educational, business, or sales promotional use. For information, please write:
Special Markets Department, HarperCollins Publishers Inc.,
10 East 53rd Street, New York, NY 10022.

Printed on acid-free paper

Library of Congress Cataloging-in-Publication Data

Shomon, Mary J.
    Living well with hypothyroidism: what your doctor doesn't tell you . . . that you need to know / Mary J. Shomon.—Rev. ed.
        p. cm.
    Includes bibliographical references and index.
    ISBN 0-06-074095-7
    1. Hypothyroidism—Popular works.   I. Title.

RC657.S56 2005
616.4'44—dc22   2004056837

            10   11   12   WBC/RRD   20   19   18   17   16

For Julia, the future

Nothing will ever be attempted if all possible objections
must first be overcome.

—SAMUEL JOHNSON

Action is the antidote to despair.

—JOAN BAEZ

It is not because things are difficult that we do not dare,
it is because we do not dare that they are difficult.

—SENECA

ACKNOWLEDGMENTS

I would like to thank Jon Mathis, my husband, who doubles as a contributing editor, for his total dedication to this book and our daughter, his good advice, his excellent brainstorming, his moral support, his backrubs after long days at the computer, and his love. I couldn't have done it without him!

I am so very grateful to my agents, Carol Mann and Gail Ross, who have helped make both the first and second editions of this book a reality. My greatest respect and admiration goes out to my editor, Sarah Durand, who has stood by this book since its inception. She intuitively recognizes the need for this book, and others like it, and is single-handedly advancing the mission of patient empowerment. She's also a superb editor, and has made this book far better for her insights and efforts.

There are so many doctors treating hypothyroidism who are out there, in the trenches, working with patients and treating hypothyroidism every day. I need to thank them all, for each and every one is a committed, caring, and smart physician. They believe that people with hypothyroidism deserve the best possible treatments and solutions. We should all be so lucky as to have these experts as our personal practitioners. Luckily, the next best thing is being able to benefit from the talent and knowledge they have so compassionately shared here in the book. So, without further ado, thanks to: Ken Blanchard, Ph.D., M.D.; David Brownstein, M.D.; Hyla Cass,

M.D.; Manelle Fernando, M.D.; Ted Friedman, M.D.; Dale Guyer, M.D.; Kent Holtorf, M.D.; Dr. Gina Honeyman-Lowe; Donna Hurlock, M.D.; Joe Lamb, M.D.; Steve Langer, M.D.; Kate Lemmerman, M.D.; John Lowe, M.A., D.C.; Ron Manzanero, M.D.; David Naimon, N.D.; Michael McNett, M.D.; Joseph Mercola, D.O.; "Doc Don" Michael, M.D.; Roby "Dr. Fitt" Mitchell, M.D.; Richard Podell, M.D., M.P.H.; Bruce Rind, M.D.; Carol Roberts, M.D.; Glenn Rothfeld, M.D.; Richard Shames, M.D.; Karilee Shames, Ph.D., R.N.; Dr. Brian Sheen; Robban Sica, M.D.; Sanford Siegal, D.O.; Bob Saieg, M.D.; Jacob Teitelbaum, M.D.; and Ken Woliner, M.D..

I must particularly single out my personal physician and friend, Kate Lemmerman, M.D., of the Kaplan Clinic in Arlington, Virginia. In addition to making excellent contributions to this book, Kate always amazes me with her open mind, caring spirit, medical talent, and her unique way with an acupuncture needle! I also wouldn't be standing tall without my trainer, Silvia Treves, or thinking calmly and clearly without Dr. Bob Umlauf.

I am indebted to James Strick, Ph.D.; Sandy Levy; Dr. Mike Fitzpatrick; Kelly Cherkes; Dana Godbout Laake; Swami Rameshwarananda; Cynthia White; David Elfstrom; Marge Tolchin; Mindy Green; Pat Rackowski; Julia Schopick; Dr. Sherrill Sellman; Dr. Viana Muller; Larry Ladd; Leonard Holmes, Ph.D.; Zafirah Ahmed, N.D.; Christina Puchalski, M.D.; Phylameana lila Désy; Dr. Barry Durrant-Peatfield; Dr. David Derry; Dr. Bruce Fife; Dr. Ann Louise Gittleman; Dr. Byron Richards; Karta Purkh Singh Khalsa; Miriam Kauk; Marie Savard, M.D.; and Ric Blake, who generously shared their thoughts, information, and research findings. And my unofficial health news bureau—Rose Apter, Kim Carmichael Cox, and James Scheer—are always there, making sure I don't miss any breaking medical or health announcements!

To the talented friends and colleagues who provide a wealth of support and assistance to me in my research, writing, publishing, and online work: Dr. William "Bud" Cline, Sharon Stenstrom, Kim

Conley, Beth Moeller, and Jody LaFerriere, I offer my heartfelt gratitude.

To my many friends, "in real life" and online, thanks to you all for bringing me encouragement and joy by phone and e-mail while I was glued to my computer writing this book. Special thanks to my spiritual sister and best friend, Jeannie Yamine, to Gen Piturro and Demo DeMartile, Faris Bouhafa, Mohammed Antabli, Jane Frank, Laura Horton, and all the wonderful Momfriends.

Thank you to my father, Dan Shomon; brother Dan Shomon, Jr.; in-laws Rus and Barbara Mathis; my aunt, Rita Kelleher, and my "favorite crazy cousins in New Jersey"—Ellen Blaze and Joan Kelleher—who are so supportive of my work. I'm blessed to have them in my lives. And much love to my mother, Patricia Rita Shomon, with me in spirit, who was so proud and supportive of my writing all of my life and, in particular, was integral to this book becoming reality.

And finally, I am forever grateful to the many thousands of people with hypothyroidism who have taken the time in the past eight years to contact me and share their wrenching, hilarious, tragic, infuriating, frightening, empowering—and always honest and heartfelt—stories for this book. While there wasn't space to include every word of every story, everyone who wrote has left an indelible mark on this project and has contributed an amazing amount of spirit, courage, energy, and passion to the book. I wrote this book *for* you, and I couldn't have written it *without* you. May you all live well!

CONTENTS

INTRODUCTION

He who enjoys good health is rich, though he knows it
not.

— ITALIAN PROVERB

Millions of Americans like you wake up each day with hypothyroidism, a condition you don't even know you have. You're fatigued, your hair is falling out, you're gaining weight and depressed. You don't even think to mention your symptoms to the doctor because you assume age, or not enough sleep, or too little exercise is to blame. Unfortunately, you don't recognize these problems as common symptoms of hypothyroidism, a condition that affects an estimated twenty million Americans, possibly even more. If you're a woman, you're up against a one-in-eight chance of developing a thyroid disorder during your lifetime. *When you're living with undiagnosed hypothyroidism, you aren't living well.*

Those of you who do mention your problems to the doctor may have a different experience. After reciting a list of symptoms right out of a Thyroid 101 textbook, you may be told by your doctor that you are suffering from depression, stress, PMS, menopause, old age, or, simply, that it's probably just "in your head." *If you're living with hypothyroidism and you've been misdiagnosed, that's not living well.*

Countless numbers of you are living unknowingly with hypothyroidism after treatments that your doctors already know can *cause* hypothyroidism. Some doctors actually forget to tell you that after you've had all or part of your thyroid removed due to Graves' disease, hyperthyroidism, nodules, or cancer, you will almost certainly need thyroid hormone replacement. If you've had radioactive iodine treatments or take antithyroid drugs to "kill" your overactive thyroid, your doctor may have forgotten to mention that hypothyroidism is usually the result. *Living with hypothyroidism that results from treatment for other thyroid conditions is not living well.*

Some of you suspect—often correctly—that you are hypothyroid, but you cannot get diagnosed. You have a long list of symptoms and a family history of thyroid problems, but you still can't even get a thyroid test. Sometimes your doctor is arrogant, sometimes ignorant; sometimes you come up against a system designed to avoid paying for medical tests. Whatever the reason, doctors repeatedly refuse to test you in the face of symptoms and history. Even if you manage to get tested, you risk being told that you're normal by doctors who believe that thyroid-stimulating hormone (TSH) test numbers don't lie—but patients, symptoms, medical history, and experience do. Your doctors rely on numbers on a page—ignoring common sense, direct examination, and overwhelming symptomatic evidence. *When you are living with undiagnosed and untreated hypothyroidism, it's impossible to live well.*

Once you are diagnosed with hypothyroidism, many of you—perhaps even a majority—do not feel well on the standard therapy. One Thyroid Foundation of America study found that up to two-thirds of hypothyroid patients still suffered symptoms—such as muscle pain, lethargy, weight gain, and depression—despite what doctors considered sufficient treatment. A survey I conducted in 2002 of nearly two thousand patients found that more than half indicated that they were not satisfied with their quality of life after treatment, and still suffered from a variety of debilitating symptoms. If my e-mail inbox is any indication, there are many of you who share these complaints. You're hypothyroid, you don't feel well, and your doctors say, "You're fine, there isn't anything else we can do for you." *Insufficient treatment that leaves you symptomatic is definitely not living well.*

Little helpful information is available. Many doctors, most of the other books about thyroid disease, the pharmaceutical company "educational brochures" and awareness programs, the thyroid patient foundations—they've all closed ranks and usually spout a standard party line: "Take your thyroid pill until your thyroid is in normal range, come back every year for a TSH test, and you're fine." The understanding is, you've got the condition, no point worrying how or why you got it, how to keep it from getting worse, or whether or not you actually feel well on the standard treatment. If you now have hair loss, depression, fatigue, weight gain, low libido, high cholesterol, or any of dozens of other unresolved symptoms that drastically affect your quality of life—symptoms you never had before your thyroid went bad—hey, what does *that* have to do with anything? You're probably lazy, eating too much, stressed out, not getting enough sleep, not getting enough exercise, getting older, have PMS, or are just plain old depressed. *Just live with it. Live with your hypothyroidism. This is not living well.*

Then there are those of you with special circumstances of hypothyroidism. If you have a baby born with congenital hypothyroidism or a child or adolescent who has become hypothyroid, you're given a prescription and sent on your way. You need information to ensure that your children *thrive* despite a disease than can profoundly affect their physical and intellectual development. You may be menopausal and need to know which thyroid symptoms can't be so easily written off to your menopausal status. You may be trying to get pregnant, are pregnant, just had a baby, or are breastfeeding, and facing the onset or worsening of thyroid problems. You desperately need information—information it's unlikely your doctor will share—to protect your own health and that of your baby, in order to ensure a healthy, normal pregnancy and child. If you are a thyroid cancer survivor who is hypothyroid due to thyroid cancer surgery, you face the special challenge of periodically going off thyroid hormone completely, allowing yourself to become extremely hypothyroid in order to ensure the accuracy of scans to detect cancer recurrence. Doctors provide little or no guidance, expecting that you will just accept living with the hypothyroidism. But there are ways to cope more effectively, to live as well as possible when going hypothyroid prior to a scan. *It's a lack of information that prevents you from living well.*

There are those of you who dare to ask questions. "Is there any thyroid hormone replacement besides levothyroxine?" "Is this really the best dose for me?" "What about the other drugs?" "How about alternative medicine?" You might be ignored, laughed at, patronized, or even in some cases fired as a patient. The consensus is that everything to be known is known, and there are no more questions to be asked, especially if a patient is doing the asking. Interestingly, some researchers have found that what have until recently been considered the "standard" treatments may not work as well as so-called alternative treatments for many patients. Instead of adopting better treatments, many doctors prefer to stick with what they learned decades ago in med school, or refuse to do anything differently until there are more studies, while patients suffer needlessly. You're expected to live with your hypothyroidism and not ask questions, quietly enduring. *Living a lifetime of silence, with your valid questions and health concerns unanswered, is not living well.*

Then, there's the future. What should we know—but don't—about diagnosing and treating hypothyroidism? What research is needed, who is looking at possible means of cure or remission, alternative drugs, and reevaluating optimum thyroid test values? What are some of the promising treatments that have yet to be formally studied? *These are questions that need to be answered—and must be investigated—if any of us is going to live well.*

Millions of people in the United States know that it's not enough to just live *with* hypothyroidism. It's time someone speaks up about how to live *well* with hypothyroidism.

■ Do You Need This Book?

An estimated twenty-seven million Americans alone have some form of thyroid disease. Almost all forms of thyroid disease lead to a single outcome: the condition of hypothyroidism—insufficiency of thyroid hormone due to an underactive, underfunctioning, nonfunctioning, partially removed, or fully removed thyroid.

This book is for you if:

- You strongly suspect you have thyroid disease, but are having difficulty getting a diagnosis by conventional means.
- You aren't sure if your various symptoms point to hypothyroidism, but you need to find out more.
- You've been diagnosed with hypothyroidism, told to take this pill and come back in a year, and want more information about how to live as well as possible with your hypothyroidism.
- You have been treated for Graves' disease, hyperthyroidism, nodules, a goiter, Hashimoto's autoimmune thyroid disease, or even thyroid cancer, and are struggling to feel well again.
- You are receiving what your doctor feels is sufficient treatment for your hypothyroidism, and yet you still don't feel well.
- You're an open-minded health practitioner looking for innovative ways to understand and help your hypothyroid patients.

Above all, this book is for you if you want to learn about living well with hypothyroidism from the perspective of empowered patients and caring practitioners.

■ About This Book

Living Well with Hypothyroidism is different. This is *your* book, written *by* a thyroid patient *for* other patients who are going through the familiar ups and downs of diagnosis and treatment.

Living Well with Hypothyroidism provides the information about hypothyroidism you probably won't find out from your doctor, pharmaceutical companies, patient organizations, or in other books about thyroid disease. I talk honestly, and without allegiance to any pharmaceutical companies or medical organizations, about the risks and symptoms of hypothyroidism, how to truly get a diagnosis, and the many treatments—conventional *and* alternative—to treat the condition and its unresolved symptoms. Ultimately, the book is about living well with hypothyroidism, having the knowledge, tools, and team of health practitioners who can ensure that you feel the best you possibly can.

In this book, you'll find out what your doctor won't tell you about risks, diagnosis, drugs, and alternative and conventional things that work—and don't work—to treat hypothyroidism and its symptoms. You'll also hear the voices of patients, real people who have struggled for diagnosis, learned to deal with doctors, tried different medicines, suffered setbacks, and enjoyed successes. Each person quoted in this book was determined to share his or her own story, ideas, humor, sympathy, hope, advice, and pain with you. I know you will recognize your own experiences, fears, and emotions, and be touched and moved by the incredibly honest and poignant stories from patients throughout the world. Above all, you'll know you are not alone.

■ My Disclaimer

I hope that what you learn in this book will help you decide what questions to ask, or what kinds of doctors to seek, or what types of therapies you might want to pursue. Although I research this subject every day, I don't try to be my own doctor or health practitioner. I ask questions, seek out caring, informed health care providers, and we work in partnership. I don't try to do it myself. Neither should you. So go find the conventional, holistic, integrative, alternative, complementary, or other practitioners to be your partners in wellness. And don't forget to show them this book.

■ My Hypothyroidism Story

Before I go any further, I think it might be useful to explain how I got interested in hypothyroidism. First, as I mentioned before, I'm not a doctor. I'm not a health professional. I have an international business degree from Georgetown University. I'm a writer. Somehow, along the way, my battle with my own health led me to manage a popular, patient-oriented Web site on thyroid disease and to launch the only monthly report on conventional and alternative thyroid-related health news and treatments. Ultimately, this has turned into a career as a health writer—including books, Web sites, newsletters, and magazine articles—and a role as a patient advocate.

Looking back, I'm fairly sure the onset of my thyroid problem occurred in early 1993, when I was thirty-two. As a teen and through my twenties, I never had a problem with weight gain. I ate what I wanted, and if I gained a few pounds, I lost it without much difficulty. I joke that in the "old days" all I had to do was cut out a package of chips with lunch every couple of days, switch to diet soda for a week or two, and I'd drop five pounds. I didn't exercise. I worked like a crazy person. I ate terribly. I also smoked a pack and a half of cigarettes a day for more than ten years.

I had about a ten-pound weight gain from age thirty to thirty-two, I grew from a size 6/8 to a size 8/10, but didn't worry much about it. Then in the winter of 1993, I published my first book. I was working an intense full-time job, then coming home and working late into the night on the new book. I had a new boyfriend. It was a period of several months of intense work/book/life excitement and stress, coupled with too little sleep, poor eating habits, and lots of cigarettes and caffeine. I ended up with the worst bronchial infection I'd ever had, which turned into a case of recurrent Epstein-

Barr virus (the virus that causes mononucleosis) so debilitating that I couldn't drag myself out of bed, couldn't go to work for a month, and was so foggy and depressed that I couldn't imagine ever feeling well enough to think clearly, much less return to work. I seriously wondered how I would even muster enough coherence to write a simple memo. I didn't have my thyroid tested at the time, but after looking at my symptoms, and talking to many others who describe similar health crises and resulting brain fog and depression, I believe this is when my thyroid problem started.

A year later—recuperated for the most part but still feeling tired—I started a slow but steady weight gain. I became engaged to my boyfriend in July 1994, and stopped smoking in September of that year. Then the weight gain escalated. I gained fifteen pounds between September and my wedding in January 1995, despite an extremely low-fat diet and thirty to forty-five minutes of exercise every night. I was a size 16 on my wedding day.

Disgusted with the weight gain and feeling increasingly depressed, I started smoking again. No weight lost, none gained, and I was still depressed. At that point, I felt dumpy, overweight, depressed, and then six months later, in July 1995, I started having trouble getting a full breath. The doctor thought I had developed asthma. At that point, I quit smoking—for good—and a few more pounds piled on. A month after I quit, the doctor decided to run some blood tests because I was again complaining that I didn't feel well. The doctor called a few days later and said that I had "low thyroid," and she'd called in a prescription for me. She put me on Thyrolar and said to come in about six weeks later for a checkup. I had absolutely no idea what a thyroid was or even where it was located.

After I was diagnosed, I continued developing all kinds of symptoms that mystified my doctor and me. My eyes were dry and gritty and my menstrual periods became heavier and more frequent. My skin started flaking. I had headaches. I asked if it could be the thyroid problem. My doctor wasn't sure about a direct connection, and sent me for second opinions from an infectious disease specialist, a pulmonary specialist, and an internist. I had an MRI. I had a consultation with an endocrinologist, who acknowledged that some of the symptoms I had probably *were* due to my thyroid. She ran an antibodies test—at my request—but said it wasn't necessary because it didn't matter *why* I was hypothyroid. I just was. The test revealed the antibodies that signal Hashimoto's disease. I asked what that meant, and the endocrinologist said it didn't change the treatment, so I didn't have to worry about it.

The endocrinologist said it was just coincidence that I was a size 8 who could eat anything I wanted before my thyroid went bad, and that less than a year later, I was thirty pounds heavier and barely staving off additional gain on even the most rigorous adherence to Weight Watchers. She suggested that the other symptoms would eventually relax. The way she put it was:

> *In four months or so, you'll look back and realize how much better you feel than you do now. It's going to be relative, and so gradual that it won't be dramatic. One day down the road, you'll just realize you feel better than you do now.*

So I waited my four months. And I still didn't feel quite well. Far better than before, yes, but still not right. So I read, and I read. And then I got a computer, and I surfed the Web. I started to disseminate information I found via the online Usenet newsgroup alt.support.thyroid, and to talk with other thyroid patients. And I found out that hair falling out, weird periods, difficulty losing weight, carpal tunnel syndrome, and depression were all utterly "normal" symptoms of hypothyroidism. Maybe some of the information wasn't what I *wanted* to hear, but I *needed* to hear it!

It was a revelation. Knowing what was and wasn't related to my thyroid was far better than not knowing. There were times I felt so sick that I secretly worried I had some incurable disease that the doctors had overlooked. Realizing that symptoms were related to the thyroid also gave me something to shoot for—fixing my thyroid—instead of running around taking pill after pill or visiting high-priced specialists for every supposedly new, but actually thyroid-related, symptom that appeared.

Later, I assembled a lot of my information and created my thyroid disease Web sites—http://thyroid.about.com—at the popular portal site About.com, and http://www.thyroid-info.com, this book's Web site and home for my thyroid newsletters, guides, and the latest developments. At the sites, I offer thousands of pages of information on thyroid disease, maintain an active bulletin board, and provide links to hundreds of online sources of conventional and alternative thyroid information. Back in July 1997, I also started a newsletter called *Sticking Out Our Necks* that offers the latest thyroid-related news on health, drugs, treatments, tests, companies, and alternative therapies for hypothyroidism and its symptoms. I expanded the newsletter, offering it also as a print version by regular mail in 2000.

In 1997, I assembled the hundreds of doctor recommendations I've received and created what is known as the Thyroid Top Doctors Directory, a state-by-state and international listing of the best doctors recommended by thyroid patients around the world. The Thyroid Top Doctors Directory still exists and is regularly updated; it is the only patient-recommendation database of thyroid doctors in existence.

And along the way, despite my hypothyroidism, I even succeeded at my most important project of all, giving birth to my wonderful daughter, Julia, in late 1997.

Every day for the past eight years I've studied as much as I can about thyroid disease and hypothyroidism, searched for information on conventional and alternative ways to diagnose and treat hypothyroidism, and turned around and put that information out via my Web pages, news reports, and guides. As part of my educational mission, I've answered many thousands of e-mails from people with hypothyroidism from the United States, Canada, England, Germany, Australia, Indonesia, Saudi Arabia, Peru, Pakistan, Brazil—

seemingly everywhere. Over and over again, people write, pouring out their hearts, sharing the same concerns, the same problems:

For five years, I suffered from increasingly debilitating symptoms, and no doctors ever correlated my list of symptoms as clear evidence of hypothyroidism. I was always feeling cold, I had unending fatigue, sometimes sleeping eighteen to twenty hours a night on weekends and twelve hours a night during the week, low blood pressure, allergy and sinus problems, bone and joint pain, depression, memory loss, a very sleepy state I now call brain fog, depression, and mood swings. You'd be moody too if you were constantly exhausted and often confused and overwhelmed by things that used to be crystal clear to you. In five years, I slowly evolved from a highly productive, very social, and caring person to someone who chose to be alone and felt like a failure in life. I was self-isolated— secretly feared that I had early Alzheimer's, or worse, undiagnosed cancer or another major illness. . . . —Alice

At the age of thirty, I thought I was dying inside. My cholesterol was 436. My doctor called me and asked, "What do you eat?" I told him I didn't eat that badly. He ran more tests and I asked him to check my thyroid. He said, "Okay, but I don't think that's it." Well it was. My TSH was 218! He said I should be in a coma. —Tracy

My family doctor referred me to a specialist, the head of the endocrinology department, suspecting hypothyroidism. I saw the specialist, complaining of my symptoms, including disgusting weight gain, depression, and lack of energy. He laughed at me and said that I was pregnant. I said, "No, I'm not . . . positively without a doubt I am not pregnant." He kept laughing, and said, "Yes, you are, I'll see you in nine months!" And he walked out of the room. That's it. I was in tears and angry when I left. I went the next day to my gyne-cologist's office, where a pregnancy blood test proved that I was not pregnant. I was referred to another doctor, who, based upon my skin, eyes, blood test, and reflexes, immedi-ately diagnosed me with Hashimoto's disease. I just want peo-ple to believe that they themselves know when their body is acting crazy. Find a doctor who will help—not think you are insane or pregnant! —LuAnn

When you receive dozens of e-mails like this every single day for years, it's obvious something is wrong, and someone needs to do something about it. That's why I wrote this book.

■ About the Internet

Throughout this book, there are references to Web sites, e-mails, and Internet-based resources. If you have access to the Internet, you can visit this book's Web site, at http://www.thyroid-info.com. The site features links to the Web sites mentioned in the book, organized as up-to-date links, along with updated information and late-breaking news.

I hope these references don't intimidate those of you who are not veteran Web surfers or who don't consider yourselves computer lit-erate. The Web has become an integral part of health research for many consumers, including me. But I wrote this book because I know that for every e-mail, bulletin board post, or fax I've received saying: "Help, I feel so alone" or "My doctor won't test me!" or "I'm gaining weight but my TSH is normal!" or "Why won't my doctor even *test* my thyroid?" there are so many more of you out there who are not online who face these same situations.

There are so many of us, millions actually. And we're finally go-ing to start talking out loud about what we have been suffering with alone, silently, for many years.

■ Challenging the Doctrine, Going Beyond the Conventional

In this book, I do express concerns about the mind-set, skills, and biases of some doctors, but I don't want you to think that I have a vendetta against doctors in general. I thank the heavens that there are doctors and practitioners who love medicine, who love the idea of caring for, healing, and curing patients. These wonderful doctors keep asking the right questions, keep looking for better answers, really listen to their patients, and are passionate about finding new ways to be our partners in the search for wellness. I have met many wonderful doctors and practitioners—including the experts who have contributed to this book, and those who care for me personally—and they are sympathetic, smart women and men whom I consider to be my friends, colleagues, and partners in wellness. They march to the beat of a different drummer, and think for themselves. I respect them completely.

Unfortunately, however, all doctors are not like them. Some doctors end up believing that they learned everything there is to be known about diagnosing and treating hypothyroidism back in med school—no matter whether that was five, fifteen, or twenty-five years ago. Scary, isn't it, that some medical professionals—the people we entrust with our lives and our health—can be so unwilling to change with the times?

You'll soon find out that many of the most forward-thinking and successful practitioners believe that relying on the TSH test as the way to diagnose hypothyroidism is an incomplete and ineffective approach that misses many cases of hypothyroidism. New research has dramatically changed the TSH blood test ranges used to diagnose and manage hypothyroidism—yet many practitioners don't know this, and are still diagnosing and treating patients according to old, outdated ranges. Other research has also demonstrated what many thyroid patients, myself included, have known for a long time—that some people don't feel as well on levothyroxine (Synthroid) alone as they do with the addition of a *second* thyroid hormone. This report was published in the *New England Journal of Medicine*. Other practitioners believe that natural, desiccated thyroid should be the primary treatment, because of its superior effectiveness with their patients. And in the midst of all these developments, the majority of doctors continue to rely exclusively on narrow interpretations of the TSH test for diagnosis, and solely use levothyroxine for treatment, condemning some people to undiagnosed or undertreated hypothyroidism and the poor health and diminished quality of life that comes along with it.

One woman with hypothyroidism asked me:

> *Why did the doctors stop listening to the patients' valid concerns and start ignoring total deterioration in health in order to devote themselves to the results of a test and treatment with only one drug?*

That is an important question, one that I try to answer in this book. The opinions of the mainstream, conventional medical establishment are well represented in the other books and patient-oriented pamphlets on thyroid disease. Pick up any pharmaceutical company pamphlet on hypothyroidism that you can get from many endocrinologists offices, buy one of the books offered by the various official thyroid groups and organizations, or visit one of their official Web sites, and you'll see the official accepted party line on hypothyroidism. Unfortunately, following the party line often leaves people desperate to feel well again.

The time is now for the millions of patients with hypothyroidism—people who actually have to live with the condition—to have a chance to be heard and, ultimately, to live well.

INTRODUCTION TO
THE REVISED EDITION

I am doing a lot of traditional, subversive things—like listening carefully to my patients.
— DONALD "DOC DON" MICHAEL, M.D.

When I first wrote this book, back in the late 1990s, I felt in some ways like a lone voice in the desert. There were a few books that talked about thyroid disease, but nothing that seemed to speak to the situation from the perspective of patients. Many publishers at the time weren't convinced that thyroid disease was of interest. I was so grateful that my publisher and editor saw the potential interest in thyroid disease, and were willing to take the risk of publishing this book.

Since that time, the book has gone into more than twenty printings. After this book spent months in the Amazon.com Top 100 Best Sellers list, a number of other books about hypothyroidism were rushed into production by other publishers. Rather than being concerned about the competition, I am thrilled. There is an epidemic of hypothyroidism out there, and the word needs to get out every way it can, and from many perspectives. This sudden surge of interest in hypothyroidism tells me that the publishers and the public are finally starting to get it. They are finally realizing that hypothyroidism is not just some easy-to-treat nuisance condition that plagues overweight, lazy, malaise-y middle-aged women, as some practitioners and members of the public wrongly believe. This ugly stigma surrounding hypothyroidism is lifting, and the awareness is starting to spread, as people begin to recognize that hypothyroidism affects more people in the United States than even diabetes, a far more visible condition that is constantly in the news.

But now, more than ever before, we need even more people and practitioners to become educated about hypothyroidism, and that is why it is time for the updated new edition of this book.

When the first edition was published, the "official estimates" of people with hypothyroidism were eight to ten million, but many of the organizations and experts I consulted said that they believed the number was more likely in the range of thirteen million. Then, a study known as the Colorado Thyroid Disease Prevalence Study was published in early 2000—about the time the first edition of *Living Well with Hypothyroidism* was released. The study looked at thyroid function in more than twenty thousand people, and based on their findings, estimated that there were as many as thirteen million Americans with *undiagnosed thyroid disease*. This study doubled the estimated total number of thyroid patients in the United States to a total of twenty-seven million. And since the vast majority of people with thyroid disease ultimately end up hypothyroid, these startling findings doubled the highest estimates of people with hypothyroidism.

And that's not all. The Colorado study used as its normal TSH reference the range of 0.3 and 5.1. But in late 2002, laboratory scientists, followed by the American Association of Clinical Endocrinologists, made a recommendation that the normal TSH range should be narrowed to 0.3 to 3.0, and that anything over 3.0 be considered hypothyroid. So the Colorado study, done before these new lab standards were recommended, actually missed millions *more* people with hypothyroidism.

And that is by the most conservative measures. Some innovative thyroid experts diagnose hypothyroidism and treat patients with TSH levels above 1.5 or 2.0. Yet others diagnose autoimmune hypothyroidism in patients with normal TSH levels, but elevated thyroid antibodies. So if you count those patients, that's millions *more* still with hypothyroidism.

Another interesting but disturbing finding from the Colorado study was that among those patients who were diagnosed as hypothyroid and taking thyroid medication, *only 60 percent were within the normal range of TSH*—again, using 0.3 to 5.1 as their range. The fact that 40 percent of patients, a number that translates to many *millions* of people, were diagnosed and already taking thyroid hormone—but not in TSH range—is of huge concern. These are patients who are likely not to feel well and have a host of symptoms—including weight gain, fatigue, depression, concentration and memory problems, infertility, even heart disease, and more—that are not being resolved by their thyroid treatment.

It's not acceptable that many millions of people with hypothyroidism are undiagnosed and untreated, and even those who are diagnosed have about a fifty-fifty chance of getting proper treatment. That's why there is no better time than now to reissue this book in an updated edition.

With increasing visibility, however, comes increasing conflict, and thyroid disease has become a bit of a minefield. On the one hand, prominent experts are quick to point out—so often and so automatically as to have become a mantra—that hypothyroidism is easy to diagnose and easy to treat. But these well-accepted new studies contradict that basic doctrine. If it's easy to diagnose, why are at least thirteen million people undiagnosed? And if it's easy to treat, why are almost half of all patients not even receiving treatment to return them to "normal" range, much less relieve them of their symptoms?

These are questions that I ask but that aren't answered by certain diehards in the mainstream endocrinology community. They have been, to put it mildly, extremely testy about being challenged in any way. And it's no secret that this book has seriously rankled mainstream endocrinologists, and some leaders of the thyroid and endocrinology professional organizations. Because I've dared to criticize them. I've suggested that they aren't always right. And I'm a patient—a *lay* person besides—so I don't have that right. I'm not a member of the medical tribe.

At one endocrinology meeting, a prominent, nationally known endocrinologist and officer of the organization opened an educational session for his fellow "thyroid experts" with some humor. His idea of hilarity? A David Letterman-like "Top Ten" list of "Top Ten Signs You Have a Crazy Thyroid Patient Walking Into Your Office." Number two was: "She comes in carrying a copy of Mary Shomon's book."

Yes, it's disturbing to know that when the endocrinology community gets together to learn, they start out by making fun of ill patients who are trying to get information to feel well. But they can make fun of me all they want! Because hearing that doctors say I'm "crazy," and that they dread patients who walk in carrying copies of my book is the *best* thing anyone could say. That means that I'm doing my job as a patient advocate . . . that the endocrinologists are taking notice, and that you will find information in this book that they *don't* want you to know! Interestingly, *not one* of these critics has ever mounted a legitimate, intelligent medical argument against the information I present. Not only is that lazy and unscientific of them, but it's quite illuminating. As Margaret Thatcher once said, "I always cheer up immensely if an attack is particularly wounding because I think, well, if they attack one personally, it means they have not a single . . . argument left."

Now, nearly five years after the first edition of this book was published, it's become even more evident that those physicians who want to protect the conventional, narrow-minded approach to thyroid diagnosis and treatment have run out of arguments. They don't have all the answers, and they resent it that patients are becoming educated, informed, empowered health consumers, willing to shop around to find the doctors who *do* have answers. Patients are hitting these doctors where it hurts—their pocketbooks *and* their egos—and what is the doctors' response? Instead of reasoned argument, they disparage their more innovative colleagues, they scoff at my book, they dismiss the information patients get on the Internet and from other books, and attack me personally.

Now, in case you think I'm taking it too personally, I'm not. If anything, I'm more encouraged than ever, because even as the narrow-minded diehards are becoming fewer, the number of physicians who are better prepared to diagnose and properly treat hypothyroidism is on the rise. In the past eight years, I've seen many doctors shift away from dogmatic "you're a lab value, not a person" decision making to practicing far more nuanced, patient-oriented medicine. Some of the innovative thyroid practitioners who weren't household names five years ago, like Dr. Ken Blanchard, have now become nationally known thyroid experts. Ken has even written his own terrific book, and has a new patient waiting list a mile long. There are many doctors' offices and wellness centers where my book is on display, and many doctors even tell their patients to read my book. And right here in these pages, you're going to meet many innovative, enlightened, and amazing practitioners who truly understand how to help us all live well.

The years since *Living Well with Hypothyroidism* was first published have been a rewarding, amazing journey. Many thousands of people have called, written, and e-mailed me to say that this book has helped them find the solutions that work for them, has helped them find the doctors who are their true partners in wellness, and helped them find the thyroid medications that truly relieve their symptoms. People have contacted me to say that *Living Well with Hypothyroidism* has allowed them, finally, to make peace with their health and get back to the business of living well. I've gotten many kind letters from doctors and practitioners, thanking me for writing the book. I am just overwhelmed by, and so grateful for, the support and kindness of so many wonderful people who make me realize that it is all worth it.

Ultimately, there is no greater gift for me than the knowledge that my book has, in even a small way, helped anyone to truly live well. And I hope that this second edition can reach out to even more people, and offer more hope for now and the future.

Live well.

PART I

1

What Is Hypothyroidism?

They do certainly give very strange, and newfangled, names to diseases.

— PLATO

The thyroid is not a particularly well-known or well-understood organ in the body. Some people have a vague idea of the thyroid as something in the neck that, when malfunctioning, makes you gain weight or develop a goiter. That's about all the information many people can muster.

The thyroid gland, however, is an essential organ, governing basic aspects of nearly every facet of your health. In the long term, you can't live without the hormones produced by your thyroid. Those hormones regulate the body's use of energy, an essential function to life and health.

■ What Is the Thyroid?

The *thyroid gland* is shaped a little like a butterfly, and is located in the lower part of your neck, in front of your windpipe. You'll know generally where the thyroid is located if you think of it as sitting be-

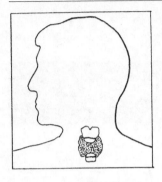

hind the Adam's apple, which usually sticks out farther from a man's neck than from a woman's.

The name "thyroid" comes from the Greek word *thyreoeides*, meaning "shield-shaped." The two "wings" of the butterfly are known as the *lobes* of the thyroid, and the area connecting the two lobes is known as the *isthmus*. It's a small gland, and normally weighs only about an ounce.

Roughly speaking, a *gland* is a discrete and separate soft body made up of a large number of vessels that produce, store, and release—or secrete—some substance. Your thyroid is one of these glands. Some glands secrete their products outside the body, some inside. Those that secrete their products on the inside of the body, and, more specifically, secrete hormonal and metabolic substances are known as *endocrine glands*. The thyroid is an endocrine gland, as are the parathyroids, the adrenal gland, the pancreas, and the pituitary gland. Diabetes, like thyroid disease, is considered an endocrine disorder. A doctor who specializes in treating patients with endocrine problems is called an "endocrinologist."

Hormones are internal secretions carried in the blood to various organs. The thyroid's main purpose is to produce, store, and release two key thyroid hormones, *triiodothyronine (T3)* and *thyroxine (T4)*. Thyroid cells are the only body cells that are able to absorb *iodine*. The thyroid takes in iodine, obtained through food, iodized salt, or supplements, and combines that iodine with the amino acid *tyrosine*, converting the iodine/tyrosine combination into T3 and T4. The "3" and the "4" refer to the number of iodine molecules in each thyroid hormone molecule. A healthy, functioning thyroid produces about 80 percent T4 and 20 percent T3. T3 is considered the biologically active hormone and is several times stronger than T4.

Thyroid hormones control *metabolism*—the process by which oxygen and calories are converted to energy for use by cells and organs. There's not a single cell in your body that doesn't depend on thyroid hormone for regulation and for energy in some form. And the T3 and T4 thyroid hormones have a number of functions as they travel through the bloodstream:

- Thyroid hormones help cells convert oxygen and calories into energy.
- Thyroid hormones help you properly process carbohydrates.
- Thyroid hormones aid in the proper functioning of your muscles.
- Thyroid hormones help your heart pump properly and effectively.
- Thyroid hormones help you breathe normally.
- Thyroid hormones help your intestinal system properly digest and eliminate food.
- Thyroid hormones help strengthen your hair, nails, and skin.
- Thyroid hormones help brain function properly.
- Thyroid hormones help with proper sexual development and functioning.
- Thyroid hormones help with normal bone growth.

The thyroid produces some T3, but the rest of the T3 needed by the body is actually formed from the mostly inactive T4 by the removal of one iodine molecule, a process sometimes referred to as *T4 to T3 conversion*, or by the more scientific term *monodeiodination*. This conversion of T4 to T3 can take place in some organs other than the thyroid, including the *hypothalamus*, a part of your brain.

Now that you have some idea of what the thyroid is and its location and function, let's look in more detail at how it fits into the overall functioning of the body.

The Thyroid Gland: Setting the Pace

When the thyroid works normally, it produces and secretes the amount of T4 and T3 necessary to keep many bodily functions at their proper pace. However, the thyroid does not do this alone. It works instead as part of a system that also includes the pituitary gland and the hypothalamus. The *pituitary gland* is another endocrine gland, located at the base of your brain.

Here's how the system works. The hypothalamus constantly monitors the pace of many of the body's functions. It also monitors and reacts to a number of other factors, including outside environmental factors such as heat, cold, and stress. If the hypothalamus senses that certain adjustments are needed to react to any of these factors, then it produces *thyrotropin-releasing hormone (TRH)*.

TRH is sent from the hypothalamus to the pituitary gland. The pituitary gland then produces a substance called *thyrotropin*, which is also known as *thyroid-stimulating hormone (TSH)*. The pituitary gland also monitors the body and can release TSH based on the thyroid hormones in the blood. TSH is sent to the thyroid gland, where it causes production, storage, and release of more T3 and T4.

Released thyroid hormones move into the bloodstream, carried by a plasma protein known as *thyroxine-binding globulin (TBG)*.

Now in the bloodstream, the thyroid hormone travels throughout the body, carrying orders to the various bodily organs. Upon arriving at a particular tissue in the body, thyroid hormones interact with receptors located inside the nucleus of the cells. Interaction of the hormone and the receptor will trigger a certain function, giving directions to that tissue regarding the rate at which it should operate.

When the hypothalamus senses that the need for increased thyroid hormone production has ended, it reduces production of TRH, the pituitary decreases production of TSH, and production of the thyroid hormone, in turn, decreases. By this system, many of the body's organs keep working at the proper pace. Think of the entire system as somewhat like the thermostat in your house. It's set to maintain a particular temperature, and when it detects that your house has become too hot, it signals to either stop blowing heat (or start blowing air-conditioning). And similarly, when the house becomes too cold, the heat will kick on (or the air-conditioning will turn off). Like a thermostat set to a particular temperature, your body is set to maintain a certain level of circulating thyroid hormone function.

■ What Is Hypothyroidism?

When your thyroid starts producing too much thyroid hormone and the balancing system doesn't function properly, then you become *hyperthyroid*. Your body goes into overdrive and speeds up, causing an increased heart rate, increased blood pressure, and burning more calories more quickly. Conversely, when the thyroid isn't functioning properly, or part (or all) of the thyroid has been surgically removed, you don't have enough thyroid hormone, and you become *hypothyroid*. Your body is moving on "slow" speed, usually with slowed thinking, slowed digestion, slowed heart rate and blood pressure, slower metabolism, lower body temperature, and you burn fewer calories and more slowly in daily living.

Dr. Sanford Siegal, an expert on weight loss, believes that the calorie burn is an essential factor in hypothyroidism. In his book *Is Your Thyroid Making You Fat?*, Dr. Siegal has said:

> *If the secretion of thyroid hormone isn't sufficient to cause the body to burn calories at a normal rate, it is hypothyroidism. If a "normal" amount of thyroid hormone is secreted but it doesn't achieve the calorie-consuming effect it should, we essentially have the same problem, and I still define it as hypothyroidism.*

■ What Causes Hypothyroidism?

Hypothyroidism is not really a disease unto itself, rather it's a condition in which there is insufficient thyroid hormone in the body, and you require thyroid hormone replacement to survive.

In primary hypothyroidism, the thyroid itself doesn't work properly, for a variety of reasons. Hypothyroidism most commonly results from the autoimmune disease Hashimoto's thyroiditis. Hashimoto's disease results when antibodies attach themselves to proteins in the thyroid tissue. The attachment process is a declaration of war to the rest of the immune system, and the thyroid is then invaded by immune cells that progressively destroy the hormone-producing thyroid tissue in a misguided effort to fend off the perceived invader.

One point of confusion that it's important to clarify: "Hashimoto's" and "hypothyroidism" are not interchangeable terms. Hashimoto's is a disease. Hypothyroidism is a condition. Hashimoto's is an autoimmune disease that *usually* causes people eventually to become hypothyroid. Hypothyroidism is a condition that can result from a number of causes and diseases.

In addition to Hashimoto's disease, hypothyroidism results from treatment for Graves' disease. Graves' disease is an autoimmune disease in which the thyroid goes into uncontrolled overproduction, or hyperthyroidism. Antithyroid drugs or radioactive iodine therapy are the typical treatments for Graves' disease. Sometimes Graves' disease requires surgical removal of the thyroid. All of these treatments partially or fully disable the thyroid's function.

In some cases, an enlargement of the thyroid, or thyroid nodules, causes the thyroid to overproduce thyroid hormone, also resulting in hyperthyroidism. Again, antithyroid drugs, radioactive iodine therapy, or even surgery are the typical treatments, usually resulting in hypothyroidism.

Sometimes nodules or goiters become large and unsightly, making it difficult to breathe or swallow. In these cases, all or part of the thyroid may be surgically removed, resulting in hypothyroidism.

Most people with thyroid cancer have their thyroid removed surgically, making them hypothyroid.

Other factors can also cause hypothyroidism. Severe deficiency of iodine, and in some cases too much iodine, can cause hypothyroidism. There are some drugs, such as lithium and amiodarone, that cause hypothyroidism. Radiation and cancer treatments to the neck and chest areas can frequently cause hypothyroidism. Pituitary tumors or imbalances can also cause hypothyroidism. A comprehensive look at the risk factors and causes of hypothyroidism is included in Chapter 2.

There is also a less conventional school of thought that identifies "cellular" hypothyroidism—hypothyroidism that may not be detected by classic blood tests, but still exhibits symptoms and responds to treatment. In these cases, it's thought that there is conversion failure—T4 is not converting to T3 properly—leaving cells starved for T3, the active hormone, and causing hypothyroidism. Some practitioners believe there may also be receptor uptake or "thyroid resistance" problems. Every cell has receptors where the thyroid hormone is meant to pass into the cell, but if there is a defect, problem, or dysfunction in the receptors, then the cells may be resistant to the thyroid hormone, and take up less than they should. Again, the end result would be hypothyroidism.

There is a tendency for people to identify themselves by the original disease, so patients will frequently say, "I'm not hypothyroid, I'm a Graves' patient" or "I don't have hypothyroidism, I'm a thyroid cancer survivor." But it's important to emphasize that while you may have started out with these diseases, the treatment you underwent—surgery to remove all or part of your thyroid, or radioactive iodine (RAI) treatment to deactivate your thyroid—almost always leaves you with a separate condition—hypothyroidism, which requires lifelong treatment. If you take prescribed thyroid hormone replacement drugs, you are hypothyroid.

■ How Is Hypothyroidism Traditionally Diagnosed?

Most conventional doctors rely on the TSH test to diagnose hypothyroidism. The TSH test is the sensitive blood test that measures the amount of thyroid-stimulating hormone—TSH—in your bloodstream. The test is sometimes also called the "thyrotropin-stimulating hormone test." Thyroid-stimulating hormone is released into the bloodstream by the pituitary gland, to tell your thyroid to release more thyroid hormone.

The TSH level remains in the normal range when the thyroid gland is healthy and functioning normally. Elevated TSH is considered indicative of hypothyroidism.

You'll need to know what the normal values are for the lab where your doctor sends your blood because "normal" varies from lab to lab. Thyroid normal ranges are in tremendous flux right now. During the 1980s and 1990s, throughout North America, the "normal" TSH range was from about 0.3–0.5 to 4.7–5.5. At the lab where they send my blood, for example, a TSH of over 5.5 is considered hypothyroid; under 0.5 it is hyperthyroid. Anywhere in between is considered "normal," or "euthyroid" (pronounced YOU-thyroid).

Values below the lower range can indicate hyperthyroidism, an overactive thyroid. Values above the top range indicate hypothyroidism, an underactive thyroid. The higher the number, the more hypothyroid you are, and therefore the less functional your thyroid is considered to be.

In November 2002, however, the National Academy of Clinical Biochemistry (NACB), part of the Academy of the American Association for Clinical Chemistry (AACC), issued new laboratory medicine practice guidelines for the diagnosis and monitoring of thyroid disease. Of particular interest were the following statements in the guidelines:

> *It is likely that the current upper limit of the population reference range is skewed by the inclusion of persons with occult*

thyroid dysfunction. . . . In the future, it is likely that the up-per limit of the serum TSH euthyroid reference range will be reduced to 2.5 mIU/L because >95% of rigorously screened normal euthyroid volunteers have serum TSH values between 0.4 and 2.5 mIU/L. . . . A serum TSH result between 0.5 and 2.0 mIU/L is generally considered the therapeutic target for a standard L-T4 replacement dose for primary hypothyroidism.

Based on these findings, in January 2003, the American Association of Clinical Endocrinologists (AACE) made the following important announcement:

Until November 2002, doctors had relied on a normal TSH level ranging from 0.5 to 5.0 to diagnose and treat patients with a thyroid disorder who tested outside the boundaries of that range. Now AACE encourages doctors to consider treat-ment for patients who test outside the boundaries of a nar-rower margin based on a target TSH level of 0.3 to 3.0. AACE believes the new range will result in proper diagnosis for millions of Americans who suffer from a mild thyroid dis-order, but have gone untreated until now.

Despite more than two years since the original NACB guidelines release, many laboratories have not yet adopted these new guidelines for normal range, and many physicians are either unaware of the AACE announcement or refuse to change their procedures until the labs revise their standards. This means that for a patient who tests above 3.0 or under 0.5, whether or not you get diagnosed and treated for hypothyroidism may depend on how up-to-date both your laboratory and practitioner are.

The idea that *low* TSH means hyperthyroidism/overactive thyroid function, and *high* TSH means hypothyroidism/underactive thy-roid—what people sometimes also refer to as "low thyroid"—can be extremely confusing. Keep in mind, the pituitary gland releases TSH

	HYPERTHYROID Numbers below range are usually considered Hyperthyroid (overactive)	LOW END OF THE RANGE (varies lab to lab)	TSH "NORMAL" RANGE Normal TSH Range means that the thyroid is considered "euthyroid," or normal, neither hyperthyroid nor hypothyroid.	TOP END OF THE RANGE (varies lab to lab)	HYPOTHYROID Numbers above range are usually considered Hypothyroid (under-active)
FORMER GUIDELINES*	Below 0.1 to 0.3	0.1 to 0.3	0.1 to 6.0	4.7 to 6.0	Above 4.7 to 6.0
NEW GUIDELINES, Per NACB and AACE, as of late 2002/early 2003	Below 0.3	0.3	0.3 to 3.0	3.0	Above 3.0

*Note: Many laboratories and practitioners are still using these outdated guidelines as of late 2004, and all evidence indicates that this will continue.

based on the amount of thyroid hormones in the blood. TSH is considered a messenger that says to the thyroid, "Produce more hormone." If you already have enough thyroid hormone, or even too much, there's no need for much TSH at all to deliver the "produce more hormone" message. You already have enough hormone, so TSH levels drop, and become *low*, when you're hyperthyroid. Conversely, if you don't have enough thyroid hormone because of an underfunctioning or nonexistent thyroid gland, more TSH will be produced in order to keep telling the thyroid, "Produce more hormone." This is why TSH levels are *high* when you're hypothyroid.

This also explains why doctors will cut your dosage if your TSH is too low, and they'll give you more thyroid hormone if your TSH is too high.

TSH tests done through your doctor's office can be expensive. They can run from $30 to $100 depending on the lab, and can cost even more if there are substantial markups by doctors' offices. Some endocrinologists have expensive analysis machines that can do a TSH test on the premises in a short amount of time, but most doctors send your blood to a lab for testing.

HYPOTHYROIDISM / UNDERACTIVE THYROID / "LOW" THYROID	HYPERTHYROIDISM / OVERACTIVE THYROID / "HIGH" THYROID
Thyroid gland is not producing enough thyroid hormone	Thyroid gland is producing too much thyroid hormone
Pituitary releases more TSH into blood to tell thyroid, "Make more thyroid hormone"	Pituitary stops releasing TSH into blood, lets levels drop below normal to tell thyroid, "Stop making thyroid hormone"
TSH GOES UP / HIGH TSH	TSH GOES DOWN / LOW TSH
Doctor raises thyroid dosage to return TSH to normal	Doctor lowers thyroid dosage to return TSH to normal

There are new, less expensive "instant" TSH tests now on the market. They are mainly used at health fairs, for on-the-spot screening. These tests mainly determine if your TSH is above "normal" range, with no specific assessment of the number itself. In my opinion, these tests might be useful for first-level, broad screening to uncover more serious hypothyroidism in people who otherwise would not be tested at all, but they should not be used for monitoring purposes.

You can get more accurate TSH testing done by using an FDA-approved home self-test. The Biosafe TSH test requires just a finger prick of blood, and you can order the test, send it back, and get results all by mail, very inexpensively. A number of companies, including HealthCheckUSA, also allow you to order your own thyroid laboratory panel directly. You get the blood drawn at a local lab—and in some cases, you can even order a lab technician to come to your home to do the blood draw. This can result in tremendous savings, especially if your doctor's office marks up tests significantly and your insurance won't cover the cost. Information on these self-ordered tests is featured in the Resources section of the appendix.

Other Blood Tests

Other levels are sometimes tested along with TSH. Be sure to ask your physician to provide you with the actual results, plus the lab's normal reference ranges, when you have any of these blood tests done.

- *Total T4/Total Thyroxine/Serum Thyroxine*—This measures the total amount of thyroxine in your blood. A low value can indicate hypothyroidism. Low T4 in combination with an elevated TSH can point to the thyroid itself as the cause of the source of the imbalance, while low T4 with normal or low TSH suggests that the problem is pituitary in nature. Total T4 levels can be artificially high at times, due to pregnancy, taking estrogen replacement or birth control pills, without hyperthyroidism.

• *Free T4/Free Thyroxine*—This test measures the amount of free, unbound T4 in your blood. Higher than normal values suggest an underactive thyroid, and lower than normal values suggest an underactive thyroid.

• *Total T3/Serum T3, Serum Triiodothyronine*—This measures the total amount of triiodothyronine in the blood. High T3 indicates an overactive thyroid. Low T3 suggests hypothyroidism.

• *Free T3, FT3*—This test measures the amount of free unbound T3 in your blood. Lower Free T3 suggests hypothyroidism.

• *T3 Resin Uptake*—When done with a T3 and T4, the T3 resin uptake test is sometimes referred to as the T7 test. This test helps determine whether variations in T4 and T3 are the result of a dysfunctional thyroid, or are related to the way the hormones are binding in the bloodstream. Results that are opposite—such as high T3 or T4 and low resin uptake, or low T4 or T3 and high resin uptake—suggest an underactive or overactive thyroid. Results that are the same—i.e., low/low or high/high—suggest that binding is the core problem.

• *Thyroglobulin Levels*—Thyroglobulin is a protein that is produced by the thyroid. With normal thyroid function, you would typically have low or undetectable thyroglobulin levels. Inflammation, as seen in thyroiditis or thyroid cancer, may also show up as elevated thyroglobulin.

• *Reverse T3 Test*—When the body is under stress, instead of converting T4 into T3—the active form of thyroid hormone that works at the cellular level—the body makes what is known as *Reverse T3 (RT3)*, an inactive form of the T3 hormone, to conserve energy. Some practitioners believe that even when stress is relieved, in some people the body continues to manufacture RT3 instead of active T3. This in turn creates a thyroid problem at the cellular level, yet the TSH lab values may well be normal. RT3 tests, therefore, have become more popular with open-minded doctors who are looking to assess a person's full range of thyroid function. RT3 can be measured with a blood test.

Antibodies Tests

Many doctors consider the TSH thyroid panel the only test needed for diagnosis of hypothyroidism. Some doctors, however, will test to determine if you have what are known as antibodies or antithyroid antibodies (sometimes abbreviated as ATA). An antibodies test determines whether you have an autoimmune thyroid problem. An autoimmune reaction is when the body acts as if one of its own organs is a foreign substance and tries to "attack" it. When this happens with your thyroid, antibodies are developed against your own thyroid that can either make it less able to function (Hashimoto's hypothyroidism) or send it into hyperfunctioning (Graves' disease/hyperthyroidism). The normal ranges for antibodies seem to vary somewhat at each lab, so be sure to find out what the normal range is for your doctor's lab.

Practitioner Robban Sica, M.D., has this to say about antibodies:

> I routinely check for anti-thyroid antibodies and am surprised by how frequently I find them, even in patients diagnosed by other doctors for hyper- or hypothyroidism.

The two most common tests for antibodies are:

• Antithyroid microsomal antibodies, also known as antimicrosomal antibodies, are often present in Hashiomoto's thyroiditis, indicating an active autoimmune process. More than 80 percent of people with Hashimoto's thyroiditis, for example, have elevated antimicrosomal antibodies in the bloodstream.

• Anti-TPO (thyroperoxidase) antibodies testing looks for antibodies to a thyroid-related enzyme. Their presence suggests thyroiditis, but their absence does not rule out Hashimoto's disease.

Dr. Gina Honeyman-Lowe, an expert in thyroid treatment, believes that testing for thyroid antibodies is essential. Says Dr. Honeyman-Lowe:

> I ask all our new patients to have thyroid antibodies checked as part of their initial evaluation. In some patients, thyroid antibodies can be elevated before we see changes in the TSH, or thyroid hormone levels. Suppression of the thyroid antibodies is necessary to avoid destruction of follicles in the thyroid gland, so rechecking the antibody levels is part of the monitoring process.

TRH Test

In the past, the TRH (thyrotropin-releasing hormone) test has been considered a particularly good blood test for detecting subtle underactive thyroid problems. In an article in *Alternative Medicine* magazine, Dr. Rafael Kellman called the TRH stimulation test the "gold standard for accurately detecting an underactive thyroid." Dr. Kellman found that when patients had three or more common hypothyroidism symptoms, some 35 to 40 percent actually tested normal on TSH, but evidenced hypothyroidism on the TRH test. While you may hear about this test occasionally, it is unfortunately not available in the United States, due to discontinued production of the TRH drug for injection. Practitioners have to rely on other means to assess subtle thyroid problems.

Imaging/Evaluation Tests

A variety of imaging and evaluation tests are sometimes used to rule out or diagnose various thyroid conditions, including hypothyroidism, and autoimmune thyroid disease.

• *Nuclear Scans/Radioactive Iodine Uptake (RAIU)*—This test involves taking a pill that contains a small amount of radioactive iodine (or other agents such as technetium). Several hours later, an

X-ray is done that can detect iodine concentrated in your thyroid. If your thyroid is overactive, it may take up higher amounts of iodine than normal, which is visible in the X-ray. If your thyroid takes up iodine, then the thyroid is considered "hot"—or overactive—and if it does not, then it's considered "cold"—or underactive. There are rare cases, however, where you can have a "cold" scan and still be hyperthyroid. This type of test can also show thyroid nodules, and whether they are taking up iodine. Hot nodules that take up iodine are rarely cancerous; however, 10 to 20 percent of cold nodules are malignant.

• *Thyroid Ultrasound*—Ultrasound of the thyroid is done to evaluate nodules, lumps, and enlargement of the gland, and to determine whether a nodule is a fluid-filled cyst or a mass of solid tissue.

• *CT Scan/Computed Tomography, CAT Scan*—This specialized type of X ray is not often used to evaluate the thyroid because it doesn't detect smaller nodules, but it is occasionally used to help evaluate an enlarged thyroid/goiter.

• *MRI/Magnetic Resonance Imaging*—MRI is done when the size and shape of the thyroid need to be evaluated. An MRI can't tell anything about the function, such as hyperthyroidism or hypothyroidism, but it may be done in conjunction with blood tests. It is sometimes preferable to X rays or CT scans because it doesn't require any injection of contrast dye, and doesn't require exposure to radiation.

• *Needle Biopsy/Fine Needle Aspiration/FNA*—This technique helps to evaluate lumps or nodules. In a needle biopsy, a thin needle is inserted directly into the lump, and some cells are withdrawn and evaluated. In some cases, ultrasound is used to help guide the needle into the correct position. Pathology assessment of the cells can often reveal Hashimoto's thyroiditis, as well as cancerous cells.

■ Alternative Tests

The Thyroid Neck Check

One self-test you can do to potentially detect some thyroid abnormalities is a thyroid neck check. To take this test, hold a mirror so that you can see your neck just below the Adam's apple and above the collarbone. This is the general location of your thyroid gland. Tip your head back, while keeping this view of your neck and thyroid area in your mirror. Take a drink of water and swallow. As you swallow, look at your neck. Watch carefully for any bulges, enlargement, protrusions, or unusual appearances in this area. Repeat this process several times. If you see any bulges, protrusions, lumps, or anything that appears unusual, see your doctor right away. You may have an enlarged thyroid or a thyroid nodule, and your thyroid should be evaluated. Be sure you don't get your Adam's apple confused with your thyroid gland. The Adam's apple is at the front of your neck; the thyroid is further down and closer to your collarbone. Remember that this test is by no means conclusive, and cannot rule out thyroid abnormalities. It's just helpful to identify a particularly enlarged thyroid or masses in the thyroid that warrant evaluation.

Basal Body Temperature Test

It's medically known that thyroid hormones have a direct effect on the basal, or resting, metabolic rate. And while hypothermia, or lowered body temperature, is a known and medically accepted symptom of hypothyroidism, the use of body temperature as a diagnostic tool is more controversial. The late Broda Barnes, M.D., made the public more widely aware of the use of axillary (underarm) basal body temperature (BBT) as a symptom and diagnostic tool for hypothyroidism. It is a diagnostic and monitoring method still used by some complementary and alternative practitioners.

To measure your BBT, use an oral glass/mercury thermometer or a special BBT thermometer available at some pharmacies. For glass thermometers, shake it down before going to bed, and leave it close by and within reach. As soon as you awake, with minimal movement, put the thermometer in your armpit, next to the skin, and leave it for ten minutes. Record the readings for three to five consecutive days. Women who still have their menstrual period should not test on the first five days of their period but can begin on day 5. Men, and girls and women who are not menstruating can test any time of the month.

If the average BBT is below 97.6 degrees Fahrenheit, some complementary practitioners would consider a diagnosis of an underfunctioning thyroid or insufficient thyroid hormone replacement. An average BBT between 97.8 and 98.2 degrees is considered normal. Temperatures from 97.6 to 98.0 degrees Fahrenheit are considered evidence of possible hypothyroidism, and temperatures less than 97.6 degrees can be even more indicative of hypothyroidism. Some practitioners, however, consider any temperature under 98 degrees to be indicative of hypothyroidism.

Use of basal body temperature is controversial, however, and even those practitioners who use the test caution that it should be part of an overall approach, and not solely relied upon. According to holistic thyroid expert and *ThyroidPower* co-author Dr. Richard Shames:

> For those who have already been diagnosed with hypothyroidism, the basal temperature test is an additional piece of observational measurement that helps determine whether a person is on the right medicine and/or the right dose, along with considering the response to medication, physical signs (especially ankle reflexes and skin temperature), and blood test results. . . . Temperature testing, however, is not infallible, and—like any other test—should never be used alone to rule in or rule out a thyroid condition, or to dictate therapy. This is simply a good piece of information that should be used wisely.

Saliva Testing

Saliva testing is another means of thyroid testing that some alternative or complementary practitioners use. I've talked with many practitioners, however, and have yet to find any who regularly use saliva testing for diagnosing or managing hypothyroidism. Even those practitioners who rely on saliva testing to evaluate adrenal function, or levels of hormones such as cortisol and progesterone, have yet to adopt saliva testing for thyroid function.

Urinary Testing

Some doctors who follow the approaches to diagnosis and treatment outlined by the late Dr. Broda Barnes use a twenty-four-hour urine collection test to evaluate for hypothyroidism. The test, which is evaluated by a laboratory in Belgium, measures the levels of T3 and T4 in twenty-four-hour urine samples. This is a controversial test, with some practitioners finding it useful, and others who say it's unproven and useless.

Thyroid and metabolism expert Dr. John Lowe has looked at these tests, and doesn't believe they are particularly valuable in diagnosing or monitoring thyroid function, as urinary T3 and T4 levels may also vary according to factors other than the effectiveness of the patient's thyroid gland in producing thyroid hormone. For example, says Lowe:

> [In one study,] researchers found that urinary T4 levels increased from 6 AM through 9 PM. The T4 level was lowest at night. The T3 level was increased in the urine only from 6 PM to 9 PM. In one study, physical and psychological stress increased the urinary excretion of T3 and T4. A patient's stress level may increase her urinary T3 and T4 levels by an unpredictable amount. If a patient remains stressed through the day and night, her excretion of T4 or T3 during that 24-hour time may be much higher than otherwise. The doctor would need to consider

this when interpreting the patient's urine test result. He'd also have to consider seasonal variations in the ambient temperature: Researchers found that the urinary excretion of both T3 and T4 was higher during the coldest months (January and February) and lowest during the hottest months (May–July). . . . Many factors, for example, nutritional deficiencies and poor diet, might alter the energy metabolism of tubule cells, and these factors might alter the T3 and T4 urine levels.

■ Prevalence

How common are hypothyroidism and thyroid disease? Officially, the American Association of Clinical Endocrinologists (AACE) 2004 estimates indicate that twenty-seven million Americans have thyroid disease—the majority of them undiagnosed. Most thyroid patients end up hypothyroid because the treatments for thyroid conditions, such as hyperthyroidism, Graves' disease, nodules, goiter, and thyroid cancer, usually leave patients hypothyroid. In addition, most people with Hashimoto's disease, the most common thyroid condition, eventually become hypothyroid as well. More than eight out of ten patients with thyroid disease are women, and women are five to eight times more likely than men to suffer from hypothyroidism. The AACE estimates that by age sixty, as many as 17 percent of women and 9 percent of men are hypothyroid.

The holistic medical community feels that hypothyroidism is underestimated, and that we are actually undergoing an epidemic. Some physicians believe that as many as 40 to 60 percent of the population experience subclinical or full hypothyroidism.

■ The Bottom Line?

While we understand what hypothyroidism is, there is no agreement on the actual number of people suffering from this condition, or how best to diagnose them—much less treat them. Those physicians on the front lines believe that there are far more than twenty-seven million people with thyroid conditions, and in particular, many more people with hypothyroidism than are typically estimated.

But one thing upon which all practitioners, both conventional and alternative, agree: There are many people with hypothyroidism who are not diagnosed. Let's turn our attention now to those risk factors that may contribute to becoming hypothyroid.

2

Are You at Risk for Hypothyroidism?

A jug fills drop by drop.

— BUDDHA

First, let's take a look at the various risk factors for hypothyroidism. Having one, or even many, of these risk factors does not necessarily mean you are or will become hypothyroid. But if you suspect you might be hypothyroid and have not been diagnosed yet, a review of the various factors that put you at risk can be an important diagnostic clue. Or if you *have* been diagnosed and wonder how you became hypothyroid, you may find some ideas here.

■ Risk Factors/Signs

A Family History of Thyroid Problems

If you have a parent, sibling, or child with any thyroid condition—including autoimmune thyroid problems, nodules, or goiters, or thyroid cancer—then you are at greater risk for developing a thyroid problem. Research shows that up to 50 percent of all first-degree relatives of people with autoimmune thyroid disease, in fact, will themselves have thyroid antibodies that may be a marker for later development of clinical autoimmune hypothyroidism.

It's likely that someone in your family has a thyroid problem and you don't know about it. He or she just doesn't mention it or is embarrassed to talk about it. For years, thyroid problems have been downplayed, misunderstood, stigmatized, and portrayed as unimportant. So it's not safe to assume you know about family thyroid problems unless you ask specifically and listen carefully.

If you ask your mother about diseases she's had, thyroid may never be mentioned. But ask about the thyroid specifically, and she might remember an episode of thyroid trouble after a pregnancy. Sometimes, your family member won't even refer to the thyroid. You might hear about a relative who is overweight because "she has a gland problem and has to take medication for it." Or a family member might tell you in passing that "goiters run in the family."

Ask questions. Ask about thyroid, goiters, metabolism, "glandular problems"—all ways people describe thyroid problems. If you suspect you might have thyroid disease, you might need to play detective a bit to get this sort of family history. In the face of a doctor who is reluctant to test your thyroid, however, a clear family history can be valuable ammunition in your search for a diagnosis.

Researching her family thyroid history, Nancy had this interesting conversation with her parents:

> I was having dinner with my folks, now seventy-five and seventy-six years old, and I was telling them of my week's events with the "Thyroid Adventure." I was asking them if they have ever had any history of thyroid problems. Dad said he just started taking thyroid meds for hyperthyroid condition, and Mom said, "Oh yes! My doctor had me on thyroid medication right after you were born in 1949 because I was anemic, but after we moved, which was a year later, I just quit taking it!" Okay, Mom, and you never thought about your low blood pressure, or the fact that you had to take a

nap almost daily and that you had an increasing weight gain for the next half century?

Needless to say, Nancy *and* her mother will be getting hypothyroidism treatment from now on.

A Personal History of Thyroid Problems or Irregularities

Having any thyroid problems in the past yourself puts you at greater risk for developing hypothyroidism. In some cases, your doctor may have told you that he or she was "monitoring" your thyroid because blood test results were inconclusive or borderline. Your doctor might have diagnosed a goiter or nodule, but decided it didn't warrant treatment. Some of you may not even remember the diagnosis, but know that years ago, you took thyroid hormone for a period of time. You may have had a short episode of thyroid trouble after a pregnancy, or after an illness, and may have had a diagnosis of something called "transient"—or temporary—thyroiditis or hypothyroidism. Past thyroid problems increase your chances of later developing hypothyroidism. A small percentage of people are born without a thyroid gland, or their thyroid gland is small, defective, or nonfunctioning. This is known as congenital hypothyroidism.

Treatment for Graves', Hyperthyroidism, Goiter, and Nodules

Amazingly, some doctors do *not* tell their patients that treatments that involve surgically removing or medically disabling the thyroid can result in hypothyroidism. Some people have all or part of the thyroid surgically removed to treat nodules, goiter, or Graves' disease. In other cases, thyroid treatment for hyperthyroidism can involve radioactive iodine (RAI) or antithyroid drugs, which make the thyroid either partially or fully inactive.

In most cases, treatment for Graves' disease, hyperthyroidism, goiter, or nodules leaves you hypothyroid.

Some of the literature given to patients overemphasizes the fact that everyone who has RAI does not necessarily become hypothyroid or need thyroid hormone replacement. It's true that some patients do not become hypothyroid after these treatments. In general, however, the vast majority do become hypothyroid and will need thyroid hormone replacement to avoid hypothyroidism symptoms.

If you have had thyroid surgery, RAI, or have taken antithyroid drugs, you should monitor yourself very carefully for the onset of hypothyroidism symptoms. At the same time, you will probably want to have regular TSH blood tests to monitor your thyroid function via your bloodwork as well.

Thyroid Cancer Surgery/Treatment

When you've had your thyroid removed in part or in full due to thyroid cancer, you become hypothyroid and require lifelong thyroid hormone replacement. You will be prescribed thyroid hormone for two reasons: first, to treat the resulting hypothyroidism and second, to prevent cancer recurrence. Most knowledgeable thyroid cancer experts recommend suppression of TSH into very low ranges as a way to prevent recurrence of the cancer. Patients having a scan to detect any cancer recurrence, however, are often required to periodically go off their thyroid medicine and experience hypothyroid symptoms because an elevated TSH is needed to get an accurate scan.

Pituitary Tumors and Pituitary Disease, Hypothalamic Disorders

A known cause of hypothyroidism is a problem with the hypothalamic-pituitary function, including diseases or tumors that cause pituitary failure and hypothyroidism. It's estimated that one out of every five adults worldwide may have a noncancerous tumor of their pituitary gland, and at least one-third of these pituitary tumors may be clinically active and causing significant health problems.

Family or Personal History of Other Autoimmune or Endocrine Diseases

If you or close family members have other autoimmune or endocrine diseases, you have a slightly increased chance of developing autoimmune thyroid disease.

One condition that is important to mention specifically is celiac disease/gluten intolerance, sometimes known as celiac sprue. Not only is hypothyroidism fairly common in celiac disease patients, but studies have shown that this particular autoimmune disease, which involves the inability to digest nutrients due to a severe allergy to gluten found in many grains, has been shown specifically to be the trigger for hypothyroidism in some people. When the celiac disease is diagnosed and treatment—a gluten-free diet—takes place, hypothyroidism can disappear in some patients.

There are also higher risks for thyroid conditions among people who have a personal or family history of:

- Insulin-dependent (type 1) diabetes
- Addison's disease
- Cushing's disease
- Polycystic ovary syndrome (PCOs)
- Premature ovarian decline/premature ovarian failure
- Alopecia
- Reynaud's syndrome
- Sjögren's syndrome
- Chronic fatigue syndrome (also known as CFS)
- Fibromyalgia

Other more common autoimmune or autoimmune-like conditions include rheumatoid arthritis, systemic lupus erythematosus (SLE), multiple sclerosis, sarcoidosis, scleroderma, vitiligo, and psoriasis.

Left-handedness and prematurely gray hair are both considered signs of increased autoimmune disease risk, and are also thought by some practitioners to be possible markers for increased hypothyroidism risk.

For more information about autoimmunity, including autoimmune thyroid diseases, I suggest you read my book *Living Well with Autoimmune Disease.*

Aging

If you are over sixty, chances are greater that your thyroid may become problematic than for a younger person. According to the American Thyroid Association (ATA), large population studies have shown that as many as one woman in every ten over the age of sixty-five has a blood level of TSH that is above normal, making her hypothyroid. According to the American Medical Women's Association, the elderly are more likely to suffer from hypothyroidism, and by age sixty, as many as 17 percent of women have an underactive thyroid. In the ever-confusing world of statistics, the American Association of Clinical Endocrinologists (AACE) states that thyroid problems affect one in eight women ages thirty-five to sixty-five and one in five women—20 percent—over sixty-five. Because the symptoms of hypothyroidism can be so similar to those related to aging, it is more difficult for doctors to spot thyroid disease in older patients.

Fertility, Pregnancy, and Hormonal Issues

Being a woman means you are more likely to develop thyroid disease than men. According to the American Medical Women's Association, women are five to eight times more likely than men to suffer from an overactive or underactive thyroid, and approximately one woman in eight will develop a thyroid disorder during her lifetime.

If you have had a baby in the past year, you are at increased risk for a variety of thyroid problems, including a short-term problem known as postpartum thyroiditis. Postpartum is also a time when underlying full-scale thyroid problems become evident and are diagnosed. Some doctors estimate that as many as 10 percent of women develop a thyroid problem after delivery. Most of these women have never had any thyroid problem in the past. Some doctors are now beginning to test carefully for hypothyroidism, as it often underlies cases of postpartum depression.

While some postpartum cases of hypothyroidism are temporary, the period after pregnancy is also a common time for permanent thyroid problems to surface. Bess was thirty-five and had just had her third child when she was diagnosed with postpartum hypothyroidism:

> At the time, I was still nursing my five-month-old son. Even though he was already taking baby food, he was still getting up in the night for feedings. I was exhausted, depressed, overweight, and looked terrible. My face was puffy and swollen, and I was always cold. I would wake up in the mornings and cry because I did not want to get out of bed. My mother urged me to see a doctor, but I dragged my feet thinking I was just unable to cope with my new infant and other children. I finally saw a doctor. He felt there was "nothing wrong with me that diet and exercise wouldn't help." However, he did run some blood tests. A couple of days later I received a call from my doctor. He needed to see me right away for a consultation in his office. That is when I found out why I was a wreck. He seemed surprised by my lab results, informing me that "I wasn't even on the charts," and that I was about as sick as I could be. Even though he explained what thyroid disease is, he felt confident that I would eventually be fine. . . . Anyway, here I sit taking Synthroid for the "rest of my life." So much for "postpartum."

Unfortunately, not all doctors are aware that there are periods when women are more prone to developing thyroid problems, such as after having a baby. One new mother who wrote to me had a doctor who clearly wasn't very informed:

> *When I went to the endocrinologist, he was adamant that I did not have a thyroid problem. His strongest statement was that "if you were hypothyroid, you could never have become pregnant."*

Miscarriage is associated in some cases with the presence of thyroid antibodies, high-normal levels of TSH, or underlying and undiagnosed hypothyroidism. The risk of miscarriage is higher when a woman is positive for antithyroid antibodies; some researchers estimate that the risk of miscarriage is twice as high. In addition, experts have found that the presence of antibodies prior to miscarriage may trigger the postmiscarriage onset of thyroid problems.

Menopause

At the start of the new millennium, an estimated fifty million American women had reached menopause, about 18 percent of the total U.S. population. Many menopausal women experience symptoms such as mood swings, depression, fatigue, weight gain, and sleep disturbances that are attributed to "menopause" but may in fact be due to undiagnosed thyroid problems. Unfortunately, according to a survey conducted by the American Association of Clinical Endocrinologists, only one in four women who have discussed menopause with their physician received a recommendation to be tested for thyroid disease.

Thyroid problems are known to surface at periods of hormonal upheaval and are more common just prior to or during menopause. As with aging, thyroid problems can be difficult to detect because symptoms are similar to menopause. If you're menopausal and having hormone levels checked, always be sure your doctor includes a thyroid TSH test as well.

Smoking and Smoking Cessation

If you are or were a smoker, you have an increased risk of hypothyroidism. Cigarettes contain thiocyanate, a chemical that adversely affects the thyroid gland and acts as an antithyroid agent. Researchers have found that smoking may increase the risk of hypothyroidism in patients with Hashimoto's thyroiditis.

If you have recently quit smoking, this may also be a time when underlying thyroid disease becomes apparent. Anecdotally, I have also heard from many women who, like me, were diagnosed with thyroid disease soon after they quit smoking. I've even wondered if there is a direct link, but that seems unlikely. More likely, I'd suspect that the nicotine "buzz" from smoking creates an artificially higher metabolism that hides the fatigue and exhaustion and weight gain commonly seen in hypothyroidism. When a smoker with underlying hypothyroidism quits, the full effects of hypothyroidism are felt, and the metabolism slows.

The nonsmoking advocates tell us that the average person gains no more than about four to six pounds after smoking. But hidden thyroid problems may explain why some who quit end up gaining far more than that. (Me, for example!) If you are a smoker with undiagnosed thyroid dysfunction, stopping smoking seems to be a metabolic/weight gain double whammy, as you lose the appetite-suppressing, metabolism-upping effects of nicotine and then experience the full effects of the hypothyroidism.

Of course, this is *not* a reason to continue smoking! You're still better off not smoking and gaining some weight than smoking. On my wish list? That the dangers of thyroid problems and the resulting lifelong battle with hypothyroidism and weight—on top of all the other dangers of smoking—were openly discussed with teenagers before they even start smoking.

Drugs

There are certain drugs that are known to have an effect on thyroid function, including causing hypothyroidism. Most common are the drug lithium, used to treat bipolar disease and other conditions, and the heart drug amiodarone (Cordarone). If you are taking these drugs now, or have taken them in the past, you are at increased risk for hypothyroidism.

Other drugs that may cause hypothyroidism in some patients include:

- Glucocorticoids/adrenal steroids like prednisone and hydrocortisone
- Propranolol, a beta-blocker
- Aminoglutethimide—a drug used for breast and prostate cancer treatment
- Ketoconazole, an antifungal
- Para-aminosalicylic acid, a tuberculosis drug
- Sulfonamide drugs, including sulfadiazine, sulfasoxazole, and acetazoleamide, which have been used as diuretics and antibiotics
- Sulfonylureas, including tolbutamide and chlorpropamide, used for diabetes drugs
- Raloxifene (Evista), a drug for osteoporosis
- Carbamazepine, oxcarbazepine, and valproate, drugs for epilepsy

Antithyroid drugs, including proplythiouricil (PTU), methimazole (Tapazole), and carbimazole can, of course, also cause hypothyroidism.

Iodine Imbalances

Severe iodine deficiency is known to cause hypothyroidism. Iodine deficiency is more common in countries that do not add iodine to salt (i.e., iodized salt), and in "Goiter Belt" areas—the mountainous or inland areas, including the Alps, Pyrenees, Himalayas, Andes, St. Lawrence River valley, Appalachian Mountains, Great Lakes basin west through Minnesota, South and North Dakota, Montana, Wyoming, southern Canada, the Rockies, and into noncoastal Oregon, Washington, and British Columbia.

At the same time, in populations where iodine deficiency is not as high a risk, such as the United States, where iodine deficiency is estimated to affect only 20 percent of the population, there is a greater risk of ingesting excessive iodine, from iodized salt, foods, and iodine-containing supplements. Too much iodine or iodine-containing herbs such as kelp, bladderwrack, or bugleweed can increase the risk of hypothyroidism.

Iodine deficiency in a pregnant woman, however, is a known factor causing thyroid problems, including hypothyroidism, in her baby.

Alcohol During Pregnancy

According to research reported on in the journal *Alcoholism: Clinical & Experimental Research*, alcohol consumption changes thyroid function and reduces the levels of thyroid hormone in both the mother and fetus. An animal study suggests that there may be strong links between thyroid function and alcohol-related birth defects. Researchers already know that children born to mothers with undiagnosed or undertreated hypothyroidism during their pregnancy can have a variety of abnormalities and birth defects, many similar to those seen in children with fetal alcohol syndrome. In the study, researchers discovered that the alcohol resulted in altered thyroid function in both mother and fetus.

Overconsumption of Goitrogenic Foods

There is a certain class of foods called "goitrogens" that can promote goiters and result in hypothyroidism by reducing the amount of iodine in the body that is available to help synthesize T4 and T3. Goitrogens are a concern only for people who still have a thyroid, and are considered a problem mainly when served raw or when overconsumed in large quantities. It's believed that thorough cooking may minimize or eliminate the goitrogenic potential. A list of some common goitrogenic foods includes Brussels sprouts, rutabaga, turnips, kohlrabi, radishes, cauliflower, African cassava, millet, babassu (a palm-tree coconut fruit popular in Brazil and Africa), cabbage, kale, soy products, horseradish, mustard, corn, broccoli, turnips, carrots, peaches, strawberries, peanuts, spinach, watercress, mustard greens, and walnuts.

Again, cooking reduces the thyroid-suppressing effects of most of these foods; and with foods that aren't typically cooked, the main concern is overconsumption. For example, people whose main dietary staple is millet are known to have higher risk of hypothyroidism, as are infants on a sole diet of soy formula.

Overconsumption of Soy Products

As noted, soy can have an effect on the thyroid. Because of its growing popularity as a food item, it deserves its own mention. Soy products, which have become increasingly popular due to a number of reported health benefits, also have a definite antithyroid and goitrogenic effect. Research is beginning to show that long-term consumption of soy products can promote the formation of goiters and the development of autoimmune thyroid disease. This is of particular concern for infants on a diet solely consisting of soy-based formula, but is also an issue for adults who regularly eat soy products in various forms, who take soy or isoflavone supplements, or who regularly use soy protein powders.

Environmental Exposures

Some experts feel that fluoride, such as that found in drinking water and toothpaste, and chlorine in drinking water can interfere with proper thyroid hormone conversion, and result in hypothyroidism. Their recommendation is to drink only distilled water to avoid this problem. This is a controversial recommendation, given that some health practitioners feel that children in particular need fluoride in order to avoid the risk of tooth decay and tooth loss. Other experts are concerned about excessive exposure to chlorine, typically found in chlorinated water supplies and swimming pools. There is also a concern on the part of some alternative practitioners that mercury, a component in dental fillings, can disable the thyroid's ability to convert T4 to T3, resulting in hypothyroidism.

X-Ray and Radiation Treatments

During the period from the 1920s through the middle of the 1960s, X-ray treatments to the head, neck, and chest were used for tonsils, adenoids, lymph nodes, and thymus gland problems, as well as for acne. There is a relationship between these treatments and irregularities in the thyroid gland, including hypothyroidism. Patients who have had radiation for head, neck, and throat cancers, either with or without chemotherapy, are at greater than normal risk of developing hypothyroidism. Among the patients evaluated in one study, within five years, 48 percent had developed hypothyroidism, and within eight years, the projected rate was 67 percent.

Nasal Radium Treatments

During the 1940s through the 1960s, "nasal radium therapy" was a treatment used for tonsillitis, colds, recurrent adenoid problems, and for military submariners and pilots who had trouble with changes in pressure. This treatment involved inserting a rod containing 50 milligrams (mg) of radium in the nose. The rod was pushed through each nostril and placed against the opening of the Eustachian tubes for six to twelve minutes. Repeated over a period of months, this would shrink tissues. An estimated sixty-seven thousand Marylanders received nasal radium therapy, and thousands of submariners, pilots, and children of military personnel got the treatments. In recent years, there have been apparent links between radium treatments and thyroid and other immune disorders and health problems.

Infection

There is a strong relationship between bacteria known as *Yersinia enterocolitica* infection, and Hashimoto's thyroiditis. *Yersinia* bacteria are found in the fecal matter of livestock and domesticated and wild animals. You can be exposed to *Yersinia enterocolitica*, therefore, via contaminated meats—especially raw or undercooked products—poultry, unpasteurized milk and dairy products, seafood—and particularly oysters—from sewage-contaminated waters, and produce fertilized with raw manure. Foods can also be contaminated by food handlers who have not properly washed their hands before handling food or utensils. Improper storage can also contribute to contamination.

Acute infection reportedly occurs most often in young children, where symptoms are typically fever, abdominal pain, and diarrhea. In older children and adults, right-sided abdominal pain and fever may be the predominant symptoms, and may be confused with appendicitis. In a percentage of cases, complications such as skin rash, joint pains, and arthriticlike symptoms can occur.

Researchers found that the prevalence of antibodies to Yersinia—evidence of exposure—was fourteen times higher in people with Hashimoto's thyroiditis than in control groups, leading to the conclusion that a sort of causative relationship exists between *Yersinia enterocolitica* infection and Hashimoto's thyroiditis.

Severe Snakebite

Not too many people will face life-threatening illness due to snakebite, but it's known that severe illness due to snakebite can result in pituitary damage that causes hypothyroidism. This is reported in people who suffered nearly fatal bites from some rare and highly poisonous vipers and rattlesnakes.

Neck Trauma/Whiplash

Some research has suggested that trauma to the neck, such as whiplash from a car accident or a broken neck, can result in hypothyroidism. Researchers speculate that this may be due to injury to the thyroid tissues themselves.

Nuclear Plant Exposure

Nuclear plants can accidentally release radioactive materials that are damaging to the thyroid. If you lived in or were visiting the area near the Chernobyl plant in the period after the nuclear accident—April 26, 1986—then you are at an increased risk for thyroid problems. The main countries at risk included Belarus, Russian Federation, and Ukraine. There is a risk, though reduced, to Poland, Austria, Denmark, Finland, Germany, Greece, and Italy.

You may also have been exposed to potentially thyroid-damaging radioactive materials if you lived near, or in the area downwind from the former nuclear weapons plant at Hanford in south central Washington State during the 1940s through the 1960s, particularly 1955 to 1965. Hanford released radioactive materials, including iodine-131, which concentrates in the thyroid gland and can cause thyroid disease.

During the 1950s and 1960s, approximately one hundred nuclear bomb tests were conducted at the Nevada Nuclear Test Site, northwest of Las Vegas. The fallout from the tests was most concentrated in counties of western states located east and north of the test site, such as Utah, Idaho, Montana, Colorado, and Missouri. Exposure to this fallout increases the risk of thyroid cancer, particularly in the Farm belt, where children drank fallout-contaminated milk. There are also cases of autoimmune thyroid problems in the United States that may be due to the iodine-131 released during these nuclear tests.

Connie's mother lived less than one hundred miles from the Nevada test site:

As a kid, my mother used to sit outside and watch the nuclear cloud float over her school. We even have home movies of her running after the "cloud." Not surprisingly, my mom now has thyroid problems I believe are directly linked to her exposure.

In the mid-1990s, the newspaper *The Tennessean* presented the results of an effort to investigate a mysterious pattern of illnesses that seem to have been concentrated around the Oak Ridge nuclear facility in eastern Tennessee. This same pattern was, according to the newspaper, repeated at other nuclear facilities in Tennessee, Colorado, South Carolina, New Mexico, Idaho, New York, California, Ohio, Kentucky, Texas, and Washington State. A number of the people interviewed for *The Tennessean*'s story reported thyroid-related illnesses they believe are a result of proximity to these nuclear facilities, and possible low-level iodine-131 exposure.

Perchlorate Exposure

Perchlorate is a chemical that blocks iodine from entering the thyroid, and prevents further synthesis of thyroid hormone. Perchlorate is a particular health concern for people with thyroid conditions, as well as for pregnant women and their fetuses. Hypothyroidism can result or be aggravated in persons who already have low thyroid function from exposure to perchlorate. Fetal and infant development can be retarded by exposure to perchlorate, including that contained in breast milk from a mother who is consuming drinking water containing perchlorate.

The source of perchlorate in the drinking water at many sites is the defense industry and the past production of solid rocket propellants and rocket fuel, with perchlorate as a by-product. Poor disposal practices, industrial accidents, and agricultural fertilizers are suspected as the sources of contamination of drinking water by perchlorate. Perchlorate has been detected in the public drinking water in at least twenty-two states. Produce grown in those states that use contaminated water for irrigation has reached around the nation.

Larry L. Ladd, a water-quality activist who lives next to America's largest rocket factory, is a key advocate for public awareness on the issue of perchlorate and its potential danger to the thyroid, and has brought perchlorate issues to national attention in the past decade. He points out that the concerns are not only for drinking water, but for produce irrigated by perchlorate-contaminated water, and especially produce irrigated with water from the tainted lower Colorado River. Crops that can contain high levels of perchlorate, according to Ladd, include:

> . . . most of the nation's winter lettuce, and a significant portion of the nation's avocados, lemons, and cantaloupes. Grapefruit, watermelon, broccoli, and onion production are also locally important for the west coast market.

Some experts believe that the safe level of perchlorate in drinking water should be set no higher than 1 part per billion. The United States Environmental Protection Agency (EPA), in a draft risk assessment made in 2002, suggested that levels higher than 1 part per billion pose a health risk, especially for fetuses and infants. In contrast, the U.S. Defense Department contends that perchlorate at 200 parts per billion has no lasting effect on humans.

Currently, eight states have advisories for perchlorate in drinking water, ranging from 1 to 18 parts per billion. Massachusetts is using the U.S. EPA guideline of 1 part per billion for its public drinking water standard, and has been advising pregnant women, children, and people with thyroid disorders not to drink water with higher perchlorate concentrations.

Exposure to Other Toxic Chemicals

Understanding how long-term exposure to toxic chemicals affects the thyroid is really just beginning. Scientists are beginning to study the effect of certain chemicals on our endocrine glands and the thyroid in particular. However, there's strong evidence that exposure to certain toxic chemicals may increase the risk of developing thyroid disease. Some chemicals of concern include dioxins, methyl tertiary butyl ether—known as MTBE—an oxygenate added to gasoline, and other chemicals that act as "endocrine disrupters."

One particular concern has been with various insecticides, including those used to treat airplanes, and popular insecticides used against the West Nile virus–carrying mosquitoes. Some of these pesticides include resmethrin, which goes by a brand name, Scourge, and sumithrin, which goes by the name of Anvil. Resmethrin and sumithrin, synthetic pyrethroid insecticides, are registered with the Environmental Protection Agency for use in mosquito control. In some people, allergic responses to pyrethroids have been reported. There are also indications that pyrethroids as a class may interfere with the immune and endocrine systems. Other adverse chronic effects, including effects on the liver and thyroid, have been reported in toxicology testing.

A long list of chemicals known to be disruptive or toxic to the immune system and/or thyroid-toxic is available at the Chemical Scorecard Web site, http://www.scorecard.org.

Other Factors?

There is no question that as researchers begin to understand more about the cause of autoimmune diseases, we'll find out more about how some thyroid diseases develop and why they seem to have become more prevalent in recent years. Deficiencies in certain vitamins, enzymes, or minerals, or overconsumption and overexposure to certain foods and chemicals, may be discovered to play integral roles in thyroid function and health. It's certain, however, that more chemicals in our water or our environment will definitely be linked to the rise in autoimmunity and thyroid dysfunction.

■ Conditions and Illnesses That Raise the Suspicion of Hypothyroidism

A number of conditions are more common in people with hypothyroidism, or may even be the triggers that caused hypothyroidism or the results of undiagnosed hypothyroidism. Some conditions are also more difficult to treat and/or resistant to standard medications when hypothyroidism is also present. When you currently have one of these conditions (particularly if it is not responding to treatment), or you have a history of a particular condition, then you have a greater possibility of being hypothyroid and should have your thyroid evaluated to rule out an underlying disorder.

Epstein-Barr Virus (EBV) and Mononucleosis

While the evidence is mainly anecdotal, some doctors suspect that there may be a relationship between having had Epstein-Barr virus (EBV) and/or mononucleosis, and later developing autoimmune thyroid disease. I had mononucleosis at seventeen and then had a very bad EBV flare-up when I was thirty-one. I suspect that the total exhaustion, and nearly two-month recuperation from the EBV, followed by the beginning of weight gain, was likely the onset of the thyroid problems for me. I have received many e-mails from people who also reported having had teenage cases of mononucleosis, only to have flare-ups of Epstein-Barr immediately preceding the diagnosis of hypothyroidism in adulthood.

Carpal Tunnel Syndrome, Tarsal Tunnel Syndrome, Tendonitis, Plantar Fasciitis

If you have carpal tunnel syndrome (CTS), there's a chance that it may be caused by hypothyroidism. CTS is what is known as a repetitive strain injury (RSI). In CTS the carpal tunnel—a tunnel of bones and ligaments in the wrist—pinches nerves that go to the fingers and thumb, with inflammation of tendons in the wrist. CTS can cause burning, tingling, pain, aching or numbness in the wrist, fingers, or forearm, as well as burning, especially in the thumb, index, and middle fingers. CTS can also make it difficult to grip, make a fist, or even hold a cup. A study in 1998 showed that many people with CTS might have unrecognized medical diseases, including hypothyroidism, as the cause of their CTS. If you have CTS (tarsal tunnel syndrome, which affects the legs), any form of tendonitis, or plantar fasciitis (pain in the balls and arches of the feet), but have not been diagnosed with or tested for thyroid disease, these new findings suggest that your doctor should order a thyroid function test—among other tests for other diseases implicated in these conditions, such as diabetes mellitus, and various arthritis conditions—before starting on other treatments for your CTS.

Polycystic Ovary Syndrome (PCOS)

Polycystic ovary syndrome (PCOS) is a common disease that affects about 5 percent of younger women. The syndrome is diagnosed when there are long-standing symptoms, such as ovulation problems, infertility, heavy/irregular/absent periods, high levels of male-type hormones (androgens), and small cysts around the ovaries. PCOS is also associated with insulin resistance and is more common in overweight women. Autoimmune thyroiditis and hypothyroidism are more common in PCOS patients.

Heart Disease/Mitral Valve Prolapse (MVP)

Having heart disease—the number one killer in America—means that there is a possibility of underlying hypothyroidism, because untreated or subclinical hypothyroidism can greatly increase the risk of developing a heart condition. One Dutch study, known as "The Rotterdam Study," found that older women with subclinical hypothyroidism were almost twice as likely as women without this condition to have blockages in the aorta. They were also twice as likely to have had heart attacks.

If you have been diagnosed with mitral valve prolapse (MVP), you also have a greater chance of also having autoimmune thyroid disorders such as Graves' disease and Hashimoto's thyroiditis. MVP is also sometimes known as "click-murmur syndrome," "Barlow's syndrome," "balloon mitral valve," or "floppy-valve syndrome." MVP is the most common heart valve abnormality. Some estimates point to two million or more Americans with MVP and most are women (about 80 percent). When you have MVP, one or both flaps of the mitral valve—one of the heart's four valves—are enlarged. Then, when the heart contracts or pumps, the flaps don't close properly, and small amounts of blood can leak backward through the valve and may cause a heart murmur. Typical symptoms of MVP are a pounding sensation, fast heartbeat, palpitations, fatigue, weakness, low tolerance for exercise, chest pain, panic attacks, headaches, migraines, sleeplessness, dizziness, fainting, intestinal problems, and shortness of breath.

I've always had fluttering heartbeat feelings, palpitations (especially after caffeine), shortness of breath, and other MVP symptoms, but my regular doctor had never heard anything unusual in my heart. My MVP was discovered by an internist during a physical. He prides himself on picking up hard-to-define murmurs. He listened to my heart for a few moments and detected the characteristic "click" of a prolapsing mitral valve. A trip to the cardiologist for an echocardiogram confirmed the murmur. The main thing I was told to do? Take antibiotics per his instruction before and after dental work and let any doctors know that I had MVP before surgeries so they can administer antibiotics. I also received a prescription for Atenolol, a beta-blocker. The cardiologist said I should take it if I was having palpitations that were noticeable or prolonged. I occasionally have used it since the diagnosis, but I do try to minimize my caffeine intake, as this seems to aggravate my MVP.

Down Syndrome

Hypothyroidism is more common in people with Down Syndrome, and most Down Syndrome patients should have their thyroid function periodically evaluated to rule this out. Miriam Kauk, mother of a daughter with Down Syndrome, had to fight to get her daughter tested, because the symptoms of hypothyroidism can be similar to those of Down Syndrome. Says Kauk:

> Some commonly recognized symptoms of Down Syndrome are a puffy face, swollen tongue, low muscle tone

(floppy), poor feeding, lethargy (lack of energy, sleeps most of the time, appears tired even when awake), persistent constipation, slow growth, thin hair, mental retardation. Every one of these is also a symptom of hypothyroidism in children. One of the biggest problems parents of Down Syndrome kids have is this brick wall we keep running into that says, "But Down Syndrome is supposed to be that way . . .

Mental Health Issues: Depression and Bipolar Disease

Depression is discussed in great depth in upcoming chapters, but it's important to note that ongoing depression, and particularly depression that is resistant to antidepressant treatments, can frequently be a symptom of hypothyroidism. As many as 52 percent of patients who suffer from major depression and do not respond to antidepressants have undiagnosed hypothyroidism. Once doctors add thyroid hormone treatment to the antidepressant, the depression often resolves.

Researchers have also found that there's a higher rate of autoimmune thyroid disease and hypothyroidism in people with bipolar disorder. This risk is separate from the increased risk some bipolar patients face when they take the drug lithium, which can cause or worsen hypothyroidism.

According to thyroid expert Ridha Arem, M.D., researchers who screened severely depressed patients for thyroid disease found that up to 15 percent of them have an underactive thyroid. The hypothyroidism was often low-grade, rather than severe. Another study found that nearly 20 percent of patients hospitalized because of severe depression had Hashimoto's thyroiditis.

Iron Imbalance Problems

Conditions related to iron levels in the blood are more common with hypothyroidism than in the average population. Iron-deficiency anemia—insufficient iron—is more common in people with hypothyroidism.

Hemochromatosis—an overload of iron in the bloodstream—is less common in general, but people with hypothyroidism are at higher risk for it. Hemochromatosis is not easy to diagnose, as it is not revealed in routine blood work, so doctors need to request specific tests to diagnose it.

Celiac Disease/Gluten Intolerance

Celiac disease is a disorder that causes the intestines to react abnormally to gluten, a protein found in wheat, rye, barley, oats, spelt, kamut, and other related grains. Celiac disease, which is sometimes referred to as celiac sprue, sprue, or gluten intolerance, makes it difficult for the body to properly absorb nutrients from foods. Symptoms include various intestinal difficulties, recurring abdominal bloating and pain; nausea; anemia; gas; tingling numbness in the legs; sores inside the mouth; painful skin rash on elbows, knees, and buttocks; cramping; hives; joint/muscle pains and aches; diarrhea; and constipation, among others. A study has shown that patients with autoimmune hypothyroidism have a far higher prevalence of celiac disease. In fact, undiagnosed celiac disease is part of the process that triggers autoimmune thyroid disease in some patients. In those where celiac disease is the trigger, researchers found that the various antibodies that indicate celiac disease—organ-specific autoantibodies (i.e., thyroid antibodies)—actually disappear after three to six months of a gluten-free diet, eliminating the autoimmune condition.

Infertility/Recurrent Miscarriage

Infertility issues as they relate to thyroid conditions are discussed at length in Chapter 15. But infertility and recurrent miscarriage are definitely more common in thyroid patients than in the general population.

Skin Problems

A number of skin problems are far more common in thyroid patients, and can be considered possible markers for hypothyroidism.

These include vitiligo, hidradenitis suppurativa, alopecia (hair loss), eczema, psoriasis, and urticaria (hives).

Vitiligo is an autoimmune condition that involves loss of pigmentation in various areas of the skin. Hidradenitis suppurativa involves painful and unsightly boils in the apocrine glands, which are located mainly under the armpits and in the groin area. These boils can frequently form, enlarge, burst, and cause scarring. Alopecia can involve hair loss, including all body hair, small circular patches of hair, or diffuse loss throughout the head and body. Eczema, sometimes called "dermatitis," is a skin condition that can range in severity from small patches of dry, itchy skin, to broken, raw, bleeding, and inflamed skin covering a large part of the body. Psoriasis, a skin condition most frequently found on the knees, elbows, scalp, hands, feet or lower back, generally appears as patches of raised red skin covered by a flaky white buildup known as plaques. Chronic hives—sometimes known as urticaria—involve raised welts, as well as dermographia, where scratches to the skin leave red swollen lines.

Urticaria is particularly common in thyroid patients. Studies have found that a significant percentage of patients with urticaria also have high levels of antithyroid antibodies, even though they may not have clinical thyroid disease. Interestingly, in one study, ten patients with chronic urticaria had normal thyroid blood test levels—but seven of the ten had elevated antithyroid antibodies and three controls had no antithyroid antibodies. After being treated with levothyroxine, the seven patients with antibodies reported that their urticaria symptoms went away within four weeks. The three controls did not respond. In five patients, symptoms recurred after treatment was stopped; these symptoms again resolved after treatment was restarted.

Premenstrual Syndrome/Difficult Menopause

Experiencing particularly debilitating premenstrual syndrome symptoms, or menopausal symptoms, can sometimes be a marker for underlying hypothyroidism. Symptoms can include:

- Extreme mood swings prior to and during menstruation
- Extreme bloating and water retention
- Depression, "brain fog" prior to and during menstruation
- Extreme mood swings prior to and during menopause
- Depression, brain fog prior to and during menopause
- Extremely low sex drive during perimenopause and menopause

Anyone with chronic PMS, or who is experiencing particularly difficult menopausal symptoms, should have her thyroid function evaluated.

Attention Deficient Hyperactivity Disorder (ADHD)

Some experts believe that people with dyslexia, a learning disability that is characterized by difficulties in reading, writing, and spelling, and attention deficit hyperactivity disorder (ADHD), are at higher risk of hypothyroidism.

Endometriosis

According to research conducted by the Endometriosis Association, women with endometriosis may also have associated disorders related to autoimmune dysregulation or pain. Almost all those studied had pain (99 percent), and more than 40 percent reported infertility. Overall, hypothyroidism, fibromyalgia, chronic fatigue syndrome, autoimmune diseases, allergies, and asthma are all significantly more common in women with endometriosis than in women in general in the United States.

Candidiasis/Yeast Overgrowth

Candidiasis is a condition characterized by an overgrowth of yeast in the body. This may manifest itself as chronic vaginal yeast infections, or thrush, intestinal problems, or other symptoms. Some experts believe that candidiasis may be a trigger for hypothyroidism, or may be more common in hypothyroidism patients.

Dr. Michael McNett sees a strong connection between candidiasis and hypothyroidism. Says McNett:

> *Something causes the immune system to aggressively attack Candida cells that most of us tolerate. This immune attack causes a rupture of the cells and release of their contents. Our bodies absorb chemicals released by the yeast, which interfere with the thyroid hormone's ability to cause its effect in the cell, and the patient develops symptoms. . . . One thing that is very interesting is that treatment for Candida hypersensitivity frequently causes all hypothyroid symptoms to disappear.*

Chronic Fatigue Syndrome and Fibromyalgia

These two conditions, which involve debilitating fatigue, chronic pain, sleep disturbances, brain fog, and depression, are more common in people with hypothyroidism, and vice versa. Indianapolis-based thyroid and chronic fatigue syndrome expert Dr. Dale Guyer estimates that more than 90 percent of his chronic fatigue syndrome patients also have an underlying thyroid problem.

Dr. Jacob Teitelbaum, an expert in chronic fatigue syndrome, fibromyalgia, and thyroid treatment, has seen that many people with hypothyroidism have developed associated fibromyalgia. In one study, conducted by Dr. Teitelbaum of sixty-four CFS patients (forty-four of whom also had fibromyalgia), thirty of the patients had overt or subclinical hypothyroidism.

Some practitioners, like Dr. John Lowe, feel that these conditions are actually manifestations of undiagnosed or undertreated hypothyroidism, or a cellular resistance to thyroid hormone:

> *Our studies suggest that perhaps 40% of fibromyalgia patients have "peripheral" tissue resistance to thyroid hormone—not pituitary or general resistance. Patients who have peripheral tissue resistance to thyroid hormone have normal*

thyroid test results before treatment with thyroid hormone. So, we don't know that they have peripheral resistance until we've treated them.

For those patients who show evidence of thyroid problems or tissue resistance, Dr. Lowe recommends a program he calls "metabolic rehabilitation." He claims to have high levels of success treating fibromyalgia patients with his protocol. According to Dr. Lowe:

When guided properly, patients whose fibromyalgia syndrome is underlain by hypothyroidism and/or thyroid hormone resistance stand a good chance of markedly improving or recovering.

For more information on chronic fatigue syndrome and fibromyalgia, I suggest you read my book *Living Well with Chronic Fatigue Syndrome and Fibromyalgia.*

Type 1 Diabetes

There is a definite linkage between autoimmune thyroid disease and type 1 diabetes, suggesting that diabetes patients should receive regular screening for thyroid dysfunction. In one study, 41 percent of the female patients and 19 percent of the male patients with type 1 diabetes developed hypothyroidism. Type 1 diabetics who were positive for thyroid peroxidase antibodies also were almost eighteen times more likely to become hypothyroid than those who tested negative for antibodies. The researchers suggested that patients with type 1 diabetes, and especially those who test positive for thyroid peroxidase antibodies, be tested annually for thyroid abnormalities.

Metabolic Syndrome/Insulin Resistance/Type 2 Diabetes

People with hypothyroidism have an increased risk of insulin resistance and the metabolic syndrome, which can progress to full-scale type 2 diabetes. The endocrine system is very much geared toward balance, and an imbalance in one area seems to set into motion a cascade of other imbalances in many people. Among these, the underlying endocrine dysfunction of a thyroid problem means that you face a higher risk of other endocrine imbalances and conditions, including insulin resistance, metabolic syndrome, and type 2 diabetes.

The characteristics of insulin resistance and metabolic syndrome are abdominal obesity (a thick waist), elevated blood fats known as triglycerides, low levels of HDL ("good") cholesterol, high blood pressure, and high blood sugar levels. These conditions, sometimes also referred to as prediabetes, frequently lead to the development of type 2 diabetes.

Holistic physician Dr. Roby Mitchell believes that evaluating metabolic syndrome symptoms may actually be a way to in part diagnose hypothyroidism and monitor treatment. Says Dr. Mitchell:

> *I'm more apt to follow a person's waist size, cholesterol profile, fasting insulin, or C-Reactive Protein than their TSH.*

High Cholesterol/Hyperlipidemia

High cholesterol—known as hyperlipidemia (high fats in the blood)—affects an estimated ninety-eight million people in the United States. Endocrinology experts estimate that as many as 10 percent of this population may have an undiagnosed thyroid problem that is contributing to the cholesterol problem. High total cholesterol, and, in particular, high cholesterol that is resistant to diet, exercise, and cholesterol-lowering medications, is a sign of possible underlying hypothyroidism.

Elevated C-Reactive Protein and Total Homocysteine Levels

Researchers have found that people with hypothyroidism often have significantly elevated levels of C-reactive protein, as well as total homocysteine. Elevations in these levels are also risk factors for developing coronary heart disease.

3

What Are the Symptoms and Signs of Hypothyroidism?

As long as one keeps searching, the answers come.
— JOAN BAEZ

If you read brochures and articles about hypothyroidism, you'll find there is a standard list of "typical" hypothyroid symptoms. For example, the Thyroid Foundation of America lists:

> *[feeling] run down, slow, depressed, sluggish, cold, tired . . . lose interest in normal daily activities . . . dryness and brittleness of hair, dry and itchy skin, constipation, muscle cramps, and increased menstrual flow in women.*

While these symptoms should raise the suspicion of hypothyroidism in any well-trained doctor, it's also safe to say that this list is just the tiniest tip of a very deep and very large iceberg.

Joyce touches upon some of the many symptoms people experience with hypothyroidism:

> *The most irritating thing about hypothyroidism is its fickle and lackadaisical onset. Go figure, a few extra pounds here, a*

feeling of sluggishness there, so what? Toss in what I affectionately coin, "Brillo hair and prune skin," and the red flags start to push through the cerebral cortex. Gradually, a few other little annoyances stealthily creep in, more bothersome than anything. When you look in the mirror in the morning you wonder, who in the hell stole the outer half of my eyebrows? What in the holy heck happened to my cheekbones? My face is so bloated, I look like a beached whale! Or your significant other asks casually, "Why do you have on two pairs of socks, an extra sweatshirt, and your bathrobe when it is seventy degrees in here?"

The symptoms of hypothyroidism can frequently become more severe as the TSH level rises. The number and severity of symptoms, however, appear to be unique to each individual. Some people suffer terribly at a TSH of 15. Others have written to me about "not feeling quite up to par," only to discover that they have a TSH of over 200.

The short symptoms lists found in the conventional brochures never seem comprehensive enough to capture the many symptoms that sufferers experience. Therefore, I conducted a survey of more than nine hundred hypothyroid patients, who described their symptoms when TSH levels rose above normal range. In addition, I used a variety of respected sources—such as *The Merck Manual, American Family Physician* magazine, the Thyroid Foundation of America, and the American Association of Clinical Endocrinologists, and the *Journal of Clinical Endocrinology and Metabolism*—to help develop this list.

■ Clinical Signs

There are a number of clinical signs that your practitioner may look for in making a diagnosis of hypothyroidism:

- Slowed Achilles reflex (Your doctor taps your Achilles tendon along the back of your heel, which causes your calf muscle to contract and your foot to jerk down. A slower than normal reaction suggests hypothyroidism.)
- Other slowed reflexes
- Low body temperature
- Slow heartbeat
- Irregular heartbeat, palpitations
- Blood pressure irregularities—low blood pressure, high blood pressure
- Loss of outer edge of eyebrow hair
- Coarse, brittle, strawlike hair
- Loss of scalp, underarm, and/or pubic hair
- Dry skin
- Dry mucous membranes
- Yellowish cast to the skin, jaundice
- Pallor, paleness of skin, pale lips
- Dull facial expression
- Protrusion of the eyeballs
- Puffiness around the eyes
- Slow movement
- Slow speech
- Hoarseness of voice
- Enlarged neck, goiter
- Edema (swelling) of the feet

■ Hypothyroidism Symptoms

The following section looks at the potential hypothyroidism symptoms you may personally experience or notice about yourself.

Hyperthyroidism Symptoms (Hashitoxicosis)

This may sound completely contradictory, but it's not uncommon that in the early stages of autoimmune Hashimoto's disease, while your thyroid is in the process of failing, it sputters periodically into overdrive, giving you bursts of hyperthyroidism, along with the accompanying symptoms. This is sometimes known as hashitoxicosis. In fact, patients need to be cautioned that any permanent treatments for hyperthyroidism should only be done after Hashimoto's disease has been ruled out, and Graves' disease or toxic nodules have been diagnosed, because there is rarely a reason to give radioactive iodine (RAI) treatment, or surgery, to someone with Hashimoto's who is cycling hyperthyroid for a short period. Some common hyperthyroidism symptoms include anxiety, panic attacks, rapid pulse, high blood pressure, sensitivity to heat, increased sweating, weight loss, increased appetite, diarrhea, muscle weakness, and insomnia.

Obesity/Weight Gain

Gaining weight inappropriately, or the inability to lose weight, are key symptoms of hypothyroidism. In my case, despite a low-fat, low-calorie diet, and an hour of stationary cycling each night, I was still gaining a pound or two a week during my most hypothyroid state. This is what I call inappropriate weight gain. Later, while still hypothyroid in the high normal TSH range for my lab (TSH of 5 to 6), I went on Weight Watchers. I followed the program to the letter and usually gained a half-pound or pound a week, while others lost two to three pounds each week.

If you find yourself suddenly gaining weight, or unable to lose weight following a reasonable diet—of course, I don't mean cutting out dessert once a week and expecting to drop pounds and inches—then this may be a symptom of hypothyroidism.

Don't always expect doctors to believe you, however. Kathryn had a long and difficult struggle with weight gain before her diagnosis of hypothyroidism:

When I mentioned the possibility of thyroid disease to a former doc, and that my maternal grandmother and mother both are and were hypothyroid, he laughed it off and told me to lay off the chips and cookies! I was barely eating at that time because I was too tired to make it to the kitchen after work.

Weight Loss

While weight gain is more common with hypothyroidism, a percentage of patients actually lose weight inappropriately. You could find it hard to maintain your weight, or lose weight faster than usual, or find yourselves eating more to maintain your weight.

Ascites/Abdominal Fluid Accumulation and Swelling

Some cases of ascites (pronounced ah-SIH-tez)—an abnormal accumulation of fluid in the abdomen—can be symptomatic of hypothyroidism. It's considered to be a fairly known but not common feature of hypothyroidism, occurring in as many as 4 percent of patients. Symptoms of ascites are rapid weight gain, abdominal discomfort and distention, shortness of breath, and swollen ankles.

Digestive Problems and Constipation

Constipation is a common symptom of hypothyroidism. Often, this type of constipation does not respond to increased dietary fiber, increased water consumption, laxatives, and fiber products like Metamucil.

Low Body Temperature, Feeling Cold

Feeling cold is a common symptom of hypothyroidism. You may feel cold when others are feeling hot, or you may always wear socks to bed, or need a sweater in the summer. In particular, you may find that your hands and feet are affected. Hypothermia (low body temperature) is also listed as a symptom of thyroid disease in many patient informational sources.

Some doctors use basal body temperature—either in conjunction with or, even, in some cases, instead of, TSH tests—as a way to diagnose hypothyroidism. This method was initially promoted by Dr. Broda Barnes. Basal body temperature is the temperature after awaking and before rising from bed and before any major movement. According to Dr. Barnes and followers of his theories, a basal body temperature lower than 97.8 to 98.2 degrees Fahrenheit can be indicative of hypothyroidism.

Some people, in addition to feeling cold or having a low temperature, notice they perspire less than usual or far less than normal.

Tiredness and Weakness

However you describe it, fatigue, exhaustion, weakness, lethargy, or feeling run down, sluggish, overtired, or just plain pooped out is one of the most common symptoms of hypothyroidism. You may find yourself needing a nap in the afternoon just to make it to dinnertime. You may sleep ten or twelve hours a night and still wake up exhausted. You may find yourself less able to exercise, and your endurance drops because of weakness or lethargy. Or you just walk around spaced out on the same amount of sleep that used to leave you feeling refreshed.

Exhaustion is also a symptom of sleep deprivation, so it can often be overlooked by doctors as a sign of a thyroid problem. Average Americans get only seven hours of sleep each night; so sleep deprivation is a common problem that doctors are likely to assume is the main reason for your chronic tiredness, not hypothyroidism.

Michele was never much of a sleeper until her thyroid started becoming underactive:

Last year, when I began feeling exhausted midafternoon, I thought something was off. Initially I actually thought I might be pregnant, as that was the only time in my life I remember feeling so drained. When it got to the point that I was taking naps in the parking lot, I headed to the doctor. Inter-

estingly enough, my mom and sister both have thyroid problems. My mom got extremely sick when she was close to my
age and my sister started at a very young age. I didn't have a
clue that thyroid problems were hereditary, so they didn't pop
up on my radar screen.

"Brain Fog"

Brain fog is that fuzzy feeling that makes it difficult to concentrate, remember things, or focus your mind. Joyce experienced severe bouts of brain fog as a symptom of her hypothyroidism:

> Before hypothyroidism hit, I made lists in my head—I re-
> membered everything, it was like my mind had a computer in
> it. As my symptoms progressed, I had lists everywhere. Lists
> that told me what I had to do because I couldn't remember.
> Lists for tasks, lists for groceries, lists for appointments, lists
> to remember where I put the lists. When your thyroid is out of
> whack, you get something I call "cotton-ball" brain syn-
> drome. That's how it feels, like your head is packed full of cot-
> ton balls and absolutely nothing else.

Slow Pulse and Low Blood Pressure

Pulse, or heart rate, varies depending on age, level of fitness, and
other factors. Generally, an average heart rate/pulse runs around 60
to 85 beats per minute. If you are not taking certain drugs that can
lower pulse, or you're not in particularly good physical condition (a
well-trained athlete can have a normal pulse of 40 to 60 beats per
minute) and your pulse is slower than 60 to 85 beats per minute, it
can be a symptom of hypothyroidism.

According to the National Institutes of Health, a blood pressure
about 120/80mm is considered a "normal" level for most adults. A
level such as 105/65 mm, for example, is considered somewhat
"low." Low blood pressure can, in some cases, be a symptom of hypothyroidism.

High Blood Pressure

High blood pressure can sometimes be a symptom of hypothyroidism. In some people, the autonomic system becomes disregulated, and this results in high blood pressure.

High Cholesterol Levels

Having unusually high cholesterol levels can be a symptom of underlying hypothyroidism. Some people have reported that despite normal diets, their cholesterol levels reached 300 to 500 points, but returned to normal or only slightly elevated levels once their underlying hypothyroidism was treated. If you have high cholesterol that is not responding to diet or cholesterol-lowering drugs, hypothyroidism may be a factor.

Skin Changes

A variety of changes to the skin are hypothyroidism symptoms. These include paleness in the skin, dry mucous membranes, easy bruising, a yellowish cast, cracked skin on elbows and kneecaps, hives or chronic urticaria, chronic itching, psoriasis, eczema, and hidradenitis suppurativa (inflamed, painful boils in the armpits and groin).

Hair Changes

Your hair—including body hair and head hair—may be falling out at the roots faster than normal and may become more brittle, breaking more easily when handled. Your hair can also look and feel very coarse, rough, and dry. You may also notice that you're losing the hair from the outer part of your eyebrow, which is considered a distinct symptom of hypothyroidism, as well as losing eyelashes.

Nail Changes

Nails can also develop problems as a symptom of hypothyroidism. They can become dry, brittle, and may break more easily than normal.

Low, Husky, Hoarse Voice

Changes in voice can be a symptom of hypothyroidism. Most typically, the voice is hoarse, husky, or gravelly. Some women even reported that when hypothyroid, they are mistaken for a man on the phone.

Muscle and Joint Aches and Pains

Pains, aches, and stiffness in various joints and muscles, particularly the hands and feet, often occur with hypothyroidism. Your aches and pains can sometimes be so severe that doctors mistake them for arthritis symptoms, or diagnose you as having fibromyalgia.

Menstrual Changes

Irregularities in your menstrual cycle are more common when you are hypothyroid. These irregularities can include longer periods than are usual for you or heavier periods than normal, a shorter cycle or a less regular cycle. For example, before I was hypothyroid, I was very regular: every twenty-eight days, with a five-day period. The first two days were heaviest, tapering to a very light flow from days 3 to 5. When I became hypothyroid and before my TSH was in the low-normal range, my periods starting coming every twenty-one to twenty-four days, lasting up to seven days, and were extremely heavy for four to five days. Now that I'm back to a low normal TSH, my period comes every twenty-six days, lasts five days, and though heavier than before my thyroid problems, the flow is not as heavy as when I am more hypothyroid.

Fertility Problems

Difficulty becoming pregnant can sometimes lead a woman to discover previously undiagnosed hypothyroidism.

Recurrent Miscarriage

Hypothyroidism can increase your risk of miscarriage. Therefore, miscarriage and in particular, recurrent miscarriage, can be considered a "symptom" of undiagnosed hypothyroidism.

Menopausal Symptoms

Premature menopause and exaggerated symptoms of menopause are both more common symptoms of hypothyroidism.

Worsened or exaggerated symptoms can include exhaustion, brain fog, poor memory, depression, lethargy, changes in mood, skin changes, hair loss, changes in hair texture, change in libido/sex drive, sleep disturbances, increased anxiety, nervousness, heart palpitations, and irregular or missed menstrual periods.

According to Dr. Richard Shames, it's a complex issue:

> *The symptoms of hot flashes, insomnia, irritability, palpitations, and the annoying "fuzzy thinking" so common in menopause can sometimes be the result of Hashimoto's thyroiditis, the most common cause of hypothyroidism. But the real complexity comes when actual symptoms of menopause are simply magnified and exaggerated because of the low thyroid situation that is now coexistent with menopause. As many thyroid sufferers are aware, low thyroid makes any illness worse. And while menopause is not an illness, it can certainly begin to feel that way when symptoms of low thyroid exacerbate the already annoying laundry list of female hormone symptoms.*

Postpartum Symptoms

The postpartum period is another time when exaggerated symptoms may point to hypothyroidism. Symptoms can include difficulty breast-feeding, difficulty losing weight, extreme hair loss, fatigue, depression, mood swings, and brain fog.

Breast Changes

Some people with hypothyroidism have imbalances in prolactin, the hormone that controls breast-feeding. One symptom that can signal hypothyroidism is lactation—or milk leaking from the breasts—in a woman who otherwise is not breast-feeding.

Mood, Depression

One of the most common symptoms of hypothyroidism is a change in mood, typically a feeling of depression. You might have periods when you feel down or sad, or may even be mistakenly be diagnosed as clinically depressed instead of hypothyroid. The mood changes associated with hypothyroidism may make you feel restless, or your moods may change easily. You may have feelings of worthlessness, have difficulty concentrating, or feel like your brain or mind is "in a fog." You may lose interest in normal daily activities, or you may be more forgetful and have a tougher time keeping up with work, or schedules, or details.

Hypothyroidism may also be the reason why your antidepressant doesn't seem to be working. In 1997, there were an estimated twenty-five million people in the United States taking antidepressants. And some studies estimate that 80 percent of people on antidepressants report a variety of unresolved symptoms—such as weight gain, lethargy, and loss of libido—that are also very common symptoms of thyroid disease. A significant percentage of people on antidepressants could actually be suffering from an undiagnosed thyroid problem.

Low Sex Drive

Having what doctors refer to as low libido—and what the rest of us refer to as low sex drive, or no sizzle between the sheets—is a common, but not as often discussed, symptom of hypothyroidism. This applies equally to men and women, and, in fact, is often the symptom that commonly leads men to a diagnosis of hypothyroidism. Interestingly, major research published in the *Journal of the American Medical Association* in early 1999 found that about 43 percent of women and 31 percent of men suffer "sexual inadequacy" for a variety of reasons, including: low desire, performance anxiety, premature ejaculation, among other concerns. Research indicated that many of these sexual concerns were probably treatable, as they are due to physical and health issues, including hormonal imbalances such as hypothyroidism.

Eye Problems

There is a form of eye disease, called "thyroid eye disease," also known as Graves' ophthalmopathy or thyroid-associated ophthalmopathy (TAO). Thyroid eye disease is most often associated with Graves' disease. Thyroid eye disease is an inflammation of the eyes, with swelling of the tissues around the eyes and bulging of the eyes. In the majority of cases, this inflammation will not cause serious or permanent trouble. Early signs include:

- Bulging or protrusion of the eyes due to inflammation of the tissues behind the eyeball (the medical term is *"exophthalmos"*)
- Blurred or diminished vision
- Red or inflamed eyes
- Double vision

Many experts believe that the swelling is caused by antibodies attacking the tissues of the eye muscles. There may also be a sensitivity to light and a continual feeling that there is something foreign or gritty in the eye. Ultimately, the eyeball may protrude because tissues behind the eye swell and become inflamed, pushing the eyeball forward. The front surface of the eye may become dry.

While thyroid eye disease is most associated with Graves' disease, hypothyroidism seems to create a variety of other irritating eye problems. You may experience the following eye symptoms:

- Eyes that feel gritty and dry
- Eyes that are photosensitive, or sensitive to light
- Eyes that get jumpy, or have more frequent tics, sometimes referred to as *nystagmus*
- A rapidly shifting gaze makes you feel dizzy or feel vertigo
- Sensitivity of eyes creates headaches
- Eyes that feel gritty or achy
- Eyes that are dry and blurry (but *may* be relieved by moisture drops or liquid tears)

Neck and Throat Complaints

A goiter, swelling or thickness in the neck, is a fairly obvious sign of a potential thyroid problem. However, even in the absence of a goiter or swelling that a doctor can feel, you may have strange feelings in your neck or throat. These feelings have been described as "fullness," discomfort with neckties or clothing around the neck, a sense of neck or throat pressure, a choking sensation, a feeling like something is stuck in the throat, or difficulty swallowing. A feeling of thickness in the tongue is also common.

Hearing Issues

According to researchers, the incidence of tinnitus can be correlated to the severity of hypothyroidism. Tinnitus is a problem that makes it seem as if you are hearing something—in some cases hissing, roaring, whistling, clicking, ringing—when there is no sound. It is most commonly referred to as "ringing in the ears." Tinnitus can be a debilitating problem for some people, and the American Tinnitus Association estimates that over fifty million Americans are affected by tinnitus to some degree, and twelve million suffer severely enough to seek medical attention for the problem.

Hearing loss, including sudden onset of hearing loss and deafness, is also a symptom, although not very common, of hypothyroidism.

More Infections and Lowered Resistance

Some doctors believe that more frequent infections, or less resistance to infection, are symptoms of hypothyroidism. Many people with thyroid problems also report getting more frequent colds, flus, and sinus infections, and have a longer, harder time recuperating from these infections.

Allergies

Development of allergies or worsening of existing allergies—including hay fever, seasonal allergies, and food allergies—have all been reported as symptoms of hypothyroidism.

Sleep Apnea and Snoring

Snoring can be a symptom of sleep apnea, and sleep apnea can be a symptom of hypothyroidism. Sleep apnea involves momentary lapses of breathing while sleeping and is accompanied by loud snoring, gasping for breath as you sleep, and feeling tired all the time, no matter how much sleep you get.

Breathing Difficulties and Asthma-like Feelings

While not reported in patient literature, a hypothyroidism symptom that many people have reported to me—and one I experience myself—is a feeling of shortness of breath and tightness in the chest. Some people describe this feeling as "I feel like I need to yawn hard to even get enough oxygen." Sometimes this can be mistaken for asthma, which is what they initially told me. But my doctor felt it was inaccurate, because it wasn't accompanied by any of the wheezing that is typical of asthma. I also noticed it was only a problem when I was in high normal range or at clinically hypothyroid TSH levels.

Some experts believe that when you are hypothyroid, not enough oxygen reaches your brain, which contributes to making thinking less efficient, reduces your concentration, and reduces muscle coordination. Dr. Stephen Langer, in his book *Solved: The Riddle of Illness*, has said:

> Hypothyroidism can cause oxygen deprivation in the brain in numerous ways: by impeding blood circulation (slowing the delivery of oxygen and nutrients); by slowing the rate of oxidation (burning) of food (glucose) to nourish brain cells; by depressing production of blood cells, by contributing to atherosclerosis (narrowing of arteries); and by limiting the amount of blood that reaches the brain.

Dizziness and Vertigo

Vertigo is dizziness with the illusion of motion. When you have vertigo, you may feel that you are moving or that things are moving around you. Lightheadedness, dizziness, and vertigo can all be symptoms of hypothyroidism. Typically, these symptoms are usually worse with higher TSH levels.

Puffiness and Swelling

Swelling, bloating, water retention, and puffiness—referred to by doctors as "edema"—of various parts of the body can be symptoms of hypothyroidism. In particular, puffiness and swelling may affect the eyes, eyelids, and face, and can sometimes be most painful and visible in the feet and hands.

Slowness

Slowness in movement and speech are both considered symptoms of hypothyroidism.

Headaches

Chronic headaches and migraines can be symptoms of hypothyroidism.

Heart Palpitations/Rapid Heartbeat

Hypothyroidism can frequently start with a short period of hyperthyroidism, or a person with hyperthyroidism may have periodic spurts of activity from the thyroid. Both situations can cause heart palpitations, heart flutters, and episodes of rapid heartbeat.

■ Infant, Children, and Adolescent Hypothyroidism Symptoms

Symptoms of hypothyroidism in infants include: a puffy face, swollen tongue, hoarse cry, cold extremities, mottled skin, low muscle tone, poor feeding, thick coarse hair that grows low on the forehead, a large soft spot, prolonged jaundice, a herniated belly button, lethargy, sleeping most of the time, appearing tired even when awake, persistent constipation, looking bloated or full to the touch, and little to no growth.

In children, symptoms are primarily a lack of growth, but can also include school problems, a diagnosis of attention deficit disorder, delayed puberty, and many of the other symptoms that adults experience, including unusual fatigue, weight gain, constipation, sensitivity to cold, dry skin, and hair loss.

Hypothyroidism sometimes appears during early adolescence, especially in girls. Symptoms to look for in prepubescent or pubescent girls include early or premature breast enlargement, unusual vaginal bleeding or vaginal bleeding before the start of menstruation, breast discharge, heavy periods, and failure to start a period or a lack of periods for long timeframes.

■ ■ ■

While the previous list of symptoms typically exceeds most of the standard symptom lists you'll find in patient educational materials, it is *still* by no means inclusive. You may have unique symptoms that are specific to your own hypothyroidism and health. One way to get to know your own symptoms better is by keeping a journal or charting your symptoms according to time of day, time of the month, and other variables, such as exercise, diet, supplements, and any blood test values you have. This can help you better understand your body's unique response to hypothyroidism.

4

Hypothyroidism Diagnosis and Symptoms Checklist

Nothing in life is to be feared. It is only to be understood.

— MARIE CURIE

The following checklist can help you communicate your risk factors and symptoms to your doctor, as an aid in getting a proper diagnosis of hypothyroidism. It can also serve as background information in your discussions regarding fine-tuning your dosage. You need to be at the optimal TSH level for your own wellness. At the end of this chapter, I've also included basal body temperature charts that you can use to track your own temperatures and show to your doctor. I suggest you make a copy of this chapter for yourself to fill out and show your doctor, and be sure to bring an extra copy for your doctor's files.

■ I Have the Following Risk Factors for Hypothyroidism:

Thyroid-Related

❑ My family (parent, sibling, child) has a history of thyroid disease.

☑ My thyroid has been "monitored" in the past due to irregularities, or I've been treated in the past for thyroid disease, including hypothyroidism, hyperthyroidism, goiter, nodules, thyroid cancer, Hashimoto's disease, Graves' disease, elevated thyroid antibodies, postpartum thyroiditis, transient thyroiditis, or another thyroid problem.

☑ A doctor has prescribed thyroid hormone for me in the past.

❑ I currently have a goiter or nodules.

❑ I have had part/all of my thyroid removed (a thyroidectomy) due to cancer.

❑ I have had part/all of my thyroid removed due to nodules or goiter.

❑ I have had part/all of my thyroid removed as a treatment for Graves' disease/hyperthyroidism.

❑ I have been treated with radioactive iodine (RAI) for Graves' disease/hyperthyroidism or thyroid cancer.

❑ I was or am being treated with antithyroid drugs (e.g., Tapazole or PTU) due to Graves' disease/hyperthyroidism.

Endocrine-Related

❑ I have or had a pituitary tumor and/or pituitary disease.

Autoimmune/Endocrine Diseases

❑ A member of my family (parent, sibling, child) or I have a history of celiac disease/gluten intolerance.

☑ A member of my family (parent, sibling, child) or I have a history of insulin-dependent (type 1) diabetes.

❑ A member of my family (parent, sibling, child) or I have a history of Addison's disease.

❑ A member of my family (parent, sibling, child) or I have a history of Cushing's disease.

❑ A member of my family (parent, sibling, child) or I have a history of polycystic ovary syndrome (PCOS). ?

☑ A member of my family (parent, sibling, child) or I have a history of premature ovarian decline/premature ovarian failure.

❏ A member of my family (parent, sibling, child) or I have a history of alopecia.

❏ A member of my family (parent, sibling, child) or I have a history of Raynaud's syndrome.

❏ A member of my family (parent, sibling, child) or I have a history of Sjögren's syndrome.

❏ A member of my family (parent, sibling, child) or I have a history of chronic fatigue syndrome (also known as CFS).

❏ A member of my family (parent, sibling, child) or I have a history of fibromyalgia.

❏ A member of my family (parent, sibling, child) or I have a history of other common autoimmune or autoimmune-like conditions, including rheumatoid arthritis, systemic lupus erythematosus (SLE), multiple sclerosis, sarcoidosis, scleroderma, vitiligo, and psoriasis.

❏ I am left-handed.

❏ I have prematurely gray hair.

Age

❏ I am over 60.

Female-Specific/Hormonal Issues

☑ I am female.

❏ I have had a baby in the past nine months.

❏ I have a history of more than one miscarriage.

❏ I have a history of infertility.

❏ I am perimenopausal.

❏ I am menopausal.

❏ I am postmenopausal.

Smoking

❏ I am currently a smoker.

❏ I've recently quit smoking.

☑ I was a smoker in the past.

Drugs and Supplements

❏ I have been treated with lithium in the past or am currently being treated with this drug.

❏ I have been treated with amiodarone (Cordarone) in the past or am currently being treated with this drug.

❏ I have been treated with glucocorticoids/adrenal steroids like prednisone and hydrocortisone in the past or am currently being treated with these drugs.

❏ I have been treated with propranolol in the past or am currently being treated with this drug.

❏ I have been treated with aminoglutethimide in the past or am currently being treated with this drug.

❏ I have been treated with ketoconazole in the past or am currently being treated with this drug.

❏ I have been treated with para-aminosalicylic acid in the past or am currently being treated with this drug.

❏ I have been treated with sulfonamide drugs, including sulfadiazine, sulfasoxazole, and acetazoleamide, in the past or am currently being treated with these drugs.

❏ I have been treated with sulfonylureas, including tolbutamide and chlorpropamide, in the past or am currently being treated with these drugs.

❏ I have been treated with raloxifene (Evista) in the past or am currently being treated with this drug.

❏ I have been treated with carbamazepine, oxcarbazepine, or valproate for epilepsy in the past, or am currently being treated with these drugs.

❏ I have been treated with antithyroid drugs, including propylthiouricil (PTU), methimazole (Tapazole) and carbimazole, in the past or am currently being treated with these drugs.

Iodine Imbalances

❑ I am or have in the past been self-treating with iodine, kelp, bladderwrack, and/or bugleweed.

❑ I have eliminated iodized salt from my diet.

❑ I live in a "Goiter Belt" area (mountainous or inland areas, including the Alps, Pyrenees, Himalayas, Andes, St. Lawrence River valley, Appalachian Mountains, Great Lakes basin westward through Minnesota, South and North Dakota, Montana, Wyoming, southern Canada, the Rockies, and into noncoastal Oregon, Washington, and British Columbia).

❑ My mother was iodine-deficient, had a goiter, or lived in a Goiter Belt area when pregnant with me.

Alcohol During Pregnancy

❑ I drank alcohol during pregnancy.

❑ My mother drank alcohol while pregnant with me.

Diet

☑ I regularly consume substantial quantities of any of the following foods: Brussels sprouts, rutabaga, turnips, kohlrabi, radishes, cauliflower, African cassava, millet, babassu (a palm-tree coconut fruit popular in Brazil and Africa), cabbage, kale, soy products, horseradish, mustard, corn, broccoli, turnips, carrots, peaches, strawberries, peanuts, spinach, watercress, mustard greens, and walnuts.

Soy Overconsumption

❑ I eat substantial quantities of soy products (i.e., tofu, tempeh, soy milk, soy nuts, edamame).

- ❑ I regularly use soy supplements in pill form.
- ❑ I regularly consume soy powders and smoothies.

Environmental Exposures

- ☑ I grew up drinking fluoridated water.
- ☑ I am currently drinking fluoridated water.
- ☑ I use fluoridated toothpaste.
- ❑ I get fluoride treatments at the dentist.
- ❑ I am regularly exposed to chlorine (i.e., I swim regularly, work at a swimming pool).
- ❑ I have mercury dental fillings.
- ❑ I regularly eat fish high in mercury.

X-Ray, Radiation, or Radium Treatments

- ❑ I have had radiation or X-ray treatments to treat my tonsils, adenoids, lymph nodes, thymus gland problems, Hodgkin's disease, or acne.
- ❑ I have had radiation treatment to my head, neck, or chest.
- ❑ I have had numerous X-ray treatments (not dental or diagnostic X-rays) to the head and neck.
- ❑ I had "nasal radium therapy" sometime during the 1940s through 1960s, as a treatment for tonsillitis, colds, and other ailments, or as a military submariner and/or pilot who had trouble with drastic changes in pressure.

Yersinia Infection

- ❑ I have recently had an episode of fever.
- ❑ I have abdominal pain, particularly right-sided abdominal pain.
- ❑ I have diarrhea.
- ❑ I have a skin rash.
- ☑ I have joint pains.
- ☑ I have arthriticlike symptoms.

Snakebite

❑ I have had a severe or life-threatening snakebite in the past.

Neck Trauma

☑ I have had serious trauma to the neck, such as whiplash from a car accident or a broken neck.

Nuclear Exposure

❑ I lived, or live, near a nuclear plant.

❑ I lived, or was visiting, in or around Chernobyl in the weeks after the nuclear accident, which occurred on April 26, 1986. (Main countries at risk included Belarus, Russian Federation, Ukraine. Lesser risk to Poland, Austria, Denmark, Finland, Germany, Greece, Italy.)

❑ I lived in, near, or downwind from the former nuclear weapons plant at Hanford in south central Washington State in the 1940s through 1960s, but particularly during the period 1955 to 1965.

❑ I lived near or in the general region of the Nevada Nuclear Test Site (NTS) in the 1950s and 1960s. According to the National Cancer Institute, the highest per capita thyroid doses of radiation were obtained in counties of western states located east and north of the NTS, such as Utah, Idaho, Montana, Colorado, and Missouri.

Perchlorate Exposure

❑ I live near a plant that produces rockets or rocket fuel, or my work exposes me to the chemical perchlorate.

❑ I drink water that comes from the Colorado River.

❑ I eat produce that is irrigated with water from the Colorado River.

Other Chemical Exposures

❑ I live in an area that has been sprayed for West Nile virus.

■ Conditions That Raise the Suspicion of Hypothyroidism

I currently have, or have in the past, been diagnosed with the following diseases or conditions, known to occur more frequently in people with thyroid disease:

❑ Epstein-Barr virus (EBV)

❑ Mononucleosis

❑ Carpal tunnel syndrome/tendonitis

❑ Polycystic ovary syndrome (PCOS)

❑ Mitral valve prolapse (MVP) (heart murmur, palpitations)

❑ Down Syndrome

❑ Depression

❑ Bipolar disease

☑ Anemia

❑ Hemochromatosis

❑ Celiac disease/gluten intolerance

❑ Infertility

❑ Recurrent miscarriage

❑ Vitiligo

❑ Hidradenitis suppurativa (painful, inflamed armpit and groin boils)

❑ Alopecia (hair loss)

❑ Eczema

❑ Psoriasis

❑ Urticaria (hives)

❑ Chronic premenstrual syndrome (PMS)

❑ Difficult menopause

❑ Attention deficit hyperactivity disorder (ADHD)

❑ Endometriosis

- ❑ Candidiasis/yeast overgrowth
- ❑ Chronic fatigue syndrome
- ❑ Fibromyalgia
- ❑ Type 1 diabetes
- ❑ Metabolic syndrome
- ❑ Insulin resistance
- ❑ Type 2 diabetes
- ❑ Elevated cholesterol/hyperlipidemia
- ❑ Elevated C-reactive protein levels
- ❑ Elevated homocysteine levels

■ I Have the Following Clinical Signs of Hypothyroidism:

- ❑ Slowed Achilles reflex
- ☑ Other slowed reflexes
- ☑ Low body temperature
- ❑ Slow heartbeat
- ☑ Irregular heartbeat, palpitations
- ☑ Blood pressure irregularities—low blood pressure, high blood pressure
- ☑ Loss of outer edge of eyebrow hair
- ☑ Coarse, brittle, strawlike hair
- ❑ Loss of scalp, underarm, and/or pubic hair
- ☑ Dry skin
- ❑ Dry mucous membranes
- ❑ Yellowish cast to the skin, jaundice
- ❑ Pallor, paleness of skin, pale lips
- ❑ Dull facial expression
- ❑ Protrusion of the eyeballs
- ❑ Puffiness around the eyes
- ❑ Slow movement
- ❑ Slow speech

❏ Hoarseness of voice
❏ Enlarged neck, goiter
❏ Edema (swelling) of the feet

■ I Have the Following Symptoms of Hypothyroidism:

Hyperthyroidism/Hashitoxicosis Symptoms

❏ Anxiety, panic attacks
❏ Rapid pulse, high blood pressure
❏ Sensitivity to heat, increased sweating
❏ Weight loss, increased appetite
❏ Diarrhea
☑ Muscle weakness
☑ Insomnia

Obesity/Weight Gain

❏ I am obese or overweight.
☑ I am gaining weight inappropriately.
❏ I'm unable to lose weight with proper diet/exercise.

Weight Loss

❏ I'm losing weight inappropriately.

Ascites/Fluid in the Abdomen

☑ I have rapidly gained weight.
❏ I am experiencing abdominal discomfort and distention.
❏ I'm experiencing shortness of breath.
❏ My ankles are swollen.

Digestive Problems/Constipation

❏ I am constipated, sometimes severely.
❏ I have frequent diarrhea.

Body Temperature

- ❑ I have been diagnosed as having hypothermia (low body temperature).
- ❑ My "normal" basal body temperature is lower than 97.8 to 98.2 degrees Fahrenheit.
- ☑ I feel cold when others feel hot. I need extra sweaters when others need air-conditioning.
- ☑ I feel cold, especially in the hands and/or feet.
- ☑ I perspire less than normal.

Tiredness / Weakness

- ☑ I feel fatigued more than normal.
- ☑ I feel weak.
- ☑ I feel run down, sluggish, lethargic.
- ☑ I feel like I can't get enough sleep, even though I'm sleeping the amount I need to feel well rested.

Brain Fog

- ☑ I find it difficult to concentrate.
- ☑ I am having trouble with my memory.
- ☑ I find it difficult to focus.

Pulse / Blood Pressure

- ❑ I have a slow pulse.
- ☑ I have low blood pressure.
- ❑ I have high blood pressure.

Cholesterol Levels

- ❑ I have high cholesterol.
- ❑ I have high cholesterol that is resistant to diet or drug treatment.

Skin Changes

☑ My mucous membranes (i.e. mouth, eyes) are dry.

❑ I have a yellowish cast to my skin.

❑ My coloring is pale, my lips are pale.

❑ I have a dull facial expression.

❑ My eyeballs are protruding.

❑ I have puffiness around my eyes.

☑ My skin is rough, coarse, dry, scaly, itchy, and thick.

❑ My skin is breaking out.

❑ I get painful, inflamed boils in my armpits or groin.

Hair Changes

❑ My hair is rough and coarse.

☑ My hair is dry.

❑ My hair is breaking, brittle.

❑ My hair is falling out more than usual.

☑ My eyebrows or eyelashes are falling out.

Nail Changes

☑ My nails are dry.

☑ My nails are brittle and break more easily.

Voice Changes

❑ My voice has become hoarse, husky, or gravelly.

Aches and Pains

☑ I have pains, aches, and stiffness in various joints, hands, and feet.

❑ I have developed carpal tunnel syndrome, or my existing carpal tunnel syndrome is getting worse.

❑ I have tarsal tunnel syndrome.

❑ I have plantar fasciitis (pain in the ball of the foot).

Fertility/Menstruation

- ❏ I am having irregular menstrual cycles (longer, or heavier, or more frequent).
- ❏ I am having trouble conceiving a baby.
- ❏ I have started to develop ovarian cysts.
- ❏ I have a history of one or more miscarriages.

Postpartum Symptoms

- ❏ I have had, or am having, difficulty breast-feeding.
- ☑ I am having difficulty losing weight.
- ❏ I am losing large amounts of hair.
- ☑ I am abnormally fatigued.
- ☑ I'm experiencing depression and mood swings.
- ☑ I'm having brain fog.

Breast Changes

- ❏ My breasts are leaking milk, but I'm not lactating or breast-feeding.

Mood/Depression/Thinking

- ☑ I feel depressed.
- ☑ I feel restless.
- ☑ My moods change easily.
- ☑ I have feelings of worthlessness.
- ☑ I have difficulty concentrating.
- ☑ I have feelings of sadness.
- ❏ I'm taking an antidepressant, but it doesn't seem to be working.
- ☑ I seem to be losing interest in normal daily activities.
- ☑ I'm more forgetful lately.
- ☑ My mind feels like I'm in a "fog."

Sex Drive

❏ I have no sex drive.

❏ I have a reduced sex drive.

❏ I have difficulty reaching orgasm.

Eyes

☑ My eyes feel gritty and dry.

❏ My vision is blurry, but eyedrops help.

❏ My eyes feel sensitive to light.

❏ My eyes get jumpy (tics in eyes).

❏ My eyes make me feel dizzy.

❏ My eyes give me headaches.

Neck/Throat

☑ I have strange feelings in my neck or throat, for example, a feeling of "fullness," or pressure, a choking sensation, or difficulty swallowing.

❏ I have a lump or what appears to be some sort of fullness or growth in my neck area.

Hearing/Tinnitus

❏ I have tinnitus (ringing in my ears).

❏ I have sudden hearing loss or deafness.

Infections/Resistance

❏ I am getting more frequent infections or infections that last longer.

❏ I get recurrent sinus infections.

Allergies

❏ I have developed allergies or my allergies have become worse.

✓ Sneeze more

Sleeping/Snoring

☑ I'm snoring more lately.

☑ I have (may have) sleep apnea.

Breathing

❑ I feel a shortness of breath.

❑ I have a tightness in my chest.

❑ I feel the need to yawn to get oxygen.

Dizziness

❑ I have vertigo and dizziness.

☑ I feel lightheaded at times.

Puffiness/Swelling

❑ I have puffiness and swelling around the eyes and face.

❑ I have swollen feet.

❑ I have swollen hands.

❑ I have swollen eyelids.

Slowness

❑ My movements are slower than normal.

❑ My speech is slower than normal.

Headaches

❑ I have chronic headaches.

❑ I get migraine headaches.

Heart Palpitations

☑ I get heart palpitations, skipped beats, and heart flutters.

❑ I have periods of rapid heartbeat.

■ Special Risk/Symptoms List for Infants

❑ My infant is on soy formula.
❑ My infant has family members (parents, siblings) with thyroid disease.
❑ My infant has a puffy face.
❑ My infant has a swollen tongue.
❑ My infant has a hoarse cry.
❑ My infant has cold extremities.
❑ My infant has mottled skin.
❑ My infant has low muscle tone.
❑ My infant is not eating well.
❑ My infant has thick coarse hair that grows low on the forehead.
❑ My infant has a large soft spot.
❑ My infant has had prolonged jaundice.
❑ My infant has a herniated belly button.
❑ My infant is lethargic.
❑ My infant sleeps most of the time.
❑ My infant appears tired even when awake.
❑ My infant has persistent constipation.
❑ My infant is bloated or full to the touch.
❑ My infant has had little to no growth.

■ Special Symptoms List for Children

❑ My child took soy formula as an infant.
❑ My child has family members (parents, siblings) with thyroid disease.
❑ My child is not keeping up with growth charts for height.
❑ My child is having school problems.
❑ My child has been diagnosed with attention deficit disorder.
❑ My child is having delayed puberty.

- ❑ My child is unusually fatigued, exhausted, or sleeping far more than usual.
- ❑ My child is gaining weight inappropriately.
- ❑ My child is severely constipated.
- ❑ My child is sensitive to cold.
- ❑ My child's hair is rough, coarse, dry, breaking, brittle.
- ❑ My child's hair is falling out more than usual.
- ❑ My child's eyebrows or eyelashes are falling out.
- ❑ My child's skin is rough, coarse, dry, scaly, itchy, and thick.
- ❑ My child's voice has become hoarse, husky, or gravelly.
- ❑ My child is complaining of pains, aches, and stiffness in various joints, hands, and feet.
- ❑ My child seems depressed.
- ❑ My child seems restless or has difficulty concentrating.
- ❑ My child seems to be losing interest in normal daily activities.
- ❑ My child seems more forgetful lately.
- ❑ My child complains of strange feelings in the neck or throat, or difficulty swallowing.
- ❑ My child seems to have some sort of fullness or growth in the neck area.
- ❑ My child gets more frequent infections or infections that last longer.
- ❑ My child is snoring more lately.
- ❑ My child yawns frequently to get oxygen.
- ❑ My child has puffiness and swelling around the eyes and face.
- ❑ My child has swollen feet, hands, or eyelids.

■ Special Symptoms List for Prepubescent/ Pubescent Girls

- ❑ My child took soy formula as an infant.
- ❑ My child has family members (parents, siblings) with thyroid disease.
- ❑ My child is not keeping up with growth charts for height.
- ❑ My child is having school problems.
- ❑ My child has been diagnosed with attention deficit disorder.
- ❑ My child is unusually fatigued, exhausted, or sleeping far more than usual.
- ❑ My child is gaining weight inappropriately.
- ❑ My child is severely constipated.
- ❑ My child is sensitive to cold.
- ❑ My child's hair is rough, coarse, dry, breaking, brittle.
- ❑ My child's hair is falling out more than usual, in particular, eyebrows, or eyelashes.
- ❑ My child's skin is rough, coarse, dry, scaly, itchy, and thick.
- ❑ My child's voice has become hoarse, husky, or gravelly.
- ❑ My child is complaining of pains, aches, and stiffness in various joints, hands, and feet.
- ❑ My child seems depressed.
- ❑ My child seems restless or is having difficulty concentrating.
- ❑ My child seems to be losing interest in normal daily activities.
- ❑ My child seems more forgetful lately.
- ❑ My child complains of strange feelings in the neck or throat, or has difficulty in swallowing.
- ❑ My child seems to have some sort of fullness or growth in the neck area.
- ❑ My child gets more frequent infections or infections that last longer.
- ❑ My child is snoring more lately.
- ❑ My child yawns frequently to get oxygen.

❑ My child has puffiness and swelling around the eyes and face.

❑ My child has swollen feet, hands, or eyelids.

❑ My child showed early appearance of breast buds.

❑ My child's breast are growing.

❑ My child has had unusual vaginal bleeding, before she has begun to menstruate.

❑ My child has a breast discharge.

❑ My child has heavy periods.

❑ My child goes without menstrual periods for long periods of time.

❑ My teenager has failed to get her period and is having delayed puberty.

■ Basal Body Temperature Chart

INSTRUCTIONS: Use an oral glass/mercury thermometer, or a special basal body temperature/fertility thermometer. Shake the thermometer down before going to bed and leave it close by and within reach. As soon as you wake up, with a minimum of movement, put the thermometer in your armpit, next to the skin, and leave it in place for ten minutes. Record the readings for three to five consecutive days. Women who still have their menstrual period should not test on days 1, 2, 3, or 4 of their period, but can begin on day 5. Men, and girls and women who are not menstruating can test any time of the month.

Day 1: _____degrees Fahrenheit   Day of menstrual cycle: _____
Day 2: _____degrees Fahrenheit   Day of menstrual cycle: _____
Day 3: _____degrees Fahrenheit   Day of menstrual cycle: _____
Day 4: _____degrees Fahrenheit   Day of menstrual cycle: _____
Day 5: _____degrees Fahrenheit   Day of menstrual cycle: _____

5-Day Average temperature: _____ degrees Fahrenheit

Day 6: _____degrees Fahrenheit   Day of menstrual cycle: _____
Day 7: _____degrees Fahrenheit   Day of menstrual cycle: _____
Day 8: _____degrees Fahrenheit   Day of menstrual cycle: _____
Day 9: _____degrees Fahrenheit   Day of menstrual cycle: _____
Day 10: _____degrees Fahrenheit   Day of menstrual cycle: _____

5-Day Average temperature: _____ **degrees Fahrenheit**
10-Day Average temperature: _____ **degrees Fahrenheit**

PART II

Conventional and Alternative Treatment Options

5

Thyroid Hormone Replacement

Medicine is not only a science; it is also an art. It does not consist of compounding pills and plasters; it deals with the very processes of life, which must be understood before they may be guided.

— PARACELSUS

Once you have a diagnosis of hypothyroidism, the first step toward living well is often your doctor writing a prescription for thyroid hormone replacement. But before you rush out to get that prescription filled, it's useful to sit down with your doctor and make sure that you get answers to some important questions about your thyroid diagnosis and treatment. Often, this is hard to do. In the course of an appointment, your doctor might say, "Hmm, I'm going to check your thyroid." A nurse draws some blood, and the next thing you know, you're getting a rushed phone call from the doctor's office, saying that your thyroid's a little low and they'd like to phone in a prescription for you. Unfortunately, all too often this is how you find out you are hypothyroid, and even more unfortunate, this may be all the information you get from your doctor.

Even if this is how you find out, call back and ask for a phone call or personal consultation with your doctor to discuss your diagnosis. And don't hang up or leave till you get answers to the following critical questions.

What Is the Normal TSH Range at the Lab Where You Send My Blood, and What Was My TSH?

In addition to your own TSH level, it is important for you to know the normal TSH values at your lab, because this number can have a major impact on your ability to live well with hypothyroidism.

What Is Your Idea of an Optimum TSH Level for Me?

This is a basic question, but it is also a loaded question. Your doctor's answer will tell you her or his philosophy about "normal" TSH.

Some doctors believe that getting you into the very top of the normal range is their sole objective, and then the job is done. Again, I need to mention the old and new "normal" TSH range. The old range had normal TSH from approximately 0.5 to 5.5. But in 2003, this range was replaced by new standards indicating that normal TSH should be 0.3 to 3.0. Unfortunately, these new standards, which are even recommended by the American Association of Clinical Endocrinologists, have not yet been widely disseminated or adopted by the majority of physicians and the laboratories they use for thyroid testing.

What that means is if you are seeing a doctor who still goes by the old 0.5 to 5.5 TSH normal range, your doctor may:

- Refuse to diagnose or treat your hypothyroidism if you have a TSH of 3.01 to 5.5.
- Treat you, but provide you with only enough thyroid hormone to get your TSH to the high end of the normal range, i.e., 5.4.
- Tell you that if you don't feel well at that high end of normal, then something *else* is wrong with you because it's certainly not your thyroid, since after all, it's *normal*.

The majority of conventional doctors, unfortunately, follow this philosophy.

Even among those doctors who have adopted the new guidelines, you may still find those who:

- Treat you, but provide you with only enough thyroid hormone to get your TSH to the high end of the normal range, i.e., 2.9.
- Tell you that if you don't feel well at that high end of normal, then something *else* is wrong with you because it's certainly not your thyroid, since after all, it's *normal.*

The idea that different people feel their best at different TSH levels has not gained widespread acceptance among many endocrinologists or conventional physicians.

There's also a tendency among some doctors to let their patients remain in the higher end of the normal range because of concerns about osteoporosis. This is controversial, and there is simply not enough medical evidence to justify this decision. Doctors are confused, however, because there *is* evidence that when untreated, the *hyperthyroidism* of Graves' disease, or that results from nodules or goiter, can put a patient at increased risk of osteoporosis. But higher doses of thyroid hormone replacement do not appear to cause a similar risk. There are numerous studies that show *no increased risk of osteoporosis* for people on thyroid hormone replacement—both those who maintain their TSH in the normal range, and even those thyroid cancer patients who have their TSH levels suppressed to nearly undetectable, technically "hyperthyroid" levels to prevent cancer recurrence. There is, therefore, no proof that low or suppressed TSH levels pose a risk of osteoporosis, and don't let your doctor tell you that there is.

According to thyroid expert Dr. Robban Sica:

> A *number of long-term studies on patients with deliberately suppressed TSH—those who have a history of thyroid cancer or multi-nodular goiter—showed no evidence of increased bone loss in follow up ranging from 3 to 27 years.*

Only with elevated T4 levels has there been increased risk of osteoporosis.

What Thyroid Hormone Replacement Have You Prescribed for Me?

Since you probably can't read the writing, you'll need to ask! The issue here is, brand name or generic? And if a brand name, did your doctor specify "daw" (dispense as written) on the prescription, meaning that the pharmacy cannot substitute a generic or cheaper brand for the brand specified? Brand-name thyroid hormone replacement is considered more reliable. Generics can be erratic and should be avoided.

How Quickly Can We Expect My TSH to Return to Normal, Given the Dosage You've Prescribed?

What you want to know is if your doctor is giving you a small dose of thyroid replacement, and intending to see what happens very slowly, or is he or she going to get you into the normal range as fast as possible. There are reasons for taking either approach, but it's important to know which one your doctor will use. Some doctors will put you on a tiny dose, then tell you you'll feel better in two weeks. When two weeks come and go, and you don't feel better, you think something's wrong with *you*. Other doctors may give you a larger starting dose, and that can sometimes cause hyperthyroid symptoms in some people. Understand the dose you are getting, and where it ranks in terms of small or large, and talk to your doctor about what to expect.

How Often Will You Test My TSH Until I Get Back to Feeling Well?

What you want to hear is that the doc is going to stay on top of your condition until you feel better. For those doctors who use normal TSH as a gauge, this means probably seeing you every six to eight weeks for a TSH test, followed up with an adjustment to your dosage, until you're feeling better and TSH results are normal.

After I'm Feeling Well, How Often Do You Suggest I Come Back for a TSH Test to Make Sure My Dosage Requirements Haven't Changed?

If the doc says once a year or once every two years, start wondering. Most doctors recommend every six months in the first year or two, and every year—at minimum—thereafter.

If I Have Questions Between Appointments, How Can I Best Get in Touch with You? Do You Return Calls Yourself or Do Your Nurses? Can I Fax in a Question? Do You Have an E-mail Address for Patient Correspondence?

Here, you can gauge how available the doctor plans to be. And if you have the option of looking for another doctor, the response here may help you decide if you'll stay or go. Some doctors will return calls themselves or even answer e-mail. Others will refer all questions to the nurses (who, by the way, often have just as good or even better information. So don't write that off as an option). But if you want personalized, hands-on service, listen to how the doctor answers so you'll get an idea of what to expect.

■ About Thyroid Hormone Treatments

When you are hypothyroid, your body doesn't produce enough thyroid hormone, and you need to replace that missing thyroid hormone. This process of treating hypothyroidism by taking external thyroid hormone drugs is called "thyroid hormone replacement."

When it comes to thyroid hormone replacement, there are several types of thyroid drugs. Here's a brief overview:

• *Natural thyroid*. This is a nonsynthetic thyroid hormone replacement produced using the thyroid gland of pigs, containing T4, T3, and other nonspecific components of thyroid hormone. The brand names in the U.S. are Armour Thyroid, Naturethroid, Westhroid, and Biotech.

- *Levothyroxine*. Pronounced lee-voe-thy-ROX-een, this is the generic name for synthetic thyroxine, also known as T4. Brand names in the U.S. and Canada include Synthroid, Levothroid, Levoxyl, Unithroid, Eltroxin, and PMS-Levothyroxine.
- *Liothyronine*. Pronounced lye-oh-THY-roe-neen, this is the synthetic form of triiodothyronine, T3. The brand name in the U.S. and Canada is Cytomel.
- *Liotrix*. Pronounced LYE-oh-trix, this is a synthetic combination of levothyroxine and liothyronine. It's a synthetic T4/T3 drug. The brand name in the U.S. is Thyrolar.
- *Compounded thyroid drugs*. Compounding pharmacies are specialty pharmacies that can make up a variety of customized thyroid drugs, including additive-free, dye-free, filler-free, and time-released versions of levothyroxine, liothyronine, levothyroxine/liothyronine, natural thyroid, and natural thyroid with levothyroxine or liothyronine. These drugs are not manufactured in bulk and do not go by particular brand names. They are prescribed by your physician, and you have the prescription filled at a special compounding pharmacy. A list of some compounding pharmacies with expertise in thyroid drugs is featured in the Resources section of this book.

Natural Thyroid

Natural desiccated thyroid drugs, made from porcine (pig) thyroid glands, contain T4, T3, and other active hormones. The top seller in this category is Armour Thyroid, which has been on the market for more than one hundred years, and for the first half of the twentieth century, was the only thyroid hormone replacement drug available. Armour, currently made by Forest Labs, is joined by Western Pharmaceuticals' products, Naturethroid and Westhroid. Naturethroid is a particular brand of natural thyroid hormone that is hypoallergenic and does not include any corn binders. Another product, Biotech, is sometimes available. There is a generic desiccated thyroid, usually referred to as "Thyroid Strong," that is available in the United States and in Canada, Parke-Davis makes a natural desiccated thyroid drug. It should be noted that these drugs are *legal, regulated, prescription-only* drugs, and should not be confused with over-the-counter, unregulated thyroid "glandulars."

In addition to being in favor with some holistic and natural practitioners as well as their patients, natural thyroid product fans also include some "old-timers," doctors who prescribed natural thyroid successfully for years, and then saw the health of their patients erode when their patients switched over to synthetics.

Periodically, rumors go around, indicating that you should be concerned about your Armour Thyroid being infected with bovine spongiform encephalopathy (BSE), also known as "mad cow disease." This rumor is unfounded. First, desiccated thyroid, such as Armour, Naturethroid, and Biotech, is made from the desiccated thyroid glands of *pigs*, not cows. Pigs have not been shown to contract BSE, the disease-causing agent. While some practitioners and patients erroneously claim that these drugs come from bovine (cow) thyroid, that is not the case. It is also highly unlikely that Armour Thyroid would transmit mad cow disease for several reasons:

- The thyroid glands used in the preparation of Armour Thyroid are obtained from pigs that are intended for consumption by humans.
- The pigs must be grain-fed and cannot be fed any animal proteins that might contain mad cow prions.
- These pigs are inspected by the USDA, and diseased animals are not used for human consumption.
- The thyroid glands are highly unlikely to have the mad cow prions in them even if the animal had been exposed to mad cow disease at the time of slaughter, since the prions do not appear to concentrate in the thyroid.

Rumors also go around periodically that indicate that these drugs are "going off the market" or "won't be available anymore," or, as one opponent of the drugs, Richard Guttler, has declared, are "heading to the Thyroid Museum for Antiquated Medicines." All signs are, however, that these drugs are here to stay, and rumors to the contrary appear to have been started by competing drug company sales representatives—the fallout from marketing wars as companies scramble to maintain profitable market share.

The issue of whether or not to use natural desiccated thyroid products like Armour is one of the major controversies in hypothyroidism treatment, and is discussed at length in Chapter 10.

Levothyroxine / Synthetic T4

Levothyroxine, a synthetic version of the T4 hormone thyroxine, has been on the market for around fifty years and came onto the scene as a synthetic alternative to the desiccated thyroid that had been available since the early 1900s. The vast majority of doctors now prescribe levothyroxine as the thyroid hormone replacement drug of choice, and when they prescribe levothyroxine, it's usually the brand-name Synthroid. Synthroid, made by Abbott Labs, is the top-selling thyroid hormone replacement in the United States, and one of the top-selling drugs in America. Since it was first introduced, Synthroid has maintained a firm hold on the top position due to its various manufacturers' extensive marketing to the medical community, and pervasive financial influence over the professional and patient thyroid organizations.

Loyalty to particular brands and the effects of financial influence have caused many doctors to recommend Synthroid over other levothyroxine brands, or to say that Synthroid is better than its competitors. While Synthroid is frequently more expensive at many pharmacies, it is not scientifically rated as more effective than other brand-name thyroid hormones, The major brands, including Mylan/King's Levoxyl, Forest Labs' Levothroid, and Jerome Steven's Unithroid, are considered equivalent. The main difference is that each

brand of levothyroxine has different fillers and binders, and some dissolve more quickly than others. Synthroid, for example, dissolves
very slowly, while Levoxyl dissolves quickly and needs to be swal-
lowed quickly, with a big glass of water, for maximum effectiveness.

Because all the brand-name levothyroxines are considered bioequivalent, you have the option of taking levothyroxine products
that are less expensive than Synthroid, as long as you remain with a
brand name. While all levothyroxine products have some ups and
downs in potency from batch to batch, brand names have fewer
variations in potency than generic brands. Most doctors do not recommend or prescribe generic levothyroxine anyway, but pharmacies
often will substitute them. Some health maintenance organizations
insist on the cheaper generic when a brand name has been prescribed. *Do not accept generic levothyroxine if at all possible*, and
always be sure to check your prescription every time you get it filled
to make sure the pharmacy hasn't substituted generic for brand
name.

A small number of patients apparently are allergic to the fillers in
one brand versus another. So if you have unusual reactions, such as
hives or rashes, or other allergic responses after taking certain
brands, you should talk to your doctor about trying a different
brand.

From 1997 well into 2003, levothyroxine drugs went through a
new drug application process with the FDA, and are now newly approved. These drugs had earlier been grandfathered in under the approval given decades earlier to Armour Thyroid, but the FDA
determined that the lack of assured potency and stability found in
levothyroxine products required that they go through a separate application process almost fifty years after their introduction to the
American market. While all the drugs currently on the market have
managed—despite their numerous deadline extensions, competitive
wranglings, and FDA warnings—to pass the FDA process, there are
still frequent recalls of most brands, due to potency and stability
problems. It appears that the approval process did not achieve much

improvement for patients in terms of product reliability. (More on the politics behind this process is included in Chapter 19.)

A general rule? If you don't do well on one brand of levothyroxine, ask to try another, rather than suffer with symptoms.

Liothyronine/Synthetic T3 and Liotrix, Synthetic T3/T4

Synthetic levothyroxine offers only T4 and depends on the body's ability to effectively convert T4 to the T3 needed at the cellular level. If the conversion works properly in the body, the levothyroxine therapy will usually work, as it does for some people with hypothyroidism who do take the pill, feel fine and normal, and only think about their hypothyroidism when they have their blood checked annually.

If there's evidence—in the form of unrelieved symptoms despite normal TSH levels—that the conversion is not optimal, some doctors will prescribe additional T3. The only brand-name drug that is T3 is a synthetic version, liothyronine, known under the brand name Cytomel and made by King Pharmaceuticals. No generic version is sold in the United States. You can, however, get time-released, compounded liothyronine by prescription at compounding pharmacies.

The synthetic T4/T3 combination drug Thyrolar (liotrix) is made by Forest Labs. Again, there is no generic version of this drug on the market.

Doctors who are more willing to work with these drugs tend to be osteopaths, naturopaths, and holistic M.D.s. There are some endocrinologists who are using these drugs when necessary for a particular patient's treatment. Psychopharmacologists are also known to use drugs with T3 as a way to help treat unrelieved depression in hypothyroid patients and in nonhypothyroid people with resistant depression.

■ Taking Your Thyroid Hormone

When you pick up your prescription for thyroid hormone, some pharmacies will send you home with a basic page of information or maybe the drug information insert. Others provide no additional information beyond the label on the pill bottle. Even if you've been taking your thyroid hormone for years or have attempted to read a pharmaceutical company product insert, you should know how to store and take your thyroid hormone and whether there are interactions with foods and other drugs.

What If You Miss a Dose?

All the package instructions say that if you miss a dose, you should take it as soon as possible. If you're close to the time for the next dose, skip the missed dose and just go back to your regular dosing schedule. Basically, you shouldn't double up if you miss a day. If I miss a dose, I usually split the dose and make it up over the next two days. But that's just me, and that's not medical advice. Ask your doctor what she or he thinks you should do if you miss a dose.

How Can You Better Remember to Take Your Medication?

The doctors call it "noncompliance." In plain English, it means "not taking your medicine" in the manner in which it was prescribed. When you need to take thyroid hormone replacement, it's critical that you take it every day as prescribed. Even a day or two's failure to take thyroid medications can throw off your treatment regimen and have a dramatic effect on your overall health. Here are some tips on how to remember to take your thyroid medication:

• Write it in your datebook. Write it in a special color that is hard to miss.
• If you use a computer or personal data assistant (PDA) like a Palm Pilot, consider putting your reminder in the scheduling program. Some programs allow you to set a regular daily "appoint-

ment" at a particular time. Some even have an alarm function you can set to remind you.

• Put a message on your computer's screen saver.

• Keep your thyroid drug pill container right on top of your alarm clock, so you can remember to take your medicine first thing in the morning. (But be careful to keep your medications away from children.)

• Link taking your medicine with key daily events, such as brushing your teeth in the morning.

• Put a note wherever you'll notice it every day—on the refrigerator, on your coffeemaker, on your toothbrush, or on your bathroom vanity mirror.

• Take your medicine the same time every day, so it becomes a habit.

• Hire a calling service to give you a daily "wake-up" call to remind you to take your pill. If you have a home voice-mail answering system such as "AnswerCall," you can program a daily reminder call at the same time each day. You can even sign up online for free services like "Mr Wakeup" or "Dr. Dose," which will make reminder calls to you.

• Use a pill sorter or a device known as a "dosette," which has compartments for different days, or even different times of the day.

• Get a special device to remind you to take your pill. You can get medication computers, vibrating watches, automatic dispensers, beepers, and other alarms that can help keep you on schedule for taking your medication.

• Enlist the aid of a family member or friend. Sometimes just a few weeks of friendly reminders can help you get into the habit of taking your medicine at the right time every day.

Should You Refrigerate Your Thyroid Hormone?

At present, the only brand of thyroid hormone replacement in pill form that requires refrigeration is Thyrolar, the brand name for liotrix, the synthetic T4/T3 product. This was a requirement started in the 1990s, though the drug has been on the market far longer. The manufacturer had its last round of evaluations and potency studies on a product that was refrigerated, so the law now requires that it list that the product requires refrigeration. Pharmacists at Forest, the drug's manufacturer, have indicated that refrigeration will actually help the product maintain optimal potency longer. If you need to travel, however, they say the product should remain stable for at least a week. So you don't have to go to extraordinary lengths to keep Thyrolar refrigerated while traveling.

The other products have no refrigeration requirement, but anecdotally some patients who have taken thyroid hormone for years have told me that they regularly keep it in the refrigerator because they feel that it keeps their prescriptions from losing their potency. Since Thyrolar is synthetic like the other products, if the pharmacists say that refrigerating Thyrolar keeps it potent longer, I wonder why that wouldn't be true for similar products that don't require refrigeration? There are no official proclamations on this from the drug companies, but I can tell you, when I was taking it, I refrigerated Thyrolar, and when I was on levothyroxine products in the past, I refrigerated them too.

Should You Take Thyroid Hormone Replacement When You're Pregnant or Breast-feeding?

I discuss these issues at greater length in the chapter on pregnancy and breast-feeding, but the simple answer is: YES! We take seriously the warnings not to take most drugs during pregnancy and, for the most part, this is good advice. However, when it comes to thyroid hormone, you're replacing something essential that your body is missing. Thyroid hormone is not something optional; it is absolutely *essential* for your body's proper functioning, and for when you are pregnant. Recent research has shown that even mild or subclinical hypothyroidism during pregnancy can increase your risk of serious problems, including premature birth, stillbirth, or lower IQ in your baby. So *do not stop taking thyroid hormone when pregnant.* There's no evidence that in proper doses it causes any harm to the baby. It is considered one of the safest things to take during pregnancy, safer than a decongestant, for example. Keep in mind, however, that 85 percent of pregnant women with hypothyroidism require an increase in thyroid hormone replacement drug to protect the baby from adverse outcomes.

When breast-feeding, you will also need to take your prescribed dosage to ensure your body's proper functioning and your ability to maintain a healthy milk supply. If you are taking your thyroid hormone in the proper dose, very little to none of it enters the baby's milk, and there's no evidence that it causes any harm to the baby whatsoever. Dosage requirements do change in the months after pregnancy for many women, however, so be sure to be checked periodically by your practitioner.

What If You Don't Tolerate Thyroid Medication?

A subset of people who are hypothyroid find that taking any amount of thyroid hormone creates problems. These people will have palpitations and extreme hyperthyroidlike symptoms after taking even the smallest standard dosage of thyroid hormone replacement medicine.

Not taking medicine is not a solution, because hypothyroidism ultimately requires treatment, but many of these patients are in a Catch-22 situation: Treat the hypothyroidism and prevent long-term illness—or suffer debilitating symptoms and side effects due to their oversensitivity to thyroid medications.

Thyroid expert Dr. Stephen Langer has worked with patients who are intolerant of thyroid medications. He works with a reputable compounding pharmacist to produce an aqueous—water-based—solution of thyroid medicine. Then, he has patients start with a daily dose as small as one drop, which is ¹/₁₀th of a quarter of a grain. He then has them go up in dosage one drop at a time. According to Dr. Langer:

> . . . with most of these patients, it takes a much longer period of time, but they can get to the right quantity of thyroid using the aqueous thyroid and can eventually be transferred over to the tablets.

Should You Take Your Thyroid Hormone with Food Versus on an Empty Stomach?

If you eat while taking certain prescription drugs, the food in your stomach may delay or reduce the drug's absorption. This is true for thyroid hormone. Food can often slow the process of the drug entering the stomach, but it may also affect absorption of the drug you're taking by binding with it. This decreases the body's ability to absorb the medication by changing the rate at which it dissolves or by changing the stomach's acid balance. Some doctors will tell you it doesn't matter, but if you want to get the most "bang for your buck," thyroid hormone–wise, you'll have best absorption if you take your thyroid hormone first thing the morning, on an empty stomach about one hour before eating.

However, if you don't take it this way, then consistency becomes the key to maintaining a stable level in your bloodstream. If you're going to take your thyroid hormone with food, take it every day with food, consistently. If you've changed from taking it on an empty stomach, you should have another TSH test about six to eight weeks later to ensure you're receiving the proper amount of thyroid hormone. While taking the drug with food might inhibit absorption somewhat, the safety check of an additional blood test will ensure that your dosage gets changed as needed. But again, *consistency* is the key. Don't take it some days with food, some days without, or you're sure to have erratic absorption and it will be harder to regulate your TSH levels.

Should You Take Your Thyroid Medication More Than Once a Day?

Some people wonder if they should take their thyroid drugs more than once a day. First, you should discuss this with your physician. But in general, if you are taking a levothyroxine/T4-only drug, there is no benefit to splitting your dose and taking it multiple times a day. The drug is dissolved so slowly, and has such a long half-life in your body, that there is no benefit to be had by taking it in staggered doses.

For drugs that contain T3, including Cytomel, Thyrolar, Armour, and the other desiccated thyroid drugs, and compounded drugs that contain T3, you may in fact want to stagger your dosage throughout the day, to help maintain a steady level. T3 is faster-acting, has a short half-life in the body, and some people report better results when they take their thyroid medications two or three times a day. In my own case, I take Armour Thyroid, and I usually take it three times a day. That said, if you are likely to forget to take it multiple times per day, you are better off taking it once a day. The compounded time-released drugs eliminate the need for split dosages by gradually releasing T3 throughout the day.

What Is the Impact of a High-Fiber Diet?

Many people on thyroid replacement therapy are fighting an additional battle to lose weight, and switching to a high-fiber diet can be a help in that weight battle. But a high-fiber diet can also affect your thyroid hormone absorption. Anything that affects your digestion speed, or speed of food absorption into the stomach, can affect your absorption of thyroid hormone. Since high-fiber diets are known to speed digestion, they can also inhibit absorption for some people. So, should you forget about eating high-fiber? Absolutely not!

Since the benefits of a high-fiber diet are known, again, the issue is consistency. If you are already eating a high-fiber diet regularly and have regular TSH testing done, your dosage level is appropriate for you, given your diet. If you are starting a new regimen of eating high-fiber, plan to get tested around six to eight weeks after you change your diet, to make sure you're receiving the proper amount of thyroid hormone. Be consistent. Don't jump around or you'll have erratic absorption, and that can wreak havoc on TSH levels . . . *and* how you feel! But again, you can bypass some of the impact by taking your thyroid hormone first thing in the morning, on an empty stomach, and waiting at least an hour to eat. This will ensure maximum absorption *whatever* you're eating!

What About Vitamins with Iron or Iron Supplements?

Iron, whether taken by itself or as part of a multivitamin or prenatal vitamin supplement, can interfere with thyroid hormone absorption. However, don't stop taking your iron. You can still take iron supplements when you're on thyroid hormone replacement. The only concern is that you should *not* take your vitamins with iron at the same time as your thyroid hormone. To ensure there's no interference with absorption, allow *at least three or more hours* between taking iron and thyroid hormone.

What About Calcium Supplements?

Many people on thyroid hormone replacement—especially women concerned about osteoporosis—also take calcium supplements. Calcium supplements are also important for thyroid cancer survivors, because the suppressive doses of thyroid hormone called for in cancer patients may increase the risk of osteoporosis. You need to be careful about calcium supplements, however. A 2001 study reported on in the journal *Thyroid* found that calcium carbonate acutely reduces the absorption of levothyroxine. In measuring those taking levothyroxine alone and levothyroxine together with 2.0 grams(g) of calcium carbonate, it was found that those taking levothyroxine alone absorbed 83.7 percent of the dose two hours after taking it. When levothyroxine was taken along with the calcium, absorption decreased to 59 percent at four hours. Over six hours, absorption was far better in those who did not take the calcium.

Another study from 1999 found that some patients taking levothyroxine experienced an increase in TSH levels after they started to take calcium supplements. When they changed their pattern and began to take the calcium and thyroid hormone *at least four hours apart*, TSH returned to the initial level. This finding can be of particular relevance to those who have had their thyroid removed and are taking calcium on doctor's orders. The calcium taken at the same time as thyroid hormone was, in some cases, raising TSH above levels recommended to prevent thyroid cancer recurrence. If you are taking calcium, it should be taken at least *four hours apart* from thyroid hormone.

What About Calcium-Fortified Orange Juice?

Taking thyroid hormone about the same time as calcium-fortified orange juice has reportedly had a similar effect as taking calcium pills with thyroid. If you want to ensure proper dosage and absorption, don't take your thyroid pills at the same time as calcium-fortified orange juice. Keep in mind that you should drink calcium-fortified orange juice and take thyroid hormone at least *four hours apart*.

Is There a Problem with Antacids?

Antacids—like Tums or Mylanta, in liquid or tablet forms—contain calcium, and may delay or reduce the absorption of your thyroid hormone. So again, they should be taken *at least four hours* apart from thyroid hormone.

When Is It Appropriate to Stop Taking Thyroid Hormone Replacement?

People frequently write in to ask me, "When can I stop taking my thyroid hormone?" Keep in mind that most people who are hypothyroid are hypothyroid for life. This is not a short-term condition, like an infection, where you take antibiotics for a while, the infection is "cured," and you're done. Occasionally, some people have a temporary thyroid problem or go into remission, but it is more likely that you will always require thyroid hormone replacement.

In certain cases, you may be asked to stop taking your thyroid hormone when switching to a new doctor. Your new doctor runs a test and finds a "normal TSH." The new doctor then tells you to *stop* taking thyroid hormone because your thyroid is "normal." Or he or she may want to see "if you still need to be taking it."

My advice? Definitely get a new doctor—or at least a second opinion—before going off any thyroid medication for your hypothyroidism. Why is it so complicated for a doctor to understand that in most cases, your test results are normal *because* you are being treated? It's as ridiculous as telling a diabetic who is taking proper care of herself and using her insulin and other medications correctly to *stop* taking insulin and other medications *because* her blood sugar levels are normal! It makes no sense.

What About Over-the-Counter Drugs Like Cough Medicines, Cold Medicines, and Decongestants That Recommend "Do Not Take If You Have Thyroid Disease"?

Most packages of over-the-counter cough and cold medicines and decongestants recommend: "Do not take if you have one of the following . . ." and then go on to list thyroid disease. While you should always check with your doctor, it's generally understood that this warning is intended mainly for people with an overactive thyroid—hyperthyroidism—rather than hypothyroidism. Stimulants like pseudoephedrine, the main ingredient in Sudafed and many other cold and allergy medicines, can be dangerous to people with hyperthyroidism, as they can add strain to an already taxed heart.

That said, is there a concern for those with hypothyroidism? There are anecdotal reports of people with thyroid disease becoming extrasensitive to stimulants. For example, some with hypothyroidism seem to develop sensitivities to caffeine, or to pseudoephedrine, and even natural ephedra, an herb that was used in diet and energy supplements, and Chinese herbal remedies. In my case, for example, I used to be able to take a Sudafed without a problem, but now even half a capsule causes heart palpitations. And I *really* have to be careful not to take it with a caffeinated beverage or I definitely have an hour of palpitations. I can take other cold products and antihistamines, for example, without a problem. I typically will choose cold medicines that don't include pseudoephedrine.

My recommendation? Talk to your doctor about these products before you try them, and if you get the go-ahead, try a much smaller dose than usual, see if it affects you, and if you feel okay, try working your way up to the normal dose.

What About Thyroid Hormone and Estrogen/the Pill?

Taking estrogen in any form, whether via controversial hormone replacement therapy or in birth control pills, can affect thyroid test results.

For example, some women taking estrogen may need to take more thyroid replacement hormone. The various hormone drugs (such as Estrace, Estraderm, Premarin, Prempro, Estradiol, and various forms of the Pill) increase a particular protein that binds thyroid hormone to it, making the thyroid hormone partially inactive. Thyroid tests can end up showing falsely increased total T4 levels. For a woman without a thyroid (i.e., surgically removed or radioactively ablated), this binding may increase your dosage requirement slightly, as you have no thyroid to compensate. Being on thyroid hormone replacement certainly does not mean you shouldn't take hormone replacement or birth control pills prescribed by your doctor. However, after beginning any estrogen therapy, you should have thyroid tests run six to eight weeks later to see if the addition of estrogen means you'll need a thyroid dosage adjustment. Also, be sure the doctor prescribing the Pill or estrogen replacement is aware that you're on thyroid hormone.

Some experts believe that estrogen has a demonstrable impact on thyroid function. According to hormonal expert Dr. David Brownstein, for example:

> . . . *any orally prescribed estrogen will result in an increase in thyroxine binding globulin (TBG), which will decrease the amount of thyroid hormone that is available for the body to use.*

Other experts have theorized that estrogen may interfere with the conversion of T4 to T3, and that the widespread use of birth control pills and the popularity—until recently—of estrogen replacement therapy drugs such as Premarin, may be contributing to our current epidemic of thyroid disease and obesity by impairing the conversion of T4 to active T3.

Are There Interactions with Antidepressants and Thyroid Hormone?

Use of tricyclic antidepressants such as doxepin, amitriptyline, desipramine, and imipramine—some brand names include Adapin, Elavil, Norpramin, and Tofranil—at the same time as thyroid hormones may increase the effects of both drugs and may *accelerate the effects of the antidepressant.* Be sure your doctor knows you are on one before prescribing the other.

Also, researchers have found that taking thyroid hormone replacement along with the popular antidepressant sertraline (Zoloft) can cause a *decrease in the effectiveness of the thyroid hormone replacement.* This same effect has also been seen in patients receiving other selective serotonin-reuptake inhibitors such as paroxetine (Paxil) and fluoxetine (Prozac).

If you are on an antidepressant or thyroid hormone and your doctor wants to prescribe the other, be sure to discuss these issues and consider getting your thyroid retested six to eight weeks after beginning antidepressant therapy to evaluate any possible interactions.

Are There Other Drug Interactions?

A number of other drugs interact with thyroid hormone or affect thyroid function.

- *Insulin*—Thyroid hormone can reduce the effectiveness of insulin and the similar drugs for diabetes. Be sure your doctor knows you are on one before prescribing the other.
- *Cholesterol-Lowering Drugs, Cholestyramine or Colestipol*—These drugs—known by brand names such as Colestrol, Questran, Colestid—bind thyroid hormones. A minimum of *four to five hours* should elapse between taking these drugs and thyroid hormones.
- *Anticoagulants ("Blood Thinners")*—Anticoagulant drugs like warfarin, Coumadin, or heparin can sometimes become stronger in the system when thyroid hormone is added to the mix. Mention it to your doctor if you are on one or the other.
- *Corticosteroids/Adrenocorticosteroids*—These include cortisone, Cortistab, and Cortone. These drugs suppress TSH and can block the conversion of T4 to T3 in some people.
- *Amiodarone HCL*—This heart drug, known by the brand name Cordarone, can cause hypothyroidism or hyperthyroidism and can interfere with T4 metabolism. People taking Cordarone should be monitored periodically for thyroid changes.
- *Ketamine*—Some people have had elevated blood pressure and a racing heartbeat when they've taken levothyroxine sodium and the anesthetic ketamine at the same time.
- *Maprotiline*—This antidepressant can increase a risk of cardiac arrhythmias when taken with thyroid hormone products.
- *Theophylline*—This drug for asthma and respiratory diseases may not clear out of the body as quickly when someone is hypothyroid, but usually clears normally when the thyroid is in the normal range.
- *Lithium*—Lithium is known actually to create hypothyroidism by blocking the secretion of T4 and T3. People taking lithium should be monitored periodically for thyroid changes.

• *Phenytoin*—This anticonvulsant, a brand of which is Dilantin, may accelerate levothyroxine metabolism, and tests may show decreased total T4 levels.

• *Carbamazepine*—This anticonvulsant pain medicine, a brand of which is Tegretol, may accelerate levothyroxine metabolism, and tests may show decreased total T4 levels.

• *Rifampin*—This antituberculosis agent may accelerate levothyroxine metabolism, and tests may show decreased total T4 levels.

What About Goitrogenic Foods?

Goitrogens are products and foods that promote the formation of goiters. They can act like antithyroid drugs in disabling the thyroid and cause hypothyroidism. Specifically, goitrogens have some ability to inhibit the body's ability to use iodine, block the process by which iodine becomes the thyroid hormones T4 and T3, inhibit the actual secretion of thyroid hormone, and disrupt the peripheral conversion of T4 to T3. If you are hypothyroid due to thyroidectomy, you don't have to be particularly concerned about goitrogens. If you still have a thyroid, however, you need to be more concerned about goitrogens and be careful not to eat them uncooked in large quantities. Some experts believe that the enzymes involved in the formation of "goitrogenic" materials in plants can be destroyed by cooking, so thorough cooking may minimize some or most goitrogenic potential. Goitrogenic foods are listed on pages 34–35.

Are There Seasonal Variations in Thyroid Hormone Requirements?

One little-known issue for thyroid patients in terms of their dosage of thyroid hormone is the seasonal variation in thyroid function.

There haven't been enough studies that evaluate exactly how the dosage requirements fluctuate and how they should be adjusted to take seasonal changes into account. Research shows, however, that TSH naturally rises during colder months and drops to low-normal or even hyperthyroid levels in the warmest months. Some doctors will adjust for this by prescribing slightly increased dosages during colder months and reducing dosage during warm periods. Most, however, are not aware of this seasonal fluctuation, and patients suffer worsening hypothyroidism symptoms during cold winter months, and hyperthyroidism symptoms during warmer months due to slight overdosage.

This seasonal fluctuation becomes more pronounced in older people and in particularly cold climates. To maintain optimal wellness, seasonal variation in TSH should be taken into consideration when evaluating the adequacy of a levothyroxine dose. Patients should insist on having twice-yearly—rather than annual—tests, especially during winter and summer months, to help assess the fluctuation, so that an adequate general replacement dosage and modification for seasonal change can be determined.

■ How Long Will It Really Take to Feel Better?

Once you're diagnosed and begin thyroid hormone replacement, the most obvious question is how long will it take until you feel better?

Many doctors and endocrinologists tell patients that it might take two weeks to start feeling better. Some people actually do feel well as early as two weeks after starting thyroid hormone replacement . . . but not most people.

For example, it took about four months for me to *start* feeling human again as my TSH crept down from a high of 15, plus several more months after that to tweak the dosages and get them even better in range.

Think of it this way. It takes months or years—*not* a few weeks—for your body to get hypothyroid in the first place. Unfortunately, your thyroid hormone replacement drug is not a magic pill like an aspirin that takes away a headache in minutes. When you start taking a T4-only medication like levothyroxine, it actually takes around two weeks for it even to be reflected in your TSH levels. Even then, your body needs to absorb, use, and apply it over time.

Knowing that I wasn't expected to feel perfect again right away was comforting in its own way. I wanted to feel better quickly, but I also had hope that I would continue to improve over time. I think having realistic expectations can make you feel better, even if you still don't feel well physically.

Some say that autoimmune diseases like thyroid disease strike "Type A" personalities more often. We want to be in control, to do more and more and more, go faster, higher, better, and this condition lays us low and forces us to give up control. Infuriating! The one thing I really learned was how patience is essential. I'm *not* good at that. But I had to try, and you do too.

While waiting for your thyroid hormone replacement to kick into action, do other things for yourself as much as possible. Try to get extra rest. Get a massage, or visit an acupuncture session for energy. Take a yoga or T'ai Chi class. Take out a temporary membership at a health club, and do some gentle exercising. Treat yourself, pamper yourself, and figure you're helping your recuperation, helping your body to heal while on your way to living well.

■ Fluctuating Thyroid Levels

People frequently write to ask about why they have different thyroid levels from blood test to blood test. For example, a TSH test three months ago may have showed a TSH level of 3.0, but the most recent test shows 1.1. Or perhaps a year ago, the TSH was 0.4, and now it's 4.0. What factors might account for thyroid levels that are changing? Are there things you may be doing that are affecting your thyroid levels? Let's take a look at some of the factors that can cause your TSH to fluctuate.

Change in Dosage

The most obvious cause of a TSH change is a change in dosage. If after your last blood test, the doctor changed your dosage, your thyroid levels may have changed in response.

Potency Fluctuations in Your Medicine

If you've had your prescription refilled since your last thyroid test, this may be a reason why your TSH has changed. Thyroid drugs, for the most part, can fluctuate significantly in terms of potency and stability, and yet still be sold. So, even from batch to batch of the same brand drug at the same dosage, filled by the same pharmacy, you may experience variance in the drug's potency level, with significant enough changes in potency to affect your thyroid levels somewhat. Then there are recalls of batches that flagged as having particular fluctuations in potency—a regular problem with the levothyroxine drugs, for example. One option to avoid these fluctuations is to consider looking into whether you can order larger quantities of pills—so that you get pills from a single batch and don't have to refill the prescription as often. Some insurance companies will actually encourage you to get longer-term supplies, via their mail-order pharmacy services, so this might be a good option.

Lab Changes or Mix-ups

Different laboratories may return slightly different results. If you have a variance from one test result to the next, be sure to check with your doctor to find out if the new test was sent to the same laboratory as the first test. If the samples went to a new lab, that may account for the next test results being substantially different; and because they are coming from a new lab, it's worth retesting to confirm that the results are accurate. Sometimes there are simply errors in lab results. Samples are switched, numbers transcribed, etc. So if the results don't make sense, don't be afraid to ask the doctor to confirm with a retest.

Timing of When You Take Your Pill on Test Day

While when you take a levothyroxine pill doesn't typically have an effect on your overall TSH levels, the timing of a T3 drug can. So ideally, on the day you have a blood test, you should try to avoid taking your thyroid hormone until after you've had your blood taken. This is particularly important if you are having T3 and Free T3 levels measured.

Timing of When You Take Your Pill Daily

If you are taking your pill at different times each day, you may sometimes be taking your thyroid hormone on an empty stomach, and sometimes with or after food. This means that you may be getting higher or lower absorption with each dose. You'll get more consistent absorption taking it either first thing the morning on an empty stomach about one hour before eating, or taking it the same time each day, with or without food.

Starting/Stopping a High-Fiber Diet

Starting or stopping a high-fiber diet since your last test can affect your TSH level, especially if you are not taking your thyroid hormone first thing in the morning, on an empty stomach, and waiting at least an hour to eat.

Starting/Stopping Calcium or Iron Supplements

If you've started or stopped taking calcium or iron supplements, or calcium-fortified juices or drinks, this may cause thyroid levels to fluctuate.

Too Much Soy

If you've been going heavy on the soy since your last test, you might try cutting out much of the soy to see if that is the reason your thyroid levels are fluctuating.

Eating Too Many Goitrogenic Foods

If you have been going heavy on goitrogenic foods (see pages 34–35), this may be contributing to fluctuating thyroid levels.

Change of Seasons

TSH will often rise during colder months in many people, and drop in hotter months, causing fluctuating levels.

Hormonal Fluctuations

Taking estrogen in any form, whether as hormone replacement therapy or in birth control pills, and the fluctuating hormones of menopause can all cause thyroid levels to fluctuate.

Pregnancy

The intense surge in estrogen during early pregnancy can increase your TSH, and increase your body's need for thyroid hormone. But in the postpregnancy period, you may have been diagnosed with a postpartum thyroid problem. For the majority of women, this condition will resolve itself, meaning that over time, you can expect the thyroid to attempt to return to normal, TSH levels will reflect these changes, and your drug dosages will need to be changed in response.

Herbs/Supplements You Are Taking

Some herbal supplements can have an impact on thyroid function. Herbs such as the Ayurvedic herb "guggul" and supplements such as selenium and tyrosine, and products containing iodine such as vitamins; or kelp and bladderwrack supplements have the potential either to increase or decrease thyroid function and cause thyroid level fluctuations.

Prescription Drugs You Are Taking

Starting or stopping one of a number of prescription drugs, especially antidepressants, cholesterol-lowering drugs, and corticosteroids among others (see the list in Chapter 2), can have an impact on your thyroid levels.

Stress and Illness

Your endocrine system is responsive to physical and emotional stress, and periods of intense stress, or the relief of such stress, may have an impact on your TSH levels. Some patients report, for example, that they will have an increase in TSH levels, and require higher doses of thyroid hormone replacement, during and after periods when they are undergoing stress, not getting proper nutrition, or are overtired due to insufficient sleep.

Progression of Your Thyroid Disease

You may have been diagnosed with autoimmune Hashimoto's disease a year ago, have been prescribed thyroid hormone, gone back six weeks later, and your TSH was 2.5. The doctor decided that your levels were fine and told you to come back in a year. And now this year's test shows your TSH at 5.7. This sort of increase may reflect the progression of the autoimmune process . . . in that as antibodies further attack the thyroid, it becomes less and less able to produce thyroid hormone on its own, therefore, TSH levels will rise.

6

Alternative Medicine for Thyroid Disease

Doctors don't know everything really. They understand
matter, not spirit. And you and I live in spirit.

— WILLIAM SAROYAN

Researchers find garlic lowers cholesterol." "Studies show acupuncture can relieve pain." "New findings indicate prayer speeds healing." Today's health headlines make it clear that alternative medicine is no longer a New Age "fad." Alternative, or what is sometimes called "complementary medicine," is an accepted part of today's mainstream health consciousness. The *Journal of the American Medical Association,* bastion of conventional medicine, reported that in 1997, Americans made more visits to alternative practitioners than to primary-care doctors. Currently, it's estimated that as many as 40 percent of Americans use some form of alternative medicine each year, an almost 50 percent increase since 1990.

Total out-of-pocket expenditures relating to complementary and alternative medical therapies are estimated at nearly $30 billion per year. Even the federal government is spending on alternative medicine, appropriating $117.7 million to the National Center for Complementary and Alternative Medicine, a division of the National

Institutes of Health, to conduct research, up from a $2 million budget in 1992. There's no question that "alternative medicine" is here to stay.

While many of us from conventionally oriented cultures find alternative medicine new, fresh, and exciting compared with the norm, it's actually old news in other cultures. Holistic medical systems, herbal treatments, and mind-body medicine have been mainstays for thousands of years in many areas of the world. In fact, only in the West does the term "alternative medicine" really mean anything. In countries like India or China, you don't usually have an either/or choice of alternatives. Day-to-day medicine in many countries simply blends Western-style medicine with what we could call "alternative approaches."

Many of these cultures have discovered what Western society is starting to realize in the twenty-first century: That the best medicine is a combination of all worlds, using effective alternative techniques *in conjunction with* conventional medicine, or what is now coming to be known as "integrative medicine."

■ What Is Alternative Medicine?

This chapter is by no means a comprehensive overview of all the possible complementary and alternative ways to help support thyroid function, relieve symptoms, or in some cases even heal thyroid disease. That's an entire book in itself. What I present here comes from the experiences of many people with hypothyroidism, my own experiences, conversations with leading doctors and alternative practitioners, and research into alternative medicine and its impact on various illnesses, especially when it relates to hypothyroidism. If a particular therapy or modality is not mentioned here, it does not mean that it doesn't work. It simply means I haven't found much research, or heard from people who have tried it, have not tried it myself, or seen it recommended by respected practitioners . . . yet! But I continue to explore every interesting possibility, and I will continue to report on any new alternative medicine developments in my newsletter and my Web sites.

A note of caution: I always recommend that you work with a practitioner in alternative or integrative treatments to help put together the right mix of approaches for you. And, if you choose to pursue these or any other complementary or alternative therapies, be sure to keep your conventional doctors informed of what you're doing, and what herbs, supplements, or drugs you might be taking. By involving your conventional practitioners, you give them a partnership role in your wellness and can potentially avoid conflicts in treatments that might arise.

■ Do You Need Alternative Medicine?

Some would call Dr. Steve Langer a practitioner of alternative medicine, but he chafes at that label. Langer will tell you, lightheartedly, "I hate the term 'alternative medicine,' because if it's right, it ain't alternative!"

And Dr. Langer is right. If something works, it works. Just because a treatment, approach, or medicine isn't written up in the *New England Journal of Medicine* doesn't make it "alternative." What you need are approaches that work, safely, to help you feel your best and live well with hypothyroidism.

If you're reading this book, then it's probably because you are one of the millions of people who have found that the traditional "take this levothyroxine pill, see me in a year" approach to managing hypothyroidism is not working for you. So, you *are* looking for alternatives.

The nature of your hypothyroidism will of course dictate how you may be able to use alternative medicine. According to Dr. Ron Manzanero:

Whether or not alternatives can be used depends on the cause of the hypothyroid state. Obviously, someone who has lost their gland to radioactive iodine treatment for Graves' disease, or had the gland removed, will need continuous thyroid hormone replacement. One could make the same argument for genetic familial hypothyroidism and for severe glandular destruction caused by autoimmune antibodies.

Even those patients who have no functioning thyroid, however, frequently find alternative medicine a helpful complement to their treatment, particularly to deal with continuing symptoms that may not be relieved by thyroid hormone replacement.

For those who still have a gland—albeit one that is not functioning optimally—it's of course important first to make sure you've done everything you can to optimize your thyroid function, be on the *right* thyroid hormone replacement for you, and at the right dosages.

But if you're still struggling, and feel that you've exhausted all the traditional medical avenues and still aren't living well, then it might be time to look at complementary and alternative medicine options.

One thing to remember is that often you need to truly commit to an alternative therapy. Some of them are not easy to follow. You may be asked to change your diet completely and give up meat, or sugar, or bread products, for example. Or you'll need to take dozens of capsules and herbal preparations a day. You also need patience. Alternative therapies rarely offer a quick fix. It may take longer to heal and normalize things using alternative therapies, so you have to be prepared for this possibility.

• If you are determined to forge ahead, start by finding an alternative practitioner recommended by your physician, trusted health advisers, or other patients. If there is licensing or certifications associated with the particular alternative therapy, it's always wise to select a practitioner who has the appropriate credentials.

■ Can Alternative Medicine Help Your Thyroid?

Karta Purkh Singh Khalsa, known as K.P. Khalsa, is one of the world's premier herbalists. As a member of the American Herbalists Guild, with more than twenty-five years of experience with medicinal herbs and natural healing, he represents one of the most astute and innovative experts on the subject of alternative medicine in America.

Khalsa, in addition to being an accomplished master of Kundalini yoga and natural healing, focuses his studies on Ayurvedic medicine, and also teaches and writes about Chinese and North American herbalism. After years in patient practice, Khalsa now concentrates his efforts on writing, speaking at conferences, providing in-person and Web training for other professional herbalists around the nation, and consulting for Herb Technology, a company that provides herbal medicines for practitioners.

Khalsa is widely known as the author of an immensely respected book that everyone should have as part of his or her health library, *Herbal Defense*. I consider *Herbal Defense* one of the truly essential works for anyone interested in alternative medicine, in particular, for those with chronic health conditions and an interest in long-term wellness. *Herbal Defense* offers a comprehensive approach to understanding health through herbs and food. The book integrates herbal information from a variety of traditions, including Chinese medicine, Ayurveda, and Native American herbalism. The book offers information on both preventing and treating conditions using herbal medicine, and a special focus on the immune system and how to support it.

When it comes to thyroid disease, Khalsa has some fascinating perspectives.

First, Khalsa believes one must identify what some of the general health triggers are that are allowing the thyroid condition to take place. Says Khalsa:

As people begin to degenerate and experience imbalance, they begin to develop inflammation in various places. Why does one person get arthritis, another thyroiditis? Because they have a particular familiar tendency, or ate a lot of something that triggers an allergic sensitivity, or for some reason, the immune system didn't have the resources it needed to support appropriate vigilance. Ultimately what works very well is to get healthy. The way to treat this disease and many of these other slipperier, obscure inflammatory and autoimmune diseases is to treat what ails them.

Next, Khalsa believes that the objective for any chronic disease such as thyroid disease is to provide overall support for the immune system herbally, and then provide support to the targeted organ—in this case, the thyroid—using herbal medicine.

At the same time, with thyroid disease, Khalsa also recommends that stretching and exercise be incorporated in the disease treatment, including yoga shoulder stands and exercises that use neck rotation and neck extension. "Anything that puts blood into and out of the thyroid can be a help," says Khalsa.

As far as specific remedies are concerned, Khalsa feels that it's a question not easily answered. Trying to pick your own herbs and self-treat is tricky, says Khalsa:

The most common story is that people are interested in herbal medicine, enthusiastic, they go to Wal-Mart and buy a particular remedy, try it, and it doesn't work. Practitioners will suggest things that are more potent, effective and really do the job.

Khalsa feels that there's not a "one size fits all" formula for thyroid disease:

You probably can't really self-treat an autoimmune disease in general, as you have to take a whole body point of view to get better results.

In fact, he doesn't feel that an alternative or herbal approach focused on the thyroid is always even called for when there is a thyroid condition. Says Khalsa:

> I don't think that the approach always needs to be specially focused on the thyroid. What people almost always have is generalized chaos in the endocrine system, a chronic endocrine dysregulation. You can see thyroid disease, or adrenal disease, or even female hormone imbalance. It depends on the lens the practitioner is looking through.

Solving the problems is doable, says Khalsa, but it points up the need for assessment and treatment by an expert. Khalsa describes the interplay of hormones as a "symphony," and "by working on the whole system, an expert can get all the glands come into play."

Says Khalsa, "I always encourage people to see a practitioner at least once or twice."

Even in the most expert of hands, Khalsa counsels patience:

> Hypothyroidism responds very slowly to natural therapies. Autoimmune conditions like Hashimoto's and Graves' disease are some of the slowest responding conditions. Expect a year for complete recovery and transition to a maintenance protocol.

Khalsa's advice—to find the triggers, support the immune system, and have a practitioner help develop your program—is sensible and applies to all of the alternative herbal medical systems that are discussed here: Chinese medicine, Ayurveda, naturopathy, and herbalism.

■ Alternative Systems

Some of the best results in dealing with hypothyroidism are experienced by patients who see a practitioner versed in a complete system of alternative medicine. These include Chinese medicine, Ayurveda, and herbalism, for example. Here is a brief look at some of these complete systems, and how they may be of help to your thyroid health.

Chinese Medicine

Chinese medicine (CM) originated from Taoism about four thousand years ago. CM is a treatment that is designed to balance the health of an individual and his or her surroundings. Central to that balance is *qi* (pronounced chee), which translates as "vital energy" or "life force." Qi flows through the body via pathways known as meridians and is exchanged with the body's surroundings. A body is in optimal health when qi is free and balanced. In addition to qi, CM relies on the concept of yin and yang, the interdependent opposites, representing different organs and health aspects. CM diagnostic techniques include observation, listening, questioning, and palpation, including feeling special pulse qualities and sensitivity of body parts. CM treatments include diet, exercises such as T'ai Chi and the Qi Gong breathing, herbal preparations, acupuncture, acupressure massage, physical therapy, and moxibustion. Moxibustion is the use of heat at specific energy points on the body—applied either directly or to the acupuncture needles—as a way to add energy.

In the United States, acupuncture is now an established practice, both as part of CM and even more so on its own. Americans make an estimated nine to twelve million visits to acupuncturists annually, and more than three thousand conventionally trained U.S. physicians also practice acupuncture.

Acupuncture requires inserting very thin, fine needles at different key energy points to regulate or correct the flow of qi and restore health. Acupuncture treatment taps into points along meridians, each having different therapeutic functions within the body. Most of the time, patients don't feel the acupuncture needles at all; occasionally, the worst they might feel is a slight pinch for a second. As a regular recipient of acupuncture treatment, and as someone who really doesn't like shots, I can tell you that when done properly, acupuncture does not hurt. It's also safe. Most practitioners use disposable needles, and it's a good idea to ask your acupuncturist to use them.

There are many verified studies conducted in Asia that show successful application of CM for immunologically based diseases, including thyroid problems. Specifically regarding hypothyroidism, a study in the *Journal of Chinese Medicine* found that the use of moxibustion along with Chinese medicinal powder at specific energy points led to recovery of thyroid function in some patients with Hashimoto's thyroiditis. Another study showed that treatment with Shen Lu Tablets, a Chinese herbal remedy, could address the underling yin deficiencies that are at the root of some hypothyroidism, actually lowering TSH levels and reducing symptoms. Various Chinese medical herbal tonics have also been studied and found to have an effect on TSH levels and hypothyroid symptoms.

In addition to herbs, Chinese medicine also incorporates acupuncture, which can also be very effective in treating the deficiency of deep energy—yin—that is so common in hypothyroidism, and in some of the symptomatic pain that can accompany hypothyroidism or related fibromyalgia.

I have personally found that regular acupuncture sessions helped me through one long episode of chronic fatigue syndrome and total exhaustion. Whenever I start suffering from unusually low energy, I go in for a few sessions, and things get back to normal and my energy becomes more balanced.

Kate Lemmerman, M.D., makes acupuncture a key part of her medical practice. She finds that 60 to 70 percent of her patients with fatigue from hypothyroidism and other causes experience benefit from acupuncture treatments. How acupuncture adds energy, however, is not easy to explain:

Asians may say that we miss the forest for the trees when we try to explain how acupuncture works in terms of endor-

phins, cortisol, and serotonin. Suffice it to say that by balancing the qi, roughly translated as energy, in someone's system, we allow improved functioning and healing. And that by using certain "tonifying" techniques, such as heating the needles, we can actually add energy. . . .

When choosing an acupuncturist, be sure he or she is licensed and certified, whether a doctor or not. For physicians, top certification is from the American Academy of Medical Acupuncture (AAMA). Acupuncturists, who are not doctors, can receive credentials known as a Diplomate in Acupuncture (Dipl.Ac.). They may be called Licensed Acupuncturist (L.Ac. or Iic.Ac.), Registered Acupuncturist (R.Ac.), Certified Acupuncturist (C.A.), Acupuncturist, Doctor of Oriental Medicine (D.O.M.), or Doctor of Acupuncture (D.Ac.) Each state has its own specific requirements for the practice of acupuncture. Either see a licensed acupuncturist or one who is nationally certified from an organization like the National Certification Commission for Acupuncture and Oriental Medicine (NCCAOM).

Ayurveda

Ayurveda (pronounced AH-yuhr-vey-duh) has been the traditional medicine of India for more than five thousand years and is probably the oldest medical system in existence. Ayurveda is a Sanskrit word that means "science of life" or "life knowledge" and is based on the premise that the body naturally seeks harmony and balance. In Ayurveda disease represents emotional imbalance, toxins, and most particularly, imbalances in what are known as *doshas*. Doshas are different regulatory systems—*vata* (movement), *pitta* (heat, metabolism, and energy), and *kapha* (physical structure and fluid balance)—that govern different aspects of health. According to Ayurveda, proper balancing of the doshas is accomplished through food and diet, herbs, meditation and breathing, massage, and even yoga poses to ensure that energy is flowing. In this way, the concept of balance and energy makes it similar to Chinese medicine.

Some naturopaths and homeopaths offer aspects of Ayurvedic treatment, or incorporate Ayurvedic herbal preparations as part of their treatments. There are also purely Ayurvedic practitioners. Typically, Ayurvedic practitioners make a diagnosis by asking detailed questions to assess your dominant dosha, and they take Ayurvedic pulses. As far as hypothyroidism is concerned, when something affects as many aspects of health as hypothyroidism does, therapies that focus on balancing all the systems can be particularly useful, and Ayurveda is no exception. Ayurveda has much to offer, and to truly benefit from it, it's worthwhile to consult a trained practitioner or Ayurvedic doctor for an evaluation and recommendations.

Ayurvedic therapy is considered particularly effective for disease brought on or exacerbated by stress, for energy and improved breathing and respiration, and for weight loss. These strengths apply to some of the most common hypothyroidism-related symptoms.

The Ayurvedic remedy z-guggulsterone, a component derived from the plant commiphora mukul, has been used as an important anti-inflammatory, antiobesity, and cholesterol-lowering agent in a popular Ayurvedic medicine known as "guggul." Guggul is considered particularly important for prevention of a sluggish metabolism, and studies have shown that Z-guggulsterone has the ability to increase the thyroid's ability take up the engines it needs for effective hormone conversion. It also increases the oxygen uptake in muscles. Some Ayurvedic practitioners have reported tremendous success with guggul.

Constipation is often a problem with hypothyroidism. One of the most basic and classic Ayurvedic herbal remedies is known as "triphala," and many thyroid patients report that daily use of triphala can have a remarkable impact on digestion and constipation problems. Various triphala preparations are available at many natural health and vitamin stores.

Ayurvedic practitioners are not officially licensed, but you should ask where and how long a practitioner was trained, how long he or she's been practicing Ayurveda, and how much of his or her practice is purely Ayurveda.

Naturopathy

Naturopathy draws on aspects of traditional Chinese medicine, Ayurveda, and other medical systems for its focus. Naturopathic philosophy aims for a balance of physical, emotional, mental, and spiritual aspects, highlighting the body's innate ability to heal itself. Naturopathic doctors act like primary-care providers for complementary therapies and are often connected to a network of alternative providers.

Naturopathy seeks to identify and treat root causes of illness or the disease process instead of symptoms. Naturopaths may recommend, or themselves practice, acupuncture, homeopathy, herbal medicine, dietary and nutritional medicine, manipulation or massage, and other techniques. It's estimated that there are more than one thousand naturopathic doctors in practice in the United States.

Since naturopathic medicine draws on many different disciplines, there are certainly arguments to be made for its effectiveness. However, since there are no specific "naturopathic" remedies or treatments, it is really up to the individual practitioner to achieve results.

If you are looking for a naturopath, stick with someone who has an "N.D." and is a licensed Doctor of Naturopathic Medicine. The Council on Naturopathic Medical Education grants this designation after completion of a four-year program at one of the several accredited naturopathic colleges in the United States.

Herbalism

When you pick up a bottle of echinacea off the supermarket shelf or drink a ginger ale to settle your stomach, you're actually practicing a form of herbal medicine. Going back to the most ancient times, there has been a well-developed understanding of the power of plants and plant products as medicine. Many of today's drugs are actually derived from herbal sources or are synthetic versions of naturally occurring herbs. According to the World Health Organization (WHO) about four billion people, or 80 percent of the world's population, use some form of herbal medicine.

While always a mainstay in the East, herbal medicine is becoming popular again in the West, with a variety of treatments taken as teas, as capsules or tablets, extracts or tinctures, and essential oils for topical use. In the United States, herbal medicine practitioners may be physicians, osteopaths, naturopaths, nutritionists, or even more traditional herbalists. Be very wary, however, of the new crop of so-called herbalists who have popped up around the massive multilevel-marketing vitamin business. Armies of salespeople are hawking all sorts of herbs and supplements, but their main credential is their membership in some sort of multilevel network marketing company, and their desire to sell you a whole boatload of products you probably don't need.

Many medical studies in the United States, Europe, and Asia have found that legitimate herbal products can have an impact on health conditions, ranging from liver repair, to enhancing the immune system, to reducing swelling, to increasing energy or aiding in weight loss.

■ Is There a Natural Treatment for Hypothyroidism?

Ultimately, many patients want to know, is there a plant or herbal replacement for thyroid hormone? The answer is no. While some people with a mild depression might decide to take the herbal remedy St. John's wort instead of going on Prozac, it's not like that with hypothyroidism. There is no natural or over-the-counter herb or plant that acts like thyroid hormone and can be taken *instead* of thyroid hormone.

Dr. Ken Blanchard feels that, for the huge majority of patients, no alternative remedy will substitute for replacing thyroid hormone. But, says Blanchard:

> *In the case of someone who is just borderline hypothyroid, I think it is possible that the various substances containing iodine, tyrosine, etc., might help.*

So, as Dr. Blanchard notes, there are some situations when supplements may help eliminate hypothyroidism. But a caution is in order. According to many alternative practitioners I've consulted, this only works for a minute fraction of patients, those who have nutritional or other deficiencies, and again, only for those with slight, borderline hypothyroidism.

Are there are things that "help" the thyroid or the immune system function better, and possibly help your thyroid function better, maybe even restore it to normal? Again, yes, there are some alternative approaches that may reduce the strain on your thyroid so you can reduce the dosage of thyroid hormone replacement. And again, in rare cases, for those who still have a thyroid that hasn't been removed in part, or given radioactive iodine (RAI), some may be able to restore function. Again, it's rare.

Is there a "natural" thyroid treatment? Yes. But when people refer to "natural" thyroid treatment, they are talking about prescription thyroid hormone replacement drugs such as Armour Thyroid or Naturethroid, considered natural because they are made from the desiccated thyroid glands of pigs, rather than synthetic reproductions of hormones. It's important to note that "natural" thyroid does *not* refer to over-the-counter "glandular" supplements, made with raw thyroid and other endocrine glands of cattle, sheep, and pigs. Only a few practitioners I've talked to over eight years have ever recommended these thyroid glandulars.

Holistic practitioner Dr. Gina Honeyman-Lowe, for example, has had a few patients benefit from over-the-counter thyroid hormone glandulars, but most of the time she finds she has to switch them to a prescription form of thyroid hormone for optimal improvement.

A concern with glandulars is that they provide very inconsistent amounts of thyroid hormone and could, in fact, pose a slight danger of variant Creutzfeldt-Jakob disease (the human form of mad cow disease) or other sorts of problems. Some people attempt to diagnose and treat themselves by taking these thyroid glandular supplements, but this can be risky. You should at least establish with a health practitioner that you do have a thyroid problem, then you can investigate alternative approaches. Glandulars should not be taken unless you are under the guidance of a knowledgeable health professional who strongly recommends them and can vouch for the safety and potency of a particular brand.

Dr. Honeyman-Lowe says this about various products for the thyroid:

> Many over-the-counter "thyroid-booster" products contain iodine, vitamins, and minerals, but I haven't seen patients get significant improvements from these products. If a person has a deficiency of the nutrients these products contain, they may be somewhat helpful. If a person has autoimmune thyroiditis, hypothyroidism, or thyroid hormone resistance, they will need to use prescription thyroid medication as part of a comprehensive treatment protocol.

The bottom line: As much as I believe in alternative medicine myself, if you are significantly hypothyroid, you will, in most cases, need to go on some form of prescription thyroid hormone replacement drug—possibly even for life.

But alternative medicine offers many options in helping support your thyroid function, alleviating other symptoms, and protecting your overall health. Optimally, then, you may want to consider integrative medicine.

■ Integrative Medicine

Integrative medicine seeks to combine the best from all traditions, including Western medicine, herbalism, Chinese medicine, acupuncture, the mind-body approach, Ayurveda, and other healing modalities. To give you an idea of some various ways that alternative medicine can be applied to thyroid disease, I've profiled several integrative practitioners, who share their approaches to hypothyroidism.

Profile: Dr. David Naimon

Dr. David Naimon is a naturopath who frequently treats thyroid patients. According to Naimon, in naturopathy the objective is to achieve a cure or a movement toward health with the least invasive intervention possible. Says Naimon:

> *While pharmaceutical medications are important and sometimes necessary, they often should be reserved for times when more natural treatments do not achieve their desired goal.*

According to Naimon, naturopathy follows a hierarchy of treatment interventions. For example, if you can achieve a cure with dietary and lifestyle modification, this would be preferable to using herbs. Likewise, if you can achieve good results with herbs, this would be preferable to using thyroid glandular products. And so on.

Dr. Naimon shared his hierarchy of intervention for thyroid disease:

1. Diet and lifestyle modification
2. Hydrotherapy and acupuncture
3. Herbs, vitamins, and minerals
4. Glandular products without hormonal activity

5. Armour Thyroid
6. Synthroid and other synthetic thyroid preparations

1. Diet and Lifestyle—Accoding to Dr. Naimon, people suffering from low-functioning thyroids should have an evaluation of their diets to determine how much is unrefined, vital, fresh food, versus refined, processed, and canned food. Says Naimon:

> *Generally, one should try to increase one's intake of whole cooked grains, fresh vegetables and fruit, legumes, nuts, seeds, and cold-water fish. At this same time, one should try to decrease the percentage of one's diet that is refined sugars and flours (sodas, breads, pastries, chips, concentrated fruit juices, high fructose corn syrup, etc.), alcohol, and coffee, and move toward whole foods. Hydrogenated oils should be avoided entirely. Cook with healthy saturated fats or mono-unsaturated fats (coconut butter, ghee, olive oil).*

Dr. Naimon feels that getting a fasting lipid profile, complete blood count, a ferritin level check, and a chemistry panel can help tailor dietary modifications to the individual. It is important to correct nutritional deficiencies, particularly iron deficiency. A woman's ferritin level should be 40 or above. A low ferritin can affect thyroid function adversely. And I would suggest correcting an iron deficiency prior to any consideration of thyroid hormone.

It is equally important to make sure liver metabolism is not compromised. The liver is the primary organ that converts T4 to T3, and there are many factors that can impair liver function (heavy metal exposure, high alcohol or coffee intake, use of certain pharmaceuticals and nonsteroidal anti-inflammatory drugs, etc.). If an overburdened liver is suspected, a liver cleanse, a fast, or an elimination reintroduction diet could be of use. Stress management and exercise are also important for maintaining healthy liver function.

2. Hydrotherapy and Acupuncture—Dr. Naimon recommends that an application of alternating hot and cold compresses to a low-functioning thyroid can help improve circulation through the gland. Says Naimon:

> *Fill one basin with hot water, another with cold. Put a wash-cloth in the hot water, wring it out and apply it to the thyroid for 3 minutes. Then take another washcloth, put it in the cold water, wring it out and apply it to the thyroid for 30 seconds. Repeat this three times, ending with the cold, once each day.*

Dr. Naimon also reports that he has had some patients with TSH levels between 4 and 6.5 see improvement in their TSH levels from regular acupuncture treatments.

3. Herbs, Vitamins, and Minerals—According to Dr. Naimon, there are many Chinese herbal formulations that can be very useful for thyroid patients. Not all patients with the same thyroid condition would receive the same formula. However, there are formulas that are more common than others. Says Naimon:

> *In menopausal women with low thyroid function, a common formula that is helpful is called Jia Jian Er Xian Tang (Golden Flower Chinese Herbs). It is a modified classical formula that addresses both kidney yin and yang deficiency. This formula would not be suited for every menopausal woman with thyroid problems, and would rarely be used for younger women with thyroid problems.*

Dr. Naimon also feels that all thyroid patients should be on 200 mcg of selenium daily.

4. Glandular Products—According to Dr. Naimon, glandular products without hormonal activity can be very useful if herbs and dietary modification are not sufficient to correct a thyroid condition. Says Naimon:

> Often you can find products that include important thyroid co-factors as well as glandulars. I often use a product from Tyler called BMR complex that contains thyroid glandular, iris versicolor, kelp, and other thyroid-enhancing substances.

5. Armour Thyroid—If thyroid function is not improving adequately with the first four steps, Naimon would then try Armour Thyroid:

> I prefer Armour Thyroid for a number of reasons. In naturopathic medicine we assume that the closer we can mimic the way the body naturally produces hormones the less chance there will be unwanted side-effects. Armour not only has T4, but also T3, T2, and T1. And while the functions of T2 and T1 are unclear, that does not mean that there are no functions. Also Armour will contain the co-factors needed for thyroid metabolism that are concentrated in thyroid tissue. Thus Armour isn't just replacing a function within the body, but could also be seen as nourishing the thyroid gland.

Only if none of the preceding steps improved a hypothyroid patient's condition would Naimon advise the patient to consider synthetic preparations of thyroid hormone.

Profile: Dr. Jacob Teitelbaum

Jacob Teitelbaum, M.D., is an author, researcher, and practitioner with expertise in fibromyalgia, chronic fatigue syndrome, thyroid conditions, and other hormonal imbalances.

Dr. Teitelbaum takes a multipronged, integrative approach to treating hypothyroidism that includes four key components.

1. **Hormonal Support**—Dr. Teitelbaum looks for any additional hormonal deficiencies in addition to thyroid. For example, says Teitelbaum:

If patients they have symptoms of low blood pressure or hypoglycemia, I recommend adrenal support with cortisol or glandulars/licorice (e.g., Adrenal Stress End by Enzymatic Therapy is excellent).

2. **Nutritional Support**—Dr. Teitelbaum typically recommends that thyroid patients decrease sugar, increase water, and take a high-quality multivitamin supplement specially designed for low metabolism conditions.

3. **Sleep**—Dr. Teitelbaum believes that thyroid patients need eight to nine hours of deep sleep a night. In some cases, this requires herbal supplements, hormones like melatonin, minerals such as calcium and magnesium, or prescription medications—i.e., Ambien and Trazodone—so that you can achieve deep, restful, stage 4 sleep—the type of sleep that is restorative and energizing.

4. **Treat Infections**—Dr. Teitelbaum feels that dealing with underlying infections is also critical to dealing with hypothyroidism. He feels that Candida (yeast) in particular can be a problem. Says Teitelbaum:

If you have sinus congestion or spastic colon (for example, gas, bloating, diarrhea and/or constipation), you likely have yeast. Avoid sugar, use acidophilus in pearl form (2 pearls, twice a day for 5 months), citricidal 100 mg 2 a day, and consider the prescription medications Nystatin and Diflucan.

In the course of Dr. Teitelbaum's research, he has developed several particularly helpful supplements, which I take and have recommended to many thyroid patients.

His customized multivitamin powder, known as the Energy Revitalization System, mixes with water to become a citrus-flavored drink, which you take along with the high-potency B-complex. The Energy Revitalization System replaces thirty-five supplement tablets a day, and includes all the key nutrients, including selenium, needed for optimal thyroid function. Dr. Teitelbaum has also developed an herbal combination supplement to aid in deep sleep. Revitalizing Sleep Formula is a mix of six herbals that helps you achieve deep sleep, without feeling groggy in the morning. Both supplements are produced by Enzymatic Therapy, one of most reputable supplement companies, and are available anywhere you can buy vitamins and supplements. (Note: Dr. Teitelbaum donates *all* his royalties from sales of these products to charity.)

Comprehensive information on Dr. Teitelbaum's approaches is available online at his Web site, http://www.vitality 101.com.

Profile: Dr. John Lowe and Dr. Gina Honeyman-Lowe

Dr. John Lowe and Dr. Gina Honeyman-Lowe take an integrative approach they call "metabolic rehabilitation," which is outlined at their Web site, http://www.drlowe.com, and in their book *Your Guide to Metabolic Health*.

According to the Lowes, the first step is a high-enough daily dose of the correct amount and type of thyroid hormone for each individual, which for most people means a combination of T4 and T3. And that is just a first step:

> *If patients are to enjoy optimal metabolic health, they must also adopt a wholesome diet, take nutritional supplements, exercise to tolerance, and abstain from the use of metabolism-impeding drugs, such as beta blockers. And, of course, other hormone imbalances or deficiencies, such as low cortisol,*

must be corrected. Each of these components is necessary to help people regain their health in the safest and most effective manner possible. Those people who consider thyroid hormone to be a "magic bullet"—and don't engage in the other health-inducing activities—may not completely recover their health.

Drs. Lowe and Honeyman-Lowe don't feel they are unique in promoting an integrated approach:

Many thoughtful, well-informed, patient-oriented alternative doctors have independently come to see the value of the integrated approach to metabolic treatment. We think this is true of most alternative doctors featured on Mary Shomon's thyroid Web sites. The consensus among these alternative doctors is meaningful. The endocrinology specialty is gradually inching its way around to the integrated approach that alternative doctors have long known works best.

7

Alternatives: Vitamins, Herbs, and Supplements

Let thy food be thy medicine and thy medicine be thy food.

— HIPPOCRATES

If you've taken a vitamin C capsule, drunk a big glass of orange juice, or popped some echinacea capsules at the sign of cold, then you are practicing vitamin, nutritional, and herbal therapy.

Diet and nutrition are basic aspects of many of the complementary and alternative medicine systems, such as Ayurveda or traditional Chinese medicine. In fact, many healing methods look on foods and herbs as medicines, much like a pill from a pharmacy.

If you take a multivitamin every day, you may think you're getting what you need for optimal health. Many nutritional experts, however, feel that "minimum daily requirements" are not sufficient to prevent chronic diseases, or help heal you when your health is compromised by an ongoing battle with hypothyroidism.

As far as nutritional and vitamin therapies for hypothyroidism are concerned, there's no way that I can tell you what particular mix of vitamins, foods, nutritional supplements, and herbs is right to address *your* hypothyroidism. You can try hit-or-miss self-medication, as many people do. But ideally, you'll save yourself time and money, and get far closer to the right combinations, if you start out with a visit to a respected and recommended nutritionist with expertise in working with thyroid problems.

Here are some vitamins, minerals, and herbs you may want to consider as part of your thyroid treatment.

■ Vitamins

Multivitamins

Everyone should take a strong multivitamin with minerals each day. This is an essential starting point. According to Drs. Richard and Karilee Shames, this should be a high-quality multivitamin, such as can be purchased from reputable health food stores, as opposed to some of the larger national drugstore brands. Grocery and drugstore multivitamins don't typically have the potency or bioavailability that thyroid sufferers need.

Vitamin A

A deficiency in vitamin A may limit the body's ability to produce thyroid hormone.

Vitamin B_2 (Riboflavin)

A shortage of vitamin B_2 can depress endocrine function, especially the thyroid and adrenals.

Vitamin B_3 (Niacin)

Vitamin B_3 helps keep cells working by aiding in respiration and delivery of energy to cells.

Vitamin B_6 (Pyridoxine)

Vitamin B_6 helps the body convert iodine to thyroid hormone.

Vitamin B$_{12}$ (Cyanocobalamin, Methylcobalamin)

Hypothyroidism makes us less able to absorb sufficient vitamin B$_{12}$ from diets. Some experts believe we should be getting 1,000 to 5,000 mg a day, even via injection when possible. Sublingual B$_{12}$ is a more effective form of delivery than other B$_{12}$ supplements.

Vitamin C

Many experts recommend that you add several grams—2,000 to 5,000 mg—of vitamin C each day. You can use capsules or powdered forms of vitamin C. A particular favorite of mine is various-flavored drink mixes known as Emer'gen-C. Very low in calories and sugar, but very flavorful (I particularly like raspberry, cranberry, and tangerine flavors), each envelope makes one drink, and the drink has a bit of fizz to it, so it functions like a soda. But it's packed with 1,000 mg (1 g) of vitamin C, as well as B$_6$, B$_{12}$, potassium, and a variety of other useful vitamins.

Vitamin D

Vitamin D appears to be necessary in order for the pituitary gland to produce thyroid hormone, and may play a role in T3 binding to its receptor. Vitamin D is part of the necessary supporting apparatus that enables the deiodinase enzyme to convert T4 (inactive thyroid hormone) into T3 (the active type). It is also thought that vitamin D is necessary for healthy immune system functioning.

Vitamin E

Vitamin E is an essential antioxidant, and it also can help with immune function.

■ Minerals

Selenium

Perhaps the most important mineral for thyroid function is selenium. Selenium activates an enzyme—hepatic type I iodothyronine deiodinase—that is responsible for controlling thyroid function by the conversion of T4 to T3. This enzyme is a selenoprotein that is sensitive to selenium deficiency. Stress and injury appear to make the body particularly selenium-deficient. After severe injury, the conversion of T4 to T3 is decreased, leading to low T3 syndrome. Another research study found that selenium levels are low after trauma, which correlates to low T3 levels, along with a decrease in the T4 to T3 conversion.

Some researchers and practitioners are beginning to believe that selenium deficiency alone can trigger autoimmune thyroid disease in some people. One study published in 2002 showed that in areas with severe selenium deficiency, there is a higher incidence of autoimmune thyroiditis. People with thyroid antibodies received 200 mcg of selenium supplementation over three months, and at the end of the test period, antibody levels had decreased by as much as 40 to 63 percent, and a small percentage of patients in the selenium-treated group had antibody levels that completely returned to normal. The researchers concluded that selenium supplementation may reduce inflammation in patients with autoimmune thyroiditis.

A 1997 study found that high intake of iodine—when selenium is deficient—could trigger thyroid damage. But sufficient intake of selenium appeared to offset the dangers of high iodine intake.

Experts recommend 200 mcg of selenium a day, but caution that selenium is one of those supplements where more is *not* better. Overdosage on selenium can be harmful, so keep your intake to 200–400 mcg, maximum.

Zinc

Zinc is needed by the thyroid for both hormone production and T4 to T3 conversion. Zinc is also necessary for proper hypothalamic functioning, an essential part of thyroid function.

Copper

When you are taking zinc, you also need to make sure you balance it out with a small amount of additional copper.

Iron

Dr. Robban Sica, a Connecticut-based holistic physician, believes that iron may be needed for some thyroid patients, and she checks ferritin (storage iron) levels to see whether additional supplementation is necessary. (Remember that if you do take iron supplements, you need to allow at least four—and some practitioners say more—hours between taking iron and taking your thyroid drugs, so that the iron doesn't interfere with the absorption of the drugs.)

Magnesium

Magnesium is an essential mineral that is often deficient in thyroid patients. It helps maintain normal muscle and nerve function, keeps heart rhythm steady, and bones strong. It is also involved in energy metabolism. If you aren't getting enough magnesium, you may have more muscle cramps and pain than usual, tingling, numbness, and abnormal heart rhythms—all symptoms that are also more common in thyroid patients.

■ Amino Acids

L-tyrosine

Tyrosine is considered the precursor to the T4 thyroid hormone. The thyroid takes in iodine and combines that iodine with the amino acid *tyrosine*, converting the iodine/tyrosine combination into T3 and T4. So, a deficiency in tyrosine means that a basic building block of good thyroid function is missing.

■ Essential Fatty Acids

Essential fatty acids are critical for thyroid patients. Many practitioners recommend essential fatty acids to reduce inflammation—particularly important in autoimmune-triggered hypothyroidism. You'll need to get a good mix of omega-3 and omega-5 acids. Some good options for getting the proper balance of good fats in a supplement include Udo's Oil—which comes as an oil and in capsule form—or Atkins Essential Oils capsules.

Evening Primrose Oil

You may also want to add some additional evening primrose oil, an essential fatty acid that contains linoleic acid. Some practitioners and patients find it can be particularly helpful with hair- and skin-related symptoms of hypothyroidism.

■ Herbs for Thyroid Support

A review of various sources regarding herbal remedies shows that many different herbs are recommended for thyroid treatment. Selecting the proper herbs for hypothyroidism is something you should do with an herbalist's help, but here are some of the herbs and supplements that may be helpful:

Siberian ginseng	Astragalus
Fo-ti root (Ho Shou Wu)	Saw palmetto berry
Triphala	Black cohosh root
Bayberry bark	Echinacea
Goldenseal	Lungwort

Motherwort

Oak, white, bark

Seawrack

Watercress

Withania somiferal
ashwagandha

Schizandra berry
(*Schizandra chinesis*)

Motherwort flowering tops

Iris (blue flag root)
(aka Iris versicolor)

Nettle

Poke root

Skullcap

Guggul/
commiphora
mukul

Ginkgo biloba

Coleus root
(*Coleus forskolli*)

Lemon balm

There are a number of thyroid-specific combination supplement formulas that typically contain tyrosine, some of the above ingredients, and often an iodine-based herb, as well as other nutrients.

■ A Special Note Re: Iodine, Kelp, and Other Iodine-Based Herbs

Use of supplemental iodine, as well as kelp, bladderwrack, and other iodine-containing herbs, is one of the key controversies in thyroid treatment. While these ingredients are frequently found in many prepackaged "thyroid formula" supplements, you'll need to decide, in conjunction with your practitioner, whether or not iodine can help—or hurt—you. Read Chapter 11's section on iodine for more information.

A partial list of herbal supplements that are iodine-based includes the following. Be on the lookout for these ingredients in thyroid-combination supplements, weight-loss supplements, and supplements for energy: bladderwrack (*Fucus vesiculosus)*, bugleweed, kelp, Norwegian kelp, kelp fronds, Irish moss, and seaweed.

■ Maca

Viana Muller, Ph.D., is an anthropologist and herbal expert. Dr. Muller has been making rainforest herb collecting/study trips to the Amazon River basin since 1989, and has dedicated herself to making research, growing, harvesting, propagation, and distribution of certified organic and wild-crafted South American medicinal herbs. What drew her close to herbs was a health crisis she suffered in 1990, from which it took several years to recover. According to Dr. Muller, her recovery period also prompted an intense study of alternative medicine, and she became passionate about healing herbs and medicinal plants. She ended up founding a company, Whole World Botanicals, in the 1990s, to help bring these native herbs and plants to other cultures outside the Amazon basin and high Andes.

One of the medicinal plants that Dr. Muller feels is particularly helpful to thyroid patients is maca root. Maca is a cruciferous root (from the same botanical family as the turnip and broccoli), which grows at 12,500 to 14,500 feet above sea level—the highest-growing food plant in the world—in the high Andean plateaus of central Peru. It is believed to be one of the earliest domesticated food plants of Peru, along with the potato. According to Dr. Muller:

> Maca almost became extinct because the Incas originally restricted its use to the royal court, then the conquering Spaniards forbid it, along with other Andean food plants used in native religious ceremonies. But the maca root has recently been rediscovered as a medicinal plant.

There have been some animal studies done on maca that found that some components might be able to stimulate the hypothalamus and pituitary gland to better balance the entire endocrine system. Dr. Muller found, while studying the impact of maca on several women who were having moderate to severe menopausal symptoms—which they reported without being asked—that they had been able to reduce their thyroid medication or in a few cases even to stop it entirely after using maca for two or three months. And they all reported feeling much better and energetic. According to Dr. Muller:

Some of the women who had hypothyroidism were taking Armour thyroid, others were taking Synthroid. What they noticed after a month or two was that they were beginning to feel some of the symptoms of an overactive thyroid, and so they cut back their thyroid medication and the symptoms went away. Some got stabilized at 50% of their former dosage of thyroid medication and some were able to stop all thyroid medication. They did this however, little by little, with frequent testing of thyroid function in order not to shock the thyroid and make their condition worse. I can't say that this was the effect with all women on thyroid medication, so it's not possible for me to give you an accurate percentage of women who had significant thyroid function improvement as a result of taking maca. The results for some, however, were so exciting and dramatic that they called me and told me. This is how I found out that taking maca could positively affect thyroid function.

8

Alternatives: Mind and Body Approaches

If you don't like what's happening in your life, change your mind.

—His Holiness The Dalai Lama

A discussion of alternative approaches would not be complete without looking at mind and body approaches. These holistic methods are often good complements to other treatments you are receiving, and may be the missing part of your complete wellness program.

■ Manual Healing/Bodywork

If you've ever had a massage and enjoyed the relaxed, warm feeling you have for many hours afterward, you've enjoyed the health benefits of manual healing and bodywork. This is a broad category that focuses on the use of touch to heal the body. Massage and manipulation are some of the oldest methods of health care. In bodywork, manual techniques, using hands, arms, elbows, and sometimes even feet, apply various types of pressure to affect the muscles, bones, joints, circulation, and other body systems.

There are so many different forms of massage and manual healing that it's hard to list them all. Swedish massage, trigger point massage (myotherapy, neuromuscular massage therapy), Rolfing, Trager, Alexander technique, Feldenkrais, myofascial-release technique, and other realignment therapies concentrate on the soft tissue surrounding the bones. Practitioners of reflexology and acupressure stimulate points to clear energy pathways that appear to be blocked. And there are many kinds of energetic work, such as Reiki and Therapeutic Touch, in which the therapist is a conduit for healing energy that is directed at the patient through the therapist's hands, sometimes without actually touching the client.

Sandy Levy is an experienced bodywork expert who runs her own myotherapy practice. She has some thoughts about choosing the right therapy:

> *Any type of bodywork can be useful. It's more important to find a good therapist with whom you are comfortable than a practitioner of a certain technique. To begin, ask yourself whether your body desires deep massage or a lighter touch . . . and follow your body's advice. Then ask around for referrals. If you want light massage, you will be looking for someone who specializes in Swedish massage and stress reduction, or one of the energy therapies like acupressure. If you crave deeper work, look for deep massage, or trigger point work, or, if you want to go all the way, Rolfing.*

Sandy has found that more than one technique can sometimes be the best solution. In her practice, she provides light, relaxing massage, deep trigger point work, plus energetic therapies like Reiki and reflexology. And she's found that many of her clients also need movement/posture work, so she refers them to Alexander or Feldenkrais practitioners.

Before choosing one, talk with several therapists about their work so you can get a feel for whether you think you can work with them. The therapist should be willing to give you at least some telephone time, but you might want to pay for a brief office consult if you have many questions.

Bodywork can be quite helpful for unresolved hypothyroid symptoms, particularly if the therapist is familiar with the disease and is able to offer a combination of techniques. Medical studies have found various forms of massage and physical therapy to be effective in dealing with pain, depression, energy, insomnia, and inflammation. Some myofascial and myotherapy experts have had particular success working with the fibromyalgia and chronic fatigue symptoms that can also plague people with hypothyroidism.

Sandy has worked with many patients with hypothyroidism:

> *Massage—deep or light, depending on the person—is very helpful in relieving muscle aches and edema, but if the therapist can also stimulate the endocrine system via acupressure or reflexology or some other energetic method, the results will be much better.*

There are different licensing and accreditation requirements for each type of bodywork. Many specialty areas—such as Rolfing and Feldenkrais—offer separate certification. Some states and areas license massage therapists. The main certification to look for, however, is N.C.T.M.B., which is granted by the National Certification Board for Therapeutic Massage and Bodywork, after completion of five hundred hours of training and the passage of an exam.

■ Osteopathic Manipulation

Osteopathic manipulation works with the musculoskeletal system as a way to treat illness, which, in osteopathic theory, can result from imbalances and misalignment in the body's structure. As part of their broader family practice functions, many osteopathic physicians rely on this osteopathic manipulation as a form of treatment. Some M.D. practitioners have also been trained in osteopathic manipulation and can provide this sort of therapy.

There is clear research supporting the use of osteopathic manipulation and techniques for musculoskeletal and nonmusculoskeletal problems. Osteopathic manipulation is particularly useful for muscular and joint pain relief and for hypothyroidism-related problems, such as carpal tunnel syndrome or chronic sinusitis. Personally, I've found osteopathic manipulation to be most useful in dealing with various muscle trauma and joint pain, such as a case of whiplash I had after being rear-ended in my car. The manipulation allowed fewer painkillers and muscle relaxants, and sped up the healing process.

Some osteopaths are now working on protocols for endocrine balancing and thyroid stimulation, so if you are interested in osteopathy, ask your prospective Doctor of Osteopathy (D.O.) if he or she has expertise in this particular area. If you want to find an osteopath, you'll definitely need someone who has a degree from a four-year institution accredited by the American Association of Colleges of Osteopathic Medicine.

■ Mind-Body Therapy/Healing/Stress Reduction

Mind-body therapy is a broad category that looks at everything from prayer to yoga to counseling to dance to breathing. Basically, they are all practices or therapies that seek to heal, establish a link between conscious thought and the body with the goal of affecting physiological processes, and trigger what's referred to as the "relaxation response."

The term "relaxation response" was coined by Harvard physician Herbert Benson, M.D., the nation's foremost mind-body expert, to describe the actual physiological changes that result from relaxation and balance. In a radio interview with public-radio host Diane Rehm, Dr. Benson articulated his thoughts:

> *We have found that when people regularly go into a quiet state, a large percentage of them feel the presence of a power, a force, an energy, God if you will, and they feel that presence is close to them, within them, then these people have fewer medical symptoms. Now, whether or not this is a physiological reaction independent of an external belief system, or whether or not there is indeed something out there, we cannot answer, but from the patients' point of view, they feel better. . . .*

Overall, mind-body techniques and the relaxation response have as their objective: calming the mind, achieving a peaceful state; coping with stress; relaxing the body and mind, generating the "relaxation response"; expressing and clearing emotions; changing negative thoughts; and controlling physical functions such as breathing.

Typically, mind-body therapies fall into two categories: physical therapies, such as dance, or mental therapies, such as biofeedback, or therapies that combine aspects of both, such as yoga or T'ai Chi. Mind-body work also includes imagery, hypnosis, transcendental meditation, psychotherapy, prayer/spiritual healing, music therapy, art therapy, breathing exercises, humor therapy, and other forms of relaxation.

Sometimes the effectiveness of these therapies is written off as the "placebo" effect, but that overlooks its effectiveness. If we believe that unconscious thought—general stress, for example, or negative self-talk—can cause illness, why wouldn't we think that conscious, positive thought could help ward off illness or heal the body? Rather than simply serving as a placebo, there is also a strong medical basis for mind-body therapy. Recent studies in the field of psychoneuroimmunology show that the mind can communicate with the nervous, immune, and endocrine systems via cells called "neuro-transmitters." Various chemical and hormonal releases can then affect health and physical function as a result of conscious thought.

Research shows that mind-body techniques are particularly useful in the stress-reduction areas, helping to reduce blood pressure, pain, headaches, asthma, and other illnesses with a strong stress component. Mind-body techniques are also empowering, involving you in your own health care as an active participant.

There are so many types of mind-body therapy that we can just touch upon a few. You'll need to research more fully those therapies that are most appealing to you and where best to participate in them.

Psychotherapy or Counseling

Psychotherapy or counseling provides an outlet for stress and anxiety, can help to calm down your overall emotional state, allowing more energy for healing, more positive thoughts and actions, which in turn speeds recovery.

Support Groups

Support groups also provide an outlet for anxiety and stress. They have the added benefit of, in many cases, providing education and information that gives you a feeling of greater control. Studies have even found that people with fatal illnesses live far longer when they are part of a support group.

Meditation Techniques

Meditation techniques are most common in Asia and are an integral part of Buddhism, Hinduism, yoga, and many Asian religions. They have gained popularity in other countries in the past thirty years. Regular meditation or *guided relaxation and imagery* have notable effects on blood pressure, anxiety, chronic pain, and can clinically reduce cortisol levels, a measure of the body's stress. Meditation training can help chronically ill patients to reduce symptoms and improve quality of life, and benefit the immune system. Researchers have also established by using magnetic resonance imaging (MRI) that meditation actually activates certain structures in the brain that control the autonomic nervous system.

Biofeedback

Biofeedback is a treatment method that uses monitoring instruments to feed back to patients various physical information—such as pulse, body temperature, and other indicators of stress—which they normally don't monitor. By wearing the biofeedback monitor, they learn to adjust their thinking and other processes to control blood pressure, temperature, gastrointestinal functioning, and brain wave activity. Biofeedback is particularly effective at treating stress, sleep disorders, headaches, and high blood pressure.

Creative Therapies

Creative therapies—such as dance, music, or art—use creative and physical activities to address health concerns. Creative therapies are particularly good for treating stress and blood pressure disorders.

Prayer and Mental Healing Techniques

Prayer and mental healing techniques usually describe an altered state of consciousness due to a spiritual experience, or the "flow of energy" or healing via another person's hands. Studies have shown these techniques can be effective, again particularly when with reference to stress and energy-related problems.

Guided Imagery

Guided imagery can be an effective technique for healing. You can use your own imagery, or follow a book, audiotape or practitioner. If you are feeling stress, you might envision progressively relaxing each part of your body as you relax on a warm, sunny beach, or you might envision the body's healing capabilities focusing on a damaged organ.

O. Carl Simonton, M.D., author of the best-selling and highly recommended book *Getting Well Again*, talks about effective mental imagery for illness:

1. Create a mental picture of any ailment or pain that you have now, visualizing it in a form that makes sense to you
2. Picture any treatment you are receiving and see it either eliminating the source of the ailment or pain or strengthening your body's ability to heal itself
3. Picture your body's natural defenses and natural processes eliminating the source of the ailment or pain
4. Imagine yourself healthy and free of the ailment or pain
5. See yourself proceeding successfully toward meeting your goals in life
6. Give yourself a mental pat on the back for participating in your recovery

Self-hypnosis

Another effective technique is self-hypnosis. One study found that the more often students practiced relaxation techniques, the stronger their immune response. Pyschotherapist Dr. Leonard Holmes believes that hypnosis can be an excellent relaxation technique for almost anyone:

> All hypnosis is really self-hypnosis—meaning that the person is putting him or herself into a trance. For most of us a trance is just a light relaxing state similar to daydreaming. Entering this state on a regular basis calms the sympathetic nervous system and reduces the levels of stress hormones in the bloodstream. Some people have even greater hypnotic ability. These are the people that you see on television acting silly

with a stage hypnotist. People with high hypnotic ability can use hypnosis as a way to change things about their mind and body.

Journaling

Have you ever written an e-mail, bulletin board post, diary entry, or letter about something bothering you, and after you were finished, felt better about the whole situation? You weren't imagining it. The act of writing about stressful events and situations can actually have a positive impact on your health. In a 1999 study published in the *Journal of the American Medical Association*, researchers reported that some patients with chronic diseases had improvements in their health after writing about major life stresses, such as car accidents or the death of a close friend or relative. The study looked at 112 patients. Each patient spent an hour each day writing, and four months after the study began, almost half of those who wrote about their stresses had experienced significant improvement in their health. The benefits of "downloading" your concerns and stresses, whether by writing in a journal or sharing your personal experiences with others who can relate via an online support group, is a natural stress reduction activity. What scientists call "expressive writing" not only gives your mind a place to unload stressful concerns or worries, it can also be a relaxation, or peaceful activity, that also helps to reduce stress by calming down your system and allowing you to focus better.

■ Spirituality and Health

Dr. Brian Sheen believes that dealing with thyroid problems may require deep healing of the mind-body influences. Says Sheen:

> *These mind/body influences consist of unforgiven grievances, unexpressed feelings and thoughts, and buried traumas*

that fester in the unconscious mind and interfere with the free movement of the body's natural healing systems . . . immune, endocrine, nervous and lymphatic . . . also re-modeling of daily living to learn to de-stress through meditation and re-think through paths such as A Course in Miracles. . . .

Others believe that there is a definite spiritual dimension to healing. In his book *God, Faith, and Health: Exploring the Spiritual-Healing Connection,* social epidemiologist Jeff Levin says:

The weight of published evidence overwhelmingly confirms that our spiritual life influences our health. This can no longer be ignored.

Some research has shown that people who are considered "religious" may live as much as seven years longer than others, on average. And a study, done by California's Human Population Laboratory, studied five thousand people for twenty-eight years and reported that frequent church attendance was linked to a 23 percent reduction in the chance of dying, versus nonchurchgoers. Other studies have found that for each of the three leading causes of death in the United States—heart disease, cancer, and hypertension—people who report a religious affiliation have lower rates of illness. Researchers at Johns Hopkins University have reported that attending religious services at least once a month more than halved the risk of death due to heart disease, emphysema, suicide, and some kinds of cancer.

Dr. Christina Puchalski, director of the George Washington Institute for Spirituality and Health in Washington, D.C., believes that attitude and spirit can have a profound impact on health:

It's important to go to a deeper level, to look at things that you're grateful for, look at the positive side. Some people actually have a mantra, some will reach out to others. Having an illness can make people self-focused, so on the spiritual side, it's important to look at what you can do with your life in spite of the fact of your illness. Think about volunteerism, your work, church, family, how you can step outside of yourself and look to others to help you and for you to help them.

Dr. Puchalski advises patients that they are going to be angry and frustrated, but the question is, how to move beyond it. What can you find that will give meaning to your life in the midst of illness?

Holocaust survivor Victor Frankl's book *Man's Search for Meaning* talks about how all of us need to find meaning in whatever we do, whether we're sick or not. Says Puchalski:

The search for meaning, however, can be seriously interrupted by illness. But ultimately, we all face this challenge. We will all get older, be laid off, retire, find ourselves less able to do things, and discover that our effort to find meaning is interrupted. Interestingly, what I've found with my younger patients is that chronic illness is a blessing in a disguise, in a weird way. Because of their health challenges, they do have to take that journey, and ask those questions a lot sooner than the rest of us. Some people ask those questions, and it causes despair. But if you can move from despair into hope, my patients say they find a much deeper, more meaningful life than ever before. Sometimes people are even grateful for their illness. . . .

While the mind-body connection is important, Dr. Puchalski cautions against the idea that illness is a manifestation of inadequacy, or that if we exercise and self-treat hard enough and long enough, we'll return to energy and wellness. Says Puchalski:

That's been some of the criticism of that work . . . that you can will yourself into healing or remission, and if you don't,

it's "I wasn't meditating hard enough, because I have a recur-
rence." I've had very religious patients who told me that "my
church group said I didn't pray hard enough because other-
wise my diabetes would have been cured." All of us have to
deal with things in our lives . . . but to say we willed a condi-
tion upon ourselves is laying a guilt trip that takes it too far.

■ Yoga

While yoga is a therapy that technically falls both into the "mind-body" category and is related to Ayurveda, I've covered it separately because I feel it is an important alternative therapy for people with hypothyroidism.

When most people think of yoga, they assume it means stretching or sitting in a cross-legged lotus position. Yoga is actually an ancient science that focuses on putting the whole body, mind, and intellect in harmony with the universe. This may sound like New Age babble, but actually yoga is quite practical, with physical exercises (asanas), breathing exercises (pranayam), and meditation techniques that help achieve that union and balance.

Some of the many health benefits of yoga have been conventionally tested and proven, and are even discussed in Western medical journals. For example, certain forms of yoga have been found to have a strong antidepressant effect. Yoga has also been found to improve lung function and breathing, and significantly reduce the amount of asthma medicines needed by asthmatic patients. Yoga is also considered an effective treatment for carpal tunnel syndrome. These are just a few of the many practical applications even mainstream medicine has found for yoga.

To find out more about yoga and its impact on thyroid disease and metabolism, I spoke with a well-respected yogi, Swami Rameshwarananda, who runs the Yoga in Daily Life Center in Alexandria, Virginia. Yoga in Daily Life is an internationally known comprehensive yoga system founded by Paramhans Swami Mahesh-warananda and includes a set of recommendations of how to achieve balance of mind and spiritual harmony. I studied for several years with Swami Rameshwarananda. In my never-ending quest for wellness—on a variety of levels—I have to say that yoga is one of the more satisfying, rewarding, and *effective* treatments I've found for energy, reduction of muscle/joint pain, and peace of mind.

Yoga is not a quick-fix solution for hypothyroidism, but it offers some overall health benefits, as well as some very specific benefits for metabolism and thyroid function. Yoga is about union of body, mind, and spirit. The word "yoga" means union, and in yoga, exercises, breath energy (prana), and meditation are all practiced in order to achieve that union and balance. In yoga, disease—such as hypothyroidism—represents a lack of unity somewhere in the "body." But to yogis, the body is not just physical. There are five distinct bodies or planes that interact with each other: nourishment/physical body; energy; mind; intellect; and causality, bliss.

In yoga a disease can represent a lack of harmony in the physical body or evidence of lack of harmony in the mind. Western medicine, on the contrary, typically focuses on the purely physical causes of illness. Swami Rameshwarananda greatly respects allopathic medicine, but feels that much of it focuses on the body of nourishment:

> *The focus is on eating, taking in nutrients, and how those nutrients are broken down to various chemicals. The other "bodies" are not considered much. The objective of yoga is balance of the whole system . . . harmony among all the bodies.*

Yoga also looks at energy and life force in a unique way. In yoga each of us has eight main chakras. While the direct translation of the word *chakra* is "wheel," it's more accurate to think of it as an energy vortex that concentrates energy in and out of our selves. Chakras are points where there is a particular accumulation of energy from the criss-crossing *nadis*—the energy pathways/vibrations—through which the prana—the cosmic energy, vitality, or life force—flows. When the nadis are not flowing freely—when there are traffic jams on the energy pathways so to speak—energy cannot then freely flow in and out of the chakras.

In yoga metabolism is closely connected with prana and is specifically linked to two chakras, the purification chakra in the throat area, and the digestive/nourishment chakra in the navel area. According to Swami Rameshwarananda, there are several ways yoga can help someone with thyroid disease. But first, he has a word of caution:

> *You can begin your practice of yoga as a way to improve your overall health, with a focus on your thyroid, but do not stop taking your thyroid medicine. Eventually, you may find that you need less medicine, or even, as some students have reported, be able to stop taking your medicine entirely. But you should only change your medicine with your doctor's monitoring and supervision.*

Swami Rameshwarananda recommends that people begin a program of basic yoga postures (exercises beneficial for everyone) that are designed to help harmonize the different bodies. These exercises are known as saraw hitta asanas and are best learned from an experienced yoga instructor. You can see them performed in a videotape demonstrated by Swami Rameshwarananda or learn similar exercises in a beginner's yoga class.

Penelope, a thirty-four-year-old with Hashimoto's thyroiditis, swears by her yoga exercises as the one thing that truly improves her health:

> *I have been studying yoga for a little over a year and am much, much more flexible and stronger than before. I was diagnosed with fibromyalgia over two years ago, and since*

starting the yoga, I have no pain or fatigue at all. The yoga has also been wonderful for muscle aches, and it even helped my libido.

There is a specific asana, or pose, that is thought to be of great benefit to the thyroid. The "half shoulder stand" (viparit karani mudra) and "shoulder stand" (sarvangasan) positions both invert and stimulate the thyroid. According to Swami Rameshwarananda, the shoulder stand is considered one of the most powerful positions in yoga, and in addition to helping the thyroid, it is thought to prolong life through its effect on metabolism and pranic energy.

In a shoulder stand, you lie flat on your back, and keeping your legs together, you raise them up until they are at a right angle to your shoulders and neck, perpendicular to the floor, chin tucked into your chest, resting the weight of your body on your shoulders and elbows, arms supporting your hips. Work up to a daily session of a full two minutes by starting with two or three shorter sessions. Swami Rameshwarananda counsels that you should always stop and consult an experienced yoga instructor if doing a shoulder stand makes you feel dizzy, uncomfortable, or interferes with your breathing.

Swami Rameshwarananda also recommends the practice of pranayam (pronounced pran-a-YAM), the breathing exercises that help to cleanse and harmonize the nadi energy pathways and clear out obstructions—physical, mental, and emotional. Many yoga centers and alternative health workshops offer this training.

The most basic pranayam of all is deep abdominal breathing. To try it yourself, lie flat on your back, or stand. Put your hand on your abdomen and take a deep breath, filling your belly with air so your hand rises, then exhale. Start basic pranayam practice by simply doing this for ten or fifteen minutes each day, and you'll be surprised at how much more relaxed, yet energetic, you'll feel.

There is also a specific breathing exercise that is designed to help the thyroid and the throat chakra. Breathe in through your nose, focusing the inhalation toward the back of your throat. Your throat should feel slightly "closed" or "blocked" while you perform this breathing exercise. Mentally, you should try to feel as if you are taking in the air *through* the front of your throat. Do this several times a day, but not for long periods, as it might make you dizzy.

More and more interest is also now focusing on specialized pranayam that have the ability to change the autonomic nervous system in various ways. For example, one study looked at three different yoga breathing techniques. One group did breathing in and out of the right nostril (the other nostril is pressed closed with a finger), one group did breathing in and out of the left nostril, and a third group did alternate-nostril breathing. Yoga experts believe that these types of breathing help balance the metabolism, generate increased energy, concentration, and mood, and help to balance endocrine disorders in particular. In one study, these practices were carried out as twenty-seven respiratory cycles, and repeated four times a day over the course of a month. At the end of the month-long practice, the "right-nostril pranayama" group showed a 37 percent increase over their baseline oxygen consumption. The left-nostril group showed a 24 percent increase, and the alternate-nostril group showed an 18 percent increase. The increase in oxygen consumption can help make the metabolism more efficient, increase energy, and potentially even help you lose weight.

Here are brief guidelines on how to do nostril breathing:

- Sit on the floor in the lotus position with legs comfortably crossed, or on a couch or chair, making sure your spine and head are straight.
- Rest your right hand on your right knee or in the lap.
- Place your index and middle fingers of your left hand at the center of your eyebrows.
- Keep the right nostril open and close the left nostril with the thumb.

- Inhale slowly and deeply through the right nostril to the count of 4.
- Hold the breath for the count of 2.
- Exhale to the count of 4.

That is one cycle of nostril breathing. Repeat the cycles, starting with one to two minutes, and working up to several sessions of ten minutes a day.

■ Energy Work/Reiki

There are many forms of energy work, where practitioners transfer "healing energy" to recipients, but one of the most popular and effective appears to be Reiki (pronounced RAY-key). Reiki teacher, practitioner, and holistic healer Phylameana lila Désy, author of *The Everything Reiki Book*, has described Reiki as a vibrational healing modality that consists of an enormous amount of what she terms "love energy." Reiki is a form of energy work—some practitioners may touch recipients, others just pass their hands over the body.

In Reiki the practitioner taps into a universal "energy force," and then passes that energy on to the recipient, who will receive it where it is most needed—mind or body. Says Désy:

> I teach my students that Reiki is a "smart energy" because it works at the level of acceptance by each individual client. Reiki will never overwhelm someone who is not accustomed to feeling energy, as it will enter the body slowly. For someone more open to the energy it will flow more quickly, but only at the level that is needed. Reiki is a balancing remedy. It will flow directly to whatever is in imbalance and nudge it back into a more balanced state. Reiki will address physical imbalances first before addressing the emotional, mental, and

spiritual problems. For this reason alone, I think the benefits someone with a chronic illness could experience from consistent Reiki treatments are the receiving of relief from the physical and emotional suffering.

Interestingly, Reiki is one of the therapies that people frequently mention as being of help to them. One patient, Jeannie, decided to learn Reiki herself after experiencing the power of a Reiki treatment:

Since being diagnosed with a thyroid problem, I give myself an hour of Reiki everyday, usually a full body treatment, as the Reiki energy is intelligent enough to know where my body needs it. I often do quite a bit of treatment on my neck and throat area and feel a lot of heat and tingling in this part of the body. I strongly believe that it is Reiki that firstly helped to diagnose the disorder and very definitely has helped to make me better.

I've had a number of Reiki treatments myself, and definitely feel that Reiki is a tremendous help, particularly when I am struggling with fatigue or stress. An hour with a good Reiki practitioner makes me feel as if I am coming away from the session with a physical, emotional, and spiritual massage. But to ensure that you get the best from this healing modality, make sure you are seeing a reputable practitioner who comes with high recommendations from others.

Guided Chakra Visualization/Affirmation

In the area of energy work, guided visualization and meditation can also help tune and balance the thyroid. To perform this visualization and meditation, you sit in a comfortable upright position (in a chair, sofa, or lotus position), eyes closed. Take a few deep, cleansing breaths. The harmonic color for the thyroid is blue, and so you should visualize a bright blue beam of light coming down through the top of your head and going right to your thyroid. Feel the blue energy infusing every cell of your thyroid, throat, and neck. Visualize the blue beam of energy enhancing the thyroid and curing its underactivity. Feel the blue light spread all around your neck and throat, softly. Now, say out loud, "My thyroid is energized and is working perfectly. I am safe, and loved, and filled with the energy of the Universe."

PART III

Challenges and Controversies

Diagnosis Challenges and Controversies

Doubt whom you will, but never yourself.

—BOVEE

Many of you have a difficult time getting a diagnosis of hypothyroidism, despite clear signs of the condition. You may have a doctor who is reluctant to test, or one who is too conservative in interpreting lab ranges, or you may face other issues that delay diagnosis. Even getting your doctor to the most basic step, the TSH test, can be a challenge for some.

Because a proper diagnosis is absolutely essential in order to live well, it's important to look at the diagnostic and treatment challenges you might encounter, and how to successfully resolve them.

■ Finding the Right Doctor or Practitioner

There is no question that the first step in getting the right diagnosis and treatment is having the right doctor or practitioner. This is not always an easy proposition.

When it comes to treating hypothyroidism, I'll tell you right up front that my bias is toward more holistic, integrative practitioners. My regular family doctor is a holistic M.D. who practices with several osteopathic physicians. She is also trained in acupuncture and osteopathy. My doctor listens, cares, is interested in learning more every day, is up on the latest developments, and never rushes, never makes me feel that I'm wasting her time, and never discards what patients think or feel in her overall process of diagnosis. And to be even-handed, on the downside, she is very popular and thus it's hard to get an appointment; you usually wait an hour or more to see her; she's expensive and not on any health insurance plans. But she's worth it!

If you're one of those who are obviously hypothyroid according to the TSH test, and you respond perfectly to levothyroxine, then almost any doctor will do. But for everyone else, the detective work that may be needed to find the hypothyroidism, not to mention the trial-and-error process of finding the right treatment, requires time, patience, persistence, and an open mind—more often characteristics of holistic, integrative physicians than the typical primary-care doctor, G.P., or endocrinologist.

Despite my bias, I have to say that there are many fine, caring, primary-care doctors, G.P.s, and endocrinologists. And there are holistic doctors and osteopaths who are narrow-minded or whose main objective is to sell you expensive vitamins, potions, and snake oil, and subject you to expensive—and even wacky—tests that put money in their pockets. So your job is to sort through and find the best—the most honest—doctors, whatever initials they have after their names, for you and your health.

As far as the right doctor is concerned, take a look at the different types of physicians you might see for your hypothyroidism and evaluate their strengths and weaknesses. I'm going to generalize here because there are always going to be wonderful doctors who break every mold and defy every stereotype. These guidelines might help, however, in making some decisions regarding your treatment.

Endocrinologists

An endocrinologist specializes in diseases of the endocrine system. Endocrinologists typically have the initials F.A.C.E. after their names, standing for Fellow of the American College of Endocrinology. The two main issues endocrinologists deal with are diabetes and thyroid problems. Some endocrinologists, however, have subspecialties such as reproductive endocrinology (fertility), nuclear medicine, growth disorders, or osteoporosis. To be honest, the big issue with endocrinologists is finding one who thinks thyroid disease is interesting. Many of them focus almost exclusively on diabetes and treat thyroid problems as a sideline. More than sixteen million Americans have diabetes, and while that's far less than the twenty-seven million people with thyroid disease, diabetes is considered to have more serious complications (i.e., risk of blindness or potential loss of a limb), and, as one doctor told me, "There are more medicines to play with," so it attracts more interest.

I sometimes refer to endocrinologists as the "accountants of medicine." They love numbers, and many are more comfortable reading lab charts and numbers off of blood test results than interacting with patients or engaging in creative problem-solving. In terms of treatment, there may not be much difference between one endocrinologist and another. All endocrinologists can read a TSH result and write a Synthroid prescription. What seems to differentiate many endocrinologists from their colleagues is, frankly, kindness, personality, sympathy, responsiveness, and bedside manner.

Thyroidologists

Some doctors—not many—refer to themselves as "thyroidologists." Officially, there really is no such thing as a thyroidologist, no official medically recognized group of professional "thyroidologists," or a specialty known as "thyroidology." Some endocrinologists and internists use the term because their practice tends to focus more on thyroid patients, versus the skew toward treating diabetes. In any case, a thyroidologist tends to be even more likely to fall into the conventional, by-the-numbers type. Don't expect much in the way of complementary or alternative approaches here. It would be rare, for example, to find a thyroidologist who came out of an osteopathic medical school, used holistic or integrative approaches, or was willing to prescribe T3 or desiccated thyroid.

Internists/General Practice/Primary-Care Physicians

Internists, general practice, family practice, and primary-care doctors are harder to characterize in terms of style or biases, because they truly do come in all shapes and sizes. For some people, an internist or G.P. can do a fine job managing hypothyroidism, ordering regular TSH tests, and writing prescriptions for conventional thyroid drugs. If the doctor is an M.D. in a conventional medical practice, and particularly an HMO, it's pretty safe to assume to a large extent that the doctor will take a traditional approach, not unlike an endocrinologist, in managing thyroid problems. For those who do well under this conventional protocol, not much more is needed. When you don't do well on the conventional approach, or when you want to understand more about the many side effects and symptoms of hypothyroidism, the fairly conventional focus of most internists and G.P.s may fall short of what you need. Rarer are the older family doctors, who diagnose using their judgment, are still versed in the use of desiccated thyroid, and are open to prescribing it, knowing the success they've had with it for years. They're few and far between, but their patients are usually very loyal.

Osteopathic Physicians/D.O.s

Currently, it's estimated that there are more than thirty-thousand American-educated and -licensed osteopathic physicians practicing in the United States. The majority of osteopath physicians are in primary care—family medicine, pediatrics, internal medicine, and obstetrics-gynecology. Osteopaths have the initials D.O. after their names, instead of an M.D. Doctors of osteopathic medicine (D.O.s) are, for the most part, pretty hard to tell from an M.D. in many ways. D.O.s are "complete" physicians, fully trained and licensed to prescribe medication and to perform surgery. D.O.s and allopathic physicians (M.D.s) are the only two types of complete physicians. D.O.s are licensed in the same way as doctors, have to attend an osteopathic medical school, and do internships and residencies. The main difference is in the philosophy of osteopathy versus conventional medicine. Osteopaths typically address people holistically, and instead of treating each symptom separately, they look for the overall cause and attempt to treat the whole person. Osteopathic physicians understand how all the body's systems are connected and related. Many osteopaths use physical manipulation of the musculoskeletal system. Osteopaths have a reputation as good listeners and believe in helping patients develop attitudes and lifestyles that don't just fight illness, but help prevent it. In treating hypothyroidism, some osteopaths are conventional TSH/levothyroxine followers, but in general, they are much more likely than an M.D. to work with nontraditional prescription thyroid medicines, such as natural thyroid or the T3-related therapies. You'll also find them more likely to be open to herbs, vitamins, supplements, and other complementary therapies to help treat the underlying immune system or persistent symptoms.

Holistic/Integrative Doctors

Holistic and integrative doctors focus on the whole person, and how he or she interacts with the environment, rather than illness, disease, or specific body parts. A small number of M.D.s, and a larger percentage of D.O.s, practice holistic and integrative medicine, following some general principles. They believe in prevention of disease when possible, and in dealing with the underlying cause of a problem versus just treating symptoms. They want to understand the patient as much as the disease or illness, and diagnose patients as individuals, rather than as "members of a disease category." They encourage patient autonomy—a doctor-patient relationship that considers the patient's needs as much as the doctor's—and the healing power of love, hope, humor, and other positive forces. Ultimately, they believe in integrating as many treatments as possible—which could include prescription drugs, herbs, vitamins, nutrition, lifestyle changes, mind-body approaches—for the greatest effectiveness.

When it comes to hypothyroidism, holistic doctors are the most likely to work with nontraditional prescription thyroid medicines, such as natural thyroid or the T3-related therapies. They are also more likely to treat you using herbs, vitamins, and supplements for your health related to the thyroid and the immune system.

I prefer a doctor who has a warm, participatory style, and is open to alternative and complementary therapies. You will have your own criteria. When looking for a doctor, Kathy, a thyroid cancer survivor, has a different focus and looks for a doctor who is particularly up-to-date:

> Now that so much information is accessible via the Internet and online support groups, I want a doctor who is up-to-date on issues, research, treatment, etc. I don't like feeling I know more than the doctor does about my condition, the prescribed medication, and the options for testing and treatment.

The Resources section contains a number of helpful organizations, referral services, and Web sites that can help you find potential doctors.

Communicating with Your Doctor

Once you've settled on a doctor, your work is not done. Now you have to manage the relationship, ensuring that you are getting the best possible care.

A productive doctor's appointment is one during which you have a chance to cover your key concerns with the doctor. In many doctors' offices, time is at a premium, so a successful appointment requires advance preparation. Following are some ways to ensure your visit is as successful as possible:

• Make up an agenda for your doctor's visit and bring two copies of it, one to share with the doctor. Be sure to include on your agenda all key questions, concerns, or unusual health symptoms. Writing down "difficult" questions sometimes makes it easier to ask them, and keeping track of key issues helps you remember all the things you want to cover with your doctor.

• Get in business mode. Act as if your appointment is a business meeting. You're the client, the doctor is the "contractor," so to speak. Doctors treat patients more respectfully when the patients dress professionally for the appointment, and when patients stay calm, relaxed, and unemotional, and do not act apologetic or passive.

• Be sure to arrive on time. If you arrive in advance, don't spend time reading old magazines, spend the time reviewing your agenda and mentally preparing for your appointment.

• Take notes. It's hard to remember what the doctor says after an appointment, so jot down notes, names of things, instructions and other information, so you have a reference.

• Bring a friend. This can help you feel more relaxed with the doctor. If your doctor gives you a hard time about having a friend with you, this is a red flag. You're the patient, you're paying the bill, and you should be able to decide who you'd like in the examining room with you. Choose a friend who is able to speak up but also is diplomatic. Friends who are health professionals—or even doctors themselves—can be of particular help. Be sure your friend knows the agenda for the appointment, so he or she can remind you of points to cover, and can help remember details of what your doctor said or agreed to do.

It's also important to keep a health diary between appointments. This can help you get the most out of appointments, and keep your health information organized. You can do this in a binder like Dr. Savard has created or in a notebook, on the computer, or in folders. The form doesn't matter. The main concern is keeping track of appointments, copies of test results, and other pertinent information.

Author and patient advocate Marie Savard, M.D., feels that having all your medical information available in one place may be one of the most important ways to help your doctor make an accurate diagnosis and recommend the best treatment. Dr. Savard's health information organizer book and binder, known as *The Savard Health Record* provides a wonderful health information tracking tool for patients. Says Dr. Savard:

> *Ask for all laboratory tests—give the doctor a self-addressed stamped envelope to send test results . . . they appreciate it and it makes the point you are serious—ask for the copies of the original, not the doctor's handwritten summaries of the information. Include blood work, X-ray reports, pathology and special study results, typed consultation reports from specialists, all heart testing and procedures, discharge summary and operative summary, if hospitalized. Remember to keep this information organized by date; store all lab work, consultations, etc., in their own section for a doctor to easily review.*

• Doctor information: Include the name, address, phone, fax, and e-mail address for every doctor you see, even periodically. Keep track of receptionists' names. And also store directions to offices you don't visit frequently.

• Pharmacy information: Include the prescription numbers and number of refills available for all current prescriptions, plus phone numbers for your pharmacy or pharmacies.

• Lab/treatment facility information: Include the name, address, and phone number of any labs or treatment facilities (radiology labs, testing locations, physical therapists, etc.).

The diary should also keep track of your key health events, including illnesses, surgeries, and other pertinent information. A detailed health diary would include: dates of visits to the doctor; dates when you've received any injections, vaccinations, or special treatments; dates and locations of diagnostic procedures (TSH tests, X-rays, MRI, bone scan); dates starting and stopping a medication, and dosage levels; blood test results—ask for a photocopy for your folder; and major emotional and physical stresses.

When It's Time to Change: Signs That You Need a New Doctor

Whether you already have a doctor, or have selected a new doctor, there may come a time to decide that you need to switch to a new physician. The decision to find a new doctor is actually more difficult than most of us might think. Our relationship with a doctor is an intensely personal one, and it's not easy to find the right match. That's why it's not easy to "fire" your doctor. You may feel intimidated by your doctor, or be afraid that you'll offend the doctor by leaving the practice.

Remember—in a doctor-patient relationship, *you* are the client, and the doctor is providing a service. And if that service is not meeting your health needs, the best thing you can do is to find the right doctor who will meet your needs. This is especially important when you have a chronic health concern that will keep you returning to your doctor regularly. Your relationship with your doctor is the foundation of your health and well-being. The wrong doctor may make it difficult—if not impossible—to return to wellness and optimal health.

How do you know when it's time for a new doctor? Here are some signs.

- Your doctor—or the doctor's staff—is disorganized, rude, or not responsive to calls or faxes.
- Your doctor's office regularly makes billing, appointment, or paperwork mistakes.
- Your doctor dismisses the Internet as a source of quackery and nonsense, or refuses to look at information you've researched.

- When you bring up a symptom or concern, your doctor assumes that it's something like "age, hormones, not enough sleep" and fails to explore other medical causes.
- If you asked for a different drug or a new drug for your condition, your doctor will usually refuse, without a reasonable explanation.
- Your doctor tries to sell you expensive products or services, i.e., vitamins, supplements, powders and potions, books, videos, or other materials the doctor claims you can only get from him/her.
- Your doctor takes phone calls, reads mail, or types on the computer during your appointment.
- Your doctor asks the same questions over and over, indicating that he or she doesn't remember or hasn't listened to what you've said.
- Your doctor has lots of drug company "swag"—the mousepads, pens, pencils, prescription pads, calendars, mugs, patient information literature, wall charts and posters, and other paraphernalia.
- Your doctor is arrogant or patronizing toward you.
- Your doctor interrupts you or acts impatient when you are speaking.

Is There a Perfect Doctor?

Ideally, we want our doctors to be kind, smart, compassionate, inexpensive, and to quickly diagnose and cure us. Sometimes this is the case. But reality check: There are times when your doctor may not be able to "cure" you. The best he or she may be able to do is help minimize symptoms, optimize your health as best as possible, or make you more comfortable given a particular condition. A great doctor is your partner in wellness, working with you to explore the situation, get the best possible diagnosis, explore treatments, fine-tune treatments as necessary—working in partnership with you.

A great doctor is one who is your partner, treats you with courtesy and respect, listens to you, and incorporates you into the decision-making process.

Remember, of course, that a great doctor won't be the perfect doctor. A great doctor may have almost every quality you want, but be a bit more costly than you'd like. Or may run late and keep you waiting. Or be so popular that there's a four-month waiting list for routine appointments. You can't expect perfection! But do expect a doctor who will make his or her best effort on your behalf. You and your health deserve it!

■ Getting Past HMO, Insurance, or Doctor Refusals to Test Your Thyroid

One challenge to diagnosis is getting past your doctor's resistance to your request for a thyroid test. Sometimes, they are protecting their ego and sense of superiority, and in other cases, they may be reacting to cost control and management measures that discourage spending for medical tests.

One patient, D.J., faced a reluctant doctor:

> I had asked for a thyroid test no less than three times over the course of nine months and was given some other test instead. She finally agreed grudgingly to a thyroid test. Imagine "our" surprise to find out my hunch was correct all along! My TSH was so high, the lab thought their analysis machine was broken!

After getting her diagnosis, D.J. found a new doctor who does not feel threatened by patients who take an active role in their health care.

Charl, a medical professional in the military, went to her military doctor to request a thyroid check:

> I was countered with, "Now, Major, not everyone who is overweight is hypothyroid [as he checked my neck manually].

Besides, who is the doctor here?!" I asked if a blood test needed to be conducted to determine whether or not my thyroid was faulty. "Do you think you can tell me my job? Your thyroid is normal. I just checked your neck!" I decided it was time to seek the advice of a civilian physician. She ordered a plethora of tests and discovered that I have Hashimoto's thyroiditis.

Some doctors discourage testing because they are in an HMO or managed care environment where their rating, reputation, or even incomes are affected by the number of tests they order. According to Dr. John Lowe:

Managed care companies provide incentives to physicians for not ordering laboratory tests, not treating patients, and not referring them to specialists. So physicians working for these companies may decline to order laboratory tests so that their income will be higher.

Some doctors simply don't have enough time to even figure out what's going on, much less order tests. According to Dr. Ken Woliner:

HMOs and PPOs pay so poorly for "time with your physician" that medical practices run people through so quickly. If a health plan only pays $25 for a visit—whether five minutes or an hour—the practice has to see six to eight patients an hour. When a doctor (or sometimes a physician assistant or nurse practitioner) spends only seven minutes per patient, they don't have time to listen to their complaints and patients get blown off. There are studies that show that the average doctor cuts off their patient after only seven seconds, finishes the visit in less than seven minutes, and leaves behind an aver-

age of 2.3 prescriptions—with the most common medications being antidepressants and sleeping pills.

When faced with a doctor who won't order tests for your thyroid, the best option is to find another doctor, even if you have to pay for the visit yourself. But if you have no options, here are a few tips:

• Be persistent. Ask for a thyroid test. Show the doctor articles about hypothyroidism that reflect your symptoms, even if he or she won't read them. Ask again and again.

• Bring your Hypothyroidism Diagnosis and Symptoms Checklist to an appointment, and ask that it be included in your medical chart after the doctor signs it, dates it, and indicates that he or she has read the checklist and discussed it with you. Make sure you get a signed and dated copy for yourself. Send a copy to the HMO's or insurance company's ombudsman or consumer liaison, along with your request that testing be approved.

• Write a simple letter that states that for the reasons listed, you have specifically requested that you be tested for thyroid disease, and that this doctor has refused. Insist that the doctor sign it, place a copy in your charts, and give you a copy. (You can then send this copy to the HMO to argue for a testing or a referral to another doctor or an endocrinologist, if needed.)

I've frequently suggested these ideas to people who write to me, and they work. Most doctors will order the test rather than officially document their decision to refuse a patient's request. Apparently, the concerns over malpractice or mismanagement charges made by patients override their reluctance to test. It may seem ridiculous that you have to fight to get standard medical tests and treatment, but it's your health that is at stake, so keep fighting.

Order Your Own Tests . . .

If you can't get anywhere with your doctor or HMO, or want to move more quickly, order your own lab tests. HealthCheck USA lets you get TSH tests, or full thyroid panels, at local laboratories, often at tremendous savings over what your doctor might charge. The results will be provided to you. You can also get an FDA-approved finger-prick TSH test from Biosafe by mail. You mail in the test kit, and the results are sent back to you. Information on how to order these tests is featured in the Resources section.

■ A Tendency Not to Trust Your Own Instincts

Many people have told me that, retrospectively, they realize something was wrong, but didn't act on it or mention it to the doctor early enough. Some people assumed weight gain was due to a change in diet, or presumed their exhaustion was due to excess obligations.

Geri, a health writer and producer in New York, was diagnosed as hypothyroid during a routine physical, but looking back, realized that she had the signs of hypothyroidism for a number of years:

> At the time I was diagnosed, I didn't think I had any symptoms. But in retrospect, I had started feeling very cold and generally sluggish and sickly for about two months before I was diagnosed. I chalked it up to general fatigue, overwork, wintertime blues, approaching thirty. Looking farther back, I think my thyroid started to go about five years ago. At that time, I stopped getting my period for twenty months and gained weight.

If you suspect or believe something's wrong, chances are you may be right. You know your body better than anyone. Trust your intuition, and go to the doctor sooner rather than later.

■ Symptom-by-Symptom Diagnosis That Misses the Big Picture

Some people go in to see the doctor over the course of months or years with symptom after symptom of hypothyroidism. The doctor treats each individual condition—cholesterol drugs for elevated cholesterol, antidepressants for depression, appetite suppressants for weight gain—but doesn't step back, look at the big picture, and say, "Aha, a classic textbook list of hypothyroidism symptoms. Maybe I should run a thyroid test."

LuAnn's experiences are a good example of what many people go through. She started with swollen eyes, then developed pins and needles in her legs, painful leg muscles, slurred speech, a thick tongue, and a swollen face. At each step of the way, her doctor said the problems were allergies, sinus problems, vitamin deficiencies, and so on. Even LuAnn's mother and husband were wondering if something was going on with LuAnn's thyroid, and when asked, the doctor said she didn't think so. Finally, after many months, the doctor agreed to test LuAnn's thyroid:

> On Friday evening I received a call from our clinic. It was the doctor on call that night. She said that my blood work results had just come in and that she was very worried and needed to get me on some medication immediately. My heart was pounding, and I think I started sobbing on the phone, just because someone was saying that, yes, there is actually something wrong with you! She said that my T4 was not even borderline. It was 0.4. And she had never seen a higher TSH, which was 460.

In this case, again, when your instincts and even other people are telling you that there's a thyroid problem, you may have to try another doctor and get a second opinion to break out of the symptom-by-symptom diagnosis rut. Your Hypothyroidism Diagnosis and

Symptoms Checklist can also present your doctor with a comprehensive and objective overview of all your possible symptoms and how they fit together into a diagnosis worth investigating.

■ Misdiagnosis and Gender Bias

The demonstrated relationship between depression and hypothyroidism is discussed in greater depth in Chapter 13. However, at the diagnostic stage, it's important to note that because depression doesn't require a lab test, you are more likely to initially walk away with a diagnosis of depression than with a thyroid test. Some researchers estimate that as much as 15 percent or more of people with a diagnosis of depression are *actually* suffering from undiagnosed hypothyroidism.

Many forward-thinking doctors believe that a thyroid test should *always* be performed to rule out thyroid disease as a cause of depression. Kate Lemmerman, M.D., says:

> *Even if someone comes in complaining specifically of depression, I believe they need to have a thorough evaluation done, including, but not limited to, thyroid testing, before being prescribed an antidepressant.*

Women face a particular risk of misdiagnosis. Some doctors don't take women's health complaints as seriously as they take those of men. This type of doctor assumes that women are more emotional or even sometimes "hysterical," and are overstating their symptoms or the severity of their symptoms. Because hypothyroidism affects women far more than men, this bias against women can also explain in part why some doctors fail to make a proper diagnosis.

There is also an issue of negative perceptions of the potential thyroid patient. Says Dr. Mike McNett:

Most people with hypothyroidism have as their primary symptoms fatigue and obesity, two conditions that carry a negative value judgment in our culture. Both of these conditions are commonly viewed as character defects, and the people who complain of them tend to be consciously or subconsciously discounted. As a result, even though a doctor may not be aware of it, he tends to give their concerns less value than, say, someone with chest pain (who gets an immediate ambulance to the emergency room).

There's often an assumption that changes in weight, mood, and energy—also frequently the symptoms of hypothyroidism—are merely a result of normal cyclical changes in a woman's "hormonal" status. It's true that weight, mood, and energy can change due to the hormonal system, but the thyroid is part of that system, too, not just estrogen.

Having your symptoms overlooked or ignored because you are a woman is particularly frustrating. Dr. Kate Lemmerman explains why this phenomenon still occurs with some doctors:

I believe that when women complain of weight gain, fatigue, dry skin, constipation, and other complaints classic for hypothyroidism it is often thought that these complaints are psychological . . . and they are prescribed an antidepressant without first checking to see if there is an organic reason for their complaints. I think we still view women as "the weaker sex" and so more easily write off their symptoms without adequately evaluating them.

While thyroid problems strike women five to seven times more often, there are still many men who develop hypothyroidism. Because hypothyroidism is less common in men, and because men are less likely to mention some of the symptoms to their doctors, getting a diagnosis can become particularly difficult for men as well.

Lee, a man in his midforties, spent most of his adulthood plagued by depression, lethargy, dry skin, and incredibly cold fingers. Typical thyroid symptoms, but like many men, he was less likely than a woman to be tested for an underactive thyroid. Eventually, the doctor tested him because he had extremely high and unresponsive cholesterol levels above 300:

> *I was going to refuse the test. That he is the first doctor to look at my description of my life and suggest that thyroid tests were needed sort of shocks me. I am overjoyed that some of the complaints I have can be dealt with so effectively for the first time.*

Tom had to go through many months of complaints and a misdiagnosis of depression before he was able to get a correct diagnosis:

> *Being a man, I have found it hard to get doctors to listen, possibly worse, because they want to categorize hypothyroidism as a "woman's disease." I have tried to explain to them that I am not trying to say I am having menstrual problems, I am not asking for a mammogram, I am asking for you to treat my thyroid, a piece of anatomy that, the last time I checked, is shared by men and women alike. I often wonder how many men are out there either too proud and macho to realize they are sick, or are being misdiagnosed as being "depressed" and being put on drugs that do not help the problem.*

Again, if you suspect that you're being written off as depressed or "hormonal"—when the real issue is an underlying thyroid condition—be persistent and repeatedly ask for thyroid testing. Insist that a copy of your hypothyroidism checklist or a letter indicating your doctor's refusal to test you be signed and included in your medical chart. Also, remember that the more businesslike and calm you can be, the more likely you will be able to make your case to the doctor.

It might be hard, and it might seem unfair or even ridiculous that you have to "convince" your doctor to do what's right, but let's get beyond what's right or fair and move on to what will result in your wellness.

■ Relying on the TSH Test as the Only Means of Diagnosis

In the past, thyroid disease was diagnosed and managed using a combination of blood tests, medical history, examination and observation of the patient, and discussion of symptoms. Some doctors also used the basal body temperature test. Today, you'll find it difficult to convince many doctors to do more than a TSH test in order to diagnose or manage your hypothyroidism. They've seemingly abandoned generations of medical knowledge and diagnostic tools, preferring to rely on one result—the TSH test, the test considered as part of many practice guidelines to be the only one that is necessary to diagnose hypothyroidism. In this purely conventional view of health, a normal TSH value—or what is referred to as being "euthyroid"—is considered normal, healthy, and not worthy of further investigation or treatment, regardless of your symptoms.

One self-described thyroidologist, Dr. Richard Guttler, shared his thoughts in a patient support group regarding the TSH test as gold standard:

> [TSH] is frankly superior to a therapy trial based on how the patient feels . . . all remaining symptoms after complete correction of the TSH to normal are not thyroid symptoms. . . .

Dr. Guttler is not alone in his total reliance on the TSH test as the only way to diagnose and monitor hypothyroidism, and his disregard for patient symptoms as part of treatment. Dr. John Lowe refers to this exclusive reliance on the TSH test as "the tyranny of the TSH" and notes that this attitude is likely to be found with most conventional practitioners.

Dr. Don Michael feels that doctors consider the TSH test as a substitute for critical diagnostic skills. Says Michael:

> *Using the lab that way misses as many cases of crippling thyroid disease as it picks up. For the most part, the labs are being used as the sole and final criteria for hypothyroidism. That is easily as foolish as using weight, apart from anything else, including seeing that patient, as the sole criterion for physical fitness.*

Dr. Sanford Siegal believes that relying on the TSH for diagnosis is problematic. Says Siegal:

> *Is the amount of thyroid hormone circulating in the blood really all that important? It is recognized that the hormone does its work only when it reaches the cells that will be affected by it. Is it possible that cells in one person react differently from those in another? Could there be a defect not in the thyroid or its hormones, but in other parts of the body so that they don't take proper advantage of the hormone?*

Perhaps no one said it better than the late Dr. Broda Barnes, author of one of the oldest—and best—books on hypothyroidism, *Hypothyroidism: The Unsuspected Illness*, published in 1976. Even back then, Dr. Barnes was one of the only practitioners to truly understand this issue of the TSH test when he wrote:

> *The efforts through the various tests to measure thyroid activity by determining the amount of hormone stored in the gland or alternatively the amount present in the bloodstream fail to do what really counts: provide an indication of the amount of thyroid hormone available and being used within*

cells throughout the body. They are somewhat akin to trying to get an idea of a thrifty man's spending habits from the amount of money in his wallet or the size of his bank account. The amounts of money in wallet or bank account, like tests for the amount of hormone in gland or bloodstream, tell us nothing about how much is being spent.

But I'll give the last word to Dr. Donna Hurlock:

We would all do a much better job if we just threw out the almighty TSH and started looking at and listening to our patients again, like docs in the 50's did.

What Can You Do?

If you've had a TSH test and been told you're normal, there's more fact-finding you need to do.

First, do not accept "you're in the normal range" as a report of your results. Ask for your specific numbers and the lab's normal ranges. Better yet, ask for a photocopy of the test results page, so you can keep it in your own file. If you have specifically requested the numbers and your doctor refuses to tell you, insisting "it's normal," or "you don't need to know the numbers," or "leave the doctoring to me," this is a *major* warning that you need another doctor. There is absolutely no valid reason for a doctor to refuse to share your lab results. If the doctor refuses, then it's due to an overinflated ego or an assumption that you deserve no role in your own health care, good reasons to look for another doctor. You pay for the lab work, you own it, and you have an *absolute* right to know your numbers.

Second, you might also want to check your health records to see if you've ever had your thyroid tested in the past. If the test occurred *before* you started to develop thyroid symptoms, you may have a true picture of what *your* normal TSH value is to compare. Sometimes, being able to see a rise from a lower-normal TSH level to one that's high normal or slightly above normal is enough for your doctor to consider diagnosing hypothyroidism.

Third, if you are one of the people who is functionally hypothyroid with a normal or high-normal TSH level, you may need additional tests—such as the Free T3 or antibodies test—to get a true diagnosis of hypothyroidism. If your doctor is willing to test for TSH and nothing else, you're not going to have much luck getting any further than this without changing doctors. In particular, if you want to pursue other testing, you'll probably need to find a more open-minded holistic doctor or practitioner.

You can order some additional tests yourself—see the Resources section for information on HealthCheck USA's service—but even if you have abnormal results, you're still stuck in a situation with a doctor who doesn't recognize the value of these additional tests. So, ultimately, moving on to a more open-minded doctor is probably a faster, more effective way to get diagnosed and move closer toward restoring your health.

Fourth, you can ask your doctor for a diagnostic trial course of thyroid hormone. According to Dr. Manelle Fernando:

> We should not be afraid to use the very useful diagnostic test of a trial period of treatment if there is sufficient clinical evidence. Of course, this has to be done with the patient's informed consent, and requires teaching and discussions, which take time, and in today's health system where talking to patients is considered a waste of time by health management, it's often difficult to do.

■ The Ever-Changing Normal Range

Even if you can get your doctor to run a test, usually the TSH test, what *is* the normal range? According to Dr. Jacob Teitelbaum, the normal range for blood testing simply means that a patient is not in the lowest or highest 2 percent of the population. According to Teitelbaum, the whole methodology for determining the normal range is flawed:

> *Normal range for thyroid hormone levels in the past has been based on statistical norms—called 2 standard deviations—out of every 100 people, those with the 2 highest and lowest scores are considered abnormal and everyone else is defined as normal. That means if a problem affects over 2% of the population (and as many as 24% of women over 60 are hypothyroid and 12% of the population have abnormal antibodies attacking their thyroid then our testing system will still miss most of them. In addition, our testing system does not take biological individuality into account. To translate how poorly this "2%" system works, this is like saying a normal shoe size would be 3 to 13. Just because this is the normal range does not mean that you can pick just any size shoe in this range for anyone. Yet, this is exactly analogous to how doctors are currently treating thyroid problems—and it is no wonder that many people respond poorly to this "one size fits all" approach. If a man got a size 5 shoe or a woman a size 12, the doctor would say the shoe sizes they were given are "in the normal range" and there is nothing wrong with it!*

Evidence that the normal range is not a monolithic, unchanging measurement was seen when, in late 2002, the announcement came out regarding a new recommended normal range. As mentioned in Chapter 5, until November 2002, doctors and labs had been using a normal TSH level ranging from 0.5 to 5.5. Recommendations from the American Association of Clinical Endocrinologists now encourage doctors to consider treatment for patients who test outside a narrower normal range of 0.3 to 3.0.

If your doctor and lab are still using the old standards, urge your doctor to read the 2002 *Medical Guidelines for Clinical Practice for* the *Evaluation and Treatment of Hyperthyroidism and Hypothyroidism*, available online at http://www.aace.com/clin/guidelines, or by calling the American Association of Clinical Endocrinologists at 904-353-7878. And be sure that you ask the doctor to tell you the specific numbers—better yet, have him/her give you a copy of the lab report, and not just say, "Your results were normal" because otherwise you have no way of telling what "normal range" your doctor is using to decide *you're* normal.

Even then, keep in mind that lab values are not the final word, and they can change yet again! Says Dr. Ken Woliner:

> *In the old days, the diagnosis of illness was made by symptoms. For example, diabetes was diagnosed if someone was thirsty, hungry and urinated a lot. Now, we make a majority of diagnoses based on some lab test "being outside the normal range: We were unable to diagnose diabetes until the fasting blood glucose (sugar) was greater than 140 mg/dl. Interestingly, this number has changed from year to year where normal glucose tolerance became < 125 mg/dl, then < 110 mg/dl, and more recently < 100 mg/dl. For thyroid, the diagnosis used to be made based upon symptoms and signs such as an enlarged thyroid (goiter) with or without nodules, fatigue, weight gain, constipation, and diminished or delayed reflexes (especially the Achilles reflex). With the first blood test, the PBI (protein bound iodine), if it was normal, doctors said, "you are not hypothyroid." They realized, however, that this test wasn't completely accurate, so it was replaced with the T4, then the T3RU. Eventually they replaced those tests with the TSH, but that missed people too. So then came the "second generation TSH," and then the 3rd generation "suprasensitive TSH." Alas, this test still was not perfect, so we now use the 4th generation "ultrasensitve TSH" and have changed the reference range to 0.3—3.0 MIU/L. The question is, If we no*

longer believe the data from those old, antiquated tests, why should we believe the tests being done now?

■ Borderline/Subclinical Hypothyroidism

The question of whether or not to treat subclinical or borderline hypothyroidism is a controversy among practitioners. Subclinical hypothyroidism is currently defined as situations where the TSH is more than 4.5, but less than 10, and levels of free thyroxine (FT4) and triiodothyronine (T3) are within the normal range.

The debate continues with an article that came out in early 2004, authored by Dr. Martin Surks and his colleagues from a consensus panel that studied subclinical hypothyroidism. Their findings, published in the *Journal of the American Medical Association*, concluded that there is little data that connects subclinical thyroid disease with symptoms or adverse health outcomes, and minimal consequences of subclinical thyroid disease.

These findings are in direct contradiction to many recent research study findings, including studies that reported that:

- Subclinical hypothyroidism treatment can reduce cholesterol levels and the risk of death from heart disease (*Journal of Clinical Endocrinology and Metabolism*, 2001 Oct;86(10):4860–66).
- Treatment of subclinical hypothyroidism reduces the risk of atherosclerosis (hardening of the arteries). (American Association of Clinical Endocrinologists 12th Annual Meeting and Clinical Congress, May 2003)
- Even when TSH levels are normal, if a patient tests positive for thyroid antibodies, treatment with thyroid hormone replacement may prevent full-blown hypothyroidism (*Thyroid*, 2001 Mar; 11(3):249–55).

Do these researchers not read their own research journals when they put together these "review" studies? Are they bound and determined to remain blind to the fact that many subclinically hypothyroid patients *do* have symptoms? Will they go against their *own* recommendations to continue to leave millions of Americans subclinically hypothyroid, suffering, and facing an increased risk of heart disease, obesity, infertility, depression, and many other symptoms?

Many people with subclinical hypothyroidism experience a variety of symptoms and risks of other health problems, including: cardiovascular disease, high cholesterol levels, weight gain and obesity, depression, reduced physical activity, and danger during pregnancy to both mother and baby.

There is even some scientific evidence that in the long term, higher TSH levels can increase the risk of thyroid cancer.

A study presented at an American Thyroid Association meeting confirmed that an underactive thyroid can result in high cholesterol levels. Gay Canaris, M.D., of the University of Nebraska Medical Center, said:

> *Each year, almost two million people suffer a heart attack or stroke. The better we can help people control their thyroid condition, the better we can help them manage or even bring down their cholesterol levels, a major risk factor to coronary artery complications.*

The primary argument doctors make against keeping the TSH level in the low end of the range is an irrational fear of osteoporosis due to unnecessary use of thyroid hormone. And this has not even been proven. Yet there is definitive research that shows the dangers of failure to treat subclinical hypothyroidism.

One self-proclaimed thyroid expert—an internist I consulted for a second opinion on my hypothyroidism—told me that as far as he was concerned a patient couldn't possibly even *have* symptoms at subclinical levels of hypothyroidism. He was adamant that no one would feel any symptoms until the TSH went well *above 10*. Speaking as someone who knows quite well, from my symptoms whether my TSH is 2 versus 5, I didn't go back to him for any more second opinions. I have received thousands of e-mails from patients who have symptoms at even normal or high-normal TSH levels, much less at levels that are actually hypothyroid by lab standards.

Diann experienced problems when she discovered that her doctor felt her TSH level was barely worth treating:

> *The doctor's office minimized my symptoms to the point of casually leaving a message on my voice mail that "your tests are a little high," when indeed the TSH level was 12. I had to retrieve my medical records to find this out. No wonder I felt like I was losing my personality, abilities, spunk, and ME. Did the internist make an effort to empathize or consult me personally?? NO! Seemingly, I wasn't suffering in his "book."*

Toy Lin also suffered with hypothyroidism needlessly for years because she didn't ask about the specific numbers, and her doctor apparently didn't believe that borderline hypothyroidism deserved treatment:

> *I'm so mad!! The last three or four years I've been on a downhill slide. I told the endocrinologist I had all these symptoms. He ignored me. I just got copies of my blood tests and see that the tests showed my TSH went from 1.6 in 1994 to 6.31 in 1996. The lab marked 6.31 as being high. The endo told me I was fine, I was normal. I have lost all this time, been a couch potato since then, because he ignored how I felt.*

Again, it's important to know the exact numbers, and the normal range the lab and your doctor are using for comparison. That way, you can see if you fall into the "subclinical" category. If your physician refuses to treat subclinical hypothyroidism, you may have to find one who will.

■ The Need for T3

A huge controversy in diagnosis is the issue of measuring T3 levels as a means of diagnosing thyroid dysfunction. On the conventional side, measurement of T3 or Free T3 is not included in any conventional guidelines for hypothyroidism diagnosis. Most practitioners rely on measuring TSH, and sometimes T4 levels, to make a hypothyroidism diagnosis. But a subsection of practitioners, including most of the innovative thyroid experts I've interviewed, feel that measuring T3 can be an important part of diagnosing hypothyroidism in some patients.

Says Dr. Ken Blanchard:

It is my belief that the majority of people with hypothyroidism need more than T4 supplementation. They also need T3 (and quite possibly the other Ts supplied only by natural thyroid). And the body requires these two hormones in physiologic doses that address deficits both in the thyroid gland and at the tissue level.

The Bunevicius-Prange Studies: 1999–2002

Fundamental to the issue of testing—or treating with—T3 is a series of controversial and conflicting research studies.

In February 1999, the *New England Journal of Medicine* published a research report that sent shock waves through the ranks of endocrinologists and left many patients cheering. The article, "Effects of Thyroxine as Compared with Thyroxine plus Triiodothyronine in Patients with Hypothyroidism," reported that adding T3 (triiodothyronine) to the standard T4 therapy improved the quality of life for most hypothyroid patients. Essentially, the research team, led by Drs. Bunevicius and Prange, took a group of thirty-three people who were hypothyroid, either due to autoimmune thyroid disease or removal of their thyroids due to thyroid cancer. All the patients were studied for two five-week periods. During one five-week period, the patient received his or her regular dose of levothyroxine (T4) alone. During the other five-week period, the patient received T4 *plus* triiodothyronine (T3). In the T4-plus-T3 phase, 50 micrograms (mcg) of the patient's typical levothyroxine dose was replaced by 12.5 mcg of triiodothyronine (T3). A variety of blood, cognitive, mood, and physical tests were conducted at various stages of research.

From the standpoint of physiological effects, the differences between pulse, blood pressure, reflexes, and a variety of other functions for T4 alone, versus T4 plus T3, were very small. Blood pressure and cholesterol, in fact, dropped slightly on the T4 plus T3. Results were dramatic, however, in mental functioning. All the patients performed better on a variety of standard neuropsychological tasks when taking the T4 plus T3. Patients' psychological state also showed improvement on T4 plus T3. At the end of the study, patients were asked whether they preferred the first or second treatments. Twenty patients said they preferred the T4-plus-T3 treatment, eleven had no preference either way, and only two preferred T4 only. The twenty patients who preferred T4 plus T3 reported that they had more energy, improved concentration, and just felt better overall.

The researchers also recommended the ideal thyroid hormone replacement program for someone without a thyroid gland or whose thyroid gland is nearly nonfunctioning: "10 mcg of triiodothyronine daily in sustained-release form . . . along with enough thyroxine to ensure euthyroidism."

Drs. Bunevicius and Prange published another study in the *International Journal of Neuropsychopharmacology* in June 2000. This study looked at hypothyroid women and replaced 50 mcg of T4 with 12.5 mcg of T3. Patients were first randomly assigned to one regimen for five weeks and then to a second regimen for an additional five weeks. After the combined hormone treatment, researchers found clear improvements in both cognition and mood. The patients who had been treated for thyroid cancer showed more mental improvement than the women with autoimmune thyroiditis, perhaps because they were more dependent on exogenous hormone.

Drs. Bunevicius and Prange went on to publish yet another study in the journal *Endocrine* in July 2002. This study looked at the difference between T4, as opposed to T4 plus T3, in treating hypothyroidism after thyroidectomy for Graves' disease. What the researchers found was that symptoms of hypothyroidism tended to decrease with the T4/T3 combined treatment.

Starting with the 1999 *New England Journal* study, this was groundbreaking research, and confirmed in the research environment what many patients, myself included, and some doctors have been claiming for a number of years: Levothyroxine-only thyroid hormone replacement does not leave a substantial percentage of hypothyroid patients feeling well, and these patients feel and function better when T3 is added to their thyroid hormone replacement. This research also offered an explanation for why patients have felt well all along on desiccated thyroid drugs like Armour Thyroid, which contains T4 and T3 naturally, and the synthetic T4/T3 drug Thyrolar.

Some open-minded conventional doctors started to successfully add T3 to their treatment options. But some of the most die-hard opponents refused. "There's no evidence that it works," they claimed. Interestingly, when the researchers found that T3 was helpful, many of the conservative doctors who had been saying, "Show me the peer-reviewed, double-blind major journal research that says T3 is good, and then I'll consider it" turned around and said, "Oh, I don't care if it's in the *New England Journal*, it's *bad* research!" They also claimed the studies were useless because they were "done in Lithuania."

The 2003 Studies

With the 1999 publication of the first Bunevicius-Prange study, some practitioners began to use T3 for the first time, and were able to point to the *New England Journal* as justification for their action.

Levothyroxine therapy is big business, however, and research that presented such a huge departure from dogma was not going to be met without resistance. Synthroid is a top-selling drug in America, and a highly profitable drug. Synthroid also contains no T3. Since anything that will take away business from the levothyroxine manufacturers has got to be a threat, it's no surprise that after the 1999 study was published, teams of researchers set out to defend against the threat and prove that levothyroxine should be the only game in town.

Two studies, published in the October 2003 issue of the *Journal of Clinical Endocrinology & Metabolism* (*JCEM*), claimed to show that combining thyroxine (T4) and T3 was *not* superior to T4 alone for the treatment of patients with hypothyroidism. One fifteen-week study looked at forty hypothyroid patients with depressive symptoms and determined that T4/T3 combination therapy did not improve either mood or personal sense of well-being. A second study compared a combination T4 and T3 therapy with T4 in a twenty-week double-blind, random-order, crossover trial of 110 hypothyroid patients. Half the patients received T4 therapy for ten weeks and then T4 and T3 therapy for ten weeks. The other half of the subjects received the combination therapy first. Once again, the researchers found no significant benefits for combination therapy compared to T4 alone.

Then, in December 2003, the *Journal of the American Medical Association* (*JAMA*) published another study, which looked at forty-six patients who were hypothyroid due to autoimmune thyroid disease (Hashimoto's disease). In the *JAMA* study, the two groups of patients either continued to receive their current synthetic T4 dose or received 50 mcg less of their current dose of T4 plus 7.5

mcg of T3, twice daily. The synthetic T4 doses of patients in both groups were adjusted to keep patients at "normal" thyroid levels, according to blood tests. After four months, there were no differences in body weight, blood pressure, or lipid levels between the two groups of patients. Additionally, no significant differences were observed in any of the standardized tests that assessed hypothyroidism symptoms or mental function. Dr. John P. Walsh, senior author, wrote:

> At the conclusion of our trial, we found no benefit of combining T4 and T3 therapy on quality of life, hypothyroid symptoms, cognitive function, subjective satisfaction with therapy or treatment preference. Furthermore, we could not identify a specific subgroup of patients who benefited from the combined therapy. Based on these findings, we believe that T4 alone should remain the standard treatment for hypothyroidism.

The Validity of the 2003 Studies

This time, instead of shock waves, cheers of support went through the endocrinology community. Conventional thyroid treatment could declare the T3 issue decided—because now they had "good" research—also known as research that supported their dogma that T3 is not needed and does not help patients. Those same defenders of the double-blind, peer-reviewed scientific method were quick to get behind results they liked, and they dismissed as "bad research" the Bunevicius-Prange studies, also double-blind, peer-reviewed research published in major medical journals—simply because they were results they *didn't* like. It's an example of the scientific method at its most flawed and political.

Aside from the politics, there is a real question about the validity and quality of the studies, and whether they prove anything about T3. Many of the experts who regularly prescribe T3 say the studies are seriously flawed and don't prove anything, for a number of reasons.

They Used the Wrong Amounts of T3—According to Dr. Ken Blanchard, author of *What Your Doctor May Not Tell You About Hypothyroidism*, the studies used too much T3. Blanchard believes that poor results will be seen with anything other than a ratio of 98 percent T4 to 2 percent T3, the percentages he uses in his protocol.

On the other hand, Dr. Kent Holtorf feels that there may not have been enough T3 used:

> It is ridiculous to point to the recent studies, in which 50 mcg of T4 was replaced with 10–12.5 mcg of T3, as evidence that T4/T3 combinations are not more effective than T4 preparations. It would not be expected that replacing 50 mcg of T4 with 10 mcg of T3 would result in significant improvement. The potency of T4 compared to T3 is actually variable. It depends on a person's ability to convert T4 to the active T3, but 10 mcg of T3 is generally less potent than 50 mcg of T4 for most people. Thus, substituting 10 mcg of T3 for 50 mcg of T4 would be expected to deliver *less* active thyroid to the patients. This was shown to be the case as evidenced by the significant increase in TSH in the group that received the 10 mcg of T3 substituted for 50 mcg of T4. There is no basis for this substitution being somehow equivalent and would not be expected to improve symptoms. It was not comparable dosing, making it an unfair comparison.

The Normal Range Used Is No Longer Normal—Blood levels of T4, T3, and TSH were maintained in the normal range in the majority of patients in those studies. However, these studies do not take into account that after they were completed, new guidelines were issued indicating that the target TSH range should be maintained between 0.3 and 2.0–3.0, rather than 0.5 to 4.6–5.0. Patients in the studies typically had TSH in the 2.0–2.5 range—which is now considered the high end of normal—throughout treatment. Some patients, however, do not achieve optimal thyroid hormone replacement results and feel relief of symptoms unless the TSH level is in the lower end of the normal laboratory range, i.e., between 0.5 and 2.0.

"One Size Fits All" Dosing Skews Results—Dr. Jacob Teitelbaum felt that the failure of these types of studies is that instead of adjusting the thyroid therapy dose to what feels best, the doctors often used a "one-size fits all" approach. Teitelbaum believes that more T3 needs to be used, or possibly the natural, desiccated thyroid drug rather than the synthetics, for optimal results. According to Dr. Teitelbaum:

> *Sadly, it seems the researchers did not consult with physicians experienced in the use of this approach. They would have noted: (1) Use an ~ 4:1 ratio of T4 to T3 (not 10:1). (2) Adjust the dose to that which feels best to the patient, while keeping the Free T4 level in the normal range. (3) If one type of thyroid does not work adequately, try another (their study posits that only one "brand" of shoe is best for everyone instead of asking the key question—"Did one form work best for some patients and the other type for others?"). (4) Do some patients benefit from split dosing (e.g., twice a day) while some do fine with once a day? (5) Are there other components of the natural thyroid that also result in a better outcome? (6) For those who still respond poorly, what other problems are being missed?*

They Contradict Clinical Experience—According to holistic practitioner Roby Mitchell, M.D.:

> *. . . we only have to look back at all the prospective, randomized, double-blinded, placebo-controlled trials "proving" that hormone replacement with Premarin and Provera would*

reduce heart disease, Alzheimer's and didn't cause breast cancer. No clinician who routinely uses T3 therapy would buy either of these studies as they just don't match up with clinical experience. That's the first criterion for establishing the validity of any study. . . .

Research Findings Don't Apply to Everyone—Drs. Richard and Karilee Shames also urge caution in interpreting the research. Say the Shameses:

It doesn't matter if 100, or 1000, studies show that most people do better with thyroxine alone. There are always some people in any of those studies who did better on thyroxine with T3 added. There are some people who do better on T3 alone. There are some who do better on Armour thyroid alone. There are some who do better with a mix of Armour and thyroxine. None of the studies will ever be 100% in any one direction. People are just too different. Which means that there are some people who may do better on the combo. You may be one of them, or you may not be. It is more likely that you are one of them if you are currently not doing all that well on thyroxine (T4) alone.

Study Size Is Too Small—None of the studies included a large number of patients. Compared to the estimated twenty-seven million-plus Americans with some form of thyroid disease, sample sizes of twenty, fifty, and one hundred are really absurd. They certainly aren't large enough to be statistically valid or applicable. Would doctors change treatments for diabetes or heart disease based on studies of twenty or fifty people?

Other Research Has Already Established the Usefulness of T3—Dr. Roby Mitchell says that there are many studies that contradict these findings. Says Mitchell:

The literature is replete with information that gainsays the notion that T3 is without merit. T3 has been shown to relieve congestive heart failure, lower blood pressure, lower cholesterol, improve serotonin production, improve outcome after cardiac bypass surgery . . . the list goes on. Anyone who looks at the literature unilaterally is not going to practice the best medicine.

Most Patients Need T3 from Desiccated Thyroid, Not Synthetic T3—Dr. David Brownstein felt that the studies weren't useful, but not necessarily because of the methodology, and more because of the drug tested. Says Brownstein:

I have not found that much benefit with just adding T3. But I have found the desiccated thyroid much more effective. My clinical experience has shown that desiccated thyroid is very effective and clinically seems to have better response than using T4 therapy alone.

Holistic physician Dr. Joseph Mercola agrees. Says Mercola:

We start all new hypothyroid patients on Armour thyroid, and switch most of those who have been on levothyroxine for the previous three years to Armour. It makes no sense to add T3 to patients who are on levothyroxine (T4) unless they are low in free T3. My experience suggests this is very common in patients who are initially started on levothyroxine as many are unable to optimally convert T4 to T3. However, with time most people seem to adjust and do not require the additional T3. However, most of this is ultimately a moot point. Clinically it is unwise to add T3 to T4 for most patients. I only need to add T3 to a very small percentage of my patients, and that is mostly restricted to individuals who are unable to tolerate desiccated (Armour thyroid).

The Studies Show That T4 Isn't the Answer—Dr. John Lowe has a different take on these new studies. Lowe feels that the studies actually demonstrate that T4-only replacement actually leaves many hypothyroid patients still suffering from hypothyroid symptoms. Says Lowe:

> *The patients included in most of the studies were chosen to participate for one reason: They were suffering from continuing hypothyroid symptoms despite their use of supposedly "adequate" T4 replacement.*

The fact that they showed no improvement still means that they were continuing to suffer symptoms on the T4. Lowe also believes that there is an even more important issue at stake:

> *Ultimately, the researchers and endocrinologists who wrote editorials on the newer study results came to a conclusion that can only be considered bizarre. That conclusion is this: Since T4/T3 replacement was no more effective than T4 replacement in relieving hypothyroid patients of their suffering, T4 replacement should remain the treatment of choice. That is, since* neither *form of replacement therapy helped the patients, they should be restricted to using only T4 replacement. On humanitarian grounds, however, I'm compelled to ask: Why restrict patients to a therapeutic approach that your own studies show continues patients' suffering?*

Studies and More Studies

There's no question that more studies will be done, looking at the impact of T3. Some will show that it helps. Some will show that it doesn't. The conventional practitioners will get behind the studies that support what they learned in medical school, and the way they practice. The holistic and integrative practitioners will keep on practicing the way they always have, with an eye toward safely achieving results in their patients.

But what can and should *you* believe? It may seem that, whether it's T3 or many other health issues, there's always a new study out that contradicts the findings from the last one. We are still seeing this with the estrogen controversy—does it help, does it hurt? And we're going to see more of it regarding estrogen, aspirin therapy, statin drugs, low-carb diets, and other continuing controversies.

Also, keep in mind that Synthroid is a top-selling, profitable drug. Its manufacturer funds medical school thyroid studies, thyroid organizations, endocrinologist groups, medical resident lunches at hospitals, thyroid research projects, thyroid researchers, and hands out millions of dollars worth of free samples, prescription pads, patient literature to doctors. Synthroid does *not* include T3, nor does Abbott, its manufacturer, make a T3 product. Who is to say that there isn't a selfish desire in the endocrinology community to maintain the status quo so they can keep enjoying the largesse of Synthroid's manufacturer?

Dr. James Strick, a professor of the history of science at Franklin & Marshall University, has some final thoughts about thyroid research:

> *Some physicians do selectively support those studies they like—or have a financial stake in . . . often the two are intertwined. That means there is no single source free of all the possible kinds of bias, as far as I can tell. Which means we depend on nongovernmental advocacy groups and, as far as thyroid patients are concerned, the work of Mary Shomon, to help make us aware of the opposing evidence and less-than-scientific conduct in the most egregious cases.*

Stay tuned, because clearly we're going to see much more information and debate about this issue in the months and years to come.

■ Antibodies and Autoimmune Thyroid Disease

You can have measurable evidence of an underlying thyroid disease, and yet test normal in the TSH test. How? You have autoimmune thyroid disease, which is measured by thyroid antibody tests. It is not uncommon to test positive for thyroid antibodies—evidence of autoimmune thyroid disease—yet have a normal TSH. When a person has antibodies, along with hypothyroidism symptoms, that usually means the thyroid is in the process of autoimmune failure. Not failed to the extent that it even registers as an elevated TSH level, but in the process of failing.

The risk of autoimmune thyroid disease is much higher when you—or a family member—already has a history of other autoimmune diseases. Some of the more common autoimmune conditions include multiple sclerosis, psoriasis, endometriosis, rheumatoid arthritis, Sjögren's syndrome, Raynaud's disease, lupus, and vitiligo, among others.

Unfortunately, many doctors believe that as long as TSH is normal, testing for antibodies is not necessary, and even then, testing positive for thyroid antibodies and autoimmune thyroid disease is *not* sufficient reason to prescribe thyroid hormone, even when you are plagued by hypothyroidism symptoms.

There are, however, some conventional doctors, and more integrative and holistic doctors and health practitioners, who believe that the presence of thyroid antibodies, along with symptoms of hypothyroidism, warrant treatment. Dr. Mike McNett is one physician who believes that antibody testing is particularly important:

> *Antibody testing is necessary to tell if a hypothyroid patient has Hashimoto's Thyroiditis, which is a prime cause of hypothyroidism. I think it's very important to do this, because Hashimoto's varies widely in activity and can cause large swings between being hypothyroid, normal, and hyper-*

thyroid. As a result, these patients should have their thyroid status monitored much more often than normal patients, possibly by a combination of basal body temperature, weights, and TSH levels.

Dr. Ken Woliner checks thyroglobulin and thyroid peroxidase antibodies on all patients he suspects of having thyroid disease:

If positive, I consider the patient to always be positive, and I stop wasting money ordering these and other thyroid blood tests again. For "research reasons" one could reorder them to determine response to therapy, but if a patient is feeling fine, despite high antibody levels—I am not going to change therapy. And if they are not feeling okay, despite having low levels of antibodies, I'm not going to keep the therapy the same and let my patient suffer. There is such a thing as "Anti-T3" and "Anti-T4" antibodies, but these tests are in the research stage. Should these tests become reliable, I may order them as well.

According to Dr. Kent Holtorf, at his nationwide network of fibromyalgia and fatigue clinics, they test for a number of antibodies:

TPO and anti-thyroglobulin are obviously useful for diagnosis of autoimmune thyroid disease. I find that individuals with autoimmune thyroid disease usually have low DHEA and testosterone levels. When these are supplemented, the levels of antibodies will usually drop, decreasing the ongoing destruction of the gland. This may explain why men are much less prone to autoimmune thyroid disease. We also test for:

- Anti-Thyrotropin Receptor Blocking Antibody—This antibody blocks the TSH activity on the thyroid and alters pituitary feedback. This results in lower thyroid levels for a given TSH level and increases the likelihood of either a missed diagnosis or an underdosing of thyroid hormone. This is another reason that the TSH is not an accurate measurement of thyroid activity.

- Anti-TSH Antibody—This is an antibody that combines with the TSH molecule. This results in an altered shape and a decreased activity of the TSH molecule with resultant less thyroid effect for a given level of TSH. This also increases the likelihood of either a missed diagnosis or an underdosing of thyroid hormone and is another reason that the TSH is not an accurate measurement of thyroid activity.

- Anti-T4 and Anti-T3 Antibodies—These are antibodies directed against the actual T4 and T3 molecules, respectively. The anti-T4 antibody alters the shape of the T4, making it unable to convert to T3, and the anti-T3 antibody alters the shape of the T3 molecule, making it unable to bind to the T3 receptor, both decreasing the thyroid effect. The antibodies also make the laboratory assays inaccurate. I have found that anti-T4 and anti-T3 antibodies are more likely to occur after a person has been on Armour thyroid; possibly because it is from a pig. This can be a cause of a person initially feeling better on Armour thyroid, but then falling back into hypothyroid symptoms despite increasing doses of Armour.

The practice of treating patients who have thyroid antibodies but normal-range TSH levels is supported by a study, reported on in the March 2001 issue of *Thyroid*. In this study, German researchers found that levothyroxine treatment for Hashimoto's autoimmune thyroiditis—where TSH had not yet elevated beyond normal range—could actually *reduce* the incidence and degree of autoimmune disease progression. In the study of patients with normal-range TSH, but elevated antibodies, half were treated with levothyroxine for a year, the other half were not treated. After one year of therapy with levothyroxine, the antibody levels and inflammation markers decreased *significantly* only in the group receiving the medication. Among the untreated group, the antibody levels rose or remained the same. The researchers concluded that preventative treatment of normal-TSH-range patients with Hashimoto's disease reduced the various markers of autoimmune thyroiditis, and they speculated that such treatment might even be able to stop the progression of Hashimoto's disease, or perhaps even prevent development of the hypothyroidism.

■ Thyroid Conversion and Resistance Problems

There are additional reasons why you may have so-called normal thyroid tests, but yet still be hypothyroid. These include the controversial concepts of thyroid hormone resistance problems, and T4-T3 conversion problems.

Thyroid Hormone Resistance

There are actually two kinds of thyroid hormone resistance. "Generalized" resistance to thyroid hormone—known as RTH—is a rare genetic disorder. Peripheral resistance however, may be a fairly common problem, say some thyroid experts.

Dr. Joe Lamb has an interesting way of looking at the issue. He believes that thyroid disease should be classified to include two distinct entities: type I and type II. Much like the way diabetes is classified, type I hypothyroidism would consist of underproduction of hormone and type II hypothyroidism would be characterized by hormone resistance. Says Lamb:

> If in diabetes, you measured insulin levels—similar to the
> standard thyroid test that only measures production—one

would find only 10% of "diabetics" have type I disease. The other 90%—those with hormone resistance—would be missed due to finding normal or even high insulin levels. So when we measure TSH and T4, we are missing the great majority of people with thyroid hormone resistance.

David Brownstein also compares the idea of thyroid hormone resistance to insulin resistance:

Thyroid hormone resistance refers to the body producing adequate amounts of thyroid hormone, but being unable to use the thyroid hormone. This occurs because the receptors where thyroid hormone is supposed to bind in the body are not working correctly. Receptors can malfunction from having vitamin and mineral deficits and heavy metal toxicities. My clinical practice has shown that excess trans fatty acids (commonly found in the standard American diet) can also cause a malfunction of these receptors. Also, the production of autoimmune antibodies, commonly found in many illnesses (e.g., Graves', Hashimoto's, Lupus, Rheumatoid Arthritis, etc.) may block thyroid receptors from properly responding to thyroid hormone. If thyroid hormone resistance is present, blood tests will indicate normal thyroid functioning, but the patient will have many signs and symptoms of hypothyroidism.

T4 to T3 Conversion

The healthy thyroid produces anywhere from 80 to 95 percent T4, and 5 to 20 percent T3. Even then, according to Dr. Glenn Rothfeld, some of the hormones are "free," and some are "bound":

T3 and T4 are present in your bloodstream in two forms, bound and free. Bound T3 and T4 are attached to proteins, which keeps them from having any action on cells, and are in plentiful supply. The supply of free T3 and free T4, the forms these hormones must be in to have an effect on your cells, is very limited—only about 1 percent of T4 and 5 percent of T3 are free. As your cells draw in free T3 and free T4, however, bound T3 and T4 break away to become free, replacing what the cells use.

After that thyroid hormone is released into your bloodstream, there are a number of steps that have to go right in order for thyroid hormone to reach your cells. Dr. Mike McNett explained the steps:

- Permeate—First, the thyroid hormone must get through the cell membrane into a cell.
- Convert—Next, most of it is in the form of T4, and since T3 is the biologically active hormone, T4 is converted to T3.
- Transport—Then, the T3 needs to be transported into the cell's nucleus.
- Bind—The T3 then needs to bind to the receptor protein in the nucleus.
- Use—And then the cell must be able to use the T3.

While Dr. McNett feels that any of these processes could be malfunctioning, many conventional doctors feel that the body almost always converts the T4 to the T3 at levels appropriate for ongoing functioning. To these doctors, even if you've had your thyroid removed, or have an underfunctioning thyroid, you would only need T4, not additional T3.

However, other practitioners feel that conversion of T4 to T3 can sometimes be temporarily, or even permanently, impaired. For example, researchers have established that the normal process of T4-to-T3 conversion can be temporarily inhibited by various stresses on the body, including illness, fasting, pregnancy, high levels of stress hormones in the body (cortisol), and other factors. And some practitioners believe that the conversion process may be permanently impaired in some people, leaving T3 levels chronically low.

Dr. David Brownstein, in his book *Overcoming Thyroid Disorders*, discusses patients he calls "poor T4 converters":

A poor T4 converter refers to the individual that has difficulty converting inactive thyroid hormone (i.e., T4) into the more active thyroid hormone (T3). My experience has been that many individuals do not adequately convert T4 into T3. That leaves these individuals suffering many of the signs of hypothyroidism, such as fatigue, poor immune system functioning, headaches, coldness, weight gain, etc. Many things contribute to a poor conversion problem including old age, vitamin and mineral deficiencies, heavy metal toxicities (e.g., mercury, lead, nickel and aluminum), adrenal problems, other hormonal imbalances and other causes as well. Many commonly prescribed drugs have also been shown to lower this conversion including birth control pills, synthetic estrogen products and beta-blockers.

Other reasons cited for poor T4 to T3 conversion include antibodies to the enzyme that *converts* T4 to T3 and infections and depression.

In his book *What Your Doctor May Not Tell You About Hypothyroidism*, Dr. Ken Blanchard explains a scenario where conversion is not optimal:

I believe that when faced with waning supplies of thyroid hormone in the bloodstream, the body compensates by stepping up the conversion of T4 to T3 at the tissue level. . . . This makes sense when you think about it: Making more powerhouse T3 is the body's way of compensating for a lack of T4. Thus, T4 becomes somewhat depleted, but T3 is relatively normal, maintained by increased conversion. The result is an imbalance of thyroid hormones that may ultimately cause or worsen hypothyroidism. Blood tests taken at this time would

show a low to normal TSH, which is interpreted as euthy-
roidism (normal thyroid function) or even hyperthyroidism.
Meanwhile, the body suffers because there isn't enough thy-
roid hormone to do the job.

In some cases, the problem may not even be in conversion, but in the cell's ability even to *use* the thyroid hormone. Says Dr. John Lowe:

Patients who are hypometabolic due to resistance to thy-
roid hormone are classified as having "partial peripheral cel-
lular resistance to thyroid hormone." These patients have
"normal" laboratory thyroid hormone levels. In other words,
they have normal amounts of thyroid hormone in their blood,
but these normal amounts are not enough to overcome the re-
sistance in their cells.

Wilson's Syndrome

In times of physical stress the body converts T4 to an inactive form of T3 known as Reverse T3. In a controversial theory, former doctor Denis Wilson theorized that the body can get "stuck" in this mode, leaving cells deficient in thyroid hormone and hypothyroid, despite normal blood test values. Wilson claims that this theoretical problem, which he named "Wilson's Syndrome" and, more recently, "Wilson's Thyroid Syndrome," is the cause of numerous health problems. Wilson believes that a major stress—such as childbirth, divorce, surgery, accident, or ongoing family/work pressure—slows the body down as a coping mechanism. The body temperature can drop as a response, which is normal. Wilson's theory says that sometimes the temperature remains low even after the stress has passed.

Wilson's Syndrome is not the same as an official, medically recognized disease known as Wilson's disease, which is a rare inability to process copper and has nothing to do with your thyroid.

A diagnosis of Wilson's Syndrome includes symptoms, as well as body temperature, taken every three hours, three times a day, starting three hours after waking, for several days (but excluding the period three days before menstruation for women, as temperatures rise during that time). If you woke at 7 a.m., then you'd take the temperature again at 10 a.m., 1 p.m., and 4 p.m. Add the temperatures together each day, and divide by three, to get an average. If the average is less than 98.6, "Wilson's Syndrome" proponents claim that you might have the problem. Wilson's protocol uses T3 to help resolve this T3 imbalance.

It's my belief that Wilson's Syndrome is not a distinct condition—it is just another manifestation of thyroid resistance or conversion problems. I also don't believe that the protocol is effective for most people. I've talked with dozens of patients and practitioners who have tried it, found it ineffective, and given up. Wilson also struggles under the weight of a questionable reputation. He does not have an active medical license, and has a history of several out-of-court settlements on a number of different complaints and charges. Wilson's site claims his legal problems have nothing to do with negligence or the protocol itself. Wilson, however, has apparently not gone back to active medical practice, instead launching his for-profit foundation, selling books, tapes, and informational binders describing his protocol.

Dr. Joseph Mercola has concerns about Wilson and his approach:

> I am surprised that someone would be so audacious to name a disease syndrome after himself that is so easily confused with a well-defined existing medical entity. Some have commented that his book for the public is of the worst of vanity-press publishing, although his doctor's manual is surprisingly well written and espouses some clever arguments, albeit based on some false premises. The Wilson protocol is so complicated and time-consuming to follow that it requires a

truly unusual patient and more time than a physician can usu-
ally afford to have any chance of being executed properly.
Unfortunately, until patients encounter something better, le-
gions of desperate patients, incorrectly treated by the "en-
docrinologist-thyroidologist technocracy," have clung onto
the hopes provided by Dr. Wilson's book.

Dr. John Lowe has said at his Web site:

I know of no scientific evidence supporting Dr. Dennis
Wilson's speculation that some patients have chronically im-
paired conversion of T4 to T3.

Dr. Kent Holtorf doesn't find Wilson's approach particularly effective for the overwhelming majority of people. Says Holtorf:

Most people will need to stay on the T3 or their symptoms
will return. The Wilson's protocol only works if a person has
very little TSH suppression and adequate T3 levels with an el-
evated reverse T3 level. This is usually not the case because
most people have a relatively suppressed TSH (0.2–2), with
low normal free T3 level and reverse T3 levels that are rela-
tively high compared to the level of free T3.

On the other hand, some aspects of what Wilson describes are
not outlandish, and some practitioners feel it may be worth investigating. Dr. Glenn Rothfeld, in his book *Thyroid Balance*, says:

Although there are no clinical studies to support or dis-
prove this protocol, it is gaining interest as a treatment.

Despite his criticisms of the approach, Dr. Joseph Mercola also
says that he needs to give some credit where credit is due:

Dr. Wilson's thoughts about "compensation" effects (and the differences therein among different patients) are useful and based on good logic and probably some quite astute clinical observations. Indeed, these dynamics are pertinent to what happens before a patient taking T3 stabilizes, and an awareness of this process may be a useful nugget to salvage from the considerable time many of us have invested into studying Wilson's approach. Of course, that does not suggest in any way that Wilson's cycling protocol with enormous doses of T3 has any merit or should be used.

For more information about Wilson's Syndrome, you'll need to visit Wilson's Web site, or invest in his manuals and patient education materials.

10

Treatment Challenges and Controversies

If everyone is thinking alike, then no one is thinking.
— BENJAMIN FRANKLIN

Diagnosis is not the only area of controversy in hypothyroidism. How to treat hypothyroidism, and what constitutes optimal treatment, is also an area where you'll find many differing opinions.

■ Optimal TSH Levels

What is the optimal TSH level? The truth is, there isn't really one level. You may feel best in the higher end of the normal range, or you may be someone who feels best with your levels suppressed to nearly 0.

Most of the time, however, doctors are likely to keep you at the high end of normal, or in the middle. And many patients and practitioners report that the lower end of normal may be where the majority of patients feel their best. So, if you don't feel well, you should discuss with your doctor the possibility of increasing your dosage of thyroid hormone replacement to target a lower TSH level.

Some doctors are reluctant to target lower TSH levels because they are concerned that lower TSH levels can increase the risk of osteoporosis. This is a very controversial issue, one that has not been decided, and is still being researched. Doctors who tell you that taking too much thyroid hormone will *definitely* increase your risk of osteoporosis are not telling you the whole story.

Dr. Bruce Rind's objective, rather than striving for "normal values," is to get his patients' lab values into an "optimal" range. Says Rind:

> I found this "optimal" range by observing what the values were of my healthiest patients. The optimal range for TSH is between 1.3–1.8 if dealing with an athlete, and between 1.0–2.0 for non-high performance patients.

Drs. Richard and Karilee Shames believe that TSH levels for someone who is undergoing thyroid treatment should be around 1.0 (or even less if antibody levels are high). Says Dr. Richard Shames:

> Some people in my practice seem to do best with a TSH that is at or just under the 0.3 level that AACE now considers the lowest end of the normal range.

In his book *Your Guide to Metabolic Health,* Dr. John Lowe cautions about using lab tests to gauge improvement. Says Lowe:

> To get optimal improvement with thyroid hormone, the patient should follow two rules. First, she should not permit her doctor to adjust her dosage according to lab thyroid test results . . . Using the results of thyroid tests to adjust a patient's dose is likely to sabotage the patient's effort to recover from her symptoms of hypothyroidism. . . . Second, the patient should enlist her doctor's assistance in adjusting the hormone

dose according to changes in her symptoms due to the last dosage increase.

Dr. Lowe is concerned that lab testing may cause some doctors to ease up on a dose simply because a patient is getting too low—or suppressed—a TSH level. According to Dr. Lowe, this may in fact be optimal for some patients, and does not mean the patient is hyperthyroid. Says Lowe:

> *An unfortunate convention in orthodox endocrinology is to define "hyperthyroidism" as a suppressed TSH level. Certainly, if the TSH-suppressive dose of thyroid hormone is too large, it will harm the patient. But many patients' TSH-suppressive doses merely induce normal metabolism in them and have no harmful effects. Depriving these patients of TSH-suppressive doses of thyroid hormone, however, is likely to harm them; they'll have chronic symptoms of hypothyroidism and may develop advanced cardiovascular disease.*

Dr. Carol Roberts also feels that suppressed levels may be best, but as far as testing is concerned, "My target is a happy patient." According to Roberts:

> *She should be feeling better, have more energy, sleep better, and the "brain fog" lifts. Then when I retest I don't pay much attention to TSH, that should be suppressed, I don't care how low. However, the T3 is important, and needs to be within the range of normal for that lab. Too high a T3 can cause heart palpitations, a dangerous condition, so even if she likes the feeling of being "high" on thyroid, I'll back her off until the T3 is within range.*

■ The Risk of Osteoporosis

Some studies demonstrate that doses of levothyroxine that suppress thyroid function—essentially causing hyperthyroidism or suppressed, extremely low TSH levels—can be a risk factor for osteoporosis. Many other major studies, however, found no significant reduction in bone mass in people with a suppressed TSH, hence no increased risk of osteoporosis. These studies looked at osteoporosis in patients who had suppressed TSH levels. Suppressed levels are typically *below* the 0.3 to 0.7 considered to be the low end of the *normal* range at many U.S. labs.

While the research is contradictory, some doctors have only heard the findings that showed very low TSH levels increase osteoporosis risk. Based on limited information, these doctors then compound the problem by employing faulty logic: If a very low TSH level poses a risk, then why not keep people at *higher* levels, and thereby avoid the risk? Hence, the current penchant to medicate patients only to high-normal TSH levels. These patients then walk around feeling unwell, being told it's not their thyroid, with the doctor refusing to prescribe a higher dose of thyroid hormone.

According to Drs. Richard and Karilee Shames, thyroid hormone is not the osteoporosis villain that it has been painted in the past:

> *The controversy started some years ago when research data on bone density and menopausal women was beginning to be collected. The results seemed to suggest that thyroid hormone treatment was associated with a lowered bone density. Both doctors and patients alike became fearful of thyroxine, and tried to treat even overt hypothyroidism with as little medicine as possible. This resulted in many people receiving a dose too low to relieve their symptoms, but it was considered a worthy tradeoff. Patients were told they would have to continue suffering through some low thyroid symptoms now in*

order to preserve their bone density for the future. However, the studies at that time lacked the data available today from third generation TSH assays and high-resolution bone densitometry. In addition, the groups of patients then being analyzed lacked the diversity necessary for accurate study. With further research now pouring in, it appears clear that thyroid medication—even in the higher doses some people need to feel best—does not increase one's fracture risk in later years. It makes no sense to soft-pedal thyroid hormone treatment in the face of this new evidence.

One 2004 review looked at sixty-three English-language studies of the thyroid-osteoporosis connection that were published from 1990–2001. Of the sixty-three studies reviewed, levothyroxine was shown to have no overall effect in thirty-one studies, partial positive and/or partial negative effects were reported in twenty-three studies, only nine studies showed overall negative effects, and three studies reported no effects.

Ultimately, this meta-review found no association between the duration of levothyroxine therapy and an associated reduction of bone mineral density, if it occurs. There was no conclusive evidence of a dose-effect relationship when all studies were considered. Not surprisingly, age-specific effects of levothyroxine on bone mineral density loss were reported by these studies, with older women experiencing the greatest effects. No significant effect of levothyroxine on bone mineral density was reported in men. In those studies, some negative impact was postulated; the adverse effects of levothyroxine on bone mineral density were reported to be greater in post-menopausal than in premenopausal women. Larger effects were noted in late-compared to early-menopausal women.

It was not clear from these studies, however, whether underlying thyroid diseases and/or their treatments are independent or additional risk factors for reduced bone mineral density. Further, there was disagreement among the studies whether a potential negative effect of levothyroxine on bone mineral density is reversible, preventable, or mitigated by drug treatment.

In summary, the reviewers conclude that all of the current evidence considered together suggests no significant effect of levothyroxine on bone mineral density, but caution that this is a preliminary conclusion limited by the nature and quality of the studies conducted on this question thus far.

What Should You Do?

If you have a family history of osteoporosis and are on thyroid hormone replacement, or you're postmenopausal and on thyroid hormone replacement—and particularly if you have a history of hyperthyroidism or Graves' disease—you should be screened for risk factors of osteoporosis; have bone densitometry, if warranted; receive counseling on diet and exercise; and receive prescriptions for osteotherapeutic drugs, if warranted.

Other practitioners would suggest you also add 1,500 to 2,000 mg of a highly absorbable bone-friendly calcium product supplements daily (remember not to take them within three to four hours of your thyroid hormone replacement drugs), eat mineral-rich foods, and consider supplementing with a trace mineral product.

■ Treatment with T3

The controversy over the need for T3 was discussed at length in the previous chapter. This is one issue where you'll need to make sensible decisions as to whether your practitioner is the right one for you, in terms of openness to various treatment options.

Some options?

• Ask your doctor for a trial course of T3, following the very precise guidelines of Dr. Ken Blanchard, as outlined in his book *What Your Doctor May Not Tell You About Hypothyroidism.* Dr.

Blanchard is an M.D., and his approach of adding just a small amount of T3 may seem more judicious and appeal to a more conservative or conventional physician.

• Ask your doctor to try adding a small amount of Cytomel to your current T4-only treatment. Some patients find that as little as 5 mcg once or twice a day is all they need.

• Ask for a switch to the synthetic T4/T3 combination drug Thyrolar. Again, because it is synthetic, it is sometimes less threatening to physicians.

• Ask to switch to a desiccated natural thyroid, like Armour. This is perhaps the most controversial way to request T3, but again, with repetition and persistence, some patients have managed to get Armour prescribed by even the most die-hard old-school Synthroid fans.

If your doctor is entirely unwilling to explore testing T3 and treating deficiencies, then it's time to consider a new physician.

And if you want something more elaborate, such as time-released T3 or a more complex dosing protocol, you will definitely need to see a thyroid expert who has experience working with T3 treatment. Note that T3 should be approached with caution, however. Heart patients, people with high blood pressure, and the elderly need to be particularly careful. Even if you have no other underlying problems, your physician should monitor you more carefully when you are on T3. It's not a "come back in a year for a test" situation—you will require more frequent monitoring.

And, according to Bruce Rind, T3 is an excellent tool if there is a poor ability to convert T4 to T3, but it should only be used if:

a. The physician is thoroughly familiar with its safe use, signs and symptoms of excessive dosage, and the patient has a similar understanding of these.

b. The adrenals can tolerate it.

c. It is used in the slow-release form (from a compounding pharmacy). I've found the fast-release form (Cytomel) extremely stressful to the adrenals.

d. The lab values are monitored. An unexpected drop in TSH suggests a decrease in adrenal tolerance to the T3.

Ultimately, T3 *can* help some patients. I can't deny my own experience, or the experience of thousands of people who have written to me, and thousands more who are the patients of the practitioners I've interviewed.

Thyroid patients have wasted enough valuable time not feeling well, living lives at half-speed, waiting to feel better, while doctors tell us that more double-blind, peer-reviewed, major medical journal research is needed. They could literally research our lives away. We already have research studies, clinical experience of thousands of practitioners, and anecdotal knowledge of millions of thyroid patients who are able to live well with the use of supplemental T3. Thyroid patients have waited long enough. Responsible doctors owe it to their patients to consider carefully whether or not T3 treatment will benefit their patients.

■ Optimal T4/T3 Balance

Optimizing the amounts of T4 and T3 given as treatment, and/or measurable in the blood, is the objective of a number of practitioners.

For Dr. Bruce Rind, the optimal ranges for Total T3 and T4, Free T3 and Free T4 are usually around the midpoint of the range given by the lab. Say Rind:

> One does need to keep in mind that if a woman is pregnant or taking estrogen (birth control pills or hormone replacement therapy) or even phytoestrogens, then the Total T3 and T4 will register a false high reading. In such cases, the Free T3

and T4 are more accurate. The reason I do use the Total T3 and T4 is that they give me a clearer picture of the thyroid values and that they are more sensitive to clinical changes.

Dr. Joseph Mercola feels that Free T3 and Free T4 levels are the only accurate measures of the actual active thyroid hormone levels in the blood, more accurate than the TSH level. Says Mercola:

The Free T3 and Free T4 levels represent the active hormones circulating in the blood. The typical thyroid tests: Total T4, T3 Uptake, and Free Thyroxine Index (FTI) are virtually worthless and should have been abandoned years ago. I believe that the Free T3 and Free T4 are not superior to TSH, but should be used in conjunction with TSH. My contention is that the reference range for TSH is inaccurate. TSH is quite a good screen and will in fact assess most cases of hypothyroidism if the new ranges are utilized. The value of Free T3 and Free T4 comes into play when one needs to diagnose secondary and tertiary hypothyroidism. These are cases of hypothyroidism due to pituitary or hypothalamic dysfunction. These are far less common than primary hypothyroidism, but nevertheless they do constitute a significant percentage of individuals.

Dr. Ken Blanchard is a perennial member of the Thyroid Top Docs list since back in 1997. Dr. Blanchard's innovative approach to T4/T3 was featured prominently in the first edition of this book. Since being featured in the book, his approach has gained such acclaim that he has presented it in great depth in his own book, *What Your Doctor May Not Tell You About Hypothyroidism.*

Dr. Blanchard has developed a very specific method—he calls it the "2 percent solution"—for determining the proper ratio of synthetic T4 and T3 needed to achieve, as he says, a "proper physiologic dose of thyroid hormone." Says Blanchard:

Over time, I began to see a pattern of success: Patients responded beautifully when the dose proportion was 2 percent T3 and 98 percent T4.

He uses a specially compounded formulation to get to that ratio, and it includes compounded T3 and/or desiccated thyroid, plus levothyroxine.

This precise dosage, according to Dr. Blanchard, resolves many of the ongoing symptoms and problems:

The fundamental reason for using T3 is that we know that the normal secretion of the thyroid gland includes primarily T4 and a smaller amount of T3. When we give small amounts of T3 along with T4, we're simply reproducing the normal physiology better.

Dr. Blanchard believes that in order to live well with hypothyroidism, patients must have their underlying thyroid problem properly treated:

When we get the people I treat on a pretty good dosage, most of them can't believe how much better they are. Many of them have almost sadness once the burden of hypothyroidism is released off of them, and they realize how many years of their lives they existed carrying this anchor around with them.

■ Treatment for Resistance and Conversion Problems

Mention thyroid hormone resistance, T4 to T3 conversion problems, Reverse T3, or Wilson's Syndrome to most conventional doctors and you'll get a lecture about quack medicine, pseudoscience, and the dangers of the Internet, among other diatribes. You may be told you can't possibly have Wilson's *disease,* or that Wilson's

Syndrome is a quack diagnosis. And if you mention "resistance," you'll come up against the idea of the difference between peripheral resistance and general resistance, and probably be told, correctly, that "generalized" resistance to thyroid hormone is extremely rare.

At worst, you might encounter hostility or even be "fired" by your doctor, the situation in which one thyroid patient, Tom, found himself:

> *I tried very hard to get the doctor to listen to me and he rolled his eyes and said, "I don't care what crap you heard on the Internet." I was just trying to ask what I felt were educated questions based on what I have read, but I got accused by the doctor of trying to "tell me how to do my job." Then he did what I still can't believe. He actually had the gall to tell me, "You're not welcome here anymore. Take your labs and your questions and comments and find another doctor. I don't want to see you again telling me how to do my job . . . if you ask me you just have a depression problem that maybe you should get looked at." I told him his bedside manner sucked, that all I was trying to do is be an advocate for myself and be involved in my own treatment.*

Ultimately, getting "fired" by his doctor was the best thing that ever happened to Tom because he went on to find a doctor that *did* diagnose his hypothyroidism, and Tom is finally feeling much better.

When you do find a physician who is willing to consider the possibility of thyroid hormone resistance, or conversion problems, treatment can include a number of options.

In some cases, when a deficiency in T3 is suspected, innovative practitioners are willing to treat patients with T3. These doctors prescribe Cytomel or time-released T3 to be added to a regimen of levothyroxine. In some cases, they prefer the combination synthetic

T4/T3 drug Thyrolar or one of the natural, desiccated thyroid products that contains T4 and T3.

Dr. Kent Holtorf believes that treatment for conversion problems, including increased levels of reverse T3—is usually time-released T3. According to Holtorf, "T4 preparations, such as Levoxyl and Synthroid, actually make this problem worse."

Dr. David Brownstein believes that the treatment for thyroid hormone resistance involves treating the underlying cause and sometimes using thyroid hormone. Primarily, he feels you need to improve your detoxification pathways, clean up your diet, and search for deficiencies of vitamins and minerals that impair conversion. In his book *The Miracle of Natural Hormones*, Dr. Brownstein lists a variety of substances and conditions that inhibit T4 to T3 conversion, including: iodine deficiency, iron deficiency, selenium deficiency, zinc deficiency, vitamin A deficiency, vitamin B_2 deficiency, vitamin B_6 deficiency, vitamin B_{12} deficiency, caffeine, beta-blockers, birth control pills, estrogen, iodine contrast agent, lithium, goitrogenic vegetables, alcohol, fluoride, and hormonal imbalances.

Brownstein's approach is customized to each patient, and may involve detoxification, supplemental vitamins or minerals, hormone balancing, and dietary changes. His books—listed in the Resources section—have more details on his approaches to dealing with conversion problems.

■ Use of Natural Thyroid

By far one of the most controversial topics in hypothyroidism is the use of natural, desiccated thyroid drugs. Many conventional endocrinologists and physicians are not only opposed to prescription natural thyroid—such as Armour, Naturethroid, Westhroid, and Biotech—but they are vehemently and vocally derisive about the drugs, about doctors who prescribe them, and patients who take them.

Thyroid.com Web master Dr. Richard Guttler has always been a particularly vehement opponent of Armour Thyroid. In a 1997 public post at an online support group, Guttler told one woman that she would not be happy with her osteopath's treatment "when your bones collapse, and heart goes out of control. . . . Get smart and go back to your M.D. and take the L thyroxin again." Later, Dr. Guttler criticized the fact that I made information available about natural thyroid, saying:

> *I'm glad all the "fringes" are filling up your e-mail, not mine. It makes my life easier dealing with only the mainstream thyroid patients who would never think of taking Armour. . . .*

Even the supposedly highest echelons of mainstream endocrinology are often opposed to natural thyroid. For example, the 2002 treatment guidelines published by the American Association of Clinical Endocrinologists (AACE) say: "In general, desiccated thyroid hormone, combinations of thyroid hormones, or triiodothyronine should not be used as replacement therapy."

And an American Thyroid Association (ATA) patient brochure on hypothyroidism states that "desiccated animal thyroid is rarely prescribed today, and there is no evidence that desiccated thyroid has any advantage over synthetic T4."

Yet, the ATA has it wrong. In 2002, more than two million prescriptions were written for Armour Thyroid alone. Clearly, practitioners do use desiccated thyroid as a replacement therapy and it is not "rarely" prescribed. Some practitioners, in fact, believe that it is an essential tool in their options to help patients live well.

Some conventionally trained physicians have shifted toward using desiccated thyroid at the same time they have moved into more holistic approaches. Carol Roberts, M.D., is a conventionally trained doctor who now practices holistic and complementary medicine. Says Roberts:

I remember being taught in school that Armour thyroid was an "old fashioned" remedy and difficult to dose. The reason I started prescribing natural thyroid was that when I opened my holistic practice ten years ago, I started getting a steady stream of little old ladies (bless their long suffering hearts) who literally begged me to "Please put me back on Armour. My new doctor put me on this synthetic stuff and I've never felt the same since!" I'm one of those renegades who listens to her patients, and soon I discovered that everyone (almost) feels better on natural thyroid. The truth is that medical education is largely controlled and funded by the pharmaceutical industry, who don't want us messing with anything natural, for fear it might become a habit!

Kate Lemmerman, M.D., is also a conventionally trained M.D. who now practices integrative medicine and acupuncture. She says:

I have come over the years to be a great fan of Armour thyroid. In medical school I learned of the "inaccuracy" and "variability" of such natural products so that when I came to trying to use T-3 to help patients with low free T-3 I first tried such products as Cytomel and Thyrolar. But several years ago there was a manufacturing shortage in Thyrolar and so I "temporarily" switched some folks to Armour. However, many of them reported clinical improvement even though their "numbers" didn't change with regard to TSH or T-3 testing. So now I routinely use Armour as my first option unless someone has an allergy to pork or does not want to take it for religious reasons.

Other physicians have been using Armour for years. Dr. Sanford Siegal has been prescribing Armour for nearly half a century.

I don't mean to suggest that synthetic thyroid doesn't work. It could hardly have achieved such widespread acceptance if it were of no value. But my own experience is that it doesn't work as well overall. If this is a personal bias, it is an honest one. My hypothyroid patients feel that natural thyroid consistently works better, and I must trust their observations.

Why Can Armour Help Some Patients?

Holistic physician Dr. Robban Sica says that, in her experience, 90 percent or more of her thyroid patients do better clinically with desiccated thyroid than with synthetic thyroid.

But why are so many practitioners like Dr. Sica reporting such success with natural thyroid? Many of these innovative practitioners who use natural thyroid believe that the reason it works better for some patients is that it contains additional hormones, as well as nutrients—known as cofactors—that may help the thyroid.

Dr. Joseph Mercola also uses Armour Thyroid. Says Mercola:

> *It is my experience the vast majority of individuals seem to empirically do better on natural hormones, rather than synthetic ones. I can't provide a definitive explanation for this observation. It may be related to the fact that the natural hormones also have T1 and T2. Little is said about these forms of thyroid hormones, but they may have some influence on optimizing thyroid function.*

Dr. David Brownstein explains some of the many hormones in desiccated thyroid in more detail:

> *Thyroid hormone is a very complex hormone. T4 is a relatively inactive form of thyroid hormone. It has to be converted into the more active T3 for the body to utilize it. If the body is lacking the ability to convert T4 into T3, the response to the T4 preparation will be suboptimal. This is the problem*

with using T4 preparations. Armour thyroid is a mixture of T4 and T3 plus many other items. These other items include minerals (selenium and calcitonin) and other hormones that help the body better convert inactive (T4) thyroid hormone to more active (T3) thyroid hormone. However, there are other thyroid hormones as well, which are known as T2 and T1 thyroid hormone. Research has shown T2 hormone to increase the body's metabolic rate. Many researchers believe T2 and T1 to be inert hormones. I don't. Our body produces them for a reason.

Dr. Dale Guyer feels that there are parallels between desiccated animal thyroid and human thyroid. Says Dr. Guyer:

It is not surprising to me however that Armour tends to work better as it contains the spectrum of hormones and metabolites one would generally find in their own thyroid anyway. Since it more closely reflects the grand design it is not surprising it works better than synthetic versions. I have always found that if you stick to the body's design blueprint, to the degree possible, things just work better.

Why Such Opposition?

Given that many practitioners and patients swear by desiccated thyroid, why is there such adamant opposition to the drug from the conventional establishment?

Dr. Roby Mitchell points to a number of reasons behind the concerns:

Most decisions in medicine are based on ignorance, emotion, tradition, and economics rather than science. Somehow it got into traditional medical lore (think economics) that Armour Thyroid is inferior to Synthroid. All the endos were then trained not to use it, which started a tradition.

Dr. Sanford Siegal did some research on the history of the subject, and shares his thoughts:

Many years ago, a batch of very inferior thyroid material was imported by a manufacturer and the finished product was distributed. It was discovered and publicized. This may have permanently tainted the reputation of desiccated thyroid. In the 1950's when the first (patented) levothyroxine was introduced (I was around then), the manufacturer did a great marketing job in convincing physicians that the product was superior. The chief argument was that it was more stable than the natural product and that the marked dosage could be relied upon. My guess is that because patent protection on desiccated thyroid had long since expired and its manufacturer had no protection from competition, it was not expedient to invest in the task of defending the product. By contrast, the producers of synthetic thyroid had every reason to promote their higher-priced patented product. Levothyroxine became the standard. Today, there are many younger doctors who do not even know that there is such a product as Armour Thyroid. In recent years the reliability of the marked levothyroxine dosage has certainly been brought into question. In my own practice, I have never felt that there was a problem with loss of potency of desiccated thyroid. With forty years of experience and literally hundreds of thousands of patients under my belt, I can state in my not-so-humble opinion that natural thyroid works better and has less side effects. As to my preference for one medication over another, what is so different about that? Is that not usual with physicians? Aren't there a dozen or so popular anti-depressants on the market and does not each have its advocates?

Dr. Dale Guyer also thinks there is an economic issue involved:

Most doctors never heard of natural thyroid (Armour). If they are familiar with Armour they usually have bought into the Synthroid gospel hook, line and sinker. This has a lot to do with the fact that you never see drug reps hanging on your door handing out free samples, fountain pens and Frisbees with a shining Armour logo! Since it only costs $6.00 (Indiana price), you just will not see the usual entourage of high paid drug reps in short skirts proselytizing about their merchandise.

Dr. Richard Shames believes that the conventional doctors think desiccated thyroid is old-fashioned and imprecise. Says Shames:

This exact same mistake was made by the doctors during the breast vs. bottled formula controversy that I witnessed in the 1950's. At that time, the precise amount of vitamins and minerals added to artificial formula exceeded the amount of vitamins and minerals in breast milk by carefully measured amounts. Young scientifically minded doctors thought this was terrific. All of the national physician organizations were behind it—but they were wrong. What could not be measured in breast milk were the antibodies and nutrient cofactors that we now recognize are what make breast milk far superior to bottled formula. I believe the same situation is what is happening with the natural thyroid.

What Can You Do?

If you think you might benefit from a course of natural, desiccated thyroid, what should you do? First, ask your physician. I've heard from some patients that even their most die-hard, conservative endocrinologists prescribed desiccated thyroid after their patients asked enough times, and persisted in insisting on at least a trial. Tell your doctor he or she can monitor lab values and other measures, but you just want a trial course of a month or two.

Second, if you have a doctor who simply will not budge, you'll need to see another practitioner to prescribe desiccated thyroid. You can check out my online *Thyroid Top Doctors Directory* (http://www.thyroid-info.com/topdrs). At this Top Doctors Directory, I also link to a Forest Pharmaceuticals database of doctors who prescribe Armour Thyroid. No better place to start than with information from patients, or the drug manufacturer, that a doctor is already willing to prescribe natural thyroid.

■ The Adrenal Connection

One common condition that frequently accompanies hypothyroidism—and may even prevent proper treatment if it is not addressed itself—is adrenal exhaustion, also known as adrenal fatigue.

Your two adrenal glands are small, triangular-shaped endocrine glands located on the top of each kidney. Each adrenal gland is approximately three inches wide and a half-inch high. Each gland is divided into an outer cortex and an inner medulla. The cortex and medulla of the adrenal gland secrete different hormones. The adrenal cortex is essential to life, but the medulla may be removed with no life-threatening effects. The adrenal cortex consists of three different regions, with each region producing a different group or type of hormone. Chemically, all the cortical hormones are considered steroids.

• Mineralocorticoids are secreted by the outermost region of the adrenal cortex. The principal mineralocorticoid is aldosterone, which acts to conserve sodium ions and water in the body.

• Glucocorticoids are secreted by the middle region of the adrenal cortex. The principal glucocorticoid is cortisol, which increases blood glucose levels.

• The third group of steroids secreted by the adrenal cortex is the gonadocorticoids, or sex hormones. These are secreted by the innermost region. Male hormones, androgens, and female hormones, estrogens, are secreted in minimal amounts in both sexes by the adrenal cortex, but their effect is usually masked by the hormones from the testes and ovaries. In females the masculinization effect of androgen secretion may become evident after menopause, when estrogen levels from the ovaries decrease.

The adrenal medulla develops from neural tissue and secretes two hormones, epinephrine and norepinephrine. These two hormones are secreted in response to stimulation by the sympathetic nerve, particularly during stressful situations. A lack of hormones from the adrenal medulla produces no significant effects. Hypersecretion—usually from a tumor—causes prolonged or continual sympathetic responses.

The adrenals produce hormones that help to balance your blood sugar, which helps your body to manage your daily ebbs and flows of energy. When blood sugar drops, the adrenals release hormones that cause the blood sugar to rise, thereby increasing energy. The adrenals also release hormones when we're under stress, releasing energy. It's the "fight or flight" response from the days when we needed to run away from wild animals, which now kicks in for everyday stressors, such as traffic jams, arguments, and work pressures. Being consistently under stress takes a toll on the adrenal glands, and eventually they run out of steam and stop producing sufficient hormones, and you can have a condition that is known as adrenal fatigue, or adrenal exhaustion. Adrenal fatigue often develops after periods of intense or lengthy physical or emotional stress, when overstimulation of the glands leaves them unable to meet your body's needs. Some other names for the syndrome include non-Addison's hypoadrenia, subclinical hypoadrenia, hypoadrenalism, and neurasthenia.

Symptoms include:

- Excessive fatigue and exhaustion
- Nonrefreshing sleep (you get sufficient hours of sleep, but wake fatigued)
- Feeling overwhelmed by or unable to cope with stressors
- Feeling run down or overwhelmed
- Craving salty and sweet foods
- Feeling most energetic in the evening
- A feeling of not being restored after a full night's sleep or having sleep disturbances
- Low stamina, slow to recover from exercise
- Slow recovery from injury, illness, or stress
- Difficulty concentrating, brain fog
- Poor digestion
- Low immune function
- Food or environmental allergies
- Premenstrual syndrome or difficulties that develop during menopause
- Consistent low blood pressure
- Extreme sensitivity to cold
- Lack of sex drive
- Dark circles under the eyes
- Lines of dark pigment in the nails
- Startling easily
- No stamina for confrontation

Interestingly, one of the most common symptoms, according to some practitioners, is *a lack of response to thyroid hormone replacement in people with hypothyroidism.*

At his Web site, http://www.drrind.com, Dr. Bruce Rind, an expert on the thyroid-adrenal connection, has a helpful chart called the Metabolic Scorecard: Symptom Matrix, with more information on adrenal symptoms. Dr. Rind feels that hypothyroidism and adrenal problems are very interrelated. Says Rind:

I've found that one of the strongest stressors to the adrenals is thyroid hormone (specifically T3). The body is designed so that under normal conditions, one organ will not destroy another. The thyroid energy is allowed to rise only to a level that will not harm the adrenals. Thus, in a stress situation, the tolerance of the adrenals usually drops and we see a corresponding drop in T3. Conversely, if fatigued adrenals just started to receive support (e.g., nutrients favorable to adrenal health, drastic reduction in stress, or even a very joyful situation) we see a rapid rise in T3. I find that most people with history of Grave's Disease or Hashimoto's Thyroiditis demonstrate weakened adrenals. Thus, the success of the thyroid therapy is limited by the health of the adrenals.

Richard and Karilee Shames agree:

If low-thyroid people with these symptoms are put on thyroid hormone alone, they sometimes respond negatively. These people may have coexistent, but hidden, low adrenal. If they take thyroid hormone by itself, the resultant increased metabolism may accelerate the low adrenal problem. The addition of thyroid hormone in this situation unmasks the also disturbing low adrenal situation. The proper approach in this case is to treat the patient with thyroid and adrenal support simultaneously. Adrenal insufficiency, especially when unmasked by the addition of thyroid hormone, is unpleasant and uncomfortable. To compound the problem, the doctor and patient then may wrongly assume that thyroid replacement has been a mistake. A tremendous opportunity for better health has now been missed.

Dr. Ron Manzanero has found that some hypothyroid patients are only relatively or "functionally" hypothyroid, and addressing the underlying adrenal problem nutritionally will actually resolve the thyroid problem. Says Manzanero:

> *Sometimes the cause of the hypothyroid state is due to something besides the thyroid, like a dysfunctional adrenal gland—in which case you have to find why the adrenals are not normal and treat the adrenals first. The most common cause is stress, with resulting excess cortisol levels. This could cause an underconversion of T4 to T3 or a suppression of T4 production. In this kind of situation I use a program of phosphatidylserine to help reestablish a normal feedback loop between the adrenals and the hypothalamus, as well as a supplement program that includes the trace minerals zinc and selenium to help with T4 to T3 conversion. Treating the patient with thyroid hormone replacement could actually make things worse by further suppressing the gland.*

Evaluating Adrenal Fatigue

Conventional endocrinologists and tests cannot diagnose adrenal fatigue because they are prepared only to diagnose extreme dysfunction in the adrenals, such as Addison's disease, a potentially fatal condition where the adrenals essentially shut down.

Your holistic or integrative practitioner, however, can do a number of tests to evaluate your adrenal function, and diagnose adrenal fatigue or other subtle dysfunctions in your adrenal glands. These tests include:

- 24-hour urine test, looking at multiple samples over twenty-four hours
- Saliva testing for cortisol levels, usually done at several points over a twenty-four-hour period.
- DHEA—since DHEA is a precursor to almost all the other adrenal hormones, low DHEA levels can often signal adrenal fatigue.

- Pregnenolone, like DHEA, is a precursor to adrenal hormones. Blood and saliva testing of pregnenolone may provide information on low adrenal function.

Dr. Kate Lemmerman tests adrenal function in her hypothyroid patients and frequently finds signs of adrenal stress, often with low DHEA-sulfate levels. Says Lemmerman:

> Often if patients are still fatigued after having idealized their thyroid functioning with appropriate thyroid replacement I find that their DHEA-S levels are less than ideal and their fatigue can be ameliorated with supplementation. I use DHEA-S levels rather than serum DHEA as I find that, as the sulfonated molecule is the active version, it is like testing for Free T-3, rather than total T-3.

Dr. Kent Holtorf typically diagnoses adrenal insufficiency using a combination of symptoms, plus blood sugar, free cortisol, and hemoglobin A1C testing. Says Holtorf:

> One must have a high clinical suspicion and not just think in terms of normal and abnormal. These normal levels are determined for healthy individuals, not the chronically ill, so the cortisol levels should be higher with this illness. 24-hour urine and saliva tests can be done, but these can also result in false positive and false negative results. Some doctors who treat these disorders have reported that cortisol is not helpful; this is totally opposite to my experience. I have found this adrenal hormone to be very helpful.

Treatments

If you are suffering from adrenal fatigue, what can you do? Here are a few tips that can help.

Physiologic Replacement Dose of Hydorcortisone—Some people with adrenal fatigue or unresponsive hypothyroidism have found that low-dose hydrocortisone at physiologic doses can help their immune system and resolve many symptoms of adrenal fatigue.

According to Drs. Richard and Karilee Shames:

> *What we are talking about is the use of small amounts of natural adrenal hormone (hydrocortisone) to bring slightly low adrenal function up to its proper normal daily range. This is in stark contrast to the high doses of powerful synthetic adrenal hormones commonly used to treat severe health problems, or to assist in building muscles.*

You will need a more open-minded, aware doctor to obtain this sort of treatment.

Adrenal Glandulars—Desiccated adrenal gland can be helpful to some people in supporting the gland, and in replacing some missing adrenal hormones. If your practitioner recommends this treatment, be sure to get a reputable brand from a reputable supplier, to ensure quality, potency, and safety.

Hormones—Pregnenolone and DHEA are hormones that can help resolve adrenal fatigue. Use of these hormones is recommended only under the guidance of your practitioner.

Dr. Kate Lemmerman uses DHEA with her patients whose test results show low levels:

> *I aim for supplementation to restore values in the mid-level of a healthy 30-year-old which is about 175–250 mg/dl in our lab. I usually start with 5–10 mg in the morning for women and 10–25 mg for men and recheck after 6–8 weeks along with recheck of the thyroid values. Once the DHEA-S levels become more ideal I have seen some patients need to decrease*

their thyroid supplementation. I DO NOT recommend that people just take DHEA without checking their levels, as excess DHEA can also be a problem with excess hair growth, acne and agitation. And because DHEA is not regulated by the FDA it is important to recheck levels because I have seen patients hardly raise their levels with certain brands, while overshooting their target level with other brands.

Natural Support—There are a variety of herbal treatments that can help support the adrenal system, including licorice and ginseng, among many.

Avoiding Stimulants—As much as you may want them, stimulants are the equivalent of giving a car too much gas and "flooding the engine." They put additional stress on the adrenals to work harder and produce more energy, and end up further depleting the adrenal glands. Things to avoid include caffeine, ephedra, guarana, kola nut, and prescription stimulants.

Balance Your Blood Sugar with Your Diet—To minimize stress on the adrenal system, and ensure maximum energy, you should consider a low-glycemic (low-sugar) diet, consisting of sufficient protein and fat; low-glycemic carbohydrates; eaten in smaller, more frequent meals throughout the day. Sugar and simple carbohydrates put stress on the adrenal glands by rapidly shifting blood sugar levels. By switching to vegetables, fruits, proteins, and high-fiber carbohydrates, blood sugar remains more stable, providing less strain on the adrenal glands.

■ Overcoming Resistance to Change, to New Information, to Empowered Patients

One of the most pervasive treatment challenges is the need to overcome the medical establishment's resistance to change, new information, and empowered patients. Some of the reasons behind this resistance include:

Medical School—Medical schools are known for being rigorous and demanding, but not tolerant of free thinking. Dr. Ron Manzanero explains:

> *Conventional medical education is not based on true analytical thinking skills, but is rather based on rote memorization of what drugs should be given for disease "x, y, or z." Everything is taught in cookbook fashion: For disease "x," use tests "a, b, or c" and treat with drugs "d, e, or f." Because of this cookbook educational process, the doctors are not thinking through the entire process of what could be going wrong with the patient; they are just going through the motions of the same failed protocols that they learned from the residents and interns before them. They are told that if you suspect a patient has thyroid disease, the only test you need to order is a TSH level. They are not taught to inquire thoroughly about symptoms or family history, or even to examine the patient for signs of thyroid disease.*

Conventional vs. Alternative "Bias"—Dr. Richard Podell feels that there is an innate bias in some practitioners. Says Podell:

> *Many patients report improvement of symptoms after taking thyroid, despite their standard thyroid tests being normal. Alternative practitioners have a bias: to believe what their patients tell them. Not just that they are sincere, but that their*

reports are fairly accurate. Traditional practitioners have a different bias: People may be sincere but they are apt to grasp at straws. They attribute coincidental ups and downs to the last placebo pill they took. They may feel better for a while, but that's just coincidence. We professionals know the truth. Most people are naïve. In theory, either view could be the more correct, and of course, both have some truth. Surely, some people who improve and stay improved with an "unproved" treatment really did respond to that treatment. Others, surely, improved by coincidence or, over the short term, with the optimism of a placebo effect.

Pharmaceutical Company Influence—The influence of free samples, educational materials, and other free items can't be underestimated. Says Dr. Ken Woliner:

There is an inherent bias towards prescribing these therapies when you allow pharmaceutical companies to give you prescription pads (laced with advertising), invite you to dinners (where their speaker talks about their drug—but not about T4/T3 therapies), give you reprints of articles (funded by their company), that were published in journals (that had advertisements for their drugs). No pharmaceutical company chooses to fund research about T4/T3 medications, to advertise in medical journals to get these articles published, nor to pay sales representatives or speakers to talk about this therapy. T4/T3 therapy is an orphan that has been (and will continue to be) ignored by most of mainstream medicine.

Lack of Information—Dr. Kent Holtorf feels that failing to stay up on the latest information is a key reason that some doctors are resistant to change. Says Holtorf:

Most doctors do not read medical journals. They just keep practicing the way they had been taught in medical school 10–20 years earlier. It has also been shown that when doctors do read medical journals, 70% of their time is spent on reading the advertisements. They rarely read the actual study, but instead, merely scan the advertisements and the study summaries. This is a major problem because whoever paid for the study, which is usually a drug company, will influence the conclusion reached. Doctors will not change the way they are treating patients unless they have overwhelming evidence.

Insurance/HMOs—Dr. Manelle Fernando feels that it is unfortunate that many physicians have lost their autonomy and the freedom to practice what she calls "the Noble Profession." Says Fernando:

Informed patients need more time. They ask more questions, and they want to take part in their treatment. This probably frustrates the physician who is working under these conditions. They also have to work too hard and too long and often have no time to keep up with the latest research, etc., and have difficulty dealing with patients who know more than they do on a particular subject.

Moving Beyond Resistance

Rather than being discouraged by some of the challenges to receiving optimal care, there are several messages to take with you.

First, thank the heavens that there *are* practitioners and doctors like these amazing folks who are willing to speak honestly, openly, and on the record about how things really are.

Second, there are lucky patients out there who are the patients of these practitioners! And there are many other practitioners, not mentioned in this book, who share the empathy, caring, curiosity, open-mindedness, humility, and wisdom of these doctors. It's just up to you to find them, so you too can be a lucky patient.

Third, doctors appear to come out of med school in one mode or the other. Clearly, there are some physicians who leave med school with their identities and ability to think for themselves intact. But some doctors don't. If your doctor tosses your Internet printouts in the trash and discourages your efforts at self-education, you are probably going up against a physician with an ingrained philosophy that differs from your own.

Ultimately, you can choose to change doctors, but you can't change the attitude and treatment approach of the doctor you choose. So, while I'd like to say that we all should be on a mission to educate the less-than-informed practitioners out there, I also think that patients should be selfish. If at all possible, don't choose a doctor who is a "fixer-upper." You need a doctor who is ready *today*—an informed, talented, and respectful partner prepared to support you in your quest to live well.

11

Other Controversies

You can't teach an old dogma new tricks.
—DOROTHY PARKER

Hypothyroidism is also not without other areas of public controversy. There are many issues—such as the use of iodine and coconut oil—that are controversies for people with hypothyroidism. There are also controversies regarding the increasing use of soy foods and supplements, as well as fluoride and its ability to trigger or worsen hypothyroidism. There is even a concern that the lack of availability of a particular supplement—potassium iodide—may be a thyroid risk for the public in the event of a nuclear incident or terrorist attack.

■ Iodine

As mentioned earlier, a deficiency of iodine is one of the basic causes of hypothyroidism and goiter. There are many millions of people worldwide who suffer from extreme iodine deficiency, as well as the serious disorders that accompany this deficiency. In fact, one-fourth of the world's population suffers from some sort of iodine deficiency disease, there are an estimated 655 million people with an enlarged thyroid and 26 million are estimated to have some thyroid-related brain damage—6 million of those suffering from "cretinism" and totally handicapped for life.

Early in the twentieth century, the use of iodized salt was thought to have almost wiped out iodine deficiency in the United States and some industrialized countries. There is, however, evidence that after decades of being nearly nonexistent, iodine deficiency is on the rise again in the United States. The October 1998 issue of the *Journal of Clinical Endocrinology and Metabolism* reported that in the previous twenty years, the percentage of Americans with low intake of iodine more than quadrupled. Researchers indicated that this trend might necessitate concerted efforts to increase iodine levels in people at risk of deficiency. The first National Health and Nutrition Examination Survey (NHANES 1), which took place from 1971 to 1974, found that just 2.6 percent of U.S. citizens had iodine deficiency. The follow-up NHANES III survey, conducted from 1988 to 1994, found that 11.7 percent are iodine-deficient. Of particular concern is the fact that the percentage of iodine-deficient pregnant women increased from 1 percent in 1974 to 7 percent in 1994. Iodine deficiency during pregnancy is particularly dangerous to a growing baby.

Researchers do not have an explanation for this change, though they suspect that reduced salt in the diet, plus a reduction in the use of iodine as a food ingredient, may be responsible. The reasons for this increasing deficiency need to be studied, and those at risk of iodine deficiency in the United States need to be made more aware of this potential risk for hypothyroidism.

Should You Take Iodine?

When you say thyroid disease, the first thing some herbalists, natural health experts and practitioners will mention is "iodine." Iodine is often cited by some alternative practitioners as an essential supplement for all thyroid patients, and particularly people with hypothyroidism.

In recent years, there's been a strong difference of opinion between some alternative practitioners and herbalists, who recommend iodine or kelp supplements for hypothyroidism, and other doctors, who argue that iodine is not only not needed, but can worsen thyroid problems, particularly autoimmune conditions.

According to David Brownstein, M.D.:

> *Adequate iodine levels must be maintained. Insufficient iodine levels will lead to thyroid problems and this is occurring in a tremendous amount of thyroid patients as I have reported in my book* Iodine: Why You Need It, Why You Can't Live Without It.

Drs. Richard and Karilee Shames offer some general criteria:

> *If you are a person who never consumes fast food, avoids salt like the plague, doesn't eat much seafood, and feels that sea vegetables are for fish, and especially if you live more than 100 miles from any coast, then you might well consider supplementation with iodine, the key mineral in thyroid hormone production.*

Dr. Carol Roberts also frequently starts out with nutritional approaches before going to prescription thyroid drugs. Says Roberts:

> *In many cases I will treat with the nutritional components (or precursors) of thyroid hormone first. Many people simply have low levels of protein in their diet, or too little iodine to be able to make thyroid hormone. If the situation is not urgent, and we can afford to try a little nutritional support, I will put the patient on tyrosine, the amino acid backbone of thyroid hormone, and kelp or other organic source of iodine,*

to see if that will give their own thyroid a chance to wake up. Putting someone on thyroid replacement often means they will have to take it for life, and that should not be done lightly.

Dr. Dale Guyer recommends iodine on a case-by-case basis. Says Guyer:

Some do better with iodine, but I have not found it necessary for most. Those who need iodine are often those with estrogen metabolism issues, prone to PMS, or disorders of the reproductive tract (fibroids, etc.). Also, I see this in those with associated adrenal disorders.

Dr. Roby Mitchell is also more cautious about iodine. Says Mitchell:

My posture has been that since most Americans have been heavily exposed to iodized salt and iodide is already contained in the thyroid molecule, iodide deficiency is an unlikely cause of thyroid dysfunction in my region of the U.S. That being said, I never dissuade a patient from doing a trial of bladderwrack or kelp to see if helps. I've been surprised more than once. The improvement or deterioration is usually not subtle.

There are practitioners, however, like Dr. Ron Manzanero, who feel that iodine is problematic. Says Manzanero:

I think the knee-jerk prescribing of iodine and kelp by the alternative practitioners is simply that: a knee-jerk response coming from an allopathic mindset. This is the same as the "cookbook" mentality that conventional doctors have, i.e., patient with disease "x" gets natural substance "a or b." In some cases, giving more iodine can shut the gland down, or, if there is an underlying autoimmune disorder like postpartum thyroiditis or Graves' disease, giving more iodine will only provoke a hyperthyroid state. So in general, I think most hypothyroid patients do not need to take extra iodine, and I generally have them avoid supplements that contain iodine.

Dr. Mike McNett agrees:

I feel that the majority of people in the US eat adequate amounts of iodine to fill their needs. I believe that the enzymes creating thyroid hormone will take the iodine they need if it's present. Putting more into the system doesn't help. The analogy I use is that, once you have gas in your car's tank, putting more gas in won't make your car run any better, and, if you overfill, you can cause a fire hazard. Iodine is the same way.

For the majority of hypothyroid patients, Drs. Richard and Karilee Shames feel that supplemental iodine is probably not necessary:

Thyroid patients have plenty of iodine in their thyroid medicine, and do not generally need to take more. Therefore, they should—unlike the general population—not take supplemental iodine in their vitamins or in their salt. Many have strong reactions against iodine, kicking off autoimmune flareup.

This was my experience. I had tried supplemental iodine in various forms—Lugol's solution of iodine, kelp supplements, and bladderwrack. Each time, it made me feel *terrible*—exhausted, brain-fogged, achy, and with a swollen neck—for two weeks, so I discontinued it. I tried again on my own with a metabolism/thyroid support supplement that contained iodine. Again, within a day or two, I was *exhausted* and barely functional. A third time, again it had a terrible effect. Personally, I've given up trying iodine.

It's hard to know if you need iodine, because there really aren't any reliable, cost-effective, easily available tests. According to Drs. Richard and Karilee Shames:

> Researchers are presently working to develop a reliable and effective test for iodine, but at this point, we are not convinced that the available tests are up for the task. In light of all this, some thyroid specialists are suggesting that you hedge your bets and simply ingest each day an amount of iodine that will help if you are too low, but won't hurt if you are already sufficient. This amount appears to be about 100 micrograms per day. However, if you find that you feel sick after taking iodine or eating iodized foods, you may want to avoid this nutrient.

What About Seaweed?

Seaweeds are actually nature's richest source of iodine, and some practitioners believe that seaweed in food form, rather than iodine supplements, may be a help to thyroid patients. There are many different forms of seaweeds, both ocean and freshwater. Each seaweed has its own unique color—browns, greens, and reds are common—and have their own particular shape and taste. They are very popular in Japanese cuisine. Nori is a red algae seaweed that turns green when toasted and is used in sushi. Kelp (known as kombu in Japan and haidai in China) is most commonly used in soups. Wakame is the seaweed used in miso soup. Dulse is a red seaweed, high in iron. Some seaweeds are used as fillers for ice cream and dressings.

Dr. Joseph Mercola is a fan of seaweed for thyroid patients. Says Mercola:

> The best source of organically bound iodine that I know of is non commercially harvested seaweeds. The dose is about 5 grams a day or about one ounce per week. So a pound would last about two months. The better seaweeds are hand picked

and dried. Kelp from the health food store may work, but it really depends on how it was harvested and there is no way to know that reliably, so I rely on seaweed harvesters who hand-pick the seaweed and reliably dry them free from contaminants.

Interestingly, some thyroid patients—myself included—who have problems taking supplemental iodine report no trouble with eating seaweed.

■ Soy

Dr. Mike Fitzpatrick is an environmental scientist and phytoestrogen researcher who has extensively researched the issue of soy formulas, and the impact of soy consumption on thyroid function. When I was initially researching this book back in the 1990s, Dr. Fitzpatrick introduced me to a controversial and little-known fact: *Overconsumption of soy products has the potential to impair thyroid function.*

Since that time, awareness of soy's impact on thyroid disease has increased, but not anywhere near as much as the media hype and marketing dollars surrounding soy, soy foods, soy pills, soy powders, and soy supplements. So it's more important than ever to bring to light the many concerns about soy.

Soy Formula

Soy formula is of particular concern to experts on phytoestrogens, like Dr. Mike Fitzpatrick. According to Dr. Fitzpatrick, since the late 1950s, it has been known that soy formulas contain antithyroid agents. Cases of goiter were reported in soy formula–fed infants until manufacturers added more iodine to their products. The antithyroid agents in soy have been identified as what are known as *isoflavones*. Soy is a rich source of isoflavones, and Dr. Fitzpatrick found that infants fed soy infant formulas receive high daily doses of these compounds. The isoflavones belong to the flavonoid chemical family, and flavonoids are considered endocrine disrupters—plants that act as hormones, disrupting the endocrine system. Flavonoids are, in particular, well-known antithyroid agents. (The grain millet, for example, contains high levels of flavonoids and is commonly known as problematic for those with low thyroid function.) Flavonoids typically act against the thyroid by inhibition of thyroid peroxidase (TPO), which disturbs proper thyroid function. Isoflavones are no exception, and they are potent inhibitors of TPO.

A preliminary study found a significant association between feeding soy formulas and the development of autoimmune thyroid disease in infants. One study found that the frequency of feedings with soy-based milk formulas in early life was noticeably higher in children with autoimmune thyroid disease. Thyroid problems were almost triple in those soy formula–fed children compared to their siblings and healthy unrelated children. Dr. Fitzpatrick raises another major concern for infants on soy formula:

> Long-term feeding of soy formulas will result in persistent inhibition of TPO and a continual tendency toward elevated TSH levels. This state is associated with the induction of thyroid cancer in laboratory animals.

In other words, infants who are exposed to high concentrations of isoflavones long-term, such as that found in a diet of primarily soy formula, may face a risk of becoming hypothyroid, as well as an increased chance of developing thyroid cancer.

In July 1996, the British Department of Health issued a warning that the phytoestrogens found in soy-based infant formulas could adversely affect infant health. The warning was clear, indicating that soy formula should only be given to babies on the advice of a health professional. They advised that babies who cannot be breast-fed or who have allergies to other formulas be given alternatives to soy-based formulas. That same year, the British government's Food Advisory Committee also asked companies to investigate the removal of soy isoflavones from soy-based infant formulas. It is technically possible to remove the actual isoflavones from soy-based infant formulas, and some companies have developed test versions of these products, but they are not readily available for consumers. It appears, however, that most formula manufacturers do not plan to modify their manufacturing process to permanently remove the isoflavones and thereby reduce the risk.

Infants are particularly vulnerable when exposed to endocrine disrupters. Because infants fed soy formula are receiving the highest exposure to isoflavones, they are at risk of chronic thyroid problems. Long-term research on this unplanned "test group" of infants, who subsisted solely on soy-based formulas, will likely reveal more to scientists in years to come. In the meantime, doctors typically advise parents of hypothyroid infants not to give their babies soy-based formulas. Additionally, all parents should seriously consider whether they want to give their infants soy formulas until manufacturers have thoroughly and adequately addressed concerns about the isoflavone component of these products.

Dr. Joseph Mercola is an opponent of soy formula. Says Mercola:

> I believe the soy issue is one of the biggest health misconceptions in the natural food movement today . . . soy formula is one of the worst foods on the planet for an infant and should be banned. It provides the hormone equivalent of five birth control pills a day and may be one of the reasons infertility and other female endocrine problems are so common today.

Soy for Adults?

There is also concern about adult consumption of soy products. One U.K. study involving premenopausal women gave the women 60 grams of soy protein per day for one month. This was found to disrupt the menstrual cycle, with the effects of the isoflavones continuing for a full three months after soy in the diet was stopped. Another study found that intake of soy over a long period causes enlargement of the thyroid and suppresses thyroid function. Isoflavones are also known to modify fertility and change sex hormone status and to have serious health effects—including infertility, thyroid disease, or liver disease—on a number of mammals.

These concerns were brought to light in a February 18, 1999, official letter of protest to the Food and Drug Administration (FDA) sent by Daniel Doerge and Daniel Sheehan, who at that time were the FDA's two key expert researchers on soy. Drs. Doerge and Sheehan were protesting the health claims for soy that the FDA had approved. They wrote in their letter:

> . . . there is abundant evidence that some of the isoflavones found in soy, including genistein and equol, a metabolize of daidzen, demonstrate toxicity in estrogen sensitive tissues and in the thyroid. This is true for a number of species, including humans. Additionally, isoflavones are inhibitors of the thyroid peroxidase which makes T3 and T4. Inhibition can be expected to generate thyroid abnormalities, including goiter and autoimmune thyroiditis. There exists a significant body of animal data that demonstrates goitrogenic and even carcinogenic effects of soy products. Moreover, there are significant reports of goitrogenic effects from soy consumption in human infants and adults.

The Weston A. Price Foundation, an organization that conducts state-of-the-art nutritional research, also has tremendous concerns regarding soy. Their Web site, www.westonaprice.org, has dozens of articles about soy, and they are part of a worldwide awareness campaign regarding the dangers of soy. They say:

> As part of our ongoing efforts to keep the public up-to-date on the problems with modern soy foods, we have com-

piled two lists of studies showing adverse effects of soy: one lists studies showing the toxicity of soy isoflavones (estrogen-like compounds in soy) and the other lists studies showing problems with consumption of soy foods in general. We looked only at studies published in scientific journals—the total was over 150! Very often, the conclusions posted in the abstracts of these studies glossed over negative findings, or even presented these findings as beneficial. Most interesting to us was the large number of recent studies showing carcinogenic and mutagenic effects of soy isoflavones.

Dr. Bruce Rind also has concerns about soy:

I think soy is unsafe. Soy can suppress thyroid function if taken in high enough quantities. No culture in the history of civilization (that we know about) has ever used soy as a food. The Asians have traditionally used it as a condiment and traditionally have made it less toxic through soaking and fermentation. We neither soak nor ferment it and instead use it as a meal.

Dr. Sherrill Sellman used to be quite a big soy fan until she started to look more into the subject. According to Sellman:

Now I err on the side of caution and actually advise women to cut way down on their soy intake. The most preferred kind of soy would be the fermented versions such as tempeh and miso because that is the most digestible form of soy. The fermentation process destroys the harmful toxins found in soy. Unfermented forms have potent enzyme inhibitors that block the action of trypsin and other enzymes needed for protein digestion. Soy, in its unfermented forms, does have an inhibiting effect on the thyroid. It is also a very allergic food and hard to digest. Contrary to the popular myth, Asians do not eat soy as

*a staple food but rather only as a condiment. I have lived for
several years in Southeast Asian and know this to be a fact.*

On the other side of the controversy, some practitioners feel that
the growing concerns about soy may be overblown. Says Dr. Ron
Manzanero:

> *I've gone back and forth on the issue simply because for a
> while there was a "paper" coming out every other month ei-
> ther for or against soy. Often the writers would have private
> agendas, such as being representatives of the dairy industry
> or having ties to the soy industry. I really do not think the
> soy question is really that much of an issue, based on what
> I've read and seen in my practice. I think it does make sense
> to eat soy the way it has been eaten for centuries in the Far
> East; i.e., fermented. On the other hand there is a large body
> of science that shows the benefits of soy isoflavones in many
> areas of the human body. I don't think that occasionally
> drinking soy milk or a soy protein shake is going to cause
> any problems.*

Internationally known holistic physician Dr. Andrew Weil has
dismissed most concerns about soy. Says Weil:

> *Excess consumption of soy can affect thyroid function, but
> only if you have a thyroid disorder to begin with or if you're
> not getting enough iodine in your diet (a rare deficiency in the
> United States). If you take medication for hypothyroidism,
> and are concerned about the effect of eating two daily serv-
> ings of soy, have your thyroid levels checked regularly. . . . All
> told, based on the evidence to date, I see no reason to worry
> about eating soy foods, whether fermented or not. I still rec-
> ommend consuming one to two servings of soy per day, an*

*amount equivalent to one cup of soy milk, or one half cup of
tofu, soy protein (tempeh) or soy nuts.*

Famous women's health writer Dr. Christiane Northrup has become a public spokesperson promoting soy as a wonder cure-all. It
should be noted, however, that Dr. Northrup has a variety of advertising relationships with various soy products, including a prominent one with a heavily marketed product called "Revival soy." She
even refers to herself publicly as "part of the 'Revival' family."

Interestingly, while a staunch defender of soy, Dr. Northrup has
reported that she herself was diagnosed as hypothyroid, "after I was
already taking Revival soy," according to her. Coincidence? Her
blood tests returned to normal only after she began taking thyroid
replacement.

More Research Is Needed

Since announcing his earlier concerns, Dr. Daniel Doerge, working at the Division of Biochemical Toxicology at the National Center for Toxicological Research, has delved further into the issue,
publishing an article in the June 2002 issue of *Environmental
Health Perspectives*. In his article research, Doerge looked at the
goitrogenic and estrogenic effects of soy in greater depth. According
to Doerge, when iodine is deficient, the antithyroid effects of soy are
intensified. Soy's ability to affect the thyroid, therefore, depends on
the relationship between iodine status and thyroid function. In animal studies, rats given a genistein-fortified diet showed an increase
in thyroid antibodies, while other measures of thyroid function apparently remained normal.

These findings have led Dr. Doerge to conclude that additional
factors appear necessary for soy to cause overt thyroid toxicity.
These factors include:

- Iodine deficiency
- Consumption of other soy components

- Other goitrogens in the diet
- Other physiological problems in synthesizing thyroid hormones

Dr. Doerge feels that more needs to be known:

> *Although safety testing of natural products, including soy products, is not required, the possibility that widely consumed soy products may cause harm in the human population via either or both estrogenic and goitrogenic activities is of concern. Rigorous, high-quality experimental and human research into soy toxicity is the best way to address these concerns.*

What Should You Do?

According to Dr. Mike Fitzpatrick, the soy industry has known about the goitrogenic and estrogenic effects of soy for more than sixty years. But in that time, far too little has been done to truly address these concerns, particularly in the United States, where the health benefits of soy are being extensively marketed, particularly to menopausal women and women at risk of breast cancer.

Dr. Fitzpatrick believes that people with hypothyroidism should seriously consider avoiding soy products, and predicts that the current promotion of soy as a health food will result in an increase in thyroid disorders:

> *It's unfortunate that awareness of this serious concern isn't greater, and that authorities haven't taken the necessary steps to study and minimize this obvious health concern.*

Other practitioners feel that some forms and quantities of soy are less dangerous than others. Says Joe Lamb:

> *I don't like pill form soy supplements aimed at treating hormonal issues—the dose of isoflavones is too high. I prefer*

soy as food products, and one serving per day, which is a lot for our society, is fine.

Dr. Roby Mitchell also doesn't strongly advise against soy in general. He says:

There are several phytonutrients in soy that are beneficial in a wide range of medical applications from reducing prostate and breast cancer to reducing vascular disease and osteoporosis. I advise patients to avoid soy supplements and encourage them to consume natural soy foods.

Dr. David Brownstein differentiates between types of soy. Says Brownstein:

Unfermented soy is a problem. I have seen it over and over in my practice. This has not been the case with fermented forms of soy. Unfermented soy needs to be limited, especially by those with thyroid problems, whether autoimmune or hypothyroidism.

Fermented soy foods include tempeh, miso, and soy sauces. Unfermented soy products include fresh green soybeans (edamame), soy nuts, soy sprouts, soy milk, and tofu, along with all of the soy pills, supplements, and soy protein powders.

My personal theory is that soy is a food, not a drug. So eating it in amounts that make it a drug can be harmful, as can eating soy in unnaturally high concentrations such as I found in supplements, soy smoothies, soy protein powders, and other similar products. I don't drink soy milk or use tofu, but I do enjoy miso soup regularly, and I use soy sauce. I also occasionally—but not regularly—enjoy a veggie burger that contains some soy, such as a Boca Burger, and I will occasionally eat soy breakfast patties, like Morningstar Farms sausage substitute.

■ Coconut Oil

If you visit thyroid disease Web sites that carry any advertising, you can't avoid the ubiquitous claims for coconut oil. Coconut oil is touted as a cure for hypothyroidism, a metabolism booster, and an easy weight-loss solution. A May 2003 article in the weekly newsstand publication *Woman's World* featured a cover story, "The New Thyroid Cure," which touted coconut oil's ability to both cure hypothyroidism and ensure rapid weight loss.

According to Dr. Bruce Fife, certified nutritionist, naturopathic physician, and author of *The Healing Miracles of Coconut Oil* and *Eat Fat, Look Thin*, coconut oil is very promising for thyroid problems and weight loss. Fife, who is a frequent contributor to the Tropical Traditions Web site selling coconut oil, says:

> *Low thyroid function has many causes and no one therapy can cure all thyroid related diseases. Coconut oil is just part of the solution. For some people coconut oil may be of little help. However, when used properly and in conjunction with other things it can have a very significant effect on the most common forms of hypothyroidism. I have developed a drugless thyroid program based on diet and lifestyle. While coconut oil is a primary feature of this program, it is not the only factor involved. I do recommend that those people who are on thyroid medication when they start the program, to continue with it under the close supervision of their doctors. Some people have reported that using thyroid medication while on my program makes their thyroid function too good and they become hyperthyroid. So a doctor must monitor the medication and gradually reduce it. This is what I'm seeing. People report that they have more energy, they lose weight, and they are able to reduce and even completely get off thyroid medication. They no longer need it.*
>
> *Is coconut oil a thyroid cure? Not by itself. Can it help*

people with low thyroid function? Yes, because it stimulates metabolism and boosts energy. For this reason, coconut oil has been a blessing to many people. In combination with other factors it has the potential to greatly improve thyroid system function. The program I am currently working on shows promise for not only improving thyroid health, but possibly helping many people end their dependence on thyroid medication.

Dr. Fife is not the only proponent of coconut oil. The Weston A. Price Foundation, a nutritional research group, is very supportive of coconut oil as a healthy fat. Researcher Mary G. Enig, Ph.D., has written extensively in support of a number of health benefits of coconut oil.

Dr. Ray Peat also recommends coconut oil. Says Peat:

An important function of coconut oil is that it supports mitochondrial respiration, increasing energy production that has been blocked by the unsaturated fatty acids. Since polyunsaturated fatty acids inhibit thyroid function at many levels, coconut oil can promote thyroid function simply by reducing those toxic effects. It allows normal mitochondrial oxidative metabolism, without producing the toxic lipid peroxidation that is promoted by unsaturated fats.

Basically, Dr. Peat believes that the medium chain saturated fatty acids in coconut oil may help energy to be used, rather than stored.

Holistic physician Dr. Ken Woliner is skeptical about claims regarding coconut oil, in particular, Dr. Fife's position. Says Woliner:

I would be happy to review any data Dr. Fife has regarding his "drugless thyroid program," but as of now, there is no evidence linking coconut oil with thyroid in the peer-reviewed medical literature, indexed on Medline or otherwise. Though

I do believe case reports to be a valid form of medical data, neither Dr. Fife nor anyone else has published any case reports in mainstream or holistic journals.

Simply, none of the data supports claims that coconut oil helps thyroid function or weight loss. I remain underwhelmed, with the exception that medium chain triglyceride oils may be healthier when substituted for—but not added to—a diet containing excess carbohydrates or unhealthy trans-fats.

■ Flu Shots

It seems that every winter, the flu is constantly in the news, and each year we hear more about the need for preventive flu shots. Should you get a flu shot?

Some alternative medicine experts recommend against the flu shot. Dr. Joseph Mercola, for example, says that:

The flu vaccine can actually weaken the immune system and make you more predisposed to the illness. I have never received a flu shot and haven't missed a day of work due to illness in over 20 years.

Dr. Mercola instead recommends immune-enhancing techniques such as avoiding sugar, getting enough rest, eating garlic, minimizing stress, exercising, and regular hand washing.

Dr. Richard Shames, co-author of *ThyroidPower*, says that:

In particular, thyroid sufferers have an immune problem that is likely to be made worse by injectible vaccinations. A person with high or low thyroid has an immune system that is TH2 predominant (T-Helper Cell Type 2). All vaccinations given by injection further stimulate this particular out-of-

balance situation and thus have the potential of making the autoimmune response and the resultant thyroid situation worse.

On the other hand, alternative medicine expert Dr. Andrew Weil recommends:

If a really virulent flu is coming, I'd take a flu shot . . . in an ordinary year I recommend flu shots only to people who have chronic respiratory illness or who are elderly, debilitated or have compromised respiration for any reason.

Weil also suggests the vaccine for anyone with a weakened immune system.

Personally, I started getting flu shots ten years ago, and I had the flu once during that time, the one year I didn't get the shot. And it knocked me out for weeks—I felt that with my thyroid, my immune system was not as good at getting rid of the flu, and so it took me far longer to recuperate than the others in my household. So I'm pretty much of a flu shot advocate, at least for my family and me. I never want to go through that misery again if it can be at all avoided.

The Nasal-Spray Flu Vaccine (FluMist)

In the 2003–2004 flu season, a new flu vaccine, the nasal-spray flu vaccine FluMist, came on the market, approved for vaccinating healthy people aged five to forty-nine years. The Immune Deficiency Foundation, which looked at the health risks posed by FluMist, says that because it is a live virus vaccine—unlike the inactived, killed virus in the injection—FluMist should not be used by people with immune deficiency diseases or weakened immune systems. The American Autoimmune Related Diseases Association (AARDA) also advises against FluMist for anyone with autoimmune diseases, including Hashimoto's disease and Graves' disease.

■ Fluoride

Fluoride, a common additive to water supplies, a frequent ingredient in toothpaste, and a common treatment given by dentists, is likely one of the reasons behind increased rates of hypothyroidism—and other health concerns—in the United States. And the tradeoff is that more research is now showing that fluoridation actually does *not* improve dental health in many people.

Fluoride is an element from the halogen group, as are iodide and chloride. It is commonly added to the water supply as hydrofluosilicic acid, silicofluoride, or sodium fluoride, and as an additive in toothpastes and some mouthwashes. Fluoride is used because it is believed to be able to fight tooth decay in children. The key initial studies purporting to demonstrate its effectiveness as an anticavity compound were performed back in the 1940s, but these studies are now being called into question. More recently, Dr. John Yiamouyiannis examined the raw data from a large study that was conducted by the National Institute for Dental Research (NIDR). He concluded that fluoride did not appear to have any decay-preventing success, as there was little difference in the DMFT values (the mean number of decayed, missing, or filled teeth) for approximately forty thousand children. It did not matter whether they grew up in fluoridated, nonfluoridated, or partially fluoridated communities.

A larger study has been conducted in New Zealand. There, the New Zealand National Health Service plan examined the teeth of every child in key age groups, and found that the teeth of children in nonfluoridated cities were slightly better than those in the fluoridated cities.

Although children's teeth have improved steadily from the 1930s to the 1990s, this improvement appears to be independent of the addition of fluoride to the water. A study has yet to be conducted that specifically addresses whether the addition of fluoride affects the quality of teeth, while controlling and accounting for other factors and other sources of fluoride.

Despite growing questions about the effectiveness of using fluoride to fight tooth decay—and increasing concerns of the safety of this practice—over 60 percent of the United States' water supply is fluoridated. Most of those cities are in the eastern part of the United States.

The Problems of Fluoride

The most recognized problem with the ingestion of too much fluoride is dental fluorosis. This condition is characterized by the failure of tooth enamel to crystallize properly in permanent teeth. The effects range from chalky, opaque blotching of teeth to severe, rust-colored stains, surface pitting, and tooth brittleness.

There are many other health concerns—including cancer, genetic damage, neurological impairment, and bone problems—that are considered possible effects of overexposure to fluoride. And even those who aren't convinced of the toxicity of fluoride are becoming increasingly concerned about the level of fluoride added to the water supply. The optimum level was set in the 1940s at approximately 1 part per million (ppm) (equal to 1 mg/1). This was based on assumptions that the total intake of fluoride would be 1 mg/day, assuming that four glasses of water were drunk per day. However, current intake of fluoride comes not just from the water supply. A study conducted by researchers at the University of Iowa and reported in the *Journal of American Dental Association* found that 71 percent of more than three hundred soft drinks contained 0.60 ppm of fluoride. Toothpaste, beverages, processed food, fresh fruits and vegetables, vitamins, and mineral supplements all contribute to the intake of fluoride. It is now estimated that the total amount of fluoride ingested per day is 8 mg/day, eight times the optimum levels.

According to Drs. Richard and Karilee Shames:

> *We know that 4 or 5 mg of fluoride per day is too much. People who exercise and drink a lot of water, who use fluoridated toothpaste, and use fluoride dental treatments thinking*

they are doing the right thing, and who drink sodas, juices,
and teas likely made from fluoridated water, including those
who bathe frequently, swim in pools, etc., may be overdosing
on fluoride all the time without realizing it. There is NO way
to measure one's exposure. Many children use gobs of tooth-
paste, and swallow it because it tastes so good.

An additional and less well-studied concern is the interaction of
the fluoride compounds added to water with other water additives.
Most studies examining the addition of fluoride to water have used
sodium fluoride; however, most communities use the less expensive
forms, such as silicofluoride, hydrofluosilicic acid, or sodium silicofluoride that are actually manufacturing waste products. A 1999
study of 280,000 Massachusetts children shows that levels of lead
in blood were significantly higher in communities using these
cheaper compounds than in towns where sodium fluoride was used
or where the water was not treated at all.

Fluoride and the Thyroid

Some experts and researchers believe that fluoride is in part the
reason for near-epidemic levels of hypothyroidism in the United
States. Fluoride had been used for decades as an effective antithyroid medication to treat hyperthyroidism, and was frequently an
effective treatment at levels below the current "optimal" intake of 1
mg/day. This is due to the ability of fluoride to mimic the action of
thyroid-stimulating hormone. The more fluoride circulating, the
more the body thinks there is TSH circulating, which shuts down
the thyroid, making it less active.

Drs. Richard and Karilee Shames have this to say about the thyroid connection:

We have come to believe that the thyroid epidemic could be
due, in large part, to the bombardment of our collective thy-
roid glands by chemicals considered to be helpful, but which

are actually harmful. Fluoride is just one of a great many such substances dumped into the environment, with deleterious human results. It is a particularly noteworthy example because it is supposed to be beneficial, as well as totally benign to even the youngest members of the society, for whom it is targeted. In fact, it appears to be neither benign nor all that effective. The EPA even admits it still has no data on the long term detrimental effects of silicofluorides.

Researcher and advocate Andreas Schuld has also found that excess of fluoride correlates with other thyroid-related issues such as iodine deficiency. Fluoride and iodine, both being members of the halogen group of atoms, have an antagonistic relationship. When there is excess of fluoride in the body, it can interfere with the function of the thyroid gland. It is possible that iodine deficiency, which is the most common cause of brain damage and mental disability in the world, could be lessened by simply cutting back on the use of fluoride.

The Future of Fluoride

Some advocates believe that the truth about fluoride does not reach the public easily because fluoride, produced as a toxic waste by-product of many types of heavy industry—such as aluminum, steel, fertilizer, glass, cement, and other industries—must be disposed of somewhere. If it's not used as an additive to water, manufacturers would have to pay millions of dollars to dispose of it properly. There is strong pressure, therefore, to keep fluoride listed as a healthy additive to water, rather than as an environmental toxin that requires costly disposal.

The U.S. government has been one of the key supporters of fluoridation. Despite the questions regarding fluoride's effectiveness and safety, there are ongoing federal health objectives to increase the number of Americans who receive fluoridated tap water.

And, given half a century of support for fluoridation, it's also not likely that the American Dental Association will backtrack on its support for fluoridation and admit it's been wrong about the dental benefits.

Some cities are taking action and making the decision to stop fluoridating their water supply—or not to fluoridate in the first place. More than ever, city officials are indicating that adding a chemical to the water supply to medicate everyone is not the right approach, and are looking into other programs to help improve the dental health of children.

The only admission that you're likely to see is the 1997 addition of warnings on toothpaste tubes, which now say: "Don't Swallow—Use only a pea-sized amount for children under six" and "Children under six should be supervised while brushing with any toothpaste to prevent swallowing." In areas where the drinking water already contains fluoride, brushing more than once daily with more than a pea-sized amount of fluoridated toothpaste can cause fluorosis, the discoloration and spotting of the teeth that affects an estimated 20 percent of children.

■ What About Children?

Most popular toothpastes for children contain fluoride, and as early as ages three and four dentists start suggesting fluoride treatments. As the parent of a young child, I don't want to neglect her dental treatment, but concerns regarding fluoride, plus the fact that I have autoimmune thyroid disease and have likely passed on that tendency to her, make me doubly concerned to expose her to too much fluoride. But I asked Drs. Richard and Karilee Shames if they feel children should be drinking bottled water, using nonfluoride toothpaste and avoiding fluoride treatments, or only those children of parents with autoimmune thyroid disease? Their thoughts:

> *Many thyroid parents would do well to tell their dentist*
> *that their child is allergic to fluoride because of the family his-*

*tory of autoimmune thyroiditis, and ask for alternative ma-
neuvers. Be sure your child brushes frequently, flosses regularly, and avoids sugar. There are many toothpastes without
fluoride when one searches carefully. We realize that it is possible that children not using fluoride could possibly have more
cavities, but this has not been proven to every doctor's satisfaction. We personally don't believe that is the case. We believe that the benefits of fluoride, even for children, have been
overstated, and the risks minimized.*

*The developing thyroid gland is particularly sensitive to
chemical assault. The stage that is set early in life can become
the backdrop for many years of adult problems—even if
there is some benefit in reduction of cavities in children's
teeth. There is also the risk of dental fluorosis, a growing
dental problem in fluoridated areas (too much fluoride is bad
for teeth). Moreover, the total health of the child is more important than the single area of baby teeth. According to John
Yiamouyiannis, Ph.D., in his book* Fluoride: The Aging Factor, *fluoride has never been shown to be helpful for adult
teeth.*

*We specifically recommend moderation, careful monitor-
ing, for those who feel a need to use some for their children's
teeth; use it sparingly and under close supervision. As with
many health matters, moderation is the key.*

What Can and Should You Do?

First, you should learn more about the effects of fluoride and get
involved in your community's decisions regarding water fluoridation.

Next, you'll need to decide how much fluoride exposure you
want for yourself and your family.

Thyroid and adrenal expert Bruce Rind, M.D., believes that thyroid patients should avoid fluoride. Says Rind:

This toxic waste product doesn't make bones stronger and it is chemically similar to iodine (both are halogens) and therefore can replace an iodine atom in T3 and T4, rendering that molecule of thyroid hormone ineffective.

Dr. Ken Woliner has some interesting thoughts on fluoride:

My father and I have done an extensive review of the medical and civil engineering literature (he is a civil engineer specializing in water treatment facilities). Topical fluoride (fluoride toothpaste, rinses, and treatments) does help prevent dental caries. Fluoridation of water supplies does nothing—absolutely nothing—to prevent dental caries. It is a myth, one that has been perpetuated by persons repeating review articles that quote "famous dentists," who quoted other review articles, which quoted theoretical arguments. In municipalities that discontinued water fluoridation, the rate of tooth decay continued to decline. Water fluoridation does increase the risk of absorbing lead out of your pipes, leading to lead toxicity (with anemia and mental retardation). It may also contribute to thyroid disorders and other conditions.

Holistic physician Joe Lamb, M.D., believes that the benefits of fluoride (prevention of decay) in toothpaste warrant its use. But says Lamb:

I think most people should drink spring water. Fluoride treatments at the dentist should not be rote but should be based upon personal dental history.

If you want to avoid fluoride, you do have options. You can buy an unfluoridated, natural toothpaste—some health food stores, vitamin stores, and natural groceries carry fluoride-free toothpaste—

particularly for young children. You can also always use baking soda as an effective alternative toothpaste.

You can also pay attention to the water you drink, and use filtered or bottled waters. Some water filters can remove fluoride from the water, but carbon-based filters such as the Brita filter do not, so be sure to find the right type of filter for fluoride. Many bottled waters contain no additional fluoride. You can find out the fluoride and other mineral content of your favorite bottled waters at Bottled Water Web's Bottlers online listing, at http://www.bottledwaterweb.com/bott. Evian and Deer Park, for example, contain no measurable fluoride, while Calistoga has 0.9 ppm.

Not everyone may need filtered or bottled water, however, if it's too expensive.

According to Dr. Ken Woliner:

> It is awfully difficult to avoid fluoridated water. It gets quite expensive to have a comprehensive water purifier or to use bottled water. For cost-effective reasons, I recommend it is important to not use fluoridated water for all lactating mothers, all babies, and children at risk for lead toxicity.

Ultimately, the decision whether to be exposed to fluoride is up to you, and there is no agreement, even among the experts. A sensible approach would be to avoid water fluoridation, and use fluoridated toothpaste or get dental fluoride treatments for yourself or your children only if you have specific dental problems that warrant such treatment.

■ Mercury

Some experts believe that mercury toxicity can be a factor in hypothyroidism. This, in itself, is controversial. There's no question that mercury can be a health hazard. But where the mercury comes from is also an area of controversy, as some experts believe that mercury dental fillings are problematic. Others believe that the main danger of mercury is from foods—primarily mercury-contaminated fish.

Mercury Fillings

According to a statement released by the International Academy of Oral Medicine and Toxicology, mercury fillings are a hazard. The statement reads:

> *Research has shown that mercury even in extremely small amounts has toxic effects, for example, low dose mercury exposure has been shown to produce neurological pathology, cytotoxicity to nerve tissue.*

Nutritional expert Dr. Edward Bauman agrees that the toxicity of dental fillings is really quite important. According to Dr. Bauman, dental mercury is in close proximity to the thyroid and the nerves that enervate the thyroid run along the same plexus. When mercury toxicity is present, Dr. Bauman feels that the straight remediation approach to treating thyroid disease isn't always enough. Says Bauman:

> *I've seen people who've had some sort of oral chelation therapy—nutrients and herbs—to try to clear out the toxins, and their thyroid normalized. This was after having tried thyroid medications, herbs, natural thyroid, etc.*

Dr. Joseph Mercola agrees:

> *Mercury is another common cause of hypothyroidism. Amalgams are 50% mercury and they are only inches away from the thyroid gland. If diagnostic testing determines mercury to be a problem then the amalgam fillings need to be removed by a biologically trained dentist and replaced with a*

*non-metal (composite) filling. The mercury needs to be elimi-
nated. I have written with Dr. Dietrich Klinghardt a comprehensive protocol for this.*

Some alternative practitioners do not believe that there's clear-cut
evidence that mercury fillings have any noticeable impact on health.
Holistic physician Dr. Andrew Weil, for example, has said:

*I don't think any study has been large enough or designed
well enough to determine for sure whether there is a long-term
effect from mercury fillings. One problem is that any harm
may be subtle and hard to detect.*

Conventional dentists maintain that mercury fillings are entirely
safe. Dental amalgam containing mercury was used extensively in
tooth fillings, and according to the American Dental Association
(ADA), in a 1995 survey, up to 76 percent of dentists say they use it
as their primary restoration material. According to a statement from
Gary C. Armitage, chairperson of the ADA's Council on Scientific
Affairs:

*The World Health Organization, FDI World Dental Feder-
ation and the American Dental Association (ADA) all support the continued use of dental amalgam as a safe, durable
and cost-effective material to restore teeth.*

Some patients report relief from some symptoms, and the ability
to reduce their level of thyroid hormone replacement after removal
of mercury fillings. Others, however, have said that the procedure
was expensive and painful, and did not result in any improvement
to their thyroid function or overall health.

Mercury in Fish

There's no question that mercury in fish can be a danger. Whether it's particularly toxic to the thyroid is not definitely established, and not likely to be studied. According to Dr. Ken Blanchard:

> *If it is ever proven that a large segment of hypothyroidism in the public is due to mercurity toxicity, then it might be possible to undergo mercury detoxification by chelation and get the thyroid working properly again. I would not hold my breath waiting for any progress in this area, however, since such studies would be very involved and prolonged and would not result in sales of a patented drug, so no funding would be available.*

Even without thyroid-specific studies, it's well known that over time, high blood levels of mercury can damage the nervous system and kidneys, causing a variety of health concerns, including memory loss and even hearing loss, neurological problems, and, at toxic levels, death. Because of their developing nervous systems, children and fetuses are in even more danger.

The general public is now being advised to avoid overconsumption of fish high in mercury, and to cut back on fish with lower mercury content. In particular, warnings are focused on pregnant women, nursing mothers, women who may become pregnant, and young children, who are being cautioned to avoid high-mercury fish. These fish include king mackerel, shark, swordfish, tilefish, striped bass, eel, albacore tuna, and bluefish. Recommendations are that adult men and nonpregnant/nonnursing women should eat them rarely, if at all.

Some experts, such as Dr. Joseph Mercola, are also concerned about other fish, including sea bass, oysters, marlin, halibut, pike, walleye, white croaker, and largemouth bass. According to the FDA and Environmental Protection Agency (EPA) canned light (not albacore) tuna, salmon, pollock, catfish, and shrimp are safer, but experts still caution that women of childbearing age and children should consume no more than twelve of these fish ounces a week. The Environmental Working group has identified the safest fish as farmed trout, farmed catfish, shrimp, fish sticks, summer flounder, wild Pacific salmon, croaker, mid-Atlantic blue crab, and haddock. Dr. Mercola, however, has a narrower list, and feels that the only safe fish are summer flounder, wild Pacific salmon, croaker, sardines, haddock, and tilapia.

■ Nuclear Incident Concerns: Potassium Iodide

The fear of nuclear accidents, as well as concerns about the potential of terrorist events, have raised the level of concern about exposure to radioactive materials. In the case of a nuclear plant accident where radioactivity is released, or a "dirty bomb" release, taking potassium iodide (KI) tablets quickly after an incident may have the ability to protect the thyroid gland from radiation damage, minimizing future risk of thyroid cancer and other thyroid diseases. Potassium iodide acts as a "blocking agent" to prevent the human thyroid gland from absorbing potentially damaging radioactive iodine.

Radioactive iodine was released during the Chernobyl nuclear accident in 1986. Post-Chernobyl exposure to the radioactive gas in the Ukraine, Russia, Belarus, and areas of Eastern Europe has resulted in a tenfold increase in thyroid cancer in children in the region, and a quadrupling of adult rates of thyroid cancer. While residents of the area around Chernobyl are still suffering from exposure, some regions of Eastern Europe that were exposed to radiation were prepared, and were able to protect their residents, because they rapidly distributed potassium iodide. For example, potassium iodide was handed out in Poland after the Chernobyl crisis, and Poland's thyroid disease rates have not increased since Chernobyl.

Some areas around nuclear plants have stockpiled potassium iodide, and plan to distribute it in the event of a nuclear incident. Other jurisdictions have actually distributed the potassium iodide pills directly to residents and schools. In a continuing controversy, other areas in the United States have refused to stockpile the potassium iodide, believing that it unnecessarily raises concerns about the safety of nuclear plants. Because children are particularly vulnerable to the effects of potassium iodide, the American Academy of Pediatrics (AAP) also recommends that households within ten miles of a nuclear power plant keep potassium iodide on hand to protect the thyroid in the event of an accidental or intentional release of radioactive iodine. Schools and child care facilities within the same radius also should have immediate access to potassium iodide, and the AAP believes that it may be prudent to consider stockpiling potassium iodide within a far larger radius because of more distant windborne fallout.

The World Health Organization is in favor of stockpiling in areas with nuclear reactors, and Japan, Canada, France, and Russia have all stockpiled potassium iodine. In most European countries—including Germany, Sweden, and Britain—potassium iodide is handed out to households in areas around nuclear plants, and it is available in central locations and emergency facilities for rapid distribution.

In the event of a nuclear incident, officials need to determine whether radioactive iodine is present. If it's not, then potassium iodide does not provide any benefit. If it is, however, the Food and Drug Administration recommends that potassium iodide be taken as soon as the radioactive cloud containing iodine is close by. There may still be some protective factors as long as potassium iodide is taken three to four hours after exposure to radioactive iodine. Depending on the extent of contamination, a single dose may be all that's recommended, or in some cases, multiple doses may be recommended. Potassium iodide is only protective for the thyroid gland—it does not protect against other radioactive substances. If officials have determined that radioactive iodine is present, they will announce when to take potassium iodide.

Potassium iodide comes in tablets of 130 mg. A one-time dose is usually all that is required. However, if a person expects to be exposed to radioactive iodine for more than twenty-four hours, another dose should be taken every twenty-four hours. Emergency management officials will provide more specific guidelines, but generally, as of 2004, officials recommended:

- Adults should take one 130-mg tablet.
- Children between three and eighteen years of age should take one-half of a 130-mg tablet (65 mg).
- Children between one month and three years of age should take one-fourth of a 130-mg tablet (32 mg).
- Infants from birth to one month of age should be given one-eighth of a 130-mg tablet (16 mg).
- Women who are breast-feeding should take the adult dose, and their infants should receive the recommended infant dose.
- Children who are approaching adult size (greater than or equal to 150 pounds) should take the adult dose regardless of their age.

Some experts recommend that family members keep enough potassium iodide on hand—at home, in cars, at work—to meet the needs of the entire family, should there be a nuclear incident. ConsumerLab has done an analysis of the quality of the key brands of potassium iodide and found them all to be effective in delivering stated quantities of the key ingredients. The products tested and found to meet quality standards include Iosat, Thyro-Block, Rad-Block KI, KI4U, Medical Corps Potassium Iodate, Potassium Iodide U.S.P. Granular, by Ruger Chemical; and Thyro-Safe.

Potassium iodide is available without prescription through some pharmacies, and via a number of Internet sources, including Iherb.com (http://www.iherb.com / phone: 888-792-0028). Only approved potassium iodide products should be purchased. Potassium iodide tablets can be stored for at least five years without losing their potency.

Note that if you have had thyroid disease, you should talk to your doctor ahead of time to find out if you should take potassium iodide in the event of an emergency, as some experts believe that the high concentration of iodine in potassium iodide can be harmful to people with thyroid conditions, including hyperthyroidism, thyroid nodules, or goiter.

Potassium iodide is also not recommended for people who are allergic to iodine or shellfish, or who have certain skin disorders (such as Dermatitis herpetiformis or Urticaria vasculitis).

PART IV

Special Concerns
of Hypothyroidism

12

Losing Weight Despite Hypothyroidism

Give me a dozen heartbreaks . . . if you think it would help me lose one pound.

— COLETTE

Totie Fields once said, "I've been on a diet for two weeks and all I've lost is two weeks." As someone with hypothyroidism trying to lose weight, you may feel like Totie was talking about you. Sometimes, it seems that nothing you do to lose weight helps. You try diet after diet, herbal diet pills, cabbage soup, low-carb, no-carb, high-carb, no-flour, no-sugar, and every latest fad and idea that comes along, and not only do you not lose weight, you may even keep gaining.

I hear from hundreds of people each week who are desperately unhappy. Brides who want to fit into wedding dresses, new mothers who can't shed the baby weight, women who aren't willing to give up feeling fit and attractive, men who don't understand why their usual workout routine or daily runs aren't keeping the weight off anymore. People like me who have a closet filled with different-sized clothing, reflecting different stages of a thyroid problem. We all are looking to answer one question: "How do I get rid of the weight???"

It's the number one complaint of people with hypothyroidism. Often, weight gain is the first symptom to tip you off that there is a thyroid problem, but it needs to be seen alongside other symptoms before doctors take it seriously. Claudia experienced this:

> *I was 115 pounds, and then I started noticing that I was gaining weight and despite trying to lose, I kept gaining. Tried everything from Nutri-System to joining exercise class. I still had energy, but I was becoming depressed. Finally, I thought I was losing my mind. They put me on Prozac. It still didn't help. I started being so tired. I continued gaining weight and was up to 140 pounds. So tired I couldn't put one foot in front of the other. People noticed I was so swollen in my face. Started with a terrible constipation I have never before had. I went to the doctor and asked him to run a test for thyroid. He did and it was very high.*

You might assume your metabolism will return to normal once you're on thyroid hormone replacement. The doctor might have told you that after the magic "two weeks"—or for some doctors "six weeks"—after starting thyroid hormone replacement your system would return to normal. You may interpret this to mean that you will be able to maintain your weight while eating and exercising as you did before you had a thyroid problem. Or you might assume you could lose weight in the same way you did before becoming hypothyroid.

Again, this does happen for *some* people. But probably not for the majority, despite what doctors say.

Katie, a marathon runner with hypothyroidism, was desperate to lose weight. She told her doctor that she was eating a healthy diet of 1,200 calories a day and jogging five miles daily. Her doctor's response? "Get off the couch and stop eating so much!"

It's mystifying, frankly. If weight gain is listed in the medical textbooks as a symptom that should trigger an examination for hypothyroidism, why does it mysteriously become an unrelated issue the minute after you fill a prescription?

Ultimately, you shouldn't expect much in the way of sympathy from the conventional doctors and endocrinologists when it comes to having difficulty losing weight. Other patients can sympathize. I can definitely sympathize. But don't be disappointed if your doctor gives you a "get off the couch" or "eat less" response. Once you're diagnosed and in the normal TSH range, they simply don't believe your thyroid has much to do with weight issues.

Don't look to the patient groups to have a handle on this issue either. Even the main patient group in the United States, the Thyroid Foundation of America, says in a brochure:

> . . . *we know that if your thyroid begins to make too little hormone, you may slow down and take less exercise—but you won't gain a lot of weight just because of having less hormone.*

For many of us, hypothyroidism is synonymous with the weight battle, and it's impossible even to separate the two problems in our minds. A hypothyroidism diagnosis is only the beginning of what becomes a lifelong battle with weight, all the while being told by doctors that weight gain or difficulty losing has *nothing* to do with thyroid disease.

But the doctors are completely wrong.

The majority of people who are hypothyroid gain weight or find losing weight far more difficult.

Just ask the millions of thyroid patients who were at perfectly normal weights—myself included—until they started to pile on pounds faster than was seemingly physically possible, only to get diagnosed with hypothyroidism shortly afterward. Of course, there are always some patients who lose weight, or who only gain a few pounds and lose them fairly easily once treated, but they are in the minority.

In my survey of more than nine hundred thyroid patients, almost 84 percent of respondents indicated that they are overweight. Among them:

- 20 percent said they are ten to twenty pounds overweight.
- 14 percent indicated that they are twenty to thirty pounds over-weight.
- 25 percent indicated that they are thirty to fifty pounds over-weight.
- 18 percent said that they are fifty to seventy-five pounds over-weight.

Interestingly, while many conventional doctors report that hypothyroidism causes no more than five to ten pounds of weight gain, only 8 percent of the respondents said they were five to ten pounds overweight.

Laura, an active fifty-one-year-old mother of two children, knew something was wrong when she started to gain weight and feel tired, moody, and achy. Says Laura:

> *I went from a vibrant, in-shape woman to a totally out-of-control, overweight couch potato!! I wanted to scream, but could not since I also lost my voice!! I did not want to leave my house and was too tired to do anything. I felt so sick I thought I would die!! I gained about forty pounds in a period of about three months. That alone was pretty scary.*

If you've had radioactive iodine (RAI) as a treatment for Graves' disease and hyperthyroidism, you are also likely to gain weight. One study found that more than 85 percent of patients receiving RAI became hypothyroid, and despite being treated with levothyroxine, their median weight gain after six months was eleven pounds, twenty pounds at twelve months, and twenty-five pounds after two years. Before the therapy, 27.5 percent were considered underweight by body mass index calculations, and 19.3 percent were obese, with a body mass index above 30. Two years after treatment, only 8.7 percent patients were underweight and a total of 51.3 percent were obese. Overall, the researchers found that there was a 32 percent increase in obesity in previously hyperthyroid patients following RAI therapy, with the main weight gain coming in the first two years.

When you're hypothyroid, you can eat less than others, and *still* gain weight. How can we thyroid patients seemingly defy all the laws of physics? If it takes 3,500 excess calories to gain a pound, how could you possibly gain ten or twenty pounds in one month? And yet, when hypothyroid—even when treated—you can. This is what happened to me, at age thirty-three, before my 1995 wedding. After going through my twenties as a slender size 8, I quickly started packing on weight—so much so that I bought a size 12 gown, and in the months before my wedding, I had to have my wedding dress let out two more sizes (Is that a horrifying thing for a bride or what?), and even after going on a reduced-calorie diet with daily exercise, I walked down the aisle as a size 16. And after the honeymoon, the weight kept piling on.

Months after my wedding, I was diagnosed as hypothyroid; my doctor put me on thyroid hormone replacement therapy. Blissfully ignorant, I assumed that all the symptoms—and, in particular, the weight—would just melt off as quickly as it had appeared, now that I was getting my thyroid back in order.

Surprise! Not so . . . Sure, as we tweaked my medicine and dosages, I felt better in some ways—less exhausted, not so moody and achy—but except for several pounds, the weight didn't budge.

In my twenties, before my thyroid apparently started to go awry, losing weight was simple. I just cut out a bag of chips with lunch a few times a week, and switched to a diet soda instead of regular, and within a few weeks, the extra pounds would be gone.

But after my hypothyroidism diagnosis, nothing I was doing moved the scale an ounce. This wasn't going to be so easy. And I'm not alone. Losing weight is *not* easy for many people with thyroid disease. It's a slow process, a far more difficult task than it is for people without metabolic problems. It is also a problem that has caused me, and *millions* of others, far more heartache than nearly any other aspect of hypothyroidism.

But remember—you're not lazy, or lacking willpower. Your weight problem is most likely *not* an emotional issue that can be shouted and bullied out of you by a television personality. You're probably not downing an entire box of donuts every night when no one else is watching. Your eating habits are probably not very different from those of your friends or family members who are at a normal weight. Your body may truly refuse to lose weight on rabbit food, Weight Watchers, or Atkins.

Your body just doesn't work the way it's supposed to, and it *does* have to do with your thyroid. When hypothyroid, for many of us, the metabolism becomes so efficient at storing every calorie that even the most rigorous diet and exercise programs may not seem to work. Your friend or spouse could go on the same diet as you, lose a pound or two—or even more—a week, and you might stay the same, or even gain weight. It's NOT FAIR!

That is the most difficult point to get past—to accept that, fundamentally, your thyroid condition may, especially in the beginning, and perhaps forever, make weight loss an unfair fight. What you suspect about your body is true. You very well may gain weight more easily than others, and you probably won't lose weight as easily or quickly as others.

The good news is, even if it's an unfair fight, it's still a fight you can win! There are answers, and there are solutions, so let's take a look at the issue of how hypothyroidism can play a role in weight problems, and what can be done to maintain a healthy weight with hypothyroidism.

■ Why Is Weight Loss Harder?

There are several key issues that make weight loss harder for people who are hypothyroid.

Metabolic Dysfunction

When we think about hypothyroidism and weight gain, we think about metabolism. The thyroid is actually the master gland of metabolism. Some people think of metabolism as the speed at which energy is burned—sort of like a car idling at 2,000 rpm will burn a smaller amount of fuel each minute than a car idling at 4,000 rpm. Actually, it's more accurate to think about metabolism as the *way*—and not the speed—that your body processes and uses the food you eat each day, more like a car that is designed to burn more fuel at the same rpm. The idea of a "faster" or "slower" metabolism is not really as accurate as the idea of an "efficient" versus a "dysfunctional" or inefficient metabolism.

In hypothyroidism the metabolism often becomes dysfunctional.

Metabolism itself is made up of several components:

• Basal metabolism—from 60 to 65 percent of calories you eat each day are spent just keeping you alive and giving you energy for basic life support. If you were to lie in bed all day, you would still need a substantial number of calories to support basic body functions.

• Physical activity—25 percent of your calories go to movement and physical activity.

• Thermic effect of food—about 10 percent of calories are spent processing the food you eat. One way to estimate how much you burn from eating is to take the total number of calories you eat in a day, and take 10 percent, to figure out how many calories you burn each day just eating. For example, if you are eating 2,000 calories a day, 10 percent of 2,000 is 200, so optimally, you would be burning 200 calories a day simply eating and digesting your food.

Overall, the calories you eat each day should equal the calories you expend.

CALORIES EATEN	=	CALORIES EXPENDED . . .
Total calories taken in		Basal metabolism +
		Activities during the day +
		Used digesting your food.

However, many hypothyroid people who are overweight do not eat any more than people of average weight—they are not taking in more calories. So it's clear that for many people, the problem must be that:

• Basal metabolism is reduced. When they are hypothyroid, even despite treatment, some people have a reduction in basal metabolism, and the basal metabolism is lower than normal. Since hypothyroidism also tends to be more common as we get older, we are also experiencing the double whammy of the thyroid's effects on the metabolism, combined with the slower basal metabolism that comes with aging.

• Activity is reduced. The ongoing fatigue of hypothyroidism causes many people to reduce activity. And remember, slowing down so that you burn even 100 fewer calories a day, perhaps the equivalent to a brisk fifteen-minute walk, means that you could gain an extra pound every month or so! Less exercise and activity also means there is less muscle, and muscle burns more calories than fat and raises metabolism.

• The thermic effect of food is blunted. In hypothyroid people, there are a variety of physiological factors that limit the thermic effect of food, and fewer calories are expended in digestion. In hypothyroidism the body can be a calorie miser, and become extremely efficient at extracting more calories than usual out of the food we eat.

So, in hypothyroid people who are overweight, all three factors may even be the case. And some hypothyroid people *also* overeat, which compounds the problem even further by adding in even more calories that aren't expended.

A Changed Metabolic "Set Point"

According to Dr. Lou Aronne, author of the best-selling book *Weigh Less, Live Longer,* when you begin to take in too many calories, you can gain a small amount of weight. Your body recognizes the starting weight as your "set point." Then, in order to maintain your set-point weight: "Your metabolism speeds up to process the excess calories, your appetite decreases, and some of the newly gained weight drops off."

According to Dr. Aronne, this self-regulating process is known as metabolic resistance. Dr. Aronne and other weight-loss experts believe that just as your body works to maintain a temperature set point of 98.6, it also appears to work toward maintaining a particular weight. His theory is that, in people with a chronic weight problem, the body puts up only modest metabolic resistance to weight gain. If you continue to take in more calories than you burn, the metabolic resistance loses strength, and your body then establishes a new, higher weight set point.

What this means is, if several years ago, a woman at five feet, seven inches and 160 pounds needed 2,500 calories a day to maintain her weight, and now, after a diagnosis of hypothyroidism and a steady weight gain, at 210 pounds, she needs 2,800 calories to maintain her weight. If she dropped her calories back to 2,500, would she lose the extra 50 pounds? No. Because as she reduces her calories and loses weight, her metabolic rate slows down. According to Dr. Aronne, she would probably drop to about 197 pounds, although she'd be consuming the same number of calories as another woman of the same height who's stayed steady at 160 pounds.

My theory is that because the body is in a state of hypometabolism—underfunctioning metabolism—in hypothyroidism, the metabolic resistance becomes impaired, allowing the body to more easily establish higher set points, making it harder to lose weight.

Changes in Brain Chemistry

Hunger is intricately tied to brain chemistry. According to Dr. Aronne, the hypothalamus in your brain senses you need energy and issues a brain chemical with the message "eat carbohydrates." That brain chemical surge is what you feel as "hunger." Once the hypothalamus senses you've eaten enough carbohydrates, it releases serotonin to tell the body, "Okay, enough carbohydrates." Serotonin is a neurotransmitter involved not only in appetite, but in depression, mood, and sleep.

This system can be dramatically altered by a process present in chronic thyroid disease:

- Thyroid disease slows down the metabolism.
- Your metabolism is then too slow for the appetite level set by your brain.
- What your brain perceives as appropriate food intake levels then exceed your body's metabolism, creating weight gain.

When you have chronic hypothyroidism, your body is under stress, which interferes with the brain chemistry and can reduce the release of serotonin. In fact, part of the weight-loss success of the recalled diet drugs Fen-Phen (fenfluramine and phentermine) for some people with hypothyroidism was the fact that they increased serotonin and created a feeling of satisfaction and fullness.

Insulin Resistance/Metabolic Syndrome

Insulin is a hormone released by the pancreas. When you eat foods that contain carbohydrates (which make up the majority of most of our diets), your body converts the carbohydrates into simple sugars.

These sugars enter the blood, becoming "blood sugar." Your pancreas then releases insulin to stimulate the cells to take in the blood sugar and store it as an energy reserve, returning the blood sugar levels to normal.

Carbohydrates can be "simple," high-glycemic (high-sugar) carbohydrates, such as pasta, bread, sugar, white flour, and cakes, or "complex," lower-glycemic (lower-sugar), higher-fiber carbohydrates, like fruits, vegetables, and whole grains. However, the important point some people miss: *Fruits and vegetables are carbohydrates.*

Some scientists speculate that sugars and starches are more easily broken down today than in our prehistoric past. They claim that many of us do not need and cannot process the amounts of carbohydrates that are considered "normal" by current dietary standards. Some scientists speculate that for as much as 25 percent of the population, eating what appears to be a "normal amount" of carbohydrates may in fact raise blood sugar to excessive levels. The pancreas responds by increasing the secretion of insulin to a level where it will drive down blood sugar. For this group, consistently eating too many carbohydrates—and remember that what is too many for this group is not necessarily too many for the average person—creates a situation called "insulin resistance."

Insulin resistance means that cells have become less responsive to the effects of insulin. So your body has to produce more and more insulin in order to maintain normal blood sugar levels. The insulin can also remain in your blood in higher concentrations. This is known as hyperinsulinemia.

In addition to those who seem to have a lowered need for carbohydrates, some people simply eat too many carbohydrates. The popularity of low-fat diets has left a large group of people with a diet that heavily emphasizes pasta, bagels, and sugary fat-free products, and most of these are high-glycemic carbohydrates. Simply overeating high-glycemic foods can in some people trigger insulin resistance and weight gain.

If you are insulin-resistant, eating carbohydrates can make you crave more carbohydrates. You'll gain weight more easily and have difficulty losing it. There are some estimates that 25 percent of the general population, and 75 percent of overweight people, are insulin-resistant.

High insulin levels can stimulate your appetite, making you feel hungrier than normal for carbohydrate-rich food, while lowering the amount of sugar your body burns as energy and making your cells more effective at storing and less able to remove fat.

When you're creating this excess insulin, it also prevents your body from using its stored fat for energy. Hence, your insulin response to excess carbohydrates causes you to gain weight or you cannot lose weight. Weight problems are not the worst aspect of insulin resistance.

Insulin resistance may set up a whole syndrome of other serious health problems, including diabetes, increased risk of coronary artery disease, high blood pressure, and high cholesterol. In particular, insulin resistance is usually the first step in metabolic syndrome, which also includes abdominal obesity (a thick waist), elevated blood fats known as triglycerides, low levels of HDL ("good") cholesterol, high blood pressure, and high blood sugar levels.

It makes sense that hypothyroidism, with its penchant for slowing down everything else in our systems right down to our cells, can also slow down our body's ability to process carbohydrates and our cells' ability to absorb blood sugar. The carbohydrates we could once eat then become too much to handle. Excess carbohydrates equals excess insulin equals excess weight. And that excess weight is a double whammy, because hypothyroidism already increases the risk of high cholesterol, heart disease, and diabetes.

Interestingly, many of the unrelieved symptoms we assume are also due to hypothyroidism—tiredness, dizziness, fatigue, exhaustion, uncontrolled hunger—may, in fact, be side effects of blood sugar swings due to insulin resistance. Any illness, such as the chronic thyroid problems we all face, also creates physical stress.

And stress raises cortisol levels. And overproduction of cortisol increases insulin levels.

All these factors mean that insulin resistance is more of a factor for overweight people with hypothyroidism than for the general population.

If you've tried conventional low-fat diets that are heavy on fruits, vegetables, pasta, rice, and grains, and low on protein and good fats, and find that you can't lose weight or even gain weight, you might be insulin-resistant.

■ Weight-Loss Challenges and Solutions

There are a number of challenges inherent in hypothyroidism that may make weight loss a challenge, but here, we discuss those challenges and talk about the solutions you can consider.

Optimize Your Thyroid Treatment

The most essential step for anyone who is hypothyroid and can't lose weight is to make sure thyroid treatment is optimized. The best diet and exercise program in the world may not allow you to lose weight if your doctor is keeping you on too low a dose of thyroid hormone replacement. Or you may be one of the many patients who can't lose weight on any dose of levothyroxine, but add in T3, or switch to natural thyroid, and your diet and exercise start working again.

Dr. Ken Blanchard, in his book *What Your Doctor May Not Tell You About Hypothyroidism*, talks about how conventional thyroid treatment actually promotes weight gain. Says Blanchard:

> In many people (but not all), treatment with synthetic 100 percent T4 can produce excessive T4 levels (at the upper end of normal) and TSH levels near the bottom of normal, nudging at hyperthyroidism. This creates a situation by

*which individuals feel hungry (from the metabolic thrust)
but very fatigued due to inadequate T4 replenishment and
conversion to T3. They ask their physicians for more T4 to
handle their symptoms, but are denied because of their near-
toxic levels.*

While optimized thyroid treatment is discussed throughout this
book, here are some key questions to review:

- Are you on the right brand of levothyroxine, if appropriate? If
  one isn't working, try another.
- Do you need additional T3, via adding in Cytomel or time-
  released T3, or switching to Thyrolar?
- Would natural, desiccated thyroid, such as the prescription drug
  Armour Thyroid, help you lose weight?
- Are you at the optimal dosage for you? (Could your TSH be
  lower?)
- Are you taking your medication properly and getting maximum
  absorption?
- Are you eating too many goitrogens or soy in your diet?
- Are you taking supplements that contain high levels of iodine?
- Are you taking supplements and vitamins that can help optimize
  thyroid function?
- Do you have any untreated, low-level infections?

Evaluate Other Drugs

Determine whether you are taking any drugs that promote
weight gain, and discuss any concerns with your physician. These
drugs can include:

- Steroid anti-inflammatories (i.e., prednisone)
- The antithyroid drug PTU
- Lithium
- Estrogen and progesterone independently, or together as the Pill

- Antidiabetic drugs, like insulin
- Various antidepressants, especially Prozac, Paxil, and Zoloft
- Mood-stabilizing and anticonvulsant drugs, such as those given for bipolar disorder, including lithium, valproate (Depakote), and carbamazepine (Tegretol)
- Beta-blockers
- Sedatives
- Tranquilizers

Check Your Blood Sugar

One thing you should consider doing is getting your blood sugar tested. At a minimum, you can get a glucose level from a home test kit, but it's preferable to get a fasting glucose to evaluate whether your blood sugar is normal, high normal, or elevated. In late 2003, the American Diabetes Association recommended that the fasting glucose range for defining "prediabetes" be changed, down from 110 mg/dl to 100 mg/dl, meaning that a value of 100 mg/dl or above would lead to a diagnosis of impaired fasting glucose/prediabetes/insulin resistance. If it is high normal or elevated, this can in part contribute to your difficulty losing weight, and also is a sign that you are either becoming insulin-resistant, are prediabetic, or are already a type 2 diabetic. If your blood sugar is elevated, you should discuss going on an antidiabetic medication such as metformin, known by its brand name, Glucophage. Metformin, along with diet and exercise, can actually help prevent the progression of your insulin resistance or prediabetes to full type 2 diabetes.

Consider Antidepressants or Supplements That Balance Brain Chemistry

Even if you do not suffer from depression, you might find that you have greater success fighting a stubborn weight problem if your doctor tries you on a course of antidepressants. A number of people have written to report that their diet/exercise plan suddenly began to work after their doctor prescribed a short course of antidepressant medication, like Prozac, Welbutrin, Effexor, or Paxil, for example. It's worth discussing with your doctor. Welbutrin, in particular, is thought to be helpful in curbing cravings and addictions, and is not as likely to cause weight gain, which can be a side effect with some antidepressants in some people.

Some antidepressants have side effects, and in some cases, people simply prefer natural supplements. Since the antidepressant herb St. John's wort may have some ability to interfere with your thyroid hormone, you may want to avoid it. Patients have reported success, however, with a supplement called 5 HTP, 5-hydroxytryptophan, an amino acid derivative and the immediate precursor to serotonin. This is one I say you should approach with caution. The only people I know who have tried this, myself included, have had energy "crashes." I don't know if our experiences are unusual, but it's worth a warning.

The CraniYums collection of supplements, which include supplements that help to balance or enhance the neurotransmitters serotonin and dopamine, may also be an aid to people who suffer from imbalances that affect appetite, energy, cravings, and mood.

Follow a Low-Glycemic Diet

An effective method to combat insulin resistance and the inability to properly process simple carbohydrates is eating a low-glycemic, fairly low-fat diet. Low-glycemic foods are foods that do not rank high on the "glycemic index," a ranking that assigns values to foods based on their effect on your blood sugar.

High-glycemic foods are sugary, starchy foods like pasta, rice, white flour breads, cereal, desserts, and sugary drinks. You may feel frustrated that there's nothing left to eat. But you need to rethink your eating habits, shifting to a diet of low-fat protein sources (like chicken, turkey, fish, leaner cuts of other meats, and low-fat dairy products) and nonstarchy, high-fiber vegetables and fruits, and certain grains.

There are numerous books and Web resources that provide information on the glycemic index of foods and beverages that you can consult. But again, if you avoid sugar in all forms, and emphasize lean sources of protein, nonstarchy vegetables, with limited fruit, and when you do eat starches, make sure they are high-fiber and eat them only in limited quantities, you are on your way toward eating low-glycemic.

Researchers have found that thyroid disease may actually be linked to increased appetite for starchy/sugary carbohydrates. This increased craving for and intake of carbohydrates appears to stem from various changes in brain chemistry and sympathetic nervous system activity that stem from the thyroid condition. As you eliminate the "bad" carbohydrates from your body, you'll eventually find the cravings are reduced. But when they strike, you may want to try some of the products that help with these carbohydrate cravings, such as CraniYums serotonin-boosting supplements, or homeopathic Craving Elimination Drops.

Eat "Enough" Calories, But Not Too Many

Many thyroid patients have already gone on extremely low-calorie "starvation" diets in their attempts to lose weight. This sort of diet wreaks havoc on the metabolism, making it think that you are facing starvation, and turning on a whole host of appetite-increasing, fat-storing hormones. Your metabolism shifts into "hoarding" mode, and slows down to prevent you from starving. While you may need to eat a lower-calorie diet to lose weight, diets that go lower than 1,000 to 1,200 calories per day are probably going to be counterproductive to most people with hypothyroidism.

At the same time, all the various calculators and guidelines that say the typical woman who weighs 150 pounds should eat 2,200 calories a day just to maintain her weight, for example, are not likely to apply to you. At one point about a year ago, I calculated the calorie levels I'm *supposed* to be able to eat in order to maintain my weight, and actually tried eating that amount every day for two weeks. I gained seven pounds. That was the end of *that* experiment!

I now eat about *half* that calorie level every day, and it's only at that level, with regular exercise, that I am able to lose weight or maintain weight lost over time.

Eat Enough Protein

Protein is needed to build muscle, and to maintain energy, and so your diet should include sufficient levels of protein. Ideally, include a portion of lean protein in every meal and snack, and never eat a carbohydrate—whether vegetable, fruit, or starch—without an accompanying protein, because it helps slow down the digestion of the carbohydrate as it converts to sugar.

Get Enough Good Fat

Essential fatty acids (EFAs) cannot be produced in the body, and so you must get them through diet or supplements. The key essential fatty acids include:

• Omega-3/alpha linolenic acid (ALA), eicosapentaenoic acid (EPA), docosahexaenoic acid (DHA)—Found in fresh fish from cold deep oceans (i.e., mackerel, tuna, herring, flounder, sardines, salmon, rainbow trout, bass), linseed oil, flax seeds and oil, black currant and pumpkin seeds, cod liver oil, shrimp, oysters, leafy greens, soybeans, walnuts, wheat germ, fresh sea vegetables, fish oil. Usually, your body can convert ALA into EPA, and then into DHA.

• Omega-6/linoleic acid/gamma linolenic acid (GLA)—Found in breast milk, sesame seeds and oil, safflower seeds, cotton and sunflower seeds and oil, corn and corn oil, soybeans, raw nuts, legumes, leafy greens, black currant seeds, evening primrose oil, borage oil, spirulina, lecithin. Linoleic acid in omega-6 can be converted into GLA.

Nutritional expert Ann Louise Gittleman, author of *Eat Fat, Lose Weight* and the best-selling *The Fat Flush Diet*, believes that good fats are essential to good health and weight loss, and that today's low-fat diets are counterproductive. Gittleman, like many other nutritional experts, believes that if you include good fats in the diet, you rev up the body's fat-burning potential and you stay full longer, allowing you to eat fewer calories without feeling hungry. In addition to adding more of the foods that contain these essential fatty acids, some of the ways you can add EFAs to your diet include:

- Omega-3/fish oil supplements—Go for a decent-tasting oil or a "burpless" capsule (Enzymatic Therapies' Eskimo Oil is my favorite).
- Omega-3/flax seeds and flaxseed oil—You can add flaxseed oil to meals, either in the oil form or as capsules. Some people like to make salad dressings out of the oil or add it to soups. Taking flaxseed oil with each meal helps slow down digestion and modulate blood sugar fluctuations (which helps with insulin levels).
- Omega-6/evening primrose oil, borage oil—These are usually taken as supplements. GLA is thought to help activate brown fat and to boost metabolic efficiency.

Gittleman is an advocate of evening primrose oil for weight loss:

In my private practice, I have seen women and men benefit time and time again from the addition of omega fats to their weight-loss plans. Many of my clients who have had at least ten pounds or more of weight to lose have reported staggeringly dramatic results with four to eight capsules of 500 mg evening primrose oil.

If you want to include a healthy balance of EFAs, select a product that includes a balance of oils, such as the Atkins-formulated Essential Oils supplement, or Udo Erasmus's Udo's Oil products.

Drink Enough Water

Hypothyroidism can cause water retention and bloating. So, because you feel or look bloated or swollen, you may not drink enough water. But the body will hold on to even more water more fiercely when you cut back on your water intake. Not drinking at least 64 ounces—or more—of water a day is counterproductive, as it will worsen bloating and cause dehydration, which slows metabolism.

Hypothyroidism also slows down digestion and elimination, which can impede weight loss. Optimize digestion by making sure you get high levels of fiber every day, and if you need help with regular elimination, consider adding a natural supplement, such as Ayurvedic triphala, to aid in regularity.

Get Enough Fiber

Fiber is another essential to digestion, and optimizing your weight-loss efforts. Fiber has minimal calories, but can fill you up by adding bulk, and when consumed with carbohydrates, it helps modulate the insulin response and normalize blood sugar. There is a fair amount of scientific support for fiber's ability to increase your feeling of fullness after you eat and reduce your hunger levels. One study found that adding 14 grams per day of fiber was associated with a 10 percent decrease in energy intake and body, and a weight loss of five pounds over four months. To add fiber, eat more raw vegetables and fruits; they have more fiber than cooked or canned. Limit cereals and breads to high-fiber only. Two slices of high-bran "health" bread, for example, has 7 grams of fiber, compared to only 2 grams of fiber for white bread. Other good sources of fiber are nuts, beans, apples, oranges, broccoli, cauliflower, berries, pears, Brussels sprouts, lettuce, prunes, carrots, and yams. Men up to fifty require 38 grams of fiber a day, and women need 25 grams. Men over fifty should get at least 30 grams, and women, at least 21 grams. If you can't get all your fiber from food, consider taking a fiber supplement.

Important Warning: If you switch from a low-fiber to a high-fiber diet, be very careful that you take your thyroid medicine at least an hour before eating in the morning, so your absorption is not impaired. High-fiber diets can change your dosage requirements, so six to eight weeks after starting a high-fiber diet, you may wish to have your thyroid function tested to make sure you don't need a dosage change.

Keep Track of What You Eat

Studies have shown that people who write down everything they eat lose weight, even if not formally dieting, simply because the act of writing it down makes you more aware and likelier to make better choices. There are special books and journals you can buy for this purpose. One particularly good diary is the *Fat Tracker Daily Diary,* from Karen Chisholm. See http://www.thefattracker.com for more information. You can also use your PDA, or a notepad, or your computer, or a calendar, or a looseleaf binder. It doesn't matter what form it takes, it's the action of sitting down and thinking about your goals, what you're going to eat, and assessing what you've eaten that makes the difference.

If you want a more formalized way to keep close track of your nutritional intake, and want a supportive community to help you follow your chosen approach, check out tools such as Ediets, Weight Watchers Online, or Physique Transformation Program's Personal Food Analyst, all of which have detailed food-tracking programs online, as well as online support communities and forums where you can share information and encouragement with others.

■ Do's and Don'ts

Things to eat and drink that may help with weight loss:

- Spicy foods and peppers, which stimulate metabolism
- Tea, especially oolong and ginseng tea, which may help stimulate metabolism

Cut back or eliminate:

- Alcohol—which is high calorie, puts stress on your liver, slows down your ability to burn fat, and interferes with your body's ability to convert T4 to T3.
- Caffeine—which can trigger production of adrenaline, which then stimulates insulin, resulting in food cravings and negative shifts in blood sugar.
- Sweeteners—in particular, try to eliminate sugar and aspartame (NutraSweet/Equal). There is a great deal of controversy over the safety of the various artificial sweeteners, but if you have to use one, you're better off using saccharin (Sweet'n Low) or sucralose (Splenda), which have safer health records, according to some holistic experts. Some natural health practitioners recommend stevia (pronounced Steve-ee-uh), a plant-derivative sweetener that has no calories and does not influence blood sugar.

■ Tips on How to Eat

Follow Some Basic Food-Combining Rules

- Try to eat protein with nonstarchy vegetables. That means you don't really want to have that baked potato with the steak. You're better off with a big salad and some sautéed mushrooms on the side.
- Avoid milk and meat at the same meal. Having milk with your meat slows down digestion.

• Eat one type of protein per meal. Don't have the beef and chicken fajita combo, or a surf-and-turf combo. Combining proteins makes them harder to digest. You can, however, add eggs to other proteins, like steak and eggs or ham quiche.

• Don't eat fruit with meat or heavy meals, as it becomes harder to digest and can raise blood sugar.

Eat a Big Breakfast

You should aim to eat a big breakfast, one that contains a substantial amount of protein. In fact, aim to eat 25 percent of your calories at breakfast. You should also eat at least 20 grams of protein at breakfast. A protein-heavy breakfast speeds up calorie burning and gets the metabolism moving. Some studies have shown that people eating a certain number of calories will lose weight if they eat more calories concentrated during breakfast, while others on the same number of calories will stay the same weight or even gain if they emphasize the calorie expenditure at lunch or dinner.

Try to Eat Three Meals Versus Multiple Mini-Meals

The controversial recommendation to eat three meals, rather than grazing, or eating five or six mini-meals, as is often suggested, comes from Byron Richards, a holistic nutritionist and author of the groundbreaking book *Mastering Leptin*. Says Richards:

> . . . if 5–6 small meals a day are needed to maintain energy, the metabolic situation is not in good shape. Eating very small meals may cause some weight loss, but metabolism will likely slow down before the weight goal is achieved. Even a low calorie snack increases insulin release, thus fat-burning mode ceases or never begins. Only by increasing the amount of time between meals will proper weight loss take place.

According to Richards, this advice to eat small, frequent meals comes from the bodybuilding and diabetic communities. Bodybuilders, says Richards, can eat more times a day because they have shortened the time that their insulin levels cycle up and down by eating consistently at high-calorie levels and burning calories intensively through their muscle development. Diabetics, according to Richards, have a malfunctioning insulin and glucagon metabolism. They have to use calories like a drug, to strictly regulate insulin levels. But these examples are not necessarily applicable for those of us who are not bodybuilders or diabetic, because, according to Richards, we need to condition our livers into better responsiveness and fitness, by balancing our leptin. And working toward having just three meals a day, with five to six hours between those meals, is Richards's solution to optimizing leptin balance.

Eat a Lighter Dinner, and Nothing Else After

Of all the meals of the day, dinner should be the lightest, whenever possible. Keep in mind that at dinner, few of us require large portions—if any—of the starchy carbohydrates, like pasta, bread, potatoes, or rice. If you are going to eat starches, you're better off eating them earlier in the day when your body needs the fuel and is more likely to burn it off safely. Byron Richards also believes that we should finish eating dinner at least three hours before bed. One his key rules to balancing leptin is:

> *Never eat after dinner. Allow 11–12 hours between dinner and breakfast. Never go to bed on a full stomach.*

Many experts agree with Richards that we should go to bed slightly hungry. Not so hungry or starving that hunger pangs will keep you awake, but your stomach should feel nearly empty. Your body is looking for fuel to burn during the night, and if you go to bed with your stomach nearly empty, and insulin levels low, your body is much more likely to seek out your fat stores for that fuel.

Eat Slowly, Chew Thoroughly

Your mother always said to chew your food, and she was right! Chewing thoroughly and eating slowly are important. When you chew thoroughly, you're letting the digestive juices in your mouth and throat do their work to properly break down and begin digesting your food. At the same time, you're helping to extend the time you're actually eating, giving your brain time to receive the "I feel full" feeling that takes about ten minutes after you start eating to generate. (How many of us are embarrassed to admit that we can eat an entire meal in *less than* ten minutes?) When we eat too quickly, we're not giving our brain enough time to receive the hormonal message that we've eaten and we're full.

■ Exercise and Breathing

As a confirmed couch potato with no athletic ability whatsoever, I'm the last person to talk about exercise. But there's no doubt that exercise is as potent a medicine as you can get *and* appears to be one of the factors that are absolutely *essential* to healthy weight loss or weight maintenance with hypothyroidism.

When you have a thyroid dysfunction, even with optimal treatment, you may feel more fatigued than normal. This level of fatigue may mean that you exercise less, and move around less, which reduces the amount of energy and calories you expend.

Thyroid disease also commonly causes joint and muscle aches and pains, carpal tunnel syndrome, tarsal tunnel syndrome, and tendonitis, all which make exercise and movement harder, and may discourage you from exercising or moving. Again, less exercise means you expend fewer calories.

In both cases, the less you exercise and less physical activity you have, the more likely you are to burn fewer calories from overall activity, but also lose muscle mass. And reduced muscle mass also reduces metabolism, because muscle burns more calories than fat, even when your body is at rest.

Muscle-Building/Strength-Training Exercise

Ideally, your exercise program should include both aerobic activities and strength training. But if you have to choose just one, make sure you incorporate strength-training activities to build muscle, as it is essential to successful weight loss while hypothyroid.

Cynthia White, a certified aerobic instructor and personal trainer from Denton, Texas, herself has hypothyroidism. Cynthia highly recommends strength training, and she likes weight lifting:

> *Muscle is more metabolically active than fat. You don't even have to go to a gym to do this. Just buy a couple of sets of dumbbells, one set in five pounds and one in ten pounds, and do the routine at home. Setting up a "circuit type" routine will kill two birds with one stone. You will be working aerobically and lifting at the same time. One myth-buster: Unless you are genetically blessed with a mesomorph body type (one that has a tendency to add muscle easily, which is rare for women) you will not "bulk up"! Trust me, I have been lifting for years and haven't bulked up yet. There are many books that can set you up with a basic weight training program. The idea is to work the muscles like your legs, back, chest, arms, and shoulders.*

Aerobic Exercise

Regular aerobic exercise is also important. First, it's a completely natural way to help the serotonin problem. Many experts recommend thirty minutes of some vigorous aerobic activity at least five times a week as a natural mood elevator and antidepressant.

Second, aerobic exercise burns calories.

Third, according to Jean-Pierre Despres, Ph.D., Professor of

Medicine and Physical Education and Director of the Lipid Research Center at Laval University Hospital, in Quebec:

> *Exercise is probably the best medication on the market to treat insulin resistance syndrome. . . . Our studies show that low-intensity, prolonged exercise—such as a daily brisk walk of forty-five minutes to an hour—will substantially reduce insulin levels.*

Geri, a health writer and television producer in New York, says keeping her weight stable requires exercise:

> *Exercise makes a* huge *difference. Even when I was at my most exhausted, I dragged my butt out of bed and did a little low-intensity exercise about five mornings a week. My schedule now is pretty crazy and I work long hours, so I don't have tons of time to exercise, but I do about twenty to thirty minutes of aerobics or light weight training about five days a week. Nothing major, but so far it seems to do the trick. When I slip off this habit a little, I find that I get more tired and slightly "hypo feeling"—sluggish, easily distracted, weak.*

Okay, it's clear that we all need to get moving!! That's not always very easy. Some people say, "But I'm hypothyroid, I'm exhausted all the time, and now you're telling me to exercise on top of it all?" The answer is: YES! But sometimes you have to start very slowly.

Cynthia White has some excellent advice regarding exercise and working activity into your life:

> *First of all, start small. Set goals that you can accomplish. It is much more motivating to continue on any new habit if you achieve small victories along the way.*

So many people with hypothyroidism fight fatigue, which makes them less energetic and motivated to exercise. According to Cynthia, there are ways to offset this:

Figure out when your peak energy period is. For some people it is in the morning, other people get their energy at night. Pinpoint your peak and do something active at that time. You also have to mentally motivate yourself. What is more motivating? Your appearance or your health? If it is your appearance, go through fitness magazines and cut out pictures of people that motivate you. (I used to paste them up on my refrigerator!) If it's your health, list all the benefits of exercise. There are too many to list here, but a sampling includes a lower risk for breast cancer, improved cardiovascular system, increased energy, increased self-esteem, and the list could go on.

If you don't enjoy working out, the trick, according to Cynthia, is to find something you enjoy doing . . . walking, tennis, racquetball, or swimming. She suggests you find an activity that you and your spouse or friend could do together, like take a walk, and think of it as precious time to talk to each other.

Cynthia also emphasizes that there are a multitude of ways to incorporate activity into the everyday tasks of life:

Take the stairs, park farther out in the parking lot. Get up off the couch and turn the channel on the TV. Don't go through the drive-through; get out of your car and go into the store. If you work in an office, find reasons to get up out of your chair. When you are sitting, wiggle or tap your foot. It may be small, but it requires energy.

It seems that people with hypothyroidism *need* exercise about as much as we need our thyroid hormone pills. Even if you're not a health spa or gym sort of person, the health experts tout the basic benefits of walking. Even a few minutes of brisk walking every day would be more exercise than a majority of us ever get and a terrific goal to accomplish. So consider this a hypothyroidism prescription for a lifetime: Rx—take a walk and get moving!

Breathe Properly

It goes by a variety of names. In yoga, it's called pranayam, the art and science of breathing. In marketing language, it's Breathercise or Oxycise. Some of the diet centers are even incorporating it into their programs. Whatever you call it, a program of deep-breathing exercises, designed to take in more oxygen and release more carbon dioxide with each breath, seems to help many people with hypothyroidism to lose weight.

We know that hypothyroidism affects the strength of your respiratory muscles. Hypothyroidism is also known to increase reactivity of the bronchial passages, even if you don't have asthma. Even when treated, a substantial percentage of people with hypothyroidism report "shortness of breath," "feeling like they're not getting enough oxygen," or even "needing to yawn to get more air" as continuing symptoms.

For many of us, the ability to take in and process oxygen may be forever changed once hypothyroidism sets in. Even when fully treated, I suspect that most of us still don't take in and process oxygen fully. That is why specific attention to breathing seems to help some people with hypothyroidism.

If you're interested in trying out better breathing, you can start by learning how to do deep abdominal breathing. Here's a simple breathing exercise:

> Lie on your back, body relaxed. Put your hand on your abdomen. Take a deep, slow breath through your nose, filling your belly, so your hand rises. Then exhale slowly, letting all the air out of your belly. Inhale again, filling the abdomen un-

til your hand rises. Again, exhale. Feel the breath energy ris-
ing from the abdomen to the throat, and back down again to
the abdomen.

You can start practicing this deep abdominal breathing anywhere: sitting in the car, standing in line, in the shower. It's a first
step toward incorporating deep breathing into your daily life. Several times a day, stop and just focus on your breathing. Take a few
deep abdominal breaths. Every time you feel tired, try taking five
deep abdominal breaths. See if these ventures in breathing practice
help you feel even a bit more energetic or alert.

A specialized type of alternate-nostril breathing to help raise the
metabolism is discussed in the book's section on yoga. This type of
breathing also appears to help with energy, and can be particularly
helpful for thyroid patients.

Pilates

In the past, I regularly did yoga, and I still do it occasionally. But
I've found that I like Pilates even better. While it involves stretching,
breathing, and some mind-body aspects like yoga, it also focuses on
the core abdominal muscles and strength building. I do an hour of
mat Pilates twice a week, and have done so for two years—the
longest I've ever kept up with *any* exercise! I also joined my local
Curves center a while back, and really enjoy their fast, thirty-
minute combination aerobic/strength-training program. I'm in and
out in forty-five minutes, and don't even have to break a sweat. In
just three months of two visits to Curves per week, I lost about ten
inches! I also try to do the alternate-nostril breathing and abdominal
breathing, at least once a day for a few minutes.

■ Other Issues

Other issues that can interfere with your ability to lose weight are discussed in various places in this book as well as in greater depth in my book *The Thyroid Diet*. These include food allergies and sensitivities, candidiasis/yeast overgrowth, celiac disease/gluten (or wheat) sensitivity, parasites, the copper/zinc balance, adrenal imbalances, and estrogen and progesterone imbalances.

■ Supplements and Herbs for Weight Loss and Metabolism

To complement your diet and exercise program, there are hundreds of vitamins, herbs, minerals, enzymes, essential fatty acids, and combination formula supplements that promote themselves as helping in increasing metabolism or making it more effective, aiding in fat burning, slowing fat storage, balancing blood sugar, and reducing appetite.

Do they work? It's a good question, because many of the supplements have never been extensively studied. Some have undergone some studies and trials, and others have been in use for centuries as part of traditional Chinese medicine or Ayurvedic remedies. There are also some that are touted mainly on the basis of anecdotal evidence. And then there is the constant battery of hype, with never-ending infomercials, bus-stop photocopied advertisements, magazine and newspaper ads, and multilevel marketers spamming you, trying to sell you the latest miracle diet supplement, the one that will finally "melt the pounds off while you sleep," or allow you to "eat anything and still lose weight," or "rev up your metabolism and burn 50 percent more fat!"

Let me let you in on a big secret. That miracle diet supplement doesn't exist. I get a thousand e-mails a week from frustrated thyroid patients who are trying to lose weight, and I guarantee you, if any of these miracle pills worked, I would be hearing from the legions of people who are thrilled with their miracle pills. So far, I haven't heard from any yet. And, yes, here and there I've fallen prey to the marketing claims, and I've tried a bottle or two of miracle pills, and they haven't solved the problem. No matter what, I'm always back to diet and exercise.

That said, there are some supplements and herbs that *may* help you in your weight-loss efforts. I emphasize *may*, because there are no guarantees, and some of the supplements will do nothing at all for you, some might actually do the opposite (and you'll be one of the few people who gains weight on something that is supposed to help with weight loss!). Some of the supplements, however, might actually be a great fit for you, and help you to lose weight.

I have reviewed these supplements in detail in *The Thyroid Diet*, where I've listed all of them and have provided my recommendation regarding whether or not they are worth trying. The most promising include alpha lipoic acid, acetyl-l-carnitine, calcium, capsaicin/cayenne pepper, chromium picolinate, conjugated linoleic acid (CLA), CraniYums, glucosol, glutamine/L-glutamine, hoodia gordonii, pantethine, pyruvate, taurine, vitamin C, and zinc.

Other supplements that are reviewed and discussed in the *Thyroid Diet* include 5-HTP, 7-KETO, caffeine, gotu kola, guaraná, green tea extract, chitosan, coenzyme Q-10, coleus, DHEA, garcinia cambogia/hydroxycitric acid (HCA), *gymnema sylvestre*, milk thistle, *phaseolus vulgaris*/starch blockers/Phase 2, and spirulina.

My Own Program

Some people ask what I take everyday, to aid with weight loss. In addition to a multivitamin, I take at least 1,200 mg of calcium, 3,500 mg or more of conjugated linoleic acid (CLA), approximately 800 mg of pure hoodia gordonii, and usually at least 1,000 mg of vitamin C.

I also particularly like a line of weight-loss supplements called "Lean for Less," from Health From the Sun/Arkopharma. When I feel like my diet needs an extra kick start, I will take all four supplements simultaneously for a few weeks, and I feel it helps get me back on track.

• Lean for Less Thermogenic is meant to burn fat and raise metabolism. It includes green tea, coleus, and citrus aurantium, but no other stimulants such as ma huang, ephedra, or guaraná.

• Lean for Less Carbo Regulator is supposed to help reduce the conversion of carbohydrates into stored fat, and reduce appetite and craving for sweets. Ingredients include chromium picolinate, hydroxy citrate acid (Garcinia cambogia fruit extract), Gymnema sylvestre leaf, and holy basil leaf.

• Lean for Less Fat Regulator is a freeze-ground preparation of nopal cactus, also known as prickly pear. Nopal cactus is reported to have a high content of gums and mucilage, giving it the unique ability to bind to fats and sugars consumed during meals and reduce their digestion and absorption into the body.

• Lean for Less Water Regulator is a combination of vitamin C, iron, magnesium, Lespedeza capitata powder, couch grass, java tea, and dandelion that decreases water retention and bloating, and acts as a natural diuretic.

Note Regarding Ephedra

While Chinese medicine practitioners have been using ma huang, an herb that contains the stimulant ephedra, for centuries, the fatal abuse of ephedra-based diet pills in a few high-profile cases has ended up causing a complete FDA ban on use of ephedra in diet formulations. Some practitioners have sworn by these products, and there is evidence that in the short term, the stimulation afforded by these supplements provided a temporary increase in metabolism along with weight loss. But over time, people can become resistant to the effects, and will need to stay at the artificially high level in order to maintain weight loss. And long-term use, or use of higher doses, also raises the risk of serious side effects, including heart attack and stroke—particularly in stimulant-sensitive thyroid patients. Ultimately, while the FDA ban was in my opinion uncalled for, these supplements don't really have a place in a safe, effective, lifelong weight-loss effort for thyroid patients.

■ Especially for People with Hypothyroidism . . .

No matter which plan you choose, when you are following a weight-loss program, there are some particular considerations you need to keep in mind that apply specifically to you as someone with hypothyroidism.

Don't expect to lose weight quickly. Celebrate your resounding *success* if you lose even a pound a week. Do *not* compare your results with anyone else. And *don't* diet with a friend, unless she or he is hypothyroid, too, because you're bound to feel frustrated if you compare your rate of loss to others.

You *have* to exercise. It's not optional. Weight-bearing/muscle-building exercise is critical to raising metabolism. And aerobic exercise helps burn calories. Even if you join a weight-loss center that says you can lose weight without exercise, it's not likely to be true for you.

If you add fiber to your diet, have your thyroid function retested about six to eight weeks after you stabilize at your new level of fiber intake. You may need a change in your dosage of thyroid hormone replacement.

If you lose more than 10 percent of your body weight, it's time to get retested to see if you need a dosage adjustment.

Many thyroid patients report that only when they dramatically cut down on starchy carbohydrates and sugars—eliminating things like bread, sugar, pasta, sodas, and desserts—and limiting carbs mainly to vegetables, with some fruit, are they able to lose weight. While there are thyroid patients who process carbs with no difficulty, and can lose weight on a more old-fashioned food pyramid diet that emphasizes cereals, grains, and bread, they seem to be the exception, rather than the rule.

Hopping on a scale to keep track of weight loss is important, but not as important as keeping track of measurements. Particularly for thyroid patients, who may have more early results in building muscle than in losing pounds, keeping track of your measurements can provide important feedback—and may even provide incentive on those other days or weeks when you don't see much movement on the scale.

■ What If Nothing Seems to Work?

Dana Laake, M.S., R.D.H., L.N., a well-respected preventive and therapeutic nutritionist, speaking at a women's health conference in 1998, was asked a question about the diets that were popular at the time. These included Sugar Busters, which is a low-glycemic diet, the ever-present Atkins diet, and Barry Sears's popular Zone diet. These diets have been criticized by conventional doctors as "radical," too "high-protein," not low-fat enough for weight loss or not balanced enough. Dana gave what I thought was excellent advice:

> No one diet is necessarily right for you. But if you're not losing weight eating the way you're eating now, change the way you're eating. You can try one of these diets, and see if it has an effect. Then, starting there, you can work your way back toward a healthier, balanced version of that diet.

This is excellent advice, recognizing that any one diet is not the answer for everyone. Conventional low-fat diets will help some hypothyroid people lose weight. High-fiber diets may be the key for others. The point is to take a look at whatever way of eating you're following now, and if it isn't working, try something very different, perhaps even radical, and see if that has an effect.

In my case, I had to try 800 calories a day, and Atkins, Zone, low-glycemic, low-carb—you name it, I've tried it, until I figured out after years of trial and error that I lose weight and feel my best on a somewhat low-calorie, controlled-fat, sufficient-protein but definitely low-glycemic diet. I cannot lose weight on an all-you-can-eat Atkins-type diet. If I had to characterize my diet, I'd say it was more like a South Beach or Zone approach, except even more customized for a thyroid patient, as defined in my *Thyroid Diet* book. If I eat bread, rice, pasta, or other starchy/sugary foods, I don't lose weight. I have to eat at least five or more servings of fruits and vegetables a day, and I have to drink a great deal of water, or I don't lose weight. I can eat limited starches, but they have to be high-fiber and must be eaten with protein (such as a high-fiber, high-protein cereal, or a high-fiber bran muffin). My diet doesn't have to be particularly low-fat, but it has to be low in saturated (bad) fats, so that most of the fat, besides that found in fish and lean meat, comes from healthy fats like olive oil, olives, avocados, and low-fat dairy products. And weight loss stalls immediately if I'm not getting in at least three to four hours a week of some sort of exercise. In my case, I prefer strength training and resistance—I go to a local Curves workout place, and work with a mat Pilates trainer.

Your options include diets that are low-calorie, low-fat, low-carbohydrate, low-glycemic, vegetarian, or vegan; aerobic exercise or strength-training exercise; or, the most likely solution—a *combination* of some of the above.

Once you determine that you lose weight on a specific type of diet, such as cutting out all meats, fish, and eggs in a vegetarian diet, or cutting out almost all fat in a very low-fat diet, you have a clue that something about that way of eating works for you and your unique metabolism. Starting from there, you can experiment by adding back in smaller amounts of the "banned" foods to find a healthy, more balanced version of that diet that works best for you, and by incorporating exercise to enhance your metabolism and weight-loss efforts.

■ ■ ■

A comprehensive approach to losing weight with hypothyroidism, including specialized diet plans, detailed food lists, and recipes, is featured in my book *The Thyroid Diet: Managing Your Metabolism for Lasting Weight Loss*. For more information about the book, see the Web site http://www.GoodMetabolism.com.

13

Depression and Hypothyroidism

Believe, when you are most unhappy, that there is
something for you to do in the world.
— HELEN KELLER

The relationship between hypothyroidism and depression is very
real and somewhat complicated. As mentioned earlier, depression can be a symptom of undiagnosed hypothyroidism. In some
cases, however, depression is diagnosed, but the actual problem is
hypothyroidism, which, when treated, will eliminate the depression.
And, most commonly, depression can persist in people with hypothyroidism, even when the thyroid problem has been treated.
Let's take a look at these issues.

■ Depression—A Misdiagnosis of Hypothyroidism

Depression is very common in the United States. According to the
National Institute of Mental Health, depression affects approximately 18.8 million American adults, or about 9.5 percent of the
U.S. population age eighteen and older.

Some researchers estimate that as many as twenty-five million people in the United States take antidepressants to treat major depression and the less severe form of depression known as dysthymia (pronounced diss-THY-me-ah). The FDA has estimated that sales of antidepressant drugs in the United States increased from 14 million prescriptions in 1992 to 157 million in 2002.

While depression is not as common as hypothyroidism, which affects more than twenty million Americans, its symptoms can be quite similar to those of hypothyroidism, including a depressed, sad and/or anxious mood, difficulty concentrating, sleeping difficulties, fatigue, loss of energy, change in weight, and irritability. Also similar is the fact that depression is more common in women: In fact, major depression and dysthymia affect twice as many women as men.

Because doctors do not realize how prevalent hypothyroidism is, they may assume that symptoms are coming from depression rather than hypothyroidism, and diagnose depression without testing for or ruling out hypothyroidism. Some doctors and managed care systems also try to avoid testing costs, and when depression is a key symptom, will go straight to a depression diagnosis and a prescription for an antidepressant, rather than perform more costly thyroid testing.

Peg's doctors were so convinced that her health problems were due to depression that she spent five years in therapy trying to get rid of her symptoms before being diagnosed and treated for hypothyroidism:

> It's funny in a way that I allowed the voice of a doctor (or anyone else for that matter) to overpower my own . . . to make me doubt what my body has been telling me, loudly, for five years. I don't regret all the therapy I've sought out, trying in vain to get to the core of why I "made myself sick." But this wasn't in my head, and so no matter how hard I tried, it wouldn't go away.

It's clear that many doctors just don't think of hypothyroidism when faced with a patient complaining of depression, *even when other hypothyroidism symptoms are present.* So there's a definite risk of misdiagnosis.

Studies have even shown that, among patients hospitalized for depression, 15 percent of them have previously undiagnosed subclinical hypothyroidism. Tom was one of those patients. When he first started getting sick, his doctor labeled him as depressed and prescribed Prozac and Xanax. Tom ended up hospitalized for depression, until a tenacious doctor decided to test his thyroid and discovered that his symptoms—mood swings, eating problems, sleep problems, weight gain, and depression—were due to serious hypothyroidism.

Mike, whose wife, Sherry, was newly diagnosed with hypothyroidism, found out firsthand how easily doctors attribute medical problems to depression:

> They could not find any medical reason for my wife's problems, so they blamed it on psychosis. The doctor said, "You need for her to see a psychiatrist." Some of her complaints were weakness, confusion, loss of appetite, frequent bladder infections, and too many other complaints to mention. I know my wife, and I knew that she was not mentally ill. I ended up taking her home after she started on the thyroid hormone, and each day I could see improvement in her condition.

Several research studies have concluded that thyroid-function screening should be required for all patients with depression, psychosis, or organic mental disorder. Instead of ending up in mental health facilities, or on antidepressant therapy that doesn't work, patients would be tested at the onset, and many could avoid months or years of inappropriate and ineffective treatment for the wrong condition. Many doctors, however, still don't routinely test for a thyroid problem when a patient first complains of depression. Why they don't is a question that I think deserves to be answered by the medical profession.

Unfortunately, when hypothyroidism is the actual cause of depression, and a person has been misdiagnosed as depressed, prescribed antidepressants may help slightly but aren't likely to resolve the symptoms. The Thyroid Society estimates that 10 to 15 percent of patients with a diagnosis of depression may have an underlying thyroid hormone deficiency. This number may actually be higher, especially if you consider that high-normal TSH values may in fact reflect subclinical hypothyroidism for some people.

Some researchers have reported that 80 percent of the people in the United States who take antidepressants still suffer a variety of unresolved symptoms—particularly weight gain, lethargy, and loss of libido. Interestingly, these are also the very same symptoms of hypothyroidism. How many of these people are misdiagnosed and are actually suffering from hypothyroidism? It's a good question that also deserves to be answered by the medical establishment.

Christine, a woman with hypothyroidism who suffered from depression before her diagnosis, recommends that you listen to your instincts: "I probably would have committed myself to a mental institution by now if I didn't know in my heart that my depression was due to my thyroid."

While we wait for answers, in the meantime, if you or someone you know has been diagnosed with depression, insist on having a thyroid test right from the start. The good news is that, in most cases, depression and psychiatric problems caused by hypothyroidism will lessen and eventually go away with sufficient thyroid hormone replacement therapy.

■ Persistent Depression with Hypothyroidism

In my survey of thyroid patients, 63 percent described depression as a continuing problem, despite being treated by their physicians for the thyroid condition.

There is no doubt that having hypothyroidism is a key risk factor for depression. According to the Thyroid Society for Education and Research, most patients with hypothyroidism have some degree of associated depression, ranging from mild to severe. Ron Pies, M.D., a clinical professor of psychiatry at Tufts University and *Psychiatric Times* columnist, estimated that as many as 40 percent of clinically hypothyroid patients have significant depression.

Dr. Pies has speculated that there may be three reasons for the link between hypothyroidism and depression. First, a malfunctioning thyroid may actually be a marker for depression. Second, having a thyroid problem may make it easier to develop depression, or worsen the symptoms of depression. And third, depression may somehow make it easier to develop autoimmune thyroid problems leading to hypothyroidism.

Whatever the causes, for many people, the depression associated with hypothyroidism is partially or fully relieved with sufficient thyroid hormone treatment. However, even after treatment for hypothyroidism, the depression can continue in some cases. This continued depression may be a coincidence, unrelated to the hypothyroidism, it may be the body's reaction to chronic illness, or it may be an indicator that the hypothyroidism is being undertreated or not treated correctly.

If all your other hypothyroidism symptoms have been relieved by the thyroid hormone replacement, and only depression remains, then it is worthwhile to discuss treatment for depression with your doctor. However, if you still suffer depression along with continued hypothyroidism symptoms, before accepting a diagnosis of depression, you may want to be extra diligent to ensure that you are receiving optimal treatment for your underlying thyroid problem.

That may involve a dosage change, a change in brand, or specifically, the addition of T3 drugs.

I'm not saying not to pursue treatment for depression when it's needed. But make sure your thyroid problem is being treated as much as possible before letting a doctor tell you that your continued symptoms are due to depression.

Doctors in the psychopharmacological community, unlike their colleagues in endocrinology, seem to be in tune with the concerns about undertreatment in the face of normal TSH values, and the need, in some cases, for T3 drugs to help relieve depression in hypothyroid patients.

■ Depression and Autoimmune Disease

In a fascinating new study that came out of Greece, researchers reported in 2004 that depression can be linked to autoimmune thyroid disease. According to the lead author, Dr. K. N. Fountoulakis, "unipolar depression might be characterized by a 'low-thyroid function syndrome.' "

This small study involved sixty control subjects and thirty patients experiencing major depression. Among the patients with depression, twenty female and ten male, and they ranged in age from twenty-one to sixty.

None of the people studied had abnormal TSH levels or abnormalities in Free T3 or Free T4—they would be considered to have no evidence of thyroid disease by many physicians. Yet all of the depressive patients had significantly higher levels of one particular measure of thyroid function, known as thyroid-binding inhibitory immunoglobulins, than did the control subjects. And among the ten out of thirty patients who had an "atypical" form of depression, all ten were found to have significantly higher levels of thyroid microsomal antibodies—a measure of autoimmune thyroid disease—than the control subjects.

This study found that there was a relationship between good response to the treatment for depression and the level of detectably thyroid dysfunction. Those with less thyroid dysfunction had greater likelihood of a good response to treatment for depression. In addition, the atypical depressives—those who had significantly higher levels of thyroid microsomal antibodies—were found to be less responsive to treatment than the other people in this study.

Overall, the researchers concluded that the fact that depressed patients in this study had increased thyroid-binding inhibitory immunoglobulins was suggestive of some sort of underlying autoimmune process in depression, and that this was independent of the type of depression. Additionally, they found that response to treatment for depression can be predicted on the basis of certain thyroid indicators, with better responses being noted when these indices were closer to normal values.

What this study potentially tells us is there appears be a relationship between the presence of thyroid antibodies and immunological dysfunction in the thyroid that predisposes us to, or perhaps even triggers, various forms of depression.

It also reinforces the fact that measuring of the thyroid's immunological factors, including thyroid antibodies, is part of a complete thyroid evaluation, and symptoms cannot be dismissed solely on the basis of normal TSH, T4, and T3 levels.

■ Other Help for Depression

If your depression is a separate, coincidental issue, or is unrelieved even by your and your doctor's best efforts at treating the underlying hypothyroidism, then the depression itself may also need to be treated. This is not something to be embarrassed about; it's just an indication that your brain chemistry is interrelated with your endocrine system, and without balance in one, it's hard to get perfect balance in the other. Antidepressant treatments—such as conventional medications, herbal drugs, therapy, exercise, and support—can help balance that brain chemistry and relieve the depression.

Antidepressant Medication

The conventional treatment is antidepressant medication. Medications include some of the newer drugs, such as mirtazapine (Remeron), venlafaxine (Effexor), nefazodone (Serzone); and bupropion (Wellbutrin); the selective serotonin reuptake inhibitors (SSRIs), such as paroxetine (Paxil), fluoxetine (Prozac), and sertraline (Zoloft); the monoamine oxidase inhibitors (MAOIs), such as phenelzine (Nardil) and tranylcypromine (Parnate); and the older tricyclic antidepressants, such as doxepin (Adapin), amitriptyline (Elavil), desipramine (Norpramin), imipramine (Tofranil); and others. Your doctor will need to discuss the best option for you. Remember that if you take an antidepressant, it can take a few weeks, or even as much as a month or more, to start seeing the benefits. Don't give up after a week or two if you don't feel a difference. Remember that some antidepressants can become stronger or weaker in the presence of thyroid hormone, or can interfere with thyroid absorption; so discuss this with your doctor.

Even after starting thyroid hormone replacement, Terri continued to suffer various mental side effects from her hypothyroidism:

My endocrinologist did not see mental side effects as valid. I thought I was losing my mind. The only way I've managed to survive this ordeal mentally is thanks to my general practitioner, who recognized my mental state. He advised that I should take an antidepressant until my thyroid becomes completely normal. This was my lifeline. My endocrinologist never suggested this, never discussed mental side effects, and even brushed off questions I asked about them as not being scientifically proven. Thanks to the combination of treatments, especially the antidepressant, I am able to cope with the mental effects of thyroid disease.

Alternative Antidepressant Supplements

Since there are side effects associated with many antidepressants, some people try supplements. While St. John's wort (*Hypericum perforatum*) is often a popular choice, some experts believe that it can interfere with thyroid hormone replacement therapy, and so should be avoided. Other supplements used for depression include 5-HTP (5-hydroxytryptophan), an amino acid derivative and the immediate precursor to serotonin, a brain chemical responsible for feelings of well-being. Another supplement some find effective is tyrosine. Tyrosine is an amino acid that is used to create norepinephrine, a brain chemical that works as an appetite suppressant, stimulant, and antidepressant; many leading-edge researchers are proposing that depression stems directly from a deficiency of norepinephrine. Most people need two to three weeks in order to begin seeing some definite benefits. And one piece of advice: Self-treating depression with supplements isn't a good idea. If you want to experiment with St. John's wort, 5-HTP, or other supplements, do it only under the guidance of a health practitioner.

Therapy

Traditional treatment for mild and moderate cases of depression can also include psychotherapy. Counseling or therapy—even short-term—can be useful in coping with depression, particularly in learning how to prevent and deal with various sources of stress in your life, and how to cope with that stress effectively. Therapy may not cure your thyroid, but emotional stress has a tremendous impact on disease. Learning and mastering skills to cope with stress helps to ensure that the stress has the least amount of impact on your health.

Bobbi found that seeing a therapist helped her greatly:

> *I was a very negative, stressed-out, worried person before, who was always an overachiever. I was experiencing some de-*

*pression due to my health problems and my inability to work
for over a year. I'm learning not to worry so much, and to let
go of things. It has helped my health.*

Exercise

Many doctors believe that aerobic exercise is the best natural antidepressant, and recommend thirty minutes of vigorous aerobics at
least five times a week. Others have found that simply walking
briskly twenty to thirty minutes daily can have a strong antidepressant effect. However you look at it, though, exercise stimulates a variety of positive things in the brain chemistry that can help to
counteract depression, and it is therefore an essential treatment in
almost every antidepressant program.

Support and Empowerment

Sue, who is a regular participant in and trained patient facilitator
for depression support group meetings, has many excellent suggestions for those who, like her, battle depression:

- Treating myself to long, soaking baths, complete with candles
and nice music.
- Taking short walks. This I had to absolutely force myself to
do, but cannot argue with the results; I always felt better afterward.
- Joining a support group for depression, just for women, sponsored by the Mental Health Association. Check your area, if interested.
- Going into therapy—with someone who specialized in depression—to work through my "issues." I really believe this is helpful
for the future, too.
- Trying positive self-talk—it works! Bought a book by Louise
Hay, and there is really something to this ability we have of breaking cyclical negative thinking with positive reinforcement. You can
use the tiniest thing you like about yourself to your extreme advan-

tage by reminding yourself of it . . . repeatedly. Do you like your eyes? Your hair? Your compassion? Anything! The best part is you don't even have to believe that it works for it to work.

• Staying in constant touch with my family physician, in case there's a possible physical cause of the depression. Such was the case with my thyroid problem.

• Getting an advocate for myself, to deal with the endless paperwork, telephone contacts (i.e., insurance), and other details.

Finally, many people like Sue find that giving and receiving support is of tremendous value in dealing with their depression. Consider getting involved in a local support group for depression, where you can exchange support and information with others.

14

Fatigue and Other Continuing Concerns

There is always a way to go if you look for it.
—ERNEST A. FITZGERALD

Of all the persistent symptoms, fatigue is one of the most common, and most difficult to resolve. In my 2002 patient survey, almost 92 percent of the patients reported feeling fatigued and more exhausted than normal.

For many patients, including me, one noticeable sign that thyroid levels are getting too high and dosages may need to be adjusted is the onset of bone-numbing fatigue. This sign of hypothyroidism often comes on suddenly, and leaves you barely able to lift your head off the pillow in the morning. You may feel like you can't get through a day without a nap, or you sleep more than usual but still feel exhausted. This fatigue, frequently seen along with other symptoms you'll find on my Hypothyroidism Symptoms Checklist, can be a sign that your hypothyroidism is undertreated.

For some hypothyroid patients, even when treatment is considered "optimal," the exhaustion continues. I get many e-mails a week from readers who are complaining that they are just plain exhausted, despite being treated for their thyroid disease, and asking *when* will they get their energy back?

Many doctors will tell you that the fatigue will be relieved by thyroid hormone replacement, and for some people, it is. But when you're *still* exhausted after you've given enough time to getting your levels back to normal, *and* you've investigated whether you are receiving optimal treatment, then it's time to look into the first line of attack—are you getting enough sleep?

■ Are You Getting Enough Sleep?

According to a survey released from the National Sleep Foundation, one in three people in the United States sleeps for six hours or less per night, substantially less than the recommended eight hours. The average person gets seven hours of sleep a night, and 40 percent of adults say that they are so sleepy during the day that it interferes with their daily activities.

"The survey findings are a source of great concern," warns Thomas Roth, Ph.D., Health and Scientific Adviser of the National Sleep Foundation and Director of the Sleep Disorders Research Center at Henry Ford Hospital, in Detroit. According to Roth: "Most of us need eight hours of sound sleep to function at our best."

I am one of those people who does *not* do well on less than 7½ to 8 hours of sleep. But just with the general business of living (particularly with a young child) getting that much sleep is a luxury I've rarely enjoyed in many years. I keep wanting to blame my thyroid, but after a few nights when I actually get eight or more hours and feel much better and more energetic, I've realized that, to a large extent, my problem is frequently sleep deprivation, compounded by an increased general need for more sleep due to the thyroid problem, even if it is treated. So if I usually needed 7½ to 8 hours, and my thyroid disease adds a bit more of a need, let's say a half hour to an hour a night, that's 8 to 8½ hours, and if I'm getting 6 to 7 hours, then I'm chronically sleep-deprived.

In addition, there is evidence that, like people with chronic fatigue syndrome and fibromyalgia, those with hypothyroidism have some sort of dysfunction in brain chemistry that prevents them from regularly getting important stage 4 delta sleep, the deep sleep that is restorative to both energy and the immune system. During typical sleep, every ninety minutes you move from light alpha sleep (stage 1), into progressively deeper sleep, beta (stage 2), gamma (stage 3), until you reach delta sleep (stage 4), the most refreshing and restorative stage of sleep. It is during this last stage that the body recovers energy and repairs muscle tissue. Without it, you can wake feeling unrefreshed and unrested. Light alpha sleep is also known as REM (rapid eye movement) sleep, when you have dreams. Stages 2, 3, and 4 are non-REM sleep.

There are so many ways that sleep problems can manifest themselves: insomnia; difficulty in falling asleep; frequent waking; difficulty in falling asleep after waking; frequent waking to urinate; failure to reach deep, stage 4 sleep; unrefreshing sleep; sleep apnea (episodes where breathing stops longer than normal), which occurs more often in people with hypothyroidism; and bruxism (grinding of teeth).

If you don't get enough sleep, particularly stage 4 delta sleep, in addition to fatigue, a number of things happen to your immune system.

• Since 80 percent of growth hormone is produced during delta sleep, insufficient delta sleep can result in growth hormone deficiencies, which can contribute to muscular pain and degeneration, and to weight gain.

• One study showed that interrupting delta sleep for three nights in a row caused test subjects to develop fatigue, aching muscles, and trigger-point tenderness.

• Stage 4 delta sleep disruptions also cause brain fog.

Diagnosing a sleep disorder can be done through a formal sleep study. Some practitioners recommend a less expensive, simpler process—set up a video camera to tape your sleeping at night, so you and your practitioner can observe common sleep behaviors.

Sleep Remedies

If you're not getting quality sleep, you should start by practicing good sleep hygiene. This involves not using your bed as a place for work, television watching, or reading; establishing regular bedtime routines; getting enough exercise; limiting napping; avoiding stimulants before bedtime; avoiding food later in the evening; minimizing noise and light in the bedroom; and other commonsense techniques.

Ultimately, however, if you are unable to reestablish healthful sleeping patterns, you may wish to try a nonprescription sleep aid. These aids can include:

- Over-the-counter drugs, such as diphenylhydramine (Benadryl, Tylenol PM, Excedrin PM), that are not habit forming. Note that some experts feel these products do not help with deep stage 4 sleep.
- Melatonin is particularly helpful if your body clock is off-kilter and you find yourself unable to go to sleep until early in the morning. Take 1 to 3 mg if you are under the age of fifty, up to 6 mg if over fifty (taken at bedtime, but if you wake up groggy, it may be too much, cut the dose back).
- Magnesium and/or calcium at night also can help with sleep.
- Doxylamine (Unisom for Sleep): 25 mg at night (an antihistamine).
- 5-HTP (5-Hydroxytryptophan): 100 to 400 mg at night. Naturally stimulates serotonin.

Some of the herbs that have been reported to help with sleep include valerian root, passionflower, and kava kava. One herbal sleep formula I particularly like was formulated by CFS/fibromyalgia practitioner Jacob Teitelbaum, M.D. His "Revitalizing Sleep Formula" contains the exact combination of ingredients he has found most effective in facilitating stage 4 sleep without morning grogginess. The supplement is available at most health food and vitamin stores, and includes valerian (*Valeriana officinalis*) root extract; passionflower (*Passiflora incarnata*) leaf flower extract; 1-theanine; hops (*humulus lupulus*) flower extract; wild lettuce (*Lactuca virosa*) leaf extract; and Jamaica dogwood (*Piscidia piscipula*) root extract.

Prescription sleep aids may also be appropriate for debilitating fatigue. These can include:

• Tricyclic Antidepressants—Antidepressants can help with pain relief and increasing serotonin levels, both functions that can facilitate improved sleep. Frequently prescribed for sleep disturbances are low-dose tricyclic antidepressants, including doxepin (Adapin, Sinequan), amitriptyline (Elavil, Etrafon, Limbitrol, Triavil), desipramine (Norpramin), and nortriptyline (Pamelor). These drugs may provide long-term benefit for improving sleep.

• Other Antidepressants—Other antidepressants that may be prescribed include sertraline (Zoloft), venlafaxine (Effexor), fluvoxamine (Luvox), fluoxetine (Prozac) paroxetine (Paxil), and Remeron (mirtazapine). Typically, it can take six weeks of using the antidepressant before it has any impact on sleep.

• Trazodone (brand name: Desyrel) is a frequently prescribed antidepressant for sleep problems, aiding with stages 3 and 4 sleep. It's particularly helpful for those who wake up every hour, or wake up and then can't go back to sleep.

• Anti-anxiety/Muscle Relaxants/Benzodiazepines—These are drugs that can help improve sleep, relax muscles, and modulate brain and brain receptor sensitivity. The most frequently recommended drug is clonazepam (Klonopin), a long-acting benzodiazepine. Others include lorazepam (Ativan) and alprazolam (Xanax). Habit-forming potential may be a concern with these drugs.

• Hypnotics—The hypnotic drugs include zolpidem (Ambien), triazolam (Halcion), temazepam (Restoril), flurazepam (Dalmane), quazepam (Doral), estazolam (ProSom). Habit-forming potential may be a concern with these drugs. The drug zaleplon (Sonata) is considered non-habit forming and may be a better option than the potentially habit-forming hypnotics.

Dr. Teitelbaum believes that you can and should, under the careful direction of your practitioner, mix as many prescription and herbal treatments as you need until you are getting seven to eight hours of sleep without waking, and are waking up refreshed.

Natural Energy Boosters

In addition to lack of sleep, if you are suffering from flagging energy, you need to make sure that you are getting enough B vitamins. Vitamin B_{12} in particular is one that is essential for energy. To ensure you're getting enough B vitamins, consider taking a B-complex, plus a separate sublingual B_{12}.

Another type of supplement useful for fatigue derives from substances that the body naturally produces for energy production. Supplements in this category include: co-enzyme Q10, also known as CoQ10, which supplies energy to muscles; l-carnitine; NADH (nicotinamide adenine Dinucleotide), which helps cells convert food into energy; and DHEA (but be sure to be tested by your practitioner before you start this hormone).

Some people have found that the South American medicinal plant maca can help with energy.

In terms of herbal remedies, while you should avoid ephedra and ma huang stimulants, you can ask your practitioner about schizandra—a Chinese herb that is used for fatigue. Ginseng, especially Siberian ginseng, as well as the supplement rhodiola, are popular for energy. Before trying any herbs, supplements, or vitamins, you should of course consult with your practitioner to ensure they are safe for you. Ginseng, for example, is not recommended for someone with high blood pressure, and many herbs and supplements are not recommended during pregnancy.

I had the opportunity to interview herbal and aromatherapy expert Mindy Green, of the Herbal Research Foundation. I asked her what, as a person with hypothyroidism, I should reach for when I'm just completely out of steam, and am ready for a giant double espresso in order to make it through the day. Mindy said, unquestionably, maté tea. Maté, pronounced, MAH-tay, is an herbal tea native to South America. Maté is considered far more nutritious than black tea or coffee, and though it also has some caffeine, its effects are described as energizing, rather than making people jittery. On the scale of bad to good, coffee should be your last choice, followed by black tea, then green tea, with maté being the best option. I have to say, maté is quite good, and it does energize you without a caffeine buzz.

Mindy Green also has some interesting recommendations about the use of herbs for energy, stimulation, or adrenal support:

> We live in a society that runs on stimulation—whether it's coffee, or violence on television—things that make us live on that edge. So while there are some excellent herbs and essential oils for adrenal support, people need to take care not to try these products along with other stimulants. When you're trying to tone your adrenals, you don't want to drink caffeine, or watch horror movies or violent news stories, for example. Instead of the stimulating effect of aerobics, do something more calming, like yoga or Tai Chi. It's almost as if you need to train your body to run more on internal energy than outside energy and stimulation.

The way Mindy describes it, taking excessive stimulants when your endocrine or adrenal systems are depleted is "like kicking a dead horse."

Other Energy Tips

To help keep your metabolism stoked, and energy high, here are some other tips:

- Make sure you eat breakfast. If you don't eat breakfast, you slow down your metabolism and send the body into "hoard mode," thinking it's starving because you're going for a long period of time frequently eight to ten hours or more, without food.
- Don't starve. Dropping your calorie intake below 1,000 calories a day will signal to your body that you are in starvation mode, and will slow down your metabolism and reduce your energy.
- Get enough exercise. As much as you can is really help for your energy, and if you do it in the morning, you're likely to raise your metabolism all day.
- Water, water, water!! You've heard it before, but drink those eight 8-ounce glasses of water every day. Dehydration causes fatigue.

Is It Chronic Fatigue Syndrome?

There is a higher incidence of chronic fatigue syndrome (CFS) among people with hypothyroidism, and the reverse is also true. To be diagnosed with CFS, however, you must have *extreme* fatigue that is medically unexplained; lasts at least six months; is not the result of ongoing exertion; is not substantially relieved by rest; and causes a substantial reduction in activity levels. In addition to extreme fatigue, for a diagnosis of CFS, there must also be four or more of the following symptoms:

- Substantially impaired memory/concentration
- Sore throat
- Tender neck or armpit lymph nodes
- Muscle pain
- Headaches of a new type, pattern, or severity

- Unrefreshing sleep
- Relapse of symptoms after exercise (also known as postexertional malaise) that lasts more than twenty-four hours
- Pain in multiple joints without joint swelling or redness

If you meet these criteria it is essential that you pursue treatment specifically for your CFS. Many of the leading-edge integrative physicians know how to address the entire picture of health imbalances and symptoms represented by CFS in combination with hypothyroidism. Your first step should be to read my book *Living Well with Chronic Fatigue Syndrome and Fibromyalgia*, and visit my associated Web site, http://www.cfsfibromyalgia, for more information and help in getting diagnosed and treated.

■ Muscle/Joint Pain

Another common symptom of people with hypothyroidism is muscle- or joint-related pain.

Hypothyroidism is known to cause what are called "myopathies"—the medical term for diseases that affect skeletal muscle. Skeletal muscles are the muscles that are connected to your bones. An example of a skeletal muscle is the biceps in your upper arm or the quadriceps in your thigh. Myopathies most often are seen in what are known as the "proximal muscles." These are the muscles, such as in the thigh and shoulder areas, that are closest to the center of the body. In myopathies caused by inflammation or metabolic conditions, such as hypothyroidism or autoimmune thyroid disease, white blood cells may attack parts of the muscle and the surrounding blood vessels, or abnormal levels of certain biochemical substances may end up accumulating in your muscles, leading to weakness or pain.

Hypothyroidism can create a variety of muscle-and joint-related symptoms. Most commonly, these symptoms are due to swelling of the muscles, or to swelling that is pressing on the nerves. Various problems include:

- General muscular weakness and pain, including cramps; and stiffness
- General joint pain, achiness, stiffness, known as "arthropathy"
- Tendonitis in the arms and legs
- Carpal tunnel syndrome—which involves pain, tingling, weakness, aching or numbness in the wrist, fingers, or forearm. It is due to swelling of membranes that compress a nerve in the forearm.
- Tarsal tunnel syndrome—similar to carpal tunnel syndrome, with pain, tingling, burning, and other discomfort in the arch of your foot, the bottom of the foot, possibly extending into the toes
- Plantar fasciitis—pain in the ball or arch of the foot, usually worse in the morning

When muscle and joint pain does not go away with proper thyroid treatment, it's time to consider several important options.

Is your thyroid treatment optimized in terms of TSH, T4, T3, Free T4, Free T3 levels, and the addition of T3, or natural thyroid, if needed? Sometimes, a change of brand, or the addition of T3, or a switch to natural thyroid can relieve this stubborn treatment.

Also, if you are receiving optimal thyroid treatment, and still suffering joint and muscle problems, should you get a referral to a rheumatologist for further evaluation and possible treatment? A trained rheumatologist can provide a more thorough evaluation for arthritis and rheumatoid arthritis. Rheumatologists are experts in joint and muscle problems; they treat arthritis, some autoimmune conditions, various musculoskeletal pain disorders, fibromyalgia, and tendonitis. To find a rheumatologist in your area, check the American College of Rheumatology's Doctor Directory.

■ Antibiotic Therapy

Holistic physician David Brownstein, M.D., sees many patients with thyroid disorders who complain of soreness and swelling in their joints. In his book *Overcoming Arthritis*, he describes how certain infections may be at the root of both autoimmune diseases—including Hashimoto's disease and Graves' disease—and various joint and muscle pain and disorders:

> My experience has shown that many individuals suffering from autoimmune illnesses often have an underlying infectious component. I began testing my patients for bacterial infections 8 years ago, and I discovered that, in the case of thyroid patients (i.e., those with Graves', Hashimoto's or thyroiditis), the infection was located in the thyroid gland.
>
> In my experience, approximately 70% of those with autoimmune thyroid disorders (i.e., Graves', Hashimoto's thyroiditis) have signs of an infection. This made perfect sense to me. Perhaps these individuals had a bacterial infection (e.g., Mycoplasma) that the body was not able to clear. Mycoplasmas are a very small bacterium that can actually get inside of the cells of the body. Because of this, the immune system cells are unable to directly attack the bacteria. In order to rid the body of the bacteria, the immune system cells will often resort to attacking the body's own tissue, which has been infected with the organism.

Dr. Brownstein uses low doses of antibiotics—often doxycycline or an antibiotic in the tetracycline family—to treat the infection. The length of treatment depends on patient response. He's had some patients who have been on treatment for years, because going off the antibiotic induces a flare-up in their symptoms.

I've been on low-dose antibiotics for a number of years. If I stop taking it, a few days later I start having a variety of aches and pains, including knee and elbow pain, carpal tunnel syndrome, forearm and shin pain, and flulike total body aches, so now I stay on it permanently. I take probiotics regularly, to ensure balance in my intestinal tract.

Is It Fibromyalgia?

If you are hypothyroid, you are at higher risk for developing fibromyalgia (pronounced fy-bro-my-Al-ja). This common and perplexing chronic condition is characterized by widespread and often severe musculoskeletal pain, fatigue, and multiple tender points. A number of leading-edge practitioners are finding high rates of hypothyroidism in their fibromyalgia patients. Some practitioners, such as Dr. John Lowe, actually believe that fibromyalgia is a manifestation of hypothyroidism.

Doctors typically use the American College of Rheumatology's 1990 criteria for classifying fibromyalgia. According to these criteria, a person is considered to have fibromyalgia if he or she has widespread pain for at least three months in combination with tenderness in at least eleven of eighteen specific tender point sites.

Pain is considered widespread when it occurs in both the left side of the body and the right side, and both above and below the waist. Cervical spine, anterior chest, thoracic spine, or low-back pain must also be present.

The "tender points" are precise areas of the body which, when pressed, generate pain. The eighteen tender point sites include:

1. The area where neck muscles attach to base of skull, left and right sides (Occiput)
2. Midway between neck and shoulder, left and right sides (Trapezius)
3. Muscles over left and right upper inner shoulder blade, left and right sides (Supraspinatus)
4. Two centimeters below side bone at elbow of left and right arms (Lateral epicondyle)

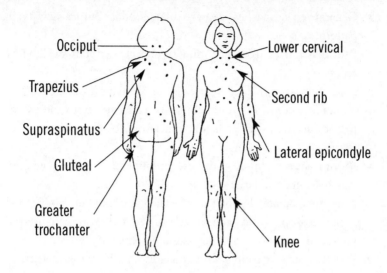

Occiput — Lower cervical

Trapezius — Second rib

Supraspinatus — Lateral epicondyle

Gluteal —

Greater trochanter — Knee

5. Left and right upper outer buttocks (Gluteal)
6. Left and right hip bones (Greater trochanter)
7. Just above left and right knees on inside
8. Lower neck in front, left and right sides (Low cervical)
9. Edge of upper breastbone, left and right sides (Second rib)

To be considered painful, pressure on the tender point must generate actual pain, not just tenderness.

Other common symptoms include:

- Prolonged fatigue after physical activity, known as a "postexertional malaise," usually lasting more than twenty-four hours
- Fatigue with or after normal activity, or fatigue after sleep (what's known as "unrefreshing" sleep)
- Mild, low-grade fever or chills
- Dry, inflamed sore throat
- Swollen or tender lymph nodes in neck or armpits
- General muscle weakness and pain

- Generalized headaches, in particular, headaches of a new type, pattern, or severity
- Pain that moves from one joint to another without swelling or redness
- Forgetfulness, difficulty remembering or saying words, excessive irritability, confusion, or inability to concentrate, to the extent that it interferes with your job, education, social, or personal activities
- More frequent illness, with susceptibility to infections, viruses, or worsening of allergies
- Neurally mediated hypotension—when you stand up, your blood pressure drops, which can make you feel faint, dizzy, nauseous; your heart rate drops and you can even pass out
- Reactivity to environmental exposures (i.e., increased sensitivity to chemicals, perfumes, odors, bug sprays, etc.)
- Night sweats
- Hypersensitivity to temperatures, sounds, sensations, confusion
- Gastrointestinal problems, such as diarrhea, constipation, bloating
- Feeling cold

If you meet these criteria, it is essential that you pursue treatment specifically for your fibromyalgia. Your first step should be to read my book *Living Well with Chronic Fatigue Syndrome and Fibromyalgia*, and visit my associated Web site, http://www.cfsfibro myalgia, for more information and help in getting diagnosed and treated.

■ Hair Loss

Hair can be considered a barometer of health because hair cells are some of the fastest growing in the body. When the body is in crisis, the hair cells can shut down to redirect energy elsewhere. The types of situations that can cause hair loss include hormonal changes, poor diet and nutritional deficiencies, a variety of medications, surgery, and many medical conditions, but noticeably, thyroid disease.

Many people notice rapid hair loss as a symptom of hypothyroidism. Some people actually say this is the worst symptom of their thyroid problem—this thinning hair, large amounts of it falling out in the shower or sink, often accompanied by changes in the hair's texture, making it dry, coarse, or easily tangled. Interestingly, some people have actually written to tell me that their thyroid problem was initially "diagnosed" by their hairdresser, who noticed the change!

It's important to understand that there are three common types of hair loss:

• General shedding is hair lost throughout the head. You'll often notice more hair in drains and in the shower, in hairbrushes, and when you brush your hair, but there are no specific patches of loss or even baldness. Typically, with hypothyroidism prior to treatment, this is the most common form of hair loss. It can occasionally continue for some people after hypothyroidism treatment, and particularly when taking levothyroxine drugs like Synthroid.

• A second type of hair loss is more commonly associated with fungal infection or autoimmune alopecia, and involves circular patches of hair loss, in some cases, complete loss of hair in these small patches. These sorts of hair-loss problems need to be evaluated by a dermatologist. Autoimmune alopecia is more common in patients who have autoimmune thyroid disease.

• A third type of hair loss is male pattern hair loss—men are most susceptible, but women can get it, too. Male pattern hair loss is concentrated on the temples and top of the head. It's caused when an enzyme starts to convert the hormone testosterone on the scalp to its less useful version, dihydrotestosterone (DHT). This makes hair follicles shrink, and then they disappear. This conversion of testosterone to dihydrotestosterone seems to be sped up in some patients with hypothyroidism, and may be the cause of hair loss that continues for thyroid patients, despite sufficient thyroid treatment. Normally, hair grows about a half-inch a month for about three years, and then it goes into a resting period. One in ten hairs is in a resting period at any one time, and after about three months a new hair pushes the old one out. When more hairs go into a resting period, or the conversion process speeds up, the balance becomes disrupted and hair loss occurs.

If you're experiencing hair loss and are just starting treatment for hypothyroidism, it's likely that the loss will slow down, and eventually stop, once hormone levels are stabilized and in the normal range. This may take a few months, however. But rest assured, I've had many thousands of e-mails from people, and have yet to hear from anyone who lost all his or her hair, or became bald, due to thyroid disease. However, people—including myself—have experienced significant loss of hair volume. In my case, I'd guess at one point, I lost almost half my hair. I had long, thick hair, and it got much thinner for a while.

If you continue to lose hair, you need to make sure that it's not your particular type of thyroid hormone replacement. Prolonged or excessive hair loss *is* a side effect of Synthroid for some people. Note: Many doctors do *not* know this, even though it is a stated side effect in the Synthroid patient literature, so don't be surprised if your doctor is not aware of this.

You also need to make sure you're getting optimal treatment, in terms of TSH level, other thyroid levels, and the need for additional T3. In my case, I have far fewer hair problems when I am taking a T4/T3 drug—like Thyrolar or Armour Thyroid—than levothyroxine.

When I have had major bouts of hair loss (despite low-normal TSH and being on a T4/T3 drug), I have taken the advice of several noted thyroid experts. In his book *Solved: The Riddle of Illness*, Stephen Langer, M.D., points to the fact that symptoms of essential fatty acid insufficiency are very similar to hypothyroidism, and recommends evening primrose oil (EPO)—an excellent source of essential fatty acids—as helpful for people with hypothyroidism. The usefulness of evening primrose oil, particularly in dealing with the issues of excess hair loss with hypothyroidism, was also reinforced by endocrinologist Kenneth Blanchard. According to Dr. Blanchard:

> For hair loss, I routinely recommend multiple vitamins, and especially evening primrose oil. If there's any sex pattern to it—if a woman is losing hair in partly a male pattern— then, the problem is, there is excessive conversion of testosterone to dihydrotestosterone at the level of the hair follicle. Evening primrose oil is an inhibitor of that conversion. So almost anybody with hair loss probably will benefit from evening primrose oil.

As someone who has had a few periods of extensive hair loss since I became hypothyroid, I can vouch for the fact that taking EPO was the only thing that calmed it down. It not only slowed, then stopped my hair loss over about two months, but new hair grew back, and it was no longer strawlike, dry, and easily knotted. When I take EPO, I usually take 500 mg twice a day.

Look at Other Alternatives

In one study, Dr. Hugh Rushton, a professor at Portsmouth University, found that 90 percent of women with thinning hair were deficient in iron and the amino acid lysine. Lysine is the most difficult amino acid to get enough of via diet. Lysine helps transport iron, which is the most important element in the body and essential for many metabolic processes. When lysine and iron levels are low, the body probably switches some hair follicles off to increase levels elsewhere. Meat, fish, and eggs are the only food sources of lysine. There are also supplements that contain lysine.

Some other natural ways to deal with hair loss include arginine, cysteine, green tea, polysorbate 80, progesterone, saw palmetto, trichosaccaride, vitamin B_6, and zinc.

■ Prescription Treatments

A dermatologist can work with you on drug treatments, including scalp injections, drugs like Rogaine (minoxidil), and Propecia, and other treatments that can help non-thyroid–related hair loss.

■ Heart Palpitations

Palpitations can be a common feature of thyroiditis attacks. According to Stephen Langer, M.D.:

> *What happens with Hashimoto's patients having thyroiditis attacks is that many wind up in the emergency room seeing cardiologists. It happens a few times and then they're written off as psychiatric cranks. They end up with large doses of anti-anxiety medications or antidepressants.*

Frequently, when not misdiagnosed as a heart problem, anxiety, or depression, palpitations may be misinterpreted as a sign that a patient is getting too much thyroid hormone. But when medical evaluation rules out hyperthyroidism that is due to too much thyroid medication, mitral valve problems, or other cardiac abnormalities, Dr. Langer has found that nutritional deficiencies may be to blame—in particular, deficiencies of calcium, magnesium or vitamin D. Says Dr. Langer:

> *There's compelling evidence coming to the surface that Vitamin D is not only a vitamin but a hormone. . . . the recommended daily allowance for Vitamin D is 400 IU, but scientists doing studies actually believe that people who do not get regular exposure to sunshine should be getting 2000–4000 Vitamin D. The Vitamin D also has profound effects on absorption of calcium and magnesium.*

Additionally, many thyroid patients have mitral valve prolapse (MVP), a defect in the heart valve that causes palpitations. An evaluation by your physician or cardiologist can diagnose MVP. If diagnosed, beta-blockers like Atenolol can help with symptoms. More severe cases of MVP may require antibiotic treatment before any dental work or surgical procedures, to help prevent infection.

■ Low Libido/Sex Drive

According to a *Journal of the American Medical Association (JAMA)* study reported on in February 1999, about 43 percent of women and 31 percent of men suffer sexual inadequacy for one reason or another. The reasons cited included low desire, performance anxiety, premature ejaculation and/or pain during intercourse. Interestingly, this finding is thought to actually underestimate the real level of sexual dysfunction in the United States.

While the study didn't look at the specific physical causes of sexual dysfunction, the research indicated that many of the sexual concerns were likely treatable, as they are due to physical and health issues. These health concerns can include common hormonal imbalances, such as hypothyroidism.

In my quality-of-life survey, 58 percent of respondents reported having no sex drive or a reduced sex drive. Low sex drive is a common—but not often talked about—symptom of hypothyroidism. It is also a symptom that for everyone, unfortunately, does *not* disappear, despite what doctors deem adequate treatment. Many people—women in particular—still complain of a lack of sexual desire even after their doctors consider the thyroid problem has been sufficiently treated.

If you suffer from sexual dysfunction, first, you need to be sure that you are getting optimal thyroid treatment—including testing for TSH and T4/T3 levels, and possible supplemental T3 or natural thyroid.

You also need to have your other hormones—not just thyroid—evaluated. Men should have testosterone, DHEA, and other androgen levels checked whenever there is any reduction in sex drive. Women should have a full hormonal profile evaluated, including estrogen levels, testosterone, and progesterone, plus DHEA. In women, adrenal function should also be checked, particularly if the testosterone levels turn out to be low. Addressing imbalances in these hormones can sometimes restore sex drive to normal. For men testosterone can be a tremendous aid in restoring lost libido. Testosterone is available in pill form (e.g., Android, Virilon, Testred, Oreton), as a transdermal patch (Testoderm, Androderm), by injection, and sometimes as transdermal pellets implanted under the skin. Some women can benefit from testosterone. Doctors frequently will provide testosterone in pill form to women, or as testosterone propionate cream. Supplementation with estrogen or progesterone can sometimes help. Ask your doctor about estradiol gel or patches, and natural progesterone supplements, rather than the conjugated estrogens that have caused so much controversy. Be careful, however, about soy-based supplements and food products that are supposed to act "like" estrogen to deal with menopausal symptoms. Many of these products contain levels of soy isoflavones that can worsen hypothyroidism in some women.

Low sex drive may be a result of other nonthyroid health conditions. Diabetes and hypertension/high blood pressure can cause low sex drive in both women and men. You should also ask your doctor to discuss the diagnosable symptoms of depression with you, so you can assess whether or not you are depressed. You should also discuss other prescription drugs you are taking, because some antidepressants, tranquilizers, and antihypertensives—as well as many illegal drugs such as cocaine and marijuana—can reduce sex drive.

Exercise improves blood flow to all body parts. Research has found that people who exercise regularly have higher levels of desire, greater sexual confidence and frequency, and an enhanced ability to be aroused and achieve orgasm—no matter what their age.

The best type of exercise is aerobic exercise because it can trigger the release of endorphins, chemicals in the brain that create a feeling of well-being.

When there are other psychological and self-esteem issues that are contributing to lower libido, therapy can sometimes help.

Drugs and Supplements

For men, the drugs Viagra and Cialis may help with both desire and performance, when there is sexual dysfunction. For women, more research is needed into prescription drugs that will help with desire.

Some herbal and natural supplements are considered helpful for low sex drive. But note: Supplements can have various—and sometimes serious—side effects, so you shouldn't self-treat . . . talk to your practitioner regarding these products. Some supplements that may help with libido include:

- Arginine—an amino acid, for both men and women
- Ashwaganda—an Indian Ayurvedic herb, typically recommended for men
- Asian ginseng (panax)—can help increase sexual energy
- Avena-sativa/oat extract—this supplement (main brand is Vigorex) reportedly does help with sex drive.
- Damiana—an aphrodisiac herb from Mexico, thought to stimulate production of testosterone. Considered most effective in women.
- DHEA (dehydroepiandrosterone)—a precursor hormone that converts to testosterone in your body.
- Ginkgo biloba—an herb that can improves sexual function in men
- Horny goat weed—used by Chinese herbalists to improve sexual functions in both men and women
- Maca—a South American herbal remedy that can help women with libido and fertility

- Kava kava—an herb most known for use in relaxation, but can also be useful as an aphrodisiac for women
- Yohimbe—an African herb that can be a very potent sex enhancer for men
- Zinc—low levels of zinc have been associated with low sex drive in women and men.

■ Thyroid Inflammation/Thyroiditis

People with hypothyroidism are more susceptible to thyroiditis attacks. Dr. Stephen Langer has referred to thyroiditis as being like an "arthritis of the thyroid." He explains that just as arthritis attacks the joints with pain and inflammation, thyroiditis can mean pain and inflammation in the thyroid for some sufferers.

During a thyroiditis attack, common symptoms you might experience are anxiety, panic attacks, heart palpitations, swelling in the thyroid area, problems swallowing and, frequently, problems sleeping.

"Thyroiditis attacks classically happen in the middle of the night," says Dr. Langer, which can be particularly troublesome in terms of your ability to sleep.

Dr. Langer suggests taking some calcium/magnesium, which are nutrients that have a sedative effect, along with a pain reliever to relieve inflammation—buffered aspirin or ibuprofen—before you go to bed. He has found that this helps about two-thirds of his patients suffering from nighttime thyroiditis symptoms.

Reducing swelling is a key aspect of dealing with thyroiditis attacks, according to Dr. Langer:

> Just as with arthritis, an anti-inflammatory pain reliever doesn't cure the problem, but it temporarily ameliorates the symptoms.

■ Perimenopause and Menopause

Perimenopause is the time frame, sometimes taking place over many years, during which the hormone levels decline and change prior to cessation of periods, causing a variety of symptoms and erratic menstrual periods. Menopause is the point when your ovaries no longer release eggs, and hormones are no longer are capable of producing a menstrual cycle. To be officially considered menopause, the menstrual period should have stopped for a year. Menopause typically occurs as early as the mid-forties up to the late fifties in women. Often, the menopausal history of a woman's mother is a good gauge as to when a daughter can expect menopause. In some women, perimenopause actually begins as early as the mid- to late thirties.

Some women go through perimenopause and menopause with few symptoms. Others experience a variety of worsening symptoms, which can range from heavy bleeding cycles, short cycles, and headaches during perimenopause, and mood swings, depression, anxiety, food cravings, weight gain, growth of fibroids, muscle and joint pain, palpitations. Menopause educator Pat Rackowski describes it as being like "permanent PMS."

Does Hypothyroidism Worsen Perimenopause and Menopause?

Some experts, including Drs. Richard and Karilee Shames, believe there is a significant relationship between hypothyroidism and increased menopause difficulties. Say the Shameses:

> Low thyroid is often the ignored factor in far too many women who are simply treated with estrogen and/or progesterone. Despite increased awareness in the medical community about the issues and interventions surrounding menopause, a disturbing number of women still suffer menopause difficulties. This underlying problem is commonly

coexistent with hypothyroidism. Not only does low thyroid become more common as women mature, but in addition, menopause and perimenopause are transition situations which require more than the usual amount of thyroid hormone.

Hypothyroidism symptoms can also be confused with menopausal symptoms. Say the Shameses:

> *The symptoms of hot flashes, insomnia, irritability, palpitations, and the annoying "fuzzy thinking" so common in menopause can sometimes be the result of Hashimoto's thyroiditis, the most common cause of hypothyroidism. But the real complexity comes when actual symptoms of menopause are simply magnified and exaggerated because of the low thyroid situation that is now coexistent with menopause. As many thyroid sufferers are aware, low thyroid makes any illness worse. And while menopause is not an illness, it can certainly begin to feel that way when symptoms of low thyroid exacerbate the already annoying laundry list of female hormonal symptoms.*

The Issue of Estrogen Dominance

Dr. Sherrill Sellman is a psychotherapist, naturopath, health researcher, and writer. She is the author of *The Hormone Heresy: What Women MUST Know About Their Hormones.* According to Dr. Sellman, the thyroid is a major player when it comes to hormonal health, because it stimulates and synchronizes all metabolic cellular functions, and is required for a most basic process: converting cholesterol into the steroid hormones pregnenolone, progesterone, and DHEA. Progesterone and DHEA are then converted into estrogen, testosterone, and cortisol.

Sellman's theory is that nature did not build a design fault into women's bodies, causing their health to deteriorate when they arrive at perimenopause or menopause. According to Sellman:

Menopause is not a downhill slide nor an "estrogen deficiency disease" as the medical world likes to call it. At menopause there is an adjustment in estrogen levels reducing the output by the ovaries by about 40–60 percent. Just low enough so that the menopausal woman won't be maturing eggs. Nature has also provided a back-up system in the estrogen department—both the fat cells and the adrenals produce estrogen. If we have any "meat on our bones," menopausal women are generally making plenty of estrogen, even if they have had a full hysterectomy! The World Health Organization has actually found that an overweight post menopausal woman has more estrogen circulating in her body than a skinny pre-menopausal woman!! Western women now have some of the highest estrogen levels ever recorded in history. In fact, we are literally swimming in a sea of estrogen exposure due medication such as the Pill and HRT, the estrogen mimics found in pesticides, herbicides, and plastics, as well as the hormones injected into feed lot cattle and farmed fish (estrogen accelerates growth and increases weight gain in animals . . . and in women, too!).

However, with menopause there is a cessation of ovulation. When we ovulate, the site, known as a follicle, from which an egg bursts forth turns into an endocrine gland that makes progesterone. When there's no ovulation, the primary supply of progesterone is not available. Thus, there is a precipitous fall in progesterone levels at menopause. However, once again, nature's backup system makes progesterone from the adrenals. When this essential and delicate balance between estrogen and progesterone is altered, causing low progesterone levels and high estrogen levels—the resulting imbal-

ance is called estrogen dominance. When estrogen is in excess, it is toxic to the body.

Symptoms of estrogen dominance can include swollen breasts, bloating, fluid retention, weight gain, food cravings, mood swings, cyclical migraine headaches, lack of sexual desire, short cycles, heavy bleeding cycles, fibroids, high blood pressure, fatigue, aging skin, thinning hair, muscle aches and pains, memory fogginess, endometriosis, depression, fibrocystic breasts, and miscarriage.

According to Dr. Sellman, when women are suffering from perimenopausal and menopausal symptoms, and in particular, when thyroid patients experience these symptoms, the problem is far more likely to be estrogen dominance. Says Sellman:

> *For the past 40 years, women have been told that menopause is a time when the ovaries fail and cease to produce estrogen, thus creating the myth of the estrogen deficient woman. It also justifies the rationale for the multi-billion dollar industry that was supplying estrogen (along with progestins such as Provera) to women not only for the relief of hot flashes and vaginal dryness but also as an anti-aging drug that was supposed to prevent skin from wrinkling, bones from disintegrating and hearts from failing, etc. It also found its way as treatment for the myriad of symptoms plaguing perimenopausal women to help boost their supposedly flagging estrogen levels. The Pill has also become a popular treatment for the perimenopausal woman.*

In perimenopause, according to Dr. Sellman, estrogen is not necessarily declining, rather, it's "doing its final hurrah" trying to stir the ovaries into action. Says Sellman:

> *Perimenopause is really a time of high but fluctuating estrogen levels along with low progesterone (perimenopausal*

women are irregular in their ovulation). High estrogen levels and low progesterone production causes an estrogen domi- nant condition. Thus, it is totally inappropriate and danger- ous to give the Pill or HRT to perimenopausal women since they already have high estrogen levels circulating through their body. Adding even more estrogen can cause many un- comfortable side-effects as well as serious health risks.

Thyroid patients are also at higher risk from estrogen domi- nance, and a worsening of symptoms, because estrogen binds to thyroid hormone, making it inactive, contributing to or worsening hypothyroidism.

Many practitioners believe that natural progesterone treatment is the optimal treatment for estrogen dominance, and that using this treatment may even help improve thyroid function. Dr. Sellman rec- ommends a good-quality natural progesterone cream.

Dr. Carol Roberts finds natural progesterone useful in her prac- tice. Says Roberts:

In almost every case of a peri- or postmenopausal woman with thyroid trouble, I will use natural progesterone to help the thyroid hormone work. Progesterone is needed to acti- vate thyroid receptors in the cell nucleus. Sometimes proges- terone alone will do the job, if the thyroid is still producing hormone.

Solutions

If you are a woman with hypothyroidism who is also going through perimenopause or menopause, it's essential that you have more frequent evaluation of your thyroid function. According to the Shameses, many women with previously normal thyroid levels will see a rise in TSH well before the rise in FSH (follicle-stimulating hormone), which is the test that usually confirms the metabolic on- set of menopause.

You may need adjustments in your thyroid medication in order to offset the hormonal changes taking place in your body.

And optimal thyroid function is essential, because, say the Shameses:

> Frequently, the underlying hypothyroidism is such a controlling factor that simply correcting it, sometimes even with homeopathic thyroid or over the counter thyroid glandular, returns the whole system to fairly normal function. Menopause continues, but it is a more mild, gradual, and comfortable process. This is because thyroid is the energy throttle for the whole body, and especially the gas pedal for all of one's coping mechanisms. Once you have the energy to go through the change more gracefully, life can become more normal.

Herbs and Supplements

A variety of vitamins and herbs may help deal with the rebalancing of hormones and perimenopausal and menopausal symptoms. Some of the most effective alternatives include Royal Maca (organic, provided by Whole World Botanicals), vitamin E capsules, vitamin E suppositories; Royal Jelly, folic acid with a B-complex, chaste tree berry (Vitex), dong quai, and black cohosh.

What About Estrogen?

While estrogen replacement therapy has been so discredited in recent years that most people are afraid of these drugs, it's important to note that all of the studies conducted used conjugated estrogens, the drug harvested from the urine of pregnant mares that was made into the formerly popular drug Premarin (*PRegnant MARe's urINe*), along with progestins. Neither falls into the category of bioidentical hormones used at small physiological replacement doses that are considered to be a safer, more effective alternative by many leading-edge experts.

If a woman is truly estrogen-deficient, then Dr. Sellman believes that estriol may be appropriate. Estriol, a bioidentical hormone, is considered the safest of all the estrogens. It is the dominant form of estrogen made during pregnancy. It is often recommended for vaginal dryness and urinary problems. Estriol, in fact, governs the harmonious workings and the suppleness of the lower third of the urethra, located in the vagina. Estriol comes in various forms, including pills, creams, and even a low-dose patch, and it's important to remember that you may only need to supplement with estrogen a few days each month.

Remember, if you do take estrogen or any hormone-balancing supplements, that you should have your thyroid tested to ensure that you don't need a thyroid drug dosage adjustment. Thyroid drug effectiveness and absorption can be affected by estrogen and estrogenlike drugs.

■ Do You Have Another Autoimmune Disease?

The thyroid conditions Hashimoto's disease and Graves' disease are two of the most common autoimmune diseases, and are the most common causes of hypothyroidism. "Autoimmune disease" refers to a category of more than eighty chronic illnesses, each very different in nature, that can affect everything from the endocrine glands—like the thyroid—to organs like the kidneys, to the digestive system. Underlying all autoimmune conditions is the concept of autoimmunity.

As late as forty years ago, medical experts believed that the immune system could only be directed against foreign invaders, and that the immune system could always distinguish our own organs and tissues, from outside "invaders" like bacteria and viruses. But researchers discovered that the immune system, which normally defends only against invaders, can become confused and attack the "self," targeting the cells, tissues, or organs of our own bodies. This concept, autoimmunity, may be taken for granted now, but it was a groundbreaking discovery at the time.

In autoimmunity the immune system's ability to recognize what's foreign and what's part of your own body breaks down in some way. Thinking that cells or tissues or organs are foreign invaders, the immune system moves into action to be rid of the invader, starting by the manufacture of antibodies—known as autoantibodies—and generation of T-cells that have as their mission the destruction of the "invader."

In some cases, damage to tissues by the immune system may be permanent, as with destruction of the insulin-producing cells of the pancreas in type 1 diabetes. While some conditions are progressive, some autoimmune diseases go into remission or even disappear. This happens, for example, in a small percentage of Graves' disease cases, or in periods of remission—sometimes months or years—in multiple sclerosis. And the hair-loss condition alopecia areata frequently resolves itself after time with no treatment.

Autoimmune diseases also target different parts of the body. For example, the autoimmune reaction targets the brain in multiple sclerosis, the intestinal and bowel systems in Crohn's disease and irritable bowel syndrome, and the thyroid in Hashimoto's and Graves' diseases. In systemic autoimmune diseases such as lupus or sarcoidosis, the tissues and organs affected may vary depending on the person. One person with lupus may have affected skin and joints, for example, whereas another may have affected skin, kidneys, and lungs.

Autoimmune diseases predominantly strike women, who suffer about 75 percent of all these diseases, according to the American Autoimmune Related Diseases Association. Autoimmune diseases are more common during childbearing years, and frequently appear in women who have just had a baby, after periods of high emotional or physical stress or accidents, during periods of hormonal change, such as perimenopause, and after starting the Pill or hormone replacement therapy.

Autoimmune diseases also can run in families. If a close family member has an autoimmune disease, then your risk of developing an autoimmune disease is somewhat increased.

The most important thing you need to know, however, is that, if you have Hashimoto's or Graves' disease, which triggered your hypothyroidism (and that is the case for most thyroid patients), then having had one autoimmune disease puts you at risk of developing others.

While there are literally hundreds of risk factors and symptoms for autoimmune disease, a closer look at them can help pinpoint and close in on more specific conditions. Across the board for the as many as eighty different autoimmune diseases beyond the thyroid conditions, there are very specific symptoms found in particular conditions.

Some of the most common conditions include rheumatoid arthritis, multiple sclerosis, Sjögren's syndrome, lupus, celiac disease/gluten intolerance, irritable bowel syndrome (IBS), alopecia areata, polycystic ovary syndrome (PCOS), Cushing's disease, Addison's disease, insulin-dependent type 1 diabetes, scleroderma, Raynaud's syndrome, psoriasis, and vitiligo.

Following is a partial checklist of the more noticeable symptoms of the most common autoimmune conditions. This list is by no means exhaustive, but it covers many symptoms and conditions. Carefully filling out this checklist and taking it to your doctor can be an important first step in getting appropriate testing and the right medical diagnosis of another autoimmune disease.

For more information on diagnosing and treating autoimmune conditions, conventionally and via holistic, alternative medicine, read my book *Living Well with Autoimmune Disease*, or visit my Web site, http://www.autoimmunebook.com.

Autoimmune Symptoms Checklist

Fever/Body Temperature
- ❑ Elevated fever, higher body temperature

Hair
- ❑ Hair loss, round bald patches on the scalp
- ❑ Hair loss, loss of facial and scalp hair
- ❑ Male pattern baldness
- ❑ Excess hair growth on the faces, necks, chests, abdomens, and thighs of women

Skin
- ❑ Hyperpigmentation, or dark tanning, in skin
- ❑ Painful skin rash, called dermatitis herpetiformis
- ❑ Fragile, thin skin
- ❑ Skin that bruises easily
- ❑ Acne
- ❑ Skin rashes, especially "butterfly rash" on the nose and cheeks
- ❑ Sun sensitivity
- ❑ Skin thickening
- ❑ Skin ulcers on the fingers

Eyes
- ❑ Blurred vision
- ❑ Dry eyes
- ❑ Eye discomfort or pain
- ❑ Nystagmus, or jerking, rapid involuntary eye movement
- ❑ Optic neuritis, inflammation of the nerves in the eye
- ❑ Unclear or double vision

Throat, Neck Voice, Mouth
- ❑ Dry mouth
- ❑ Hoarseness, husky or gravelly voice

- ❏ Difficulty in swallowing
- ❏ Mouth and nose sores
- ❏ Pale sores inside the mouth

Fatigue, Sleep

- ❏ Chronic fatigue
- ❏ Exhaustion after minimal effort or exercise

Muscles, Joints, Tendons

- ❏ Pain and tenderness throughout the body
- ❏ Muscle weakness
- ❏ Joint stiffness
- ❏ Bone, joint, and muscle aches, inflammation, and pains
- ❏ Backaches, unexplained rib and spinal column fractures
- ❏ Deformed joints

Hands and Feet

- ❏ Raynaud's phenomenon (extreme sensitivity to cold in the hands and feet)
- ❏ Swelling in hands and feet

Weight Changes

- ❏ Weight loss
- ❏ Weight gain
- ❏ Weight gain in upper body, abdomen
- ❏ Rounded or puffy face
- ❏ Increased fat around the neck
- ❏ Thinning arms and legs

Digestion, Gastrointestinal

- ❏ Nausea, vomiting, or diarrhea
- ❏ Recurring abdominal bloating and pain
- ❏ Pale, foul-smelling stool

❏ Gas
❏ Increased urination

Pulse/Blood Pressure
❏ Low blood pressure
❏ High blood pressure
❏ Fast pulse

Mood, Thinking
❏ Irritability, anxiety, and depression
❏ Brain fog, difficulty concentrating, forgetfulness

Balance, Coordination, Neurological Symptoms
❏ Lack of coordination or unsteady gait
❏ Dizziness, vertigo
❏ Numbness, weakness, tingling or paralysis in one or more limbs
❏ Tremor

Food/Drink and Cravings
❏ Craving of salty foods
❏ Increased thirst
❏ Loss of appetite

Menstruation/Gynecological
❏ Irregular or absent menstrual periods
❏ Cysts on ovaries

Fertility and Sex Drive, Pregnancy
❏ Infertility or decreased fertility in women
❏ Decreased fertility in men
❏ Reduced sex drive

Especially in Children
- ❑ Delayed growth in children, failure to thrive in infants

Blood Changes
- ❑ Unexplained anemia (low count of red blood cells)
- ❑ High cholesterol levels

Blood Sugar Changes
- ❑ Hypoglycemia/low blood sugar
- ❑ High blood sugar

15

Infertility, Pregnancy, and Breast-feeding

Of all the rights of women, the greatest is to be a mother.

— LIN YÜ-TANG

I take a particular interest in the issues of fertility, pregnancy, and breast-feeding because I was diagnosed with Hashimoto's thyroiditis six months after I got married. Two years later, my husband and I decided we'd try to have a baby. At the time, I was thirty-four, and though I was being treated for my thyroid problem, I was still dealing with symptoms of hypothyroidism. I figured if there was ever a poster child for fertility problems, it would be me. So I read relentlessly, talked to a number of doctors, and tried to find out exactly how I could, first, maximize my chance of getting pregnant, and, second, ensure a healthy pregnancy and a healthy baby.

To be honest, underlying it was my concern that I'd need to show evidence that we'd specifically tried to get pregnant and had documented all the cycles and such. That way, I wouldn't have to go through the requisite year of trying to get pregnant, only to be told to start charting temperatures and testing for ovulation for another six months before I could *finally* be labeled "infertile" and start investigating fertility treatments.

I started with the books on thyroid disease. Unfortunately, most of the patient-oriented literature was not much help. The books mentioned that untreated hypothyroidism increases the risk of infertility, miscarriage, or complications, but that once treated, these issues would no longer be a problem. End of discussion.

For a disease that affects mainly women, this glossing over of the disease's effect on reproduction—a very important time for a woman, healthwise—seems irresponsible, indicative of how little the medical profession seems to understand the impact that hypothyroidism has on a woman's ability to live well and live normally. With little information available, I was determined to research the issue myself to make sure that I had the best possible outcome. Once I did my homework, the whole process, charting my cycles, getting the TSH level optimized, and getting pregnant, took four months. I'm not going to say this is typical or normal, but it was a pleasant surprise for us, and I think being prepared, knowing when I ovulated, and being sure my thyroid function was optimal were all factors in the success.

The result is the information I've included here in this chapter—and my lovely daughter, born in 1997!

■ Hypothyroidism, Autoimmune Thyroid Disease, and Pregnancy

Hypothyroidism, and the autoimmune thyroid disease that is frequently the cause, can make it harder to get pregnant, or can make positive outcomes somewhat more difficult.

For example, there are a number of common reproductive problems that are more prevalent in thyroid patients, and make it more difficult to get pregnant, including:

Failure to ovulate: Untreated or undertreated hypothyroidism can cause your body to fail to release eggs. Even though you may still have periods, don't assume that you're ovulating. Check with an ovulation predictor kit or talk to your doctor about testing for anovulation.

Menstrual Irregularities: Hypothyroidism can cause what's known as a short luteal phase, which refers to the time frame between ovulation and menstruation. The luteal phase needs to be a certain length—thirteen to fifteen days is considered normal—to nurture a fertilized egg. Doctors may diagnose you as infertile, when in reality you can get pregnant but simply fail to sustain the fertilized egg. The egg miscarries, right around the same time as your period would normally begin.

Prolactin Excess: Some women with hypothyroidism have an excess of prolactin, the hormone responsible for the production of breast milk. While it would seem that this is a good thing, too much prolactin during the conception period can actually impair fertility.

Ovarian Cysts: Hypothyroidism has been linked with an increased risk of polycystic ovaries, which can also decrease fertility by causing irregularities in the menstrual cycle, and sometimes no periods at all.

Dangers to mother and baby in women who are untreated or undertreated for hypothyroidism are also not uncommon. One study showed that among pregnant women with either overt or subclinical (low level) hypothyroidism:

- 21 percent of the overtly hypothyroid and 15 percent of the subclinically hypothyroid had pregnancy-induced hypertension.
- 16.6 percent of the overtly hypothyroid and 8.7 percent of the subclinically hypothyroid had low birth weight newborns.
- 6.6 percent of the overtly hypothyroid and 3.5 percent of the subclinically hypothyroid had postpartum hemorrhage.
- 5 percent of the overtly hypothyroid and none of the subclinically hypothyroid had placenta abruptio.
- 3.3 percent of the overtly hypothyroid and none of the subclinically hypothyroid had congenital malformations.

Another well-known concern is for the brain development of the baby. In order for the fetal brain to develop properly, an adequate supply of thyroid hormones is vital. Lack of such a hormones—as may occur in women who haven't been treated for their underactive thyroid—can cause negative effects on the baby, including a lower I.Q. and possible learning problems. In a 1999 study in the *New England Journal of Medicine,* children born to mothers whose hypothyroidism was not being treated scored several points lower on an I.Q. test than children of nonthyroid patients. The study went on to note, however, that children whose mothers were undergoing treatment for an underactive thyroid scored almost the same as children born to mothers with normal thyroid function.

According to thyroid expert Steven Langer, M.D.:

Baby I.Q. problems result because the mother supplies all thyroid hormones for growth and development of the fetus for the first 12 weeks of pregnancy. After twelve weeks, the fetus develops its own thyroid gland; however, the mother-to-be is still the source of thyroid hormone. During those first twelve weeks, a hypothyroid mother can't always assure enough thyroid hormone for proper brain development. In some cases, miscarriage occurs at this point.

Miscarriage and stillbirth are also concerns. One report in the *Journal of Medical Screening* showed that pregnant hypothyroid women who are not receiving treatment have nearly four times the risk of a late miscarriage (second trimester or later) than other women. Another study found that 6.6 percent of overtly hypothyroid mothers, and 1.7 percent of subclinically hypothyroid mothers, have stillbirths.

There are also numerous studies indicating a relationship between thyroid autoimmunity—as determined by the presence of elevated antithyroid antibodies—and infertility and recurrent miscarriages. According to an article in the journal *Obstetrics and*

Gynecology, the presence of antithyroid antibodies increases the risk of miscarriage. Several studies have indicated that women with Hashimoto's disease are as much as two to five times more likely to have a miscarriage in the first twelve weeks of pregnancy, as opposed to women without thyroid autoimmunity.

Elevated TPO (thyroperoxidase) antibodies are also linked to an increased risk of recurrent miscarriage rate. One study found that as much as 31 percent of women experiencing recurrent miscarriages were positive for either ATA (antithyroid antibodies), TPO, or both. Researchers at the Pacific Fertility Center in California have shown that antithyroid antibodies can also make in vitro fertilization less successful. Dr. Gregory Sher has said:

> *The presence of antithyroid antibodies is associated with a variety of manifestations of poor reproductive performance. These range from infertility, through early miscarriage to prematurity, intrauterine growth retardation, other serious complications of late pregnancy, and even fetal death.*

Key Issues

All this information is to underscore how important it is that:

- All women considering pregnancy should have thorough thyroid testing, including antibodies.
- All women experiencing infertility or recurrent miscarriage should have thorough thyroid testing, including autoimmune and antibody profiles.
- The workup for all newly pregnant women should include thyroid testing.
- Women who have a thyroid problem should be particularly prepared and vigilant about their thyroid condition before, during, and after pregnancy.
- Women who don't have a diagnosed thyroid condition but who are pregnant should be educated regarding the possible signs of

hypothyroidism during pregnancy, so that they can seek out and receive treatment as early as possible, to protect their own health and the health of the baby.

Early diagnosis, frequent testing, and proper treatment throughout pregnancy dramatically reduce the risk that hypothyroidism and thyroid autoimmunity present to both mother and baby, and can help ensure the best chance of a healthy outcome.

■ Infertility

If you're struggling with infertility or recurrent miscarriage, could thyroid disease be the reason behind your problems? Of course, there are many causes of infertility and recurrent miscarriage that have nothing to do with the thyroid. But if you have had difficulty conceiving, and have no diagnosed problems (i.e., abnormally shaped uterus, scarred fallopian tubes, genetic conditions, etc.), your thyroid could be to blame.

Unfortunately, many women have been diagnosed as infertile, or have suffered miscarriage after miscarriage, only to be told there is no earthly explanation for their difficulties and losses and to simply "keep trying." These women are often not tested for an underlying thyroid or autoimmune condition. Don't assume that even the most elaborate infertility workups by experts will include thyroid tests. Despite thyroid disease being not only common, but a known cause of infertility and miscarriage, some practitioners inexplicably do not include this testing as part of standard fertility assessments! And, even if you have a thyroid problem and are having trouble getting pregnant, are you aware of the reasons why your thyroid can make it more difficult, or what you can possibly do to help?

Hypothyroidism and Infertility

If you are having difficulty getting pregnant, or experiencing miscarriages and you have not had your thyroid tested, as the most basic starting point, you may want to do a self-test for your thyroid. You can do a home TSH (thyroid-stimulating hormone) test, which will assess the TSH levels. A company called Biosafe received FDA approval for an accurate, affordable (less than $40) home TSH test. Biosafe's test kit requires an almost painless finger prick, using their special finger lancet. All you need is a couple of drops of blood, which you put into their collection device, and send to Biosafe's labs for analysis. Results are mailed back to you quickly. You can also order your own complete thyroid blood panel at a local laboratory through HealthCheck USA. For information on Biosafe or Health-Check USA, see the Resources section.

Ideally, however, your physician should do a comprehensive thyroid workup, which would include TSH, total T4, free T4, total T3, free T3, antithyroid antibodies (ATA) (thyroglobulin and microsomal antibodies), and antithyroid peroxidase antibodies (anti-TPO).

What are you looking for? Realistically, you are looking for a TSH level of 2.0 or less. Unfortunately, most laboratory tests and experts are still working off outdated lab standards that view TSH levels as high as 5.5 or 6 as normal, however these have been shown to negatively affect fertility.

In November 2002, the new *Laboratory Medicine Practice Guidelines*, issued by the National Academy of Clinical Biochemistry, stated:

> *A serum TSH result between 0.5 and 2.0 mIU/L is generally considered the therapeutic target for a standard L-T4 replacement dose for primary hypothyroidism. . . . Thyroxine requirements increase during pregnancy. Thyroid status should be checked with TSH + FT4 during each trimester of pregnancy. The L-T4 dose should be increased (usually by 50 micrograms/day) to maintain a serum TSH between 0.5 and*

2.0 mIU/L and a serum FT4 in the upper third of the normal reference interval.

If you have a TSH above 2, you may wish to find a sympathetic and innovative practitioner who is aware of these more recent findings.

Antibodies/Autoimmunity

If you or someone you know is having difficulty getting pregnant, or is suffering recurrent miscarriage, thyroid function and thyroid antibodies should both be tested. While the patient-oriented literature overlooks this entirely, some of the more pioneering medical researchers and fertility specialists understand that even high-normal range TSH, and/or the presence of antithyroid antibodies—even in the absence of an elevated TSH or symptoms of hypothyroidism—can be a factor in infertility or early miscarriage. A variety of immunological adjustments need to take place in a pregnant woman, and the existence of underlying autoimmune thyroid problems may set in motion a mechanism that results in a greater incidence of infertility, lower success rates with in vitro fertilization, or more frequent miscarriage.

Many doctors do not appear to know about this link between antibodies and infertility, yet it is published in conventional research journals. The respected journal *Obstetrics and Gynecology* reported that the presence of antithyroid antibodies increases the risk of miscarriage. According to U.S. research reported in the *Journal of Clinical Endocrinology and Metabolism*, that risk of miscarriage can be twice as high for women who have antithyroid antibodies.

Researchers have also demonstrated that antithyroid antibodies can cause greater difficulty conceiving after in vitro fertilization, regardless of whether or not there are clinical symptoms of hypothyroidism. Researchers had greater success in achieving successful pregnancies when they gave low doses of heparin (an antiblood clotting agent) and aspirin and/or intravenous immunoglobulin-G

(IVIG) to women who had antithyroid antibodies. Dr. Geoffrey Sher and colleagues at Pacific Fertility Centers performed this research.

Keep in mind that if you are monitoring your ovulation and cycle, and have your thyroid and TSH levels regulated, and you still don't get pregnant after the requisite six months to a year, you probably should consult with a fertility specialist for additional treatment and ideas.

Colleen was diagnosed as hypothyroid when she went to see her doctor about her inability to get pregnant:

> Through my entire time of having a "cycle" it was rarely regular. I could go for a year without my period and my previous doctor had said not to worry about it until you are ready to try to have a baby. My new doctor was very concerned about this. Through all the blood tests it was discovered that I was hypothyroid. My TSH was 15. I was put on Synthroid and am monitored every six weeks. I was still not pregnant, even though my level was just checked at .8 and I am on Synthroid .75 mcg.

Because more than her thyroid may be involved, Colleen ended up deciding to pursue more aggressive fertility efforts, taking Clomid and Provera to induce ovulation and a cycle, and going to see a reproductive endocrinologist.

Some experts believe that as many as one out of five women with thyroid antibodies will not be correctly identified when standard blood tests are used. For women who have had recurrent pregnancy loss, they recommend more sensitive tests, such as enzyme-linked immunosorbent assays (ELISAs) or gel agglutination tests. A reproductive endocrinologist with expertise in autoimmune issues would be necessary to help conduct and evaluate these tests.

If you have tested positive for thyroid antibodies, there are a number of treatments that may help you become pregnant and have a healthy pregnancy. These include:

Low-Dose Heparin—In some cases, using low-dose heparin (an anticoagulant produced naturally by the body) with aspirin and, less commonly, prednisone (a steroid) before getting pregnant can help ensure higher pregnancy rates.

IVIG—Another method for dealing with the antibodies is intravenous immunoglobulin G (IVIG). In IVIG you would receive a transfusion of antibodies from thousands of donors, drawn from the general population. The influx of immunoglobulin distracts your immune system, so to speak, preventing the antibodies from attacking your developing baby. According to Dr. Gregory Sher of the Pacific Fertility Center, in California, women with antithyroid antibodies have a higher success rate with in vitro fertilization when they are treated with low doses of heparin and aspirin and/or IVIG.

Thyroid Hormone Treatment—In one study of women who had thyroid antibodies, borderline hypothyroidism according to TSH levels, and a history of recurrent and early miscarriages, thyroid hormone was given before and during pregnancy. This significantly reduced the miscarriage rate, and 81 percent of the women had live births, as opposed to only 55 percent of the women who were given IVIG injections.

What You Can Do

If you are experiencing infertility or recurrent miscarriage, you should first insist on having your complete thyroid profile, including antibodies, evaluated thoroughly.

Second, consider pursuing treatment if:

- Your TSH is 0.3 or below.
- Your TSH is above 2.
- You have borderline-low or high free T4.
- You have borderline-low or high free T3.
- You have tested positive for thyroid antibodies.

Luckily for some women, proper thyroid treatment and optimal TSH levels can raise the likelihood of a successful pregnancy. A number of women have written to me saying that after extended periods of what their doctors had diagnosed as infertility, they found my information and finally insisted that their doctors test them for thyroid disease, treat high-normal TSH levels in the presence of antibodies, and/or increase their dosage of thyroid hormone to get their levels down to the 1-to-2-TSH range. And every one of those women is now a mother for the first time!

■ Preparing for Pregnancy

Any woman who knows she is hypothyroid should take key steps to prepare for her pregnancy.

Know Your Cycles

Before I planned to get pregnant, I needed to make sure that all the reproductive bases were covered, meaning I needed to answer key questions: Was I ovulating? Was my luteal phase long enough? In my case, after twenty years of having periods every twenty-eight days like clockwork, once I was hypothyroid, my periods came every twenty-three to twenty-six days, irregularly, so I didn't know what my cycles were actually telling me.

I started by charting my basal body temperature in order to monitor fertility signs and ovulation, and determine my luteal phase. My bible was a book that is, in my opinion, absolutely essential for all women. It's called *Taking Charge of Your Fertility*, by Toni Wechsler, M.P.H. With this book, I learned (for the first time I might add) the real story about the menstrual and hormonal cycles. This book is definitely a far cry from those *Now You're a Woman* pamphlets and films in grade school. I learned how to use basal temperature and other fertility signs to chart my monthly hormonal cycle. While charting allowed me to estimate ovulation, I also used an over-the-counter ovulation predictor kit, available for around $10 at the drugstore, to make sure I knew what I was doing with the charting. After three months, according to my charts and testing, it was obvious I was ovulating, and I had a long enough luteal phase to sustain pregnancy. That was a good start.

Have a Preconception Visit to the Doctor

I had a "preconception" appointment with the doctor a few months earlier, which resulted in my getting an overdue measles/ mumps/rubella booster vaccination and a prescription for the extra folic acid that helps a woman prevent birth defects if taken in the period prior to and during pregnancy. All women—not just ones with a thyroid condition—who are getting ready to conceive should take a folic acid supplement for several months before attempting conception. Studies have shown that numerous birth defects, such as spina bifida, anencephaly, and other neural tube defects, have been linked to low levels of folic acid in pregnant women. Both the CDC and the March of Dimes recommend that women take 400 mcg (0.4 mg) of synthetic folic acid every day. Neural tube defects typically appear in the growing fetus at four weeks of age—long before many women even know they're pregnant, which is why you need to start taking them before you even try to get pregnant.

I also started taking a prenatal vitamin at that time. Many doctors prescribe prenatal vitamins with iron to their preconception patients, and that's fine, for thyroid patients as well as women with no thyroid problems. However, because iron interferes with the absorption of thyroid hormone, you should *not* take your prenatal vitamin with iron within three to four hours of your thyroid medication. This allows the thyroid hormone to be fully absorbed without interference from the iron.

You also want to make sure your prenatal vitamin has enough iodine. Iodine is particularly important for thyroid health, and proper iodine intake is even more essential during pregnancy. Until recently, it was assumed that iodine deficiency is not a particular problem in the United States, Japan, and some European countries, where iodine supplementation programs have been in place for many years. Recently, however, studies have shown that iodine intake has dropped significantly in the U.S., for example, and as many as 15 percent of women of childbearing age and almost 7 percent of women during pregnancy were iodine-deficient. Mild iodine deficiency during pregnancy can contribute to hypothyroidism, and significant iodine deficiency during pregnancy—which is seen in some countries that do not have routine iodine supplementation—can cause significant birth defects and even cretinism in children. The recommended dietary allowance for iodine in 200 mg/day during pregnancy and 75 mg/day while breast-feeding. A good prenatal vitamin should have enough iodine to avoid deficiency. But if you have cravings for seaweed or seafood, go ahead and indulge them (as long as you avoid the more mercury-toxic fish), because they may be a sign that your body wants more iodine.

Optimize Your TSH Level

What's the best TSH level in order to achieve a successful pregnancy? That's a tough question because different doctors have different answers. Some women may have been told that their TSH level is "normal," and they shouldn't have any trouble getting pregnant, yet they suffer years of "unexplained" infertility or miscarriages. Others may be told not even to attempt conceiving until the thyroid levels stabilize at 1 or 2.

Part of the source of the confusion stems from the definition of "normal," and much of it depends on what numbers the laboratory considers "high," "normal," and "low." While it's a relief to get a diagnosis of "normal," if you're still feeling sick, or still having problems, it's no help at all to you. Insist on getting the exact number, and the normal range for your lab. While the new standards indicate that "normal" range is somewhere around 0.3 to 3 (with over 3 being considered hypothyroid, or underactive, and under 0.3 being hyperthyroid, or overactive), many labs and practitioners are still using outdated lab guidelines, which put normal range at 0.5 to 5.5.

It's also important to note that even within the range of numbers set by labs, individual factors can't be overlooked. Some women might feel absolutely great with a TSH level of 3, and have no difficulties getting and remaining pregnant. Other women, with the exact same TSH levels, may feel sick, in a constant fog, and have trouble conceiving.

When I started doing my preconception workup, my TSH level at the time was 4.1. I was feeling okay, not perfect but pretty well, and thought because I was in normal range, this would be a good time to finally try to get pregnant. My endocrinologist (a woman with more than twenty years' treating women with thyroid problems and thyroid-related infertility) believed *firmly* that most women do not normalize unless their TSH is between 1 and 2 (considered low by some doctors), and that a woman with evidence of thyroid disease can't get pregnant and/or maintain a pregnancy at a TSH higher than 1 to 2. At that time, the new "Laboratory Medicine Practice Guidelines" indicating a TSH target range of less than 2 for pregnant women had yet to be issued by the National Academy of Clinical Biochemistry.

Also at that time, my doctor said there weren't any specific journal papers to back up her own findings, but she said she'd even been treating fellow physicians suffering from infertility who'd been able to get pregnant once their TSH was lowered to the 1-to-2 level. She said I might be able to get pregnant at my current level, but to sustain a pregnancy would be more difficult. So she upped my dosage of thyroid hormone replacement, targeting the TSH range of 1 to 2.

Interestingly, there was some research that backed up her opinions on normal levels during early pregnancy. A study was reported on in 1994 in the *Journal of Clinical Endocrinology and Metabolism* that looked at pregnant women with thyroid antibodies and TSH in the normal range. This study found that women with autoimmune thyroid disease had TSH values that were significantly higher, though still normal, in the first trimester than in women with healthy pregnancies who were used as controls. The higher TSH level of the women with autoimmune thyroid disease?: 1.6. The normal TSH level for the control group of pregnant women without autoimmune thyroid disease?: 0.9. A TSH of 0.9 is a far cry from the so-called normal TSH levels of 3 or 4 or 5 that some doctors feel are no impediment whatsoever to getting—or staying—pregnant.

Within a month of treatment with a slightly increased dose, my thyroid was down to a TSH level of 1.2, and a month later, I became pregnant!

■ Managing Pregnancy with Hypothyroidism

Once you're pregnant, it's not time to relax, because you still need to be your own advocate and stay vigilant and knowledgeable.

Find Out as Early as Possible That You're Pregnant

Make sure that you find out you are pregnant as early as possible. One way is to use a home pregnancy test kit. Some kits (I like the E.P.T. kits) are sensitive as early as ten days postconception, and you don't even have to wait for a missed period in order to get a positive result. I suggest you test as early as possible, because the earlier you confirm the pregnancy, the earlier you can start ensuring that your hypothyroidism is properly monitored. I can't emphasize enough how important it is that you and your physician manage your hypothyroidism carefully throughout the pregnancy, and as early as possible in the pregnancy. Recent research has shown that even mild or subclinical hypothyroidism during pregnancy can increase your risk of serious problems, including premature birth, stillbirth, and breech birth, as well as lower IQ and other developmental problems in your baby.

In my case, I tested positive via the home pregnancy test only nine days postconception. This is fairly unusual . . . some women who are pregnant still don't test positive until around fourteen days postconception or later. I had a blood test to confirm the pregnancy at my regular doctor's office, and knew I was officially pregnant at only three weeks postconception, which is when I called to schedule my first obstetrician (ob-gyn) appointment. Definitely, though, experts recommend that as soon as you miss that first period, you should have a thyroid test to evaluate thyroid function.

Have Your First Doctor's Visit Right Away

The first thing you should do if you suspect you're pregnant and/or have a positive pregnancy is call your doctor's office and push to be seen as early as possible. Some doctors don't like to see pregnant patients until *well* into the first trimester. For some women, this is fine, but as a patient with a thyroid condition, it's absolutely vital that you get seen—and start the process of monitoring thyroid hormones and antibody levels—as soon as possible.

Many obstetricians will tell you that they don't see pregnant patients until nine or ten weeks after their last menstrual periods. But by that time your medication dosage may already need drastic adjustment, to account for dangerously high TSH levels and worsening hypothyroidism. One study found that the thyroid hormone requirements of hypothyroid women increase by 25 percent to 50 percent soon after conception. How much of an increase in thyroid drugs you'll need may depend in part on how you became hypothyroid. Typically, women who have had RAI for hyperthyroidism need the greatest increase—a mean increase of 46 percent, according to one study. In Hashimoto's disease, the mean dose increase was 26 percent. According to research published in 2004 in the *New England Journal of Medicine,* as many as 85 percent of pregnant women with hypothyroidism require an increase in thyroid hormone replacement drug to protect the baby from adverse outcomes. Interestingly, the need for an increase in dosage of thyroid medication during pregnancy was seen as early as the fifth week of gestation, and some researchers recommend that you take two additional doses of thyroid medication each week immediately after you've confirmed your pregnancy, and contact and see your health-care provider right away so that a program of test-guided dose adjustments can be started.

My ob-gyn wanted to schedule me to come in sometime in the eighth or ninth week. I insisted on scheduling the first visit at five weeks postconception. At that time, I also asked that they run a TSH test. Interestingly, in just the five weeks since conception, my TSH had gone up to 3, from 1.2. In keeping with my endocrinologist's directions, my dosage was upped slightly, I was retested two weeks later, and my TSH returned to around 1.4.

There are a number of medical and hormonal reasons why your thyroid hormone requirements go up so dramatically, but the most important one is that your baby's thyroid health depends completely on you. In the first trimester, your baby develops arms, legs, a beating heart, and a brain, but an as-yet nonworking but fully formed thyroid gland. He or she needs a steady, appropriate supply of hormones to ensure proper development, and the only place to can get it is from YOU! If it's not readily available, your baby's development can suffer.

Frequent Testing

Many guidelines say that a pregnant woman with hypothyroidism should, in addition to being tested as soon as she confirms the pregnancy, also have her thyroid function checked at least once during each trimester, at minimum.

Normal TSH, but low Free T4 (FT4), can also be problematic during pregnancy. If you are a pregnant woman who is hypothyroid, you should have your doctor check not only your TSH levels, but also your Free T4 levels. According to research presented at the June 2000 Endocrine Society conference, there is increasing evidence that even normal Free T4 levels that fall into the lowest tenth percentile during the early stages of pregnancy can be associated with poor infant development. Low-normal free T4 is not defined as maternal hypothyroidism when TSH is normal, but these outcomes indicate that screening and treatment for thyroid problems may be warranted in all women. The study concluded that women with a low-normal Free T4—in the lowest tenth percentile at twelve weeks' gestation—are at risk for children with developmental delay. Further, the researchers found that "TSH, during early gestation, seems to be without any value to pick up these women at risk."

So, you may wish to consult with a cutting-edge endocrinologist or thyroid expert who is willing to monitor not only your TSH but your Free T4 levels throughout your pregnancy.

After the first trimester, I had my thyroid tested every two months or so, and it varied no more than a few tenths of a point, requiring no adjustment in my medication throughout the entire pregnancy. It's never been so stable before or since.

Take Your Thyroid Hormone!

Some women wonder if they should even continue to take their thyroid hormone during pregnancy. Corinne, newly pregnant, wrote to me asking: "I'd like to know if I should stop my thyroid hormone because I really don't want to take any drugs during pregnancy that might harm the baby."

Over the last few decades, many women like Corinne have become more aware of the cautions against use of prescription and nonprescription drugs during pregnancy. While these cautions are often warranted, this warning should *never* apply to hypothyroidism. Your thyroid medication, such as Synthroid, Levoxyl, Levothroid, Armour, Thyrolar, etc., is safe to take during pregnancy, and in fact you could be doing your baby much more harm— irreparable brain damage, for instance—if you *don't* take your prescribed thyroid drugs at the levels indicated by your physician. Much like an insulin-dependent diabetic cannot stop taking insulin during pregnancy, a woman who is hypothyroid should not stop taking her thyroid hormone replacement unless specifically directed to do so by her physician.

Not to take your thyroid hormone is a danger to your health, to your pregnancy, and to your child. Thyroid hormone, in proper doses, is replacing something your body needs in order to maintain a healthy pregnancy. Insufficient thyroid hormone in early pregnancy can increase the risk of miscarriage. Later in pregnancy, it can increase the risk of stillbirth or premature delivery. And throughout the pregnancy, having an elevated TSH level can create a substantially increased risk of negatively affecting your child's psychological development, and can result in substantially lower I.Q. levels, reduced motor skills, and problems with attention, language, and reading throughout life. Research reported in the *New England Journal of Medicine* in 1999 demonstrated, in fact, that women with untreated underactive thyroids during pregnancy are nearly four times more likely to have children with lower I.Q. scores. Overall, the greatest danger for you and your unborn baby is to think that taking thyroid at the proper dosage of hormone is bad for your baby and discontinuing your thyroid hormone replacement. Thyroid hormone is one of the few drugs in pharmaceutical category "A" (low risk) for pregnant women. Studies in pregnant women show that when taken in the proper dosage, there are no adverse effects on the fetus.

Take Your Thyroid Hormone Properly

You may be taking your thyroid hormone, but you also need to take it properly. Here is a recap of some tips on how to ensure that you are getting maximum benefit from your thyroid medicine:

• Always check the prescription against what you receive. Don't allow generic substitutions.
• Most doctors feel that taking thyroid hormone on an empty stomach allows for maximum absorption. If you can, take your thyroid medicine first thing in the morning, at least an hour before eating, to allow for maximum absorption.

- If you start or stop eating high-fiber foods, get your thyroid rechecked, because it may change your absorption of thyroid medicines.

- Take vitamins or supplements with iron—including prenatal vitamins—at least two to three hours apart from your thyroid hormone. Iron can interfere with thyroid hormone absorption if taken too close together.

- Many pregnant women are told to add more calcium to their diet. Be careful about taking calcium and calcium-fortified orange juice at the same time as thyroid hormone. Allow at least four hours between taking calcium and your thyroid hormone, so absorption is not affected.

- Many pregnant women take antacids, due to heartburn during pregnancy. But don't take antacids within two hours of your thyroid hormone. Allow at least four hours, so absorption is not affected.

- Consistency is vital to your success. If nausea prevents you from taking your pills on an empty stomach, take your thyroid pill every day with food, rather than miss taking it, or taking it erratically—some days with food, some days without. You may stabilize at a slightly higher dosage than if you weren't taking your pill with food, but you'll get to the right dosage.

Enjoy the Feeling!

Most people I've talked to who have autoimmune hypothyroidism say they've actually felt *better* while pregnant. I have to say that when pregnant I felt the best I had since being diagnosed as hypothyroid. Naturally, I had the typical tiredness most pregnant women experience, but it was a different feeling, not the bone-numbing fatigue and brain fog I'd had with untreated hypothyroidism, but more of a sleepiness that was relieved by naps and nighttime sleep. My allergies were near nonexistent, I didn't get a single cold, flu, or other ailment. I've heard doctors speculate that some women with autoimmune diseases have immune systems that function almost perfectly during pregnancy, and I seemed to be one of them.

Eat Healthily, and Don't Gain Too Much Weight

My main pregnancy concern? More weight gain that I'd have liked, which led to a borderline blood sugar problem that the doctor said wasn't gestational diabetes but was close to it, late in the pregnancy. I ate very healthily—I thought—but looking back, I realize my diet was very heavy in carbohydrates and fruits. I think that hypothyroidism's tendency to give some people an exaggerated insulin response and near diabetic blood sugar levels may make some pregnant women with hypothyroidism more susceptible to greater weight gain, and borderline or full-blown gestational diabetes. If I had another baby, I would ask for a consult with a nutritionist to devise a low-glycemic diet that would provide sufficient nourishment for my baby and me, but would balance blood sugar and minimize unnecessary weight gain.

Heading to the Hospital

I have one important tip for hypothyroid mothers-to-be. When you go to the hospital to have your baby, pack your thyroid hormone in your hospital overnight bag. Otherwise, it can be a major hassle to get them to issue you your thyroid medicine, especially if you take anything besides Synthroid.

Delivery

Delivery is not usually any different for a hypothyroid mother. In my own situation, I had an uncomplicated, planned C-section (my baby was completely breech), and my daughter Julia was born a healthy 8½ pounds.

What About the Baby?

You may worry that if you are hypothyroid, or have an autoimmune disease like Hashimoto's, your baby will too. It's rare, but it can happen. However, since Hashimoto's typically doesn't appear until the second decade of life, it's not likely to be seen in infants. Congenital hypothyroidism appears in one per four thousand or five thousand newborns. If thyroid therapy is started during their first three months, most of these children will have normal intellectual development. Untreated, however, their hypothyroidism can lead to serious mental and physical impairment. In the United States, all newborns are required to be tested for low T4 levels; the test is typically done along with the heel stick for PKU (phenylketonuria). But you will want to double-check at the hospital, or with your child's pediatrician at her/his first posthospital visit, to ensure that the thyroid test was performed.

■ Managing Your Hypothyroidism After Birth

The period following childbirth—the postpartum period—is difficult for any new mother, regardless of whether or not you have thyroid difficulties. There's sleep deprivation, pain—especially if you've had a difficult or prolonged labor or a C-section—worry, and simply the emotional upheaval of adding a baby to your household. Fluctuating hormones—signaling the end of pregnancy, the beginning of lactation, etc.—can make you subject to dramatic mood swings. And we've all heard about the "baby blues," a period of time when you may feel unexplainably sad or depressed.

Monitor Thyroid Levels

In my case, my postpartum TSH levels bounced around like a rubber ball. I went from hyperthyroid immediately postpartum, to the top of the normal range, nearing hypothyroid levels, just weeks later, back up to hyperthyroid, and back down to hypothyroid, with only tiny dosage adjustments. It appeared that my hormones were fluctuating wildly.

Diane was on thyroid hormone replacement for two years before she became pregnant with her third child:

> *The obstetrician monitored my thyroid hormones through the pregnancy and the baby was born big and healthy. Shortly after his birth, the symptoms came back in full force. My doctor's office was undergoing staff changes again. I went to one young doctor just out of school. He ran the regular tests and told me they were in the "normal ranges" again. But he did adjust my Synthroid. I was almost down to nothing.*

Monitor Other Hormones

For thyroid patients, the postpartum period can be a rollicking roller-coaster ride of hormones, and an imbalance can have consequences. Progesterone, also dubbed the "pregnancy hormone," is roughly three hundred times higher than normal during pregnancy, in order to sustain the growth of your baby. Estrogen also rises significantly, with estradiol one hundred times higher than normal, and estriol to about one thousand times the nonpregnant level. Generally, because of the higher hormonal level, most—but certainly not all—pregnant women report feeling happy and healthy. Shortly after delivery, however, hormone levels come crashing down drastically, throwing the new mother into an emotional upheaval.

In my case, when my daughter was around five months old, I still couldn't shake the exhaustion and a moody feeling that had descended on me about a month after her birth. I went to my regular doctor, sure that I must be suffering from postpartum depression. The doctor, however, decided to run some hormone tests before recommending an antidepressant. It's a good thing she did, because she discovered that I had various hormonal imbalances in addition to my thyroid edging out of normal range into hypothyroid TSH levels again. She prescribed some natural progesterone and changed my thyroid hormone dosage, and soon it was as if the fog had lifted and the world was a happy place again.

■ Temporary Thyroid Problems Postpartum

As many as 10 percent of all new mothers may suffer from postpartum thyroid problems, including the thyroid inflammation called "postpartum thyroiditis." Frequently, the result of this thyroiditis is hypothyroidism. Sadly, though, many doctors are not cognizant of the incredible changes a damaged thyroid gland can cause in a new mother. You may go to your doctor with complaints of mind-numbing fatigue, depression, anxiety, heart palpitations, and irritability, and you may condescendingly be told it's normal for new mothers and to "go home and try to rest and relax, and enjoy your baby."

The body's immune system—in which antibodies would normally seek out and "attack" foreign bodies, such as a fetus—is typically suppressed during pregnancy, in order to protect the baby. After childbirth, however, the body's seek-out-and-attack functions return, although this time turning on its own glands and tissues. Postpartum thyroiditis happens when the body starts manufacturing antibodies against the thyroid gland. The antibodies frequently damage or stun the thyroid, making it unable to produce enough thyroid hormone, and you become hypothyroid. For some women, postpartum thyroid problems can be temporary, lasting anywhere from several months to as long as a year, and for some, the thyroid imbalances after birth can be the beginning of a lifelong autoimmune condition.

If you tested positive early in your pregnancy for antithyroid antibodies, you have a 33 percent to 50 percent chance of developing thyroiditis after childbirth. However, postpartum thyroid problems also can appear in women who tested negative for the antibodies. Typically, postpartum thyroid problems can begin with a short period of hyperthyroidism, including feeling overheated, weakness in muscles, anxiety, nervousness, rapid pulse rate, rapid weight loss, diarrhea, unusual fatigue, insomnia, and milk supply problems. All of these symptoms, however, can be easily mistaken as normal symptoms after pregnancy, making it harder to detect in some patients. The hyperthyroidism symptoms typically shift into hypothyroidism symptoms, including exhaustion, constipation, memory and concentration problems, feeling cold, muscle cramps, and weight gain. Sometimes, the postpartum symptoms will cycle back and forth between hypothyroidism and hyperthyroidism.

For some women, no treatment is necessary, and the condition resolves on its own. A majority of women return to normal, several months to as much as a year after postpartum thyroid diagnosis, and never have another problem. Other women have postpartum thyroid problems after every pregnancy, but otherwise things return to normal, until menopause, when thyroid problems appear again. Some women—possibly as many as 30 percent—remain hypothyroid, because their thyroid glands are too damaged by the imbalance or because the pregnancy has activated an inherent case of autoimmune thyroid disease.

If you have had a gradual return to normal, you and your doctor will need to do frequent TSH tests in order to monitor your drug dosages and gradually taper you off as your TSH returns to normal. For women with postpartum hypothyroidism, doctors can prescribe thyroid replacement hormones, such as Synthroid or Armour, until their TSH levels stabilize. Keep in mind, however, that once you've had an episode of postpartum thyroid problems, you are much more likely later to develop a thyroid problem during a period of stress, subsequent pregnancy, or during menopause.

■ Breast-feeding Challenges

No doubt you are well aware of the benefits of breast-feeding your child. Breast-fed infants reportedly score better on I.Q. tests, are sick less often, and enjoy better overall health. Breast-feeding supposedly lowers your own risk of breast cancer and other types of cancer, and uses up more calories, helping you return to your prepregnancy weight sooner. But will your thyroid condition prevent you from nursing your baby? Not necessarily. The likelihood is, if you are hypothyroid, and taking the proper dose of thyroid hormone replacement, you will be able to nurse your baby. However, La Leche League's *Breastfeeding Answer Book* says, "Women with a history of thyroid problems may need to be retested if their nursing baby is slow in gaining weight, as changes in metabolism can affect milk production."

The hormone prolactin is responsible for the production of breast milk. It is stimulated by TRH (thyrotropin-releasing hormone), which in turn stimulates TSH. When your levels of TRH are low, as they are in hypothyroid women, prolactin is insufficient and you may have difficulty producing enough breast milk to nourish your baby.

Some women who are hypothyroid, myself included, do have problems with milk supply. In my case, I very much wanted to breast-feed my daughter, and prior to her birth, I had read several books, gone to a La Leche meeting, had some advance training from my doula (birth attendant), and after my baby was born, had several sessions with the hospital's lactation consultant.

I felt thoroughly prepared to nurse my daughter, and after she was born, all the experts assured me that she had latched on fine and we were doing well. After a week, however, she hadn't had many wet or dirty diapers, and had lost weight. I was not becoming engorged between nursings, and after more visits to the lactation consultants and the doula, they theorized that I didn't have a sufficient milk supply, and my daughter didn't have a very strong sucking re-flex. After trying many methods of increasing milk supply recom-mended by the various resources I called on—everything from herbs like fenugreek, a nursing vacation, and nursing every two hours—my daughter continued to lose weight. At the three-week point, the pediatrician insisted that I add supplemental formula. My baby im-mediately began gaining weight. At that point, I also turned to pumping to help increase my milk supply and despite a program of pumping, nursing and using the supplemental nursing system, I was able to pump only about half the typical milk supply of other moth-ers at this postpartum stage. It was clear then that I had a low milk supply, and had probably had it from the beginning.

Suspecting my thyroid was out of whack, I was tested, and they discovered that I'd become hyperthyroid, with a TSH level of less than .05. My dosage was readjusted to return me to the 1-to-2 TSH range, but this never resulted in a rebound in milk supply. It may have been too late to kick-start it. So my recommendation is that new mothers might want to get their TSH tested a few days after de-livery, so dosage modifications can be made right away, if needed. Despite the low milk supply, I did manage to successfully pump about half of my daughter's needed milk until she was six months old, when my supply stopped. I am still proud of this accomplish-ment, given the challenges.

One concern some women have is whether they should continue taking thyroid hormone drugs (i.e., Synthroid, Levoxyl, Armour, Thyrolar) when breast-feeding. You need to continue taking your medication—you actually need sufficient thyroid hormone in order to properly produce healthy breast milk. Thyroid hormone replace-ment, when provided in proper dosage level, crosses into breast milk in only minute quantities and has no adverse effect on the baby. That said, if too much thyroid hormone is being taken and levels be-come hyperthyroid, then excess thyroid hormone can pass into the breast milk. For this reason, you must take medication exactly as prescribed by your physician. The period following delivery is also one where thyroid levels can fluctuate, so frequent testing is very important, because your dosage and TSH level may be just right three months postpartum, but three months later, the same dosage could be making you hyperthyroid. So, plan to get blood levels drawn frequently (at least every three months) as long as you are nursing your baby.

Dealing with Low Milk Supply

My milk-supply issues are apparently not uncommon for women with underlying thyroid problems. Often, a period of low milk supply may, in fact, be a sign of postpartum thyroid problems. After suffering from a period of low milk supply after the birth of her son, Sharon began to develop other symptoms, including sore and numb wrists and arms, and major fatigue, which she would discover were related to a case of postpartum hypothyroidism:

> I saw my internist and asked for a referral to a physical therapist for what I believed was carpal tunnel syndrome. He listened to my symptoms and said that while he would give me the referral for the splints he also wanted me tested for hypothyroidism. It turned it out I was hypothyroid. The doctor later on said, "I bet you are tired and depressed, and think that's how a new parent should feel." He explained to me about postpartum thyroiditis and Hashimoto's thyroiditis, and told me, in answer to my question of when did it start, that he had no way of knowing, but he absolutely agreed that my thyroid disease was the cause of my declining milk supply.

Not content to leave it at that, Sharon decided to get the word out about how the onset of low-milk supply had coincided with the hypothyroidism:

> I took my best articles to my hospital-based midwife and asked her if she or any of the ob-gyns warn women about thy-

roid disease in the first year of pregnancy. She admitted they did not and probably should. I commented that the new mother gets lost in the system. If she has had a routine pregnancy and postpartum period, her last visit is six weeks after the baby is born and probably before signs of thyroid disease are noticeable. Monitoring should be done at six-month and one-year periods to see if the new mother is in a hypothyroid or hyperthyroid state. I then contacted the lactation consultant, who proved to be the most open to ideas. When she heard the outcome of my saga, she said, "We always focus on getting the baby to nurse or to reestablish the mother's milk supply. We never think to have the mother examined."

If your newborn isn't gaining weight after the first week, and isn't having the requisite number of soiled and wet diapers each day, he or she might not be getting enough milk.

Assuming that you've gone back to your doctor, and had a full panel of hormone and thyroid tests done, and medications adjusted as needed, your next step is to visit a professional, if you are still having difficulties. A certified lactation consultant can check the baby's latch onto the nipple, give you ideas for different positions to hold your nursing infant, and suggest a number of helpful ways to increase your milk supply and get your baby sucking more vigorously and efficiently.

You can find a certified lactation consultant at your hospital, a birthing center, through a recommendation from your pediatrician, in the Yellow Pages, or from La Leche League.

In addition to professional assistance from someone who is knowledgeable about breast-feeding, there are some other approaches that may help with your milk supply. These include:

Nursing Vacations—Where you focus totally on resting, eating and drinking properly, and nursing the baby on demand. This can sometimes help rejuvenate a flagging milk supply.

Switch Nursing / "Burp and Switch Nursing"—This technique involves allowing your baby to feed on the first breast until his sucking lessens in intensity and he begins to get sleepy. Gently take him off your breast, burp him, and get him started again on the other breast. When his sucking slows, repeat the process, switching again, so he nurses at least twice at each breast. Breast milk contains a watery foremilk at the beginning of a feeding, designed to quench the baby's thirst, and the high-fat, creamy, satiating hindmilk, which is produced as the baby continues to suckle. It could be that your baby is not gaining well because he or she is not getting enough of the hindmilk.

Getting Enough Food and Liquids—A nursing mother needs to continue the healthy diet she had during pregnancy. Most lactating mothers need an extra 500 calories a day. Now is not the time to go on a crash diet to get back into those prepregnancy jeans, particularly when your baby is not feeding and gaining well. You also need at least eight to twelve glasses of water a day, and you should avoid caffeinated drinks when possible.

Herbs and Teas to Increase Milk Supply—There are numerous medicinal herbs out there that are "galactogogues," meaning they boost milk supply. Some may be effective for you. Check with your practitioner before starting any of these herbs or teas. Some of the most recommended include fenugreek, blessed thistle, alfalfa (but note, alfalfa is *not* recommended if you have an autoimmune problem).

Prescription Drugs—There are medications that some doctors will prescribe to women with a low milk supply, provided all other avenues to breast-feeding success have been exhausted. Reglan (metoclopramide) is available in the United States and is sometimes used to increase milk production. If you get a prescription for it, the typical dose is 10 to 15 mg, three times a day. It's a temporary drug, to be used no longer than four weeks. One important caveat: If you suffer from depression, as many thyroid patients do, particularly in the dicey postpartum period, this drug is probably not for you. Some of the side effects include depression and mood swings.

Sometimes, in spite of your best plans, things don't work out with simple breast-feeding. After exhausting all possible ways to get your baby gaining directly at the breast, you may need to, as I did, supplement nursing or pumped breast milk with bottles, cups, tubes, or syringes of formula while trying to get baby nursing and gaining better. Whatever happens, know in your heart that you gave breast-feeding the best effort that you could, and please don't feel guilty if it doesn't work. You are not a failure, nor does the fact that you are not nursing reflect poorly on your mothering skills or your love for your baby. You tried everything you could possibly do, you sought out help from professionals, you followed their advice to the letter. No guilt allowed! Instead, pat yourself on the back for giving your baby the best start in life he or she could get!

Infant Formula Issues

How can you choose which formula to give your baby? Some studies suggest that staying away from soy formulas for infants is a good idea, particularly if you have thyroid conditions in your family. Why? According to environmental scientist Dr. Mike Fitzpatrick, infants fed a steady diet of soy formula are more at risk for developing thyroid disease. Soy baby milks—and other soy products, for children and adults alike, he attests—have high levels of isoflavones, which are strong antithyroid agents.

Fitzpatrick has spoken on behalf of the New Zealand Ministry of Health regarding their position:

> *The Ministry of Health has found that infants with a history of thyroid dysfunction should avoid soy formulas and soy milks. Additionally, there is potential for isoflavone exposure to cause chronic thyroid damage in all infants fed soy formulas.*

Fitzpatrick stated that exposing infants to isoflavones was unnecessary, and that the risk of harm could be avoided if manufacturers removed isoflavones from soy formulas. "In the interim," he stated, "it is appropriate for medical practitioners to monitor the thyroid status of infants fed soy formulas."

Scientists, lactation consultants, and health care professionals agree that "breast is best" for a plethora of reasons, not the least of which is that breast milk contains certain fatty acids that are linked to brain and visual development. Babies who are breast-fed—or babies fed a formula supplemented with DHA (docosahexaenoic acid)—score significantly better on I.Q. tests, studies show. But if you do need to use a baby formula, try to choose one that has supplemental DHA.

■ Moving Forward

I hope that this chapter has not frightened you. Despite the possibility of hormonal ups and downs, and breast-feeding challenges, I just want to offer hope that you can get pregnant and have a healthy baby while you're being treated for hypothyroidism. I had my wonderful little girl and she was worth all the hormonal flip-flops in the world!

When it comes to being hypothyroid and having successful pregnancies, you can't get a happier ending than Jeanne's story:

> I have been taking Armour thyroid since I was two years old. I have seven kids, six girls and one boy. They were all born within ten years. The only problems that I noticed while pregnant was that my thyroid had to be upped to four grains a day. I am now back to taking only one grain a day. My oldest is twenty-three and my youngest is thirteen. Sometimes I wouldn't have minded if my fertility were on the low side!

16

Hypothyroidism in Infants and Children

So long as little children are allowed to suffer, there is
no true love in this world.

—ISADORA DUNCAN

Congenital hypothyroidism—hypothyroidism at birth—affects
an estimated one in four thousand newborns. The disease used
to be a major cause of mental retardation in children because development of the brain, as well as normal growth of the child, is dependent upon normal levels of thyroid hormone. Now routine
testing for hypothyroidism—usually part of the heel stick test given
to newborns in the United States, Canada, and many other nations—
has prevented many of the long-term problems that developed as a
result of undetected and untreated hypothyroidism.

It's always worthwhile to verify that your baby has had the
newborn-screening tests and that the test screened for congenital
hypothyroidism. I remember when I had my baby, I asked the
nurses specifically if the heel stick test they were giving her covered
hypothyroidism. Not one maternity ward nurse had any idea what
the test covered, and I insisted on getting a copy of the state's
brochure that explained the test in full. I was relieved to discover

that the test did cover hypothyroidism. But frankly, hospitals aren't perfect, and things can get overlooked; this is one question I recommend that everyone ask.

Because congenital hypothyroidism is not so common, it's not always easy to get information about the problem. Early on in my work as a patient advocate, I had the pleasure of interviewing Kelly Cherkes, who at that time was Thyroid Division Director for the MAGIC (Major Aspects of Growth in Children) Foundation for Children's Growth and Related Adult Disorders. While no longer with MAGIC, Kelly has been a strong advocate for parents, providing a wealth of information and resources related to infant and childhood hypothyroidism. She herself is the mother of a hypothyroid child.

According to Kelly, even with the screening program, it's important for parents to watch for the symptoms of congenital hypothyroidism in infants:

- Puffy face, swollen tongue
- Hoarse cry
- Cold extremities, mottled skin
- Low muscle tone (floppy, no strength)
- Poor feeding
- Thick coarse hair that grows low on the forehead
- Large fontanel (soft spot)
- Prolonged jaundice
- Herniated belly button
- Lethargic (lack of energy, sleeps most of the time, appears tired even when awake)
- Persistent constipation, bloated, or full to the touch
- Little to no growth

According to Kelly, children with congenital hypothyroidism are usually diagnosed within the first couple of weeks of life due to the newborn-screening programs:

More often than not symptoms are not apparent at birth but can become visible by the time of diagnosis. Most parents feel they have been blessed with a "good" baby because they sleep so much and fuss so little.

When hypothyroidism is discovered in an infant, it is typically due to one of three reasons: (1) failure of a normal thyroid gland to function properly; (2) a congenital thyroid malformation—including failure to develop properly, position in the wrong location, or undersized; or (3) an enzyme defect in iodine metabolism that makes them unable to make thyroid hormone.

Once diagnosis is made, your child should be referred to a pediatric endocrinologist. Kelly has found that for some parents, it can be difficult to find a local pediatric endocrinologist, but even if it means traveling a bit out of your area, it is very important to have your child seen by a specialist at least once. Then, after the pediatric endocrinologist has seen your child, he or she may follow up with your child's pediatrician to ensure proper treatment.

Doctors should, according to Kelly, perform other tests to find out more about your child's condition, including a thyroid scan to tell if your child has a thyroid gland or not. Some children have a gland in the wrong place or one that isn't fully developed. This is important because if your child has a gland and it's in the right place, the condition may be temporary, what's known as transient hypothyroidism. If your child does not have a gland or the gland is misplaced, your child will need thyroid replacement medication for life. It is good to have this information early on instead of waiting till your child is three, at which point you might have to take her or him off medication to get an accurate scan at that time. Your child will also likely have a bone-age X-ray done. This is an X-ray of the ankle and/or wrist to show the growth of the bones. It is a diagnostic tool used to let doctors know the possible severity of the disorder by determining the time of onset in utero.

In addition to congenital hypothyroidism, children can also develop what's known as acquired hypothyroidism. Typically, this is hypothyroidism that develops in children due to autoimmune thyroid disease such as Hashimoto's disease. It's more common as children reach puberty or teenage years, but can still appear in young children. It is also more common in girls than in boys. According to Kelly, when children acquire hypothyroidism, it can be more damaging than to an adult. In most instances, when a child develops hypothyroidism it goes unnoticed for quite some time. Unfortunately, children change so much during childhood that tiredness, mood swings, weight gain, and health problems are often attributed to other causes. Most parents mainly notice the deficit hyperactivity disorder (ADD/ADHD). Many children also suffer from upper respiratory infections and have been diagnosed asthmatic until they are on a proper regimen of thyroid replacement hormone.

Kelly believes that anyone with a family history of hypothyroidism should have their children routinely screened, especially if they test positive for thyroid antibodies. Children who acquire hypothyroidism are treated similarly to those who are born with it. A bone-age X-ray and thyroid scan are necessary, and very close monitoring of their levels is also a must.

However your baby or child has become hypothyroid, Kelly recommends that parents keep the results of all tests, along with blood test results and specific values in a journal or record book. Your journal should also include the normal ranges for these tests, so you have a way to gauge where your child falls compared to the normal values. You can use this journal to keep track of the child's symptoms as well, with the goal of becoming familiar with how these levels coincide with your child's health and well-being. Keep in mind that lab levels change depending on your child's age. Once your child reaches twelve, he or she will typically have the same normal ranges as adults.

Treatment for congenital and acquired hypothyroidism involves replacing the missing thyroid hormone in pill form. It is absolutely essential that these pills be taken daily for life, because thyroid hormone is critical for all the body's functions. This is *particularly* important for infants and children in order to ensure normal physical, mental, and intellectual development.

When it comes to medication for infants and children, there are various brands of thyroid hormone replacement that can be prescribed. Kelly has some excellent tips that you might want to discuss with your child's doctor:

> For children I recommend the soft pills, Levoxyl or Levothroid. These two dissolve easily in water and/or crush easily. Synthroid is a very hard pill which is hard to crush, then when you add water it clumps up, I found it to be extremely difficult to work with. There is not a liquid form of levothyroxine sodium at present. Some pharmacists will take thirty days of medication, crush the pills and add them to a "simple syrup" which is administered daily. The problem with this is a potency issue. You don't really know day to day how much hormone your child is receiving because the powder settles and needs vigorous shaking so it's a guess how much each actual dose is. I believe this method, although easier, is not the best for infants.

Kelly has these suggestions for parents on how to give the medication:

1. *Dissolve or crush pill in 1 cc of water, breast milk, or milk-based formula. (Do not mix with soy-based formula.) Draw liquid into syringe. Place tip of syringe far back on the inside of infant's cheek and slowly squeeze into child's mouth.*

2. *Crush pill, wet your finger, roll finger into powder, let baby suck the powdered pill from your finger. This method*

works the best and ensures the infant gets all the medication.

It is best to administer on an empty stomach. It can be difficult with newborns because they feed so frequently. If this is a problem, remember that consistency is the key, it is more important to be consistent in how and when you administer. If there are any kind of malabsorption issues, the blood test will reflect that and your pediatric endocrinologist can adjust the dose accordingly. When your child is older, around two, he or she can chew the pills instead of having to crush them. Most children like them and this becomes part of their daily routine.

A normal starting dose for infants is approximately 50 mcg, and the goal is to get the child euthyroid (normal thyroid levels) as soon as possible to avoid any developmental delays or potential brain damage.

According to Kelly, as your child grows, it is of the utmost importance to keep close track of thyroid levels. Any child who is hypothyroid—congenital or acquired—will need periodic changes in dosage. Doctors often recommend that the child have blood tests at least every six months and even more frequently while an infant. Also, schedule a special thyroid checkup for a girl with hypothyroidism about the time she first begins to menstruate. Hormonal fluctuations may warrant a modification in her thyroid hormone dosage. With early, proper, and regular treatment, your child can grow and develop normally. But keep in mind some additional advice from Kelly:

Thyroid disorders in children can create a number of symptoms that seem unrelated to the thyroid. As you care for your children, please be aware, it is not just a pill a day. We as parents are the only advocates for our children and empowering ourselves with knowledge of this disorder is the only way we can truly do what's best for them.

17

Hypothyroidism After Thyroid Cancer

Fall seven times, stand up eight.

— JAPANESE PROVERB

In most cases of thyroid cancer, the gland is surgically removed, either all or in part. For some the thyroid or any remaining thyroid tissue is ablated, using radioactive iodine. The treatment usually results in hypothyroidism, and a lifelong need to be on thyroid hormone replacement.

Because thyroid cancer survivors take suppressive doses of thyroid hormone, designed to keep TSH levels at 0 or nearly undetectable levels, they often don't consider themselves "hypothyroid." But if you have had thyroid cancer, have had all or part of your thyroid removed, and need to be on thyroid hormone replacement, your condition is now hypothyroidism.

There are a number of unique issues related to thyroid cancer. These are concerns that are not applicable to people who are hypothyroid due to autoimmune illness or surgical removal or RAI for noncancerous thyroid conditions.

■ TSH Suppression

The first unique issue is what is known as TSH suppression, the practice of giving sufficient dosage of thyroid hormone to keep the TSH low, sometimes almost undetectable, in the hyperthyroid range. This is done as a way to prevent thyroid cancer recurrence. Making sure that thyroid cancer survivors are aware of the need for suppression is a mission of Kathy, a thyroid cancer survivor herself. Kathy, who has been an active member of ThyCa, the Thyroid Cancer Survivors' Association and the associated online e-mail support lists, has some excellent advice that is very specific to her fellow thyroid cancer survivors:

> If you lost your thyroid gland to thyroid cancer and you believe you have symptoms of hypothyroidism, the most important question is: has your doctor explained to you that in order to prevent recurrence or spread of papillary or follicular thyroid cancer you must suppress TSH to a below-normal level, meaning that your bloodwork should be more indicative of hyperthyroidism than hypothyroidism? If your answer is "no," call or fax your doctor as soon as possible.
>
> No doctor ever told me that I was taking Synthroid to do more than replace the functions previously performed by the gland. I had to hear from fellow patients that TSH needed to be suppressed below normal to prevent thyroid cancer recurrence! Ask whether suppression of TSH to a below-normal level has been your doctor's goal, and ask what your TSH is on your current dosage of thyroid replacement hormone. The conservative approach is to suppress TSH below 0.1, but, depending on the circumstances of the case at hand, some endocrinologists will allow TSH of up to 0.3 or 0.5 if the patient feels poorly at lower levels. If, upon talking to your doctor, you learn that your TSH has not been suppressed to below-normal levels, consider either encouraging your doctor to in-

crease your dosage or change to a doctor with more thyroid cancer experience.

■ "Going Hypo"

The second issue is becoming hypothyroid prior to thyroid scans, or a process sometimes referred to as "going hypo." As part of the process of thyroid cancer follow-up, periodic scans look for any reappearance of the cancer. Most people are required to stop taking their thyroid hormone and become clinically hypothyroid with elevated TSH levels in the weeks prior to the scan. This is often the most difficult aspect of thyroid cancer follow-up treatment, in that people actually become and remain hypothyroid for weeks in order to ensure the most accurate scan.

Megan, an upbeat young thyroid cancer survivor, has this to say about "going hypo":

> *I'm not looking forward to being off the pills because those days will pass slowly, and I'll be feeling pretty bad. Not easy for someone like me who is normally very active and has a to-do list a mile long. Being off the thyroid pills made me absolutely exhausted, like I've been to several all-night parties without the fun. Even my elbows were tired. How do you have tired elbows??? Every day I felt more like a dishrag. I told that to a friend, a psychotherapist, who asked, "What color dishrag are you?" I replied, "A yellow one, because I am cheerful and positive, even though I feel limp." After that, just thinking about being a yellow dishrag made me smile and feel better. There are days when I can't find the energy to turn on the computer, but when I do, I also sure love to read e-mail jokes. I am keeping my spirits up by laughing. It's good medicine and it doesn't taste bad, except for the tasteless jokes!*

Bob, a survivor of papillary thyroid cancer, has some excellent tips gleaned from his two trips to what he calls "Hypoland":

- Work: Tell your boss ahead of time what to expect and when. When I had a treatment schedule with dates, I followed up with an e-mail.

- If you start feeling crappy sooner than expected, contact your doctor and see if you can get your TSH level checked early. I was originally scheduled to have blood drawn on the 11th and if my TSH was greater than 40. I would take my tracer dose of RAI on Monday the 14th. As it turned out, I called on Tuesday the 8th and my TSH was 114. I took my 3 mci dose on Wednesday, found I had less than 1 percent uptake on Thursday and a clean scan on Friday the 11th.

- Dealing with other people: When you're hypo, your face will be puffy, your speech will be slurred, and you won't be moving quite as purposefully as normal. As a result, it is likely strangers will respond to you differently than you're used to. I found myself "under observation" at the library and in a couple of stores. I'm also afraid I scared a lady at my daughter's pre-school.

When thyroid cancer survivors "go hypo," doctors typically target a fairly elevated TSH level for the scan. Getting to a TSH of 30 or 40, or over 100 as Bob described, can mean more than your fair share of full-scale hypothyroid symptoms. It makes sense not to plan important, stressful, or taxing events during this period, and to avoid taking on too much during this time.

Ric Blake is a thyroid cancer survivor and the dedicated founder and organizer of the first Thyroid Cancer Survivors Conference in 1998, and one of the founders of the Thyroid Cancer Survivors' Association (ThyCa). Ric has some lighthearted—but quite valid—ideas to share as well, in his "Tips for Thyroid Cancer Survivors While Hypothyroid":

In hypo-hell, one is much like a cat, an old and cranky cat. For those preparing to go off your hormones in preparation for a body scan, we offer this guide for you and your significant other.

• As with any old cat, hugs and snuggles works wonders.

• As with any cranky cat, keeping your distance is a smart idea.

• Change the balance of household responsibilities: Your partner can take on more; you can sleep.

• Add more physical activity to your schedule: Your partner can rub your back; you can purr.

• Consider separate vacations: Your partner can go to Hawaii; you can go someplace warm.

• Divide up household chores: Your partner can do them all; you can sleep.

• Reschedule cooking responsibilities: Your partner can go out; you can eat salt-free between naps.

• Change your recreation schedule: Your partner can go dancing; you can keep the bed warm.

• Rent videos. Your partner can rent *Fatal Attraction 2*; you can rent *Sleeping Beauty*.

• Rethink making major decisions: Make no decision more complicated than which shoe to put on first.

Ric has also developed what he refers to as "the more serious version":

> *Forewarned is forearmed has much merit for thyca survivors. In the three and a half years since my diagnosis and surgery, I've had body scans and RAI four times. On average, I've been hypothyroid every ten months, making me a reluctant expert on journeys to hypo-hell and back. The last two times have been easier because by 1997 I had met other survivors and learning from others' experiences is the best resource we have for living well with thyca.*
>
> *My doctors told me I would feel increasingly worse as I became more and more hypothyroid. What they didn't tell me was just* how *much worse I would feel. If they had, I would have been better able to plan my life. Each time I followed the same sequence: six weeks off hormones, scan, RAI, then begin hormones four days or so after the radiation. Here are the survival tips I've learned along the way.*
>
> *Working: If possible, don't work full time the last week before and the first week after your scan. Use your vacation time and plan lots of naps. If you must work, negotiate with your employer and work half-days if possible.*
>
> *During this two-week period, don't: drive a car; operate dangerous equipment; sign important papers; make significant decisions; start a new job; move to a new house or apartment; or tell your boss what you really think.*
>
> *Avoid: stressful conversations; difficult people; malls; and rush-hour commuting, even if you're sitting on the passenger's side of the car.*
>
> *Put off: working on important projects; anything requiring clear thinking and organizational skill; and everything that can be put off.*
>
> *Do: drink lots of water to prevent constipation; eat lots of*

fruits and vegetables for the same reason; exercise even when you don't feel like it; cut down on calories to avoid weight gain; plan on being very good to yourself; buy yourself something special; plan on seeing lots of movies, plays, and concerts that require no thinking on your part; buy new batteries for the television remote: channel surfing is therapeutic; and weed your garden before you're severely hypo.

Expect to: be very cold; carry a sweater at all times, even in the summer; be a jerk to the people around you; apologize ahead of time; lose your car and house keys often; forget the names of your spouse and children; and get lost driving familiar roads.

When preparing for scans, you should: wear warm clothes (sweats are best) and take a blanket; and if possible, take a portable radio, tape, or CD player.

Not everyone has a full-scale reaction to the hypothyroid period before a scan. Margie found that despite being off her thyroid hormone for a total of more than five weeks and reaching a TSH of 95, she didn't suffer hypothyroidism symptoms throughout the entire period. Her symptoms only began a few days before she was due to start back on her thyroid hormone replacement. She has some theories about why she didn't experience the full brunt of "going hypo":

I attribute this to serious workouts, mainly weights and stationary gym bike, at least five days a week, which I started over four months ago. I was doing five miles a day on the bike. The symptoms I have experienced are quick sudden weight gain—fifteen pounds in two weeks—problems concentrating and being irritated at things that do not normally bother me much. Also sudden exhaustion, then rebounding.

Thyrogen Scans

It's important to mention Thyrogen to thyroid cancer survivors. A product approved in 1998, Thyrogen, the brand name for recombinant TSH, allows some patients to avoid the process of withdrawal from thyroid hormone replacement. Patients switch from their thyroid hormone replacement to Thyrogen prior to the scan, and don't suffer the experience of going hypothyroid. It's certainly something to discuss with your doctor. Thyrogen is a very expensive drug, and only certain patients are good candidates. Some experts do not believe that the scan results done while taking Thyrogen are as sensitive as results for patients who have "gone hypo," and so some practitioners feel that a Thyrogen scan is not as reliable as the full hormone withdrawal; however, this is currently a point of debate. Thyrogen scans can be highly useful for those patients who have had several clear scans, and thus a limited likelihood of cancer recurrence.

■ The Low-iodine Diet

A third issue is the low-iodine diet. Many patients are required to go on a low-iodine diet for at least two weeks before the scan to ensure the greatest accuracy. This diet increases the reliability of the test. Doctors often ask patients to continue the diet through the testing procedure and during any subsequent treatment with radioactive iodine, so some people can be on it for a number of weeks.

You should get specifics from your doctor regarding how to follow the low-iodine diet, and download or request a copy of the latest low-iodine diet guidelines from the Thyroid Cancer Survivors' Association. As far as general guidelines are concerned, however, it's basically fine to eat fresh meats, fresh poultry, fresh or frozen vegetables, fresh fruits, as long as you don't cook with or add specific condiments and other foodstuffs that contain iodine. So, generally, here are the low-iodine diet guidelines:

- *Avoid iodized salt and salty foods:* You'll want to avoid all iodized salt and sea salt products as well. You can use noniodized salt, kosher salt is noniodized, for example. Be aware that most salty foods like pretzels, chips, popcorn, and nuts may have iodized salt, so you should avoid them. Also, most restaurant and fast foods contain salt, and there's no way to determine which outside salt is iodized. Your best bet is to avoid most salty foods. (Unfortunately this means you need to be careful about most restaurants.)
- *Avoid seafood:* Fish, shellfish, seaweed, and kelp are all high in iodine.
- *Avoid dairy products:* including milk, ice cream, cheese, cream, yogurt, butter, egg yolks, and milk chocolate. The only exception is egg whites and chocolate made without milk.
- *Avoid foods with the following additives:* carrageen, agar, algin, alginates.
- *Avoid cured, corned, or spicy meats:* Avoid bacon, ham, sausage, salami, lox, corned beef, sauerkraut, etc. Fresh meat is acceptable.
- *Avoid commercial bakery products:* Since commercial baked goods often contain iodine, you'll need to have only homemade or local bakery products.
- *Avoid vitamins and food supplements:* If they contain iodine—and most multivitamins do—you'll need to stop taking them.
- *Avoid red, orange, or brown food, pills, and capsules:* Many red, red-orange, and brown food dyes contain iodine.
- *Avoid other foods that may contain iodine dyes and preservatives:* These include soy products, molasses, instant coffee and tea, canned fruits and vegetables.

While we don't have the space to present menu ideas and all the various tips and tricks used by thyroid cancer patients to make food interesting on the low-iodine diet, here are a few excellent tips from Bob to help you follow the guidelines:

Start shopping for staples ahead of time. I had a little trouble finding margarine with neither salt nor dairy this year. The supermarket that carried Fleischmann's version last year now carries Mother's. Some stores I tried don't carry any. All the supermarkets I checked had noniodized salt next to the regular salt. I found salt-free peanut butter in the dietetic food section.

Try a few days on the diet before you're hypo. That way, you'll find out what does and doesn't work while you still have your wits about you and can do something about it. You also won't find yourself, as I did last year, standing in the middle of Best Buy, hypo and hungry with heavy metal blaring while you're trying to pick out a bread machine.

Get a vegan cookbook. Vegans don't use any eggs or dairy. They also don't use much salt, so don't be surprised if things taste pretty bland at first. You can always add noniodized "salt and pepper to taste" after you cooked it. I was amazed at the difference between my first and second bite of vegan chili. Another good source is the Vegetarian Resource Group (Web site: http://www.vrg.org). Their recipes aren't all vegan, but they do give directions for things like mixing cashews and water in a blender to substitute for milk in cooking (i.e., "I cup raw cashews, 3 cups water, blend both for 5 minutes and refrigerate. Shake well before use.")

Don't view this as an opportunity to lose weight, go vegetarian, or make any other dietary changes not related to iodine. You're going through enough. Do try to notice if you're allergic to dairy. I seem to be. My nose stopped running about a week into the diet and started again shortly after eating pizza last night.

■ T3 for Thyroid Cancer Patients?

A fourth issue is related to thyroid hormone replacement. While the T4 versus T3 drug battle wages on between conventional and complementary practitioners and their patients, nowhere is the battle fiercer than when it comes to the issue of thyroid cancer suppression.

Most doctors treating thyroid cancer survivors are adamant in their insistence that levothyroxine is the only drug of choice for thyroid cancer suppression and feel that there is absolutely no role for the T4/T3 synthetic or natural drugs as part of the management of thyroid cancer. They have a concern that there may be ups and downs in TSH levels due to the use of T3, and that even small fluctuations in TSH could fail to prevent cancer recurrence.

I'll be honest here. There's no research regarding whether taking added T3, or a synthetic or natural drug with T3, is or isn't a problem with thyroid suppression or increases the risk of cancer recurrence. Ultimately, what thyroid hormone replacement you take for thyroid cancer suppression and how you feel on that drug is an extremely important matter for you to take up with your doctor. Just keep in mind that in terms of the right treatment and program for total wellness, each patient is ultimately an individual, and some doctors recognize this more than others.

Gail is a sixty-year-old woman who has lived half her life as a thyroid cancer survivor and now provides support to newly diagnosed thyroid cancer patients. Bucking the convention, she takes Armour Thyroid, prescribed by her conventional doctor. Gail found that, unlike today, there was little information available to her when she was diagnosed in 1968. Now she is active in the medical community and well informed about thyroid disease. Even more so since becoming active on the Internet.

I never knew there were issues with T3 replacement. I had no idea that the endocrinology community frowned on the use of Armour thyroid or, for that matter, any replacement with a T3/T4 combination. Although I had a very active and potentially fatal situation in my battle with thyroid cancer, I have been on a T3/T4 drug for 27 of the last 31 years.

I recently asked my endocrinologist how can it be that I survived, against some steep odds, on a drug that was supposed to be inadequate for suppression and not good for me? His reply, though not completely to the point, indicated his flexibility against the T4-only theory. And then he said, "You feel good, don't you? We are not going to fool with success!" On the whole my endocrinologist does not advocate the use of T3. But in my situation he stands firm. I hardly ever experienced the dilemmas that patients go through with their T4 medication. My TSH suppression came right in on target through all the years. The "bounce" that we hear about with T3 never was apparent in my blood testing. The variable times and circumstances when that blood was taken over the years are many. It makes me wonder why T3 is not looked at a bit differently by the medical community.

■ General Wellness

The final issue is general wellness after thyroid cancer. At low TSH levels, thyroid cancer survivors can experience symptoms of hyperthyroidism, and even though TSH is suppressed, at times, also experience hypothyroidism. While some symptoms are no doubt due to the thyroid, there can also be a tendency to attribute most health problems to the underlying thyroid issues.

Again, Kathy feels that if your TSH is being adequately suppressed, but you are still having symptoms, you'll need to look at some other issues:

Have you talked to your primary care doctor or a counselor as well as your endocrinologist about your symptoms?

Perhaps there is a valid medical reason for your symptoms that is totally unrelated to your thyroid cancer and hormone suppression therapy. Perhaps there is other bloodwork that should be ordered. Perhaps the fears and uncertainty related to a cancer diagnosis have led to anger, depression, or other emotional trauma for which psychotherapy is indicated.

Kathy also feels that it may be important to have a partnership with an endocrinologist in which you feel comfortable suggesting alternative or unconventional approaches to thyroid hormone suppression therapy:

If you have ruled out any causes other than thyroid suppression therapy for your hypothyroidlike symptoms, then explore the feasibility of working with your endocrinologist to modify the current approach to alleviate the symptoms. Perhaps, if you have had a history of negative scans and favorable Tg readings, your doctor would be willing to lower your thyroid hormone dosage slightly and allow your TSH to rise. Perhaps, if you are taking only levothyroxine, your doctor would be willing to add supplemental T3 or switch to a T4/T3 combination.

One aspect of thyroid cancer aftercare is the fact that, if your care is properly managed, you will never again have a "normal" level of thyroid hormone in your system:

Remember, you are different than someone with thyroid disease. While the thyroid disease patient strives to attain normal thyroid hormone levels, you are striving for optimal adaptation to abnormal levels. The payoff is increased odds of avoiding recurrence or spread of your thyroid cancer.

Suppressed TSH levels mean that you may have to pay more attention or take a different approach, to things like diet, exercise, relaxation, or supplements than you did before having your thyroid removed. Kathy suggests taking advantage of all the information available at the library, bookstore, on the Internet, or in patient/survivor support groups to develop a customized, individual program for adapting to the reality of TSH suppression. Just be sure to keep in touch with your doctor about the approach you develop, and get bloodwork done soon enough after any major dietary changes to ensure that your TSH remains adequately suppressed.

Long-term thyroid cancer survivor Gail has some thoughts about life with and after thyroid cancer:

My journey with thyroid cancer was tumultuous in the early years when I had five major surgeries in four years. Since then I have lived an active, healthy life, raising three wonderful children and doing volunteer work with cancer patients. Cancer became a steppingstone to a better life and understanding of what is important. I put the fears behind me and let the joys of life become my focal point.

PART V

Living Well Now and in the Future

18

Living Well with Hypothyroidism: Creating Your Plan

Drugs are not always necessary, but belief in recovery always is.

— NORMAN COUSINS

For most of us, there's no one magic pill that ensures that we can live well with hypothyroidism. Rather, the secret is an approach that blends the science *and* the art of living well.

Hopefully, this book has already provided enough information to help you get on the right thyroid hormone replacement at the right dosage for you. This is essential to living well. The *science* of living well also relies on resolving any other hormonal or chemical imbalances and health issues that might get in the way of being well and living well. For this, a productive partnership with caring, smart health care practitioners will take you a long way.

The *art* of living well opens up a whole additional world of opportunities. You can find the right alternative therapies and integrate them into your overall treatment, learn to develop a positive attitude, choose foods to nourish mind and body, or learn how to empower yourself to move forward on your own behalf.

Ultimately, your success begins with a fundamental belief in your own recovery. Yes, hypothyroidism may not be the easiest condition to resolve completely, and, yes, many doctors may not invest much energy in the problem . . . but leave that behind. *You* must have faith and believe that *you* can recover and go on to live well.

This chapter looks at some various approaches to help you live well. These ideas mainly come from the best possible source: people living well with hypothyroidism themselves. Some advice comes from doctors and health care practitioners who have demonstrated their ability to help people live well. You'll find many ideas to consider as part of your own effort to live well.

An endocrinologist, the practice of T'ai Chi, and a vegetarian diet might be the answer for one person. Or the addition of a T3 drug, aerobic exercise, and participation in a chronic disease support group at the local hospital may work for another. Each person's optimal approach is likely to be different. Your job is to find the mix of ideas that works best for *you*.

In my case, for example, I've found that a holistic doctor; use of natural thyroid; periodic acupuncture; yoga; weight-bearing exercise; a low-glycemic diet; online support; a nutritionist advising me on vitamins, supplements, and diet; and a sense of humor constitute the best mix for me.

Sherry Ann has found an approach that works for her:

> *I pray a lot and I thank the Lord that I am where I am to-day and that I am not as I was years ago. I really thought then that I was going to die. I believe humor is great. It keeps our spirits up, and we need to laugh because Lord knows I have shed my share of tears. Learn all you can about this, and if your doctor doesn't understand, you find another one. Keep prayer in your life. Try to find a support group to go to and take your family with you.*

As you read through the various suggestions on living well with hypothyroidism, I hope you find ideas about approaches that might work for you. And as you read the ideas and hopes of other thyroid patients, give some thought to what you'd like *your* personal philosophy to be.

My personal philosophy is that even if I can't resolve every single thing about my hypothyroidism, I keep looking for answers I can find. This makes me feel I have some control over the situation. Along the way, I even try to have a laugh or two! And I find great comfort in sharing whatever information I have with others.

■ Living Well Tip #1:
Find the Right Hypothyroidism Therapy

There's no doubt that the right therapy for hypothyroidism is a basic requirement for living well. No amount of Synthroid is going to solve your problem, if what you really will thrive on is Armour. You can add time-released T3 therapy to your Levoxyl, but that won't help if you don't need the added T3 and start to feel jittery. Finding the right drug at the right dosage is not an automatic process for everyone, and may require a bit of experimenting and patience while your doctor fine-tunes and tweaks your thyroid hormone regimen.

When I was first diagnosed, my doctor put me on Thyrolar. A year later, after reading all the medical literature and initially buying into the marketing spiels, I told the doctor I wanted to go on Synthroid. She reluctantly agreed. Within a month, my hair started falling out rapidly, and a thyroid test showed that I'd become hyperthyroid on an equivalent dose. My dose was reduced slightly, the hair loss increased, and I developed an ovarian cyst. Another TSH test a month later showed that I had become hypothyroid. Back to hyperthyroid, then hypothyroid again. After four more months of wildly fluctuating TSH levels, and further hair loss, we decided to go back to Thyrolar. Things calmed down right away. My doctor and I didn't need any medical textbook or double-blind study to tell us that I was doing better on Thyrolar than on Synthroid. Later on, we did a similar test with natural thyroid, and I flourished, leading to a permanent switch to Armour Thyroid. You may have to go through this process periodically, but it's worth it to ensure you're getting the right medicine and dosage you need.

■ Living Well Tip #2:
Find a Great Doctor (and Get Rid of a Bad One)

The right doctor is an important—almost essential—part of living well. You probably can live well *despite* your doctor, if you truly have no option but to work with an HMO doctor you're stuck with or the only endocrinologist within five hundred miles. When you have a choice, however, one of the most important things you can do is find a great doctor and leave the bad ones behind.

Renee is one patient who needed to find a more positive doctor to help her live well:

> I like to be an informed medical consumer. My doctor claimed to be okay with it. Then, I started having some chest pains. I have read that when taking thyroid hormones, chest pains can be a serious concern. When I saw my doctor to get a refill on my thyroid prescription, I told him that I've been having some chest pains. He listened to my heart and called me a "neurotic fruitcake." No kidding . . . his exact words! He said it several times. I refused to respond. I just wanted to get out of that office! I am looking for a new doctor. I am not a "fruitcake," and I highly doubt that I am "neurotic." I think a doctor needs to listen to (even unfounded) concerns and reassure patients (even "neurotic" ones) without humiliation. I have lost trust and he has lost a patient!"

In her path toward wellness, Geri also found it was time for a new doctor:

The primary-care physician (PCP) who diagnosed me has since been fired (by me) because she had a horrible *attitude. She never answered my questions, didn't take my concerns seriously, generally acted like she had no time for me, and treated me like an uninformed idiot, which I'm definitely not. I'm a health/medical/science writer on a TV science news show, so I deal with this type of information every day. I found another PCP on a referral from friends, and so far so good.*

Sometimes, you'll find a fresh perspective after changing doctors. For years Yobeth's regular physician conducted an annual blood test for her hypothyroidism and never changed her dose. Yobeth decided to start seeing an endocrinologist:

As it turned out, my medication needed adjusting. However, while I was there I learned a lot that I'd never known. I learned there were links to thyroid disease, diabetes, and high cholesterol. This came as a total shock. I'd never been told [that] or checked [for it] by any of my other doctors. I do have high cholesterol and my three-month average glucose test was high, but I'm not diabetic yet. Maybe I'm overreacting, but it seems doctors should take this a little more seriously and also educate patients more thoroughly.

Personally, I have to say that I am extremely lucky in that I have a wonderful doctor who is my partner in the search for wellness. My physician, Kate Lemmerman, M.D., has these thoughts about the key characteristics of her patients who live well with a chronic and, sometimes, debilitating and exhausting condition like hypothyroidism:

The key characteristic to living well with any chronic condition is setting the stage for healing in your life. You try to provide ideal conditions for the body to heal. And what we need for those ideal conditions is a combination of proper nutrition, appropriate exercise, and a healthy mental attitude. I think it is very helpful to find a physician whom you trust and with whom you can communicate. Even if they are not "experts" in the field, if they are dedicated to your well-being, they will learn along with you the best way to enhance your health.

Dr. Lemmerman's point is valid. She is not an endocrinologist or thyroid expert. But she is always learning, always trying to keep up with new information and is a talented, open-minded, and caring physician who practices medicine as an art. She is dedicated to my well-being, and you can't ask for anything more.

Chapter 9 offered a number of tips on how to find a doctor and communicate well with him or her. If you have doubts about your current doctor, don't forget that your doctor works for you, and just like a plumber or accountant, if he or she isn't doing a good job or treats you like a second-class citizen, it's time to shop around.

■ Living Well Tip #3:
Educate Yourself About Hypothyroidism and Health

I can't emphasize enough how important it is for you to really understand hypothyroidism. So often, people contact me, complaining that they don't feel well after a year or more on Synthroid, and ask, "What should I do?" When I ask them what their TSH level is, they say, "What level? I don't know about this. I just want to feel well." Inevitably, it turns out that they are high normal, or even clinically hypothyroid, or have an extremely low T3 level, and a discussion with the doctor allows for some dosage modifications or a change in medication, and they are feeling better soon. If you don't feel well, you simply can't afford to say, "I don't know—or don't want to know—about this." You *must* take it upon yourself to understand what's going on, so you can ask the right questions, discuss options with your doctor, and find another doctor if yours doesn't make sense.

Allyson has this to say about the need for self-education:

> *Doctors who see five patients an hour do not have time for explanations and questions. Thyroid patients must learn to ask questions, due to the very nature of this illness. I obtained the information I possess today from two sources: books written by patients and doctors, as well as the Internet.*

Megan, a thyroid cancer survivor, prides herself on being knowledgeable about her health issues:

> *Read everything you can get your hands on. Knowledge is power. The more informed you are, the less fear you have. Do whatever you can to feel you have some power in an out-of-control situation. Even if that only means learning more about your disease or its treatments. Know that you have choices.*

Geri, a health-and-science writer and TV producer, has this to say about dealing with doctors:

> *Most of my conflicts with doctors have arisen because I'm a very good researcher and have a medical/science background that lets me investigate things more than most patients do. Most docs don't like it when you demonstrate that you have actual knowledge about something. And, frankly, I think this is the fault of patients almost as much as it is of the doctors . . . most patients blindly accept what a physician*

tells them and consider themselves too dumb to know other-
wise. So when informed patients like us come along, the docs
have no idea what to do with us!

Who knows what developments may be announced tomorrow regarding hypothyroidism? And who knows when—or even if—your
doctor will hear about those developments? The Resources section
in this book includes many useful Web sites, newsletters, books, and
practitioners to help you educate yourself. If you want to live well,
your responsibility is to be aware of available options. You can't afford not to stay up-to-date, because you just might miss hearing
about a new drug or new therapy that could be the answer for you.

■ Living Well Tip #4: Help Educate Others

One important thing everyone with hypothyroidism can do is help
educate others and correct common misconceptions about the condition.

Few people know much about hypothyroidism, beyond unfairly
characterizing it as "a disease that makes middle-aged women fat."
This unfair, inaccurate characterization is part of the reason the disease is so often overlooked and underdiagnosed by doctors, and
why there is so little interest in finding better treatments and cures.
Part of living well is making sure that others understand, and doing
your part to raise awareness.

Sometimes, education starts at home. The most appalling letter
I've ever received was from the husband of a woman just diagnosed
with hypothyroidism. This man was clearly in the dark about the
condition:

> *Is there really such a thing as a thyroid disease? Is it conta-*
> *gious? The women on my wife's side of the family all seem to*
> *have it. Is it hereditary? Does my wife's lack of ambition and*

motivation have anything to do with it . . . or is it simply the result of this "so called" disease? Will she be more ambitious or self-motivated if she takes Synthroid?

Honestly, I felt for his wife. Hypothyroidism seemed the least of her problems. But after sending him extensive information about hypothyroidism, he actually wrote back to say that he was trying to be more patient and understanding with his wife. So perhaps even *he* was capable of being "educated"!

When you encounter lack of understanding or misconceptions, take the time to explain the situation. One woman said that she was so convinced that some of her co-workers were suffering from hypothyroidism that she filled them in on the symptoms and convinced nine of them to be tested. Amazingly, six of the nine were hypothyroid, with TSH levels ranging from 18 to the hundreds. A little education can go a long way toward helping others.

■ Living Well Tip #5: Be Both Patient *and* Persistent

Patient is a confusing word. The word "patient" derives from a Latin verb that means "to suffer." According to the dictionary, patient, as an adjective, means putting up with pain or provocation without complaint. The noun refers to an individual awaiting or under medical care and treatment, or "one that is acted upon." I'm not going to suggest that you should be a "patient patient," putting up with pain without complaint while you are "acted upon" by doctors! Rather, I prefer another definition: "remaining steadfast despite opposition, difficulty, or adversity."

You may need patience just to endure the diagnosis process, much less the search for effective treatment. During the years she tried to get diagnosed, Cathi kept a journal, which helped her remain hopeful:

Each day I would write out "SURVIVAL" on the top of the page and list the things I'd have to do to make it through the day with the pain, the fatigue, holding-on-to-furniture just to stand up. I would list the things I was going to do when my mystery problem was cured and simply fantasize about a future free of pain and what that would be like.

With diagnosis and treatment of her hypothyroidism, Cathi was able to stop fantasizing, move beyond just surviving, and start really living well.

Even with the best therapies or the right drug, you can't expect miracles overnight, so patience is essential at all stages of treatment. However, patience doesn't mean inaction. One of the hardest aspects of a chronic condition like hypothyroidism is the need to be both patient *and* persistent at the same time. You can't give up trying to find the right answers, the right doctor, or the right treatment.

Carol, a fifty-two-year-old woman with hypothyroidism, feels that patience and perseverance are the words that best depict her experience with hypothyroidism:

Patience to wait for the slow response of the medication. Perseverance to go back for repeated blood tests. Patience with myself when I can't do anything after working all day. Perseverance to search for a new GP doctor after finding out that my GP didn't know how to read the lab results and had not treated my hypothyroidism. Patience to wait for two and a half months to get in to see a top endocrinologist. Perseverance to make up all the time I missed at work to go to doctors and labs. Patience with insensitive friends and co-workers. Perseverance with doctors that prescribed tests that were detrimental or inappropriate after telling them I was hypothyroid.

Susan sums it up perfectly when she says: "It is so frustrating that when you are feeling your worst you have to fight the hardest." But that is exactly the point. Living with a chronic disease is a marathon, not a hundred yard dash. Hypothyroidism is one of those "slow and steady wins the race" situations.

■ Living Well Tip #6: Surround Yourself with Personal Support

One aspect of living well with any chronic disease is surrounding yourself with supportive people. Spouses, family members, friends, children, co-workers, support group members—all can play a part in helping to encourage your return to good health. The last thing you need is someone who doesn't believe you are ill, makes fun of you, or doesn't cut you some slack when you're not feeling well.

Rachel, a woman in her early twenties, emphasizes the importance of the right kind of friends and support in her life:

> I have discovered who my true friends are, as some believe I'm "being ill" just to get attention. I've actually realized my priorities are to take care of myself—and to get much more sleep than I used to! Needless to say, I've lost several friends, just because I couldn't go out at night with them. While that hurts, I realize there are better friends out there, friends who support me. My boyfriend and I had only started dating when I first got sick, so I said to him, "I don't know how long I'll be sick for, but you may leave now," and he told me I was being silly. He has stuck by me. . . .

Some of the best spouses and friends are those who take the time to understand hypothyroidism, so they can understand you. Tom has this recommendation for spouses and partners of people with hypothyroidism:

Go to the doctor, ask questions, and find out what they are going through. It will make those times when they seem unbearable understandable, and understanding and love from you is the best medicine they can get . . . and the quickest.

It's very important to open up and share your experiences with others. Renee had this to say about the importance of personal support:

I hope that fellow patients have and rely on a strong personal support network. The reason I say this is that when I was hypo and depressed . . . I didn't even have the self-esteem to tell my husband how bad it was for me. The isolation was part of the depression for me . . . not a good thing at all. I got myself into a place where I felt very alone. It was weird, and it took several weeks to get back to feeling like myself again after I started my thyroxine.

If, like Renee, you don't feel comfortable talking to your spouse or partner, it's worthwhile discussing your situation with someone else. If you're not comfortable talking with family and friends, consider seeing a therapist for a few visits, or get online where you can remain anonymous while you exchange information, support, and camaraderie with others going through similar experiences.

Personally, my husband has always been interested in understanding more about hypothyroidism, and has been extremely supportive. I also found tremendous support by participating at alt.support.thyroid, the online newsgroup. I was amazed to find other people dealing with the same thyroid concerns I had and really enjoyed the interchange, benefiting from information and support. In recent years, I've also turned to the community at my own thyroid bulletin board, an active group of people who provide mutual support and information, spiced up with a sense of humor and a great deal of compassion. I never fail to find a smile, or an uplifting story, or some empathetic grumbling when I need it.

The value of support is never so great as when we discover that friends know us better than we do at times. Joyce found this out when her hypothyroidism took a turn for the worse:

> When I hit menopause, my thyroid became the roller-coaster ride from hell. Up, down, and all around, sometimes with dramatic drops within a two-week span. Not understanding why, my family physician would increase and decrease my medications, hoping to get me level. After a gentle push, or perhaps a shove in this case, by a dear friend, Rosy, I finally decided I needed to take control of my own body. Rosy didn't beat around the bush when she said, "I am very concerned for you. I want my friend Joyce back, you need to pursue other options and take control of your body and your life, whatever it takes!" I promised her I would begin researching my disease and in desperation, I began doing research on the Web, all the while giving Rosy intermittent reports on my progress. I read somewhere on the Web that some vitamins or other prescription medications might interfere with the absorption of thyroid replacement medications. After a thorough examination by an endocrinologist, with a few simple directions, turned my upside-down life around. "Take your vitamins and other prescription medications in the morning and your Synthroid at night." My recovery was very dramatic. Within days, I began remembering things; I felt like working out again, I was smiling, happy, and creative. In other words, Joyce was back! I am happy to report that several months later, Rosy's friend Joyce is as feisty and tenacious as she once was, full of vim, vigor, and a little vinegar on the side. Thank you, my friend.

The message here? Every person with hypothyroidism needs a Rosy—a supportive friend, spouse, family member, or even cyber-pal. Treasure each and every Rosy in your life!

That said, be careful that you are part of a support group that doesn't just focus solely on symptoms, to the exclusion of solutions. You don't want a group that has a particular agenda—i.e., to purchase particular supplements—or a group that has a bias against or rule preventing discussion of all of your options. There are, for example, some support groups online, sponsored by patient organizations, where moderators discourage or even prevent discussion of natural and alternative treatments. Be sure to check out groups before joining.

Note: My list of support groups in the Appendix are all groups that do not have strict moderation of topic restrictions.

■ Living Well Tip #7: Dont Be Afraid to Stick Up for Yourself

The buzzword for this is "empowerment," but let's call it what it is—being able to stick up for yourself with doctors and medical professionals. This is an absolutely essential skill for anyone with a chronic health problem, because you're going to spend some time with health practitioners. No point wasting time and money being lectured at or cowed by your doctor. Learn to stick up for yourself, speak up, and say your piece.

Carla, in her early fifties, has some thoughts about being an empowered patient:

> When I had to start on replacement therapy, I was, of course, given Synthroid. I felt terrible on this medication and my blood pressure, normally quite low, shot through the roof. My doctor was baffled. While researching, I found that a certain number of the general public has a metabolism that does not convert synthetic T4 to T3 when the brain calls for it. I

asked my doctor to prescribe Cytomel. He did, and I felt much, much better. If I had not had the capability and resources to investigate this matter on my own, I shudder to think where I would be today.

Tom has some unique advice from the man's perspective:

The most important thing to remember, man or woman, is that you alone are in charge of your body, and you must not ever let anyone, no matter how many degrees, not keep you informed and involved. Take one day at a time, allow your spouse to help, and ask for help, too. Both are problems men seem to have. This disorder and our modern-day beliefs about "what makes a man" conflict with each other in the worst sort of way. Your life is not worth being macho over.

Peg, a teacher, has realized that it isn't always simple to be an empowered patient. She's tapping her desire to be well as a motivator:

I have a master's degree and am currently undergoing postgraduate training that I will apply to my doctorate, which I plan to pursue and obtain. Yet nobody has listened to me. Blame it on doctors not taking women seriously or what have you. The bottom line is: I neglected some of my own power by allowing myself to be "talked out" of my feelings, intuition, and instincts. But I'm taking that power back, empowering myself and advocating for myself by collecting information to support me. Yes, I am passionate about this. This is my life, and I believe (hope and pray) that it won't be too long until I get it back!! No more passive role for this lady. I'm climbing over from the backseat I've been in and taking over the driving. And I will not stop until I find the doctor who has the expertise to help me. I'm not cured yet, but I haven't felt this good in years.

Dr. Don Michael has some advice:

> I tell all my patients, "Don't believe any doc blindly, not even me. Listen, ask questions, bring a friend or relative or spouse, pick your doc more carefully than your mechanic, don't be afraid to go elsewhere. This is not your parent, you are not a little kid, and you deserve respect and answers." After having lost a mother, a brother, and about 20 years of my life to undiagnosed, untreated hypothyroidism, I really feel that this is a battle for our lives. Take no prisoners, fight like your life depends on it . . . it does.

■ Living Well Tip #8: Listen to and Trust Your Own Body

Listening to and trusting your own body and instincts is an important part of living well. This can be hard if you're not yet diagnosed and are told time and time again, "It's in your head," or "It's not your thyroid." After suspecting thyroid disease for many months, but being told by her doctor that there was no reason even to test for hypothyroidism, LuAnn simply *knew* there was something more there. She finally demanded a full thyroid test:

> On Friday evening I received a call from our clinic. It was the doctor on call that night. She said that my bloodwork results had just come in and that she was very worried and needed to get me on some medication immediately. My heart was pounding and I started sobbing on the phone, because someone was saying that, yes, there is actually something wrong with you! She said that my T4 was not even borderline. It was 0.4. And she had never seen a higher TSH, which was 460. But my doctor shocked me when we saw her that Monday. She said, "See, aren't you glad that we checked for thyroid. I kind of thought that that was what was wrong." I

told her, "But you said it wasn't thyroid!" She just said, "Well, now we know, don't we? Maybe we should have communicated a little better with each other." Oh, was I mad!!! I have never set foot in their clinic again.

Leanne, a thirty-three-year-old thyroid cancer survivor, feels it is important to listen to her body:

I guess just as important as being informed is being tuned into your own body. I was feeling stressed and short-tempered, so I called my doc and asked her to order some bloodwork because I felt I was taking too much Synthroid. That was, in fact, the case. And then a few months later, I told my husband I was still a little high, and the bloodwork verified that. Remember, nobody knows the normal you better than you do. Trust yourself.

My doctor is often amazed at how accurate I can be in estimating my TSH levels. I can definitely tell the difference between a TSH of 1.5 versus 4 versus 5.5. If you listen to your body and trust your own instincts, you can probably become quite good at monitoring your own thyroid levels as well.

■ Living Well Tip #9: Develop Some "Perspective"— The Ability to Look Beyond Your Thyroid Problem

When you have something like hypothyroidism, which can affect so many aspects of your health, there's a tendency to take it to an extreme. You'll sometimes want to blame everything from your latest toothache to an ingrown toenail on your thyroid.

Ted—an alt.support.thyroid regular—has this to say about having some perspective:

As you know, in alt.support.thyroid, we can find a reason for any symptom to have a root in thyroidland. It is easy to place blame with the thyroid. Many of us get caught up blaming everything on our thyroids. I blame my exhaustion on my thyroid. I blame my memory lapses on my thyroid. I blame my bald head on my thyroid. I blame the fact that my washing machine loses socks on my thyroid. . . . You would think that the thyroid is god.

Ted feels that elevating the thyroid to this level of importance can lead to a sense that tweaking the thyroid dose can cure everything. And if it doesn't, we can end up feeling a sense of hopelessness. That's when it's useful to take a step back when therapy seems to fail, and look at the various interrelated functions of the body, before assuming that the thyroid is at the core of all the problems.

In my own case, I have a tendency to assume everything goes wrong because of the thyroid. But sometimes the several days of unrelenting headache is just a plain old sinus infection. Aches and pains can actually be the flu, rather than a developing case of rheumatoid arthritis. And while I assumed I was going to be a standard infertility case and would find it near impossible to get pregnant due to my hypothyroidism, I was pleasantly surprised when I became pregnant quickly. The point is, don't assume the worst, and don't always assume it's your thyroid.

■ Living Well Tip #10: Reduce Stress in Your Life

Stress has a major effect on a chronic health concern like hypothyroidism. Stress changes body chemistry and changes your body's need for thyroid hormone, a need that can't always be met on a fixed dosage. Stress also generates brain chemicals that contribute to depression and other diseases and make them impossible to heal.

When you lower stress, you cause changes in the brain and the immune system that actually increase the ability to fight disease.

Look at the various stressors in your life with an eye toward reducing or eliminating as many as possible. Do you dread weekly housecleaning sessions? Figure out a less stressful way to get them done—perhaps involving your family or hiring a cleaning person. Learn to say "no" to extra obligations and requests from other people. It's one thing to serve as a class-trip chaperone or take on extra projects at work once in a while. But if you can't say "no," and then find yourself overloaded with other people's hand-me-down projects, focus on learning to say "no" and put your own health and priorities first. "Sorry, I would love to, but I can't possible do that. I have other plans," is a good multipurpose excuse. There's no reason to explain that your other plans include a well-deserved nap or relaxing bath or energizing walk.

Sometimes, reducing the stress in your life may require more dramatic changes, particularly in your job. Bobbi felt it was necessary to switch careers in order to gain more control and less stress in her life:

> I've recently started my own business. I'm cleaning houses and I love it. I used to be a legal/executive secretary stressed out to the max and now I basically work for myself with flexible hours. It's great. I felt like a prisoner and a victim of this disease before. Therapy and a good doctor have made all of the difference in the world! Having an understanding husband, family, and friends have also contributed to my healing process.

Diann is another person who decided to change her job to control her stress:

> I have just made a "courageous" choice in life: I have given up my very stressful career of several years, and next week I

start clerking at a discount store. I am simplifying my life, pay-
ing the credit cards off, eliminating car payments, and just plain
getting back to basics. My personal philosophy these days: Life
is way too short to struggle past fifty! I grew a fantastic garden
this summer. I incorporate all the items in foods I make from
"scratch." Our food budget has never looked so good.

Another major source of physical stress is not getting enough
sleep. According to a survey released in 1998 by the National Sleep
Foundation, one in three people in the United States sleeps for six
hours or less per night, substantially less than the recommended
eight hours. Sleep is an important way to help restore immune function, and if you used to need seven or eight hours, once hypothyroid, you may need somewhat more on a regular basis to be truly
rested. Don't compromise on sleep or it will definitely add to your
stress levels.

In addition to changing careers, learning to assertively say "no,"
and getting enough sleep, there are many other ways to reduce stress
effectively. Exercise, mind-body practices like yoga and T'ai Chi,
deep-breathing techniques, meditation, relaxation tapes, and prayer
can all be extremely effective. Some people find that alternative therapies like aromatherapy or listening to relaxation tapes work to reduce stress. It's important to find methods that work for you and to
practice them actively, while at the same time removing or reducing
those stress factors that you can control.

Other helpful ways to beat stress? Cut down on caffeine, stop
multitasking all the time, avoid people who are "stress carriers" or
"energy vampires," take a "news" fast and avoiding watching the
news for a day or a week, adopt a pet, drive less aggressively, be
flexible and recognize that things don't always go as you plan and
pray/speak to God/your higher power/nature/your inner guide.

■ Living Well Tip #11: Exercise

Exercise has so many positive benefits to everyone, including thyroid disease patients, that it should be included in everyone's wellness efforts. Unless you are trying to lose weight, the type of exercise is not as important as simply incorporating some daily activity into your life. Gardening, dancing, housework—all can be considered exercise. But it's likely that you'll stick to it if it's an activity you truly enjoy. And remember, any exercise is a help. Whether it's something fairly relaxing like T'ai Chi or yoga, or marathon running, find the exercise you like and do it regularly.

■ Living Well Tip #12: Get Tested as Often as Needed

Most of the standard operating manuals for thyroid disease recommend having your thyroid checked once a year—sometimes even once every two years. More frequent testing, however, may be better for you. If you have ongoing problems with symptoms, or unusual symptoms appear, don't wait for your next annual or semiannual thyroid check. Go in right away.

Renee was glad she had a test earlier than scheduled:

> The doctor I'd been seeing since moving to a new city said every six months would be often enough to check my TSH. In July, my TSH was 2.04 (normal range 0.2–6). Three months later, I went back and asked for a test because I was exhausted, sleeping, and depressed, mostly. My TSH had shot up to 58 within three months.

Being tested is particularly important to remember when you're going through any hormonal changes, such as postpregnancy, perimenopause, menopause, or stopping/starting the Pill or hormone replacement therapy. Drs. Richard and Karilee Shames underscore the need for frequent evaluation:

> *Keep in mind that whatever treatment you arrive at for doing well currently may change in the future. Optimal dosing—whether natural or prescription for thyroid patients—is a moving target.*

■ Living Well Tip #13: Try New Ways of Taking Your Medicine

How and when you take your thyroid hormone may have an impact on its effectiveness for you. If things aren't working, and you're taking your thyroid hormone with food, try taking it on an empty stomach. If you take your dose once a day in the morning, try taking it in the evening. If you can split your pill, talk to your doctor about taking some in the morning, some in the evening. The most important message? When things aren't working, it's time to try something different.

■ Living Well Tip #14: Maintain Your Sense of Humor

Doris Lessing wrote: "Laughter is by definition healthy." She was right. A sense of humor goes a long way in dealing with illness.

William F. Fry, M.D., of Stanford University, an expert for the past thirty years on the physiological effects of humor, believes that laughter may actually trigger physical changes that help ease pain. It's thought that laughter causes the brain to release hormones that cause the release of endorphins, the body's natural painkillers. Other scientists have actually documented increased immunity and a reduction in stress hormones during laughter. In one Japanese study, reported on in the *Journal of the American Medical Association*, a significant reduction in their allergic response was seen in patients who had their allergy triggered and then watched a comedy film. The researchers concluded that laughter may play some role in helping the immune system to alleviate the allergic response.

All in all, it's clear that humor acts as a critical *vaccine*, protecting your emotional and mental immune system, and can help protect your body from the effects of stress, particularly stress that is due to long-term chronic illness. Humor helps bolster your immune system and resilience, and should be a part of your overall program—including nutrition, exercise, rest, and emotional satisfaction—for wellness. And beyond the technical, medical reasons, laughter simply does feel good.

I've tried to incorporate humor at my thyroid Web site. You might ask, What's so funny about thyroids? It's actually not that hard to find things to laugh about when it comes to thyroid problems, doctors, or HMOs. But no one says you need to laugh *about* your thyroid. A funny book, movie, song, or just a good laugh with a friend—all have the same healthful effects.

Find something to make you laugh . . . laughter is the best medicine.

■ Living Well Tip #15:
Men—Realize That You're Not Alone

So many of you men with hypothyroidism feel that you are alone. Dealing with most of the same symptoms that plague women, you also cope with the extra stigma of having what people think of as a "woman's disease." You may feel that no one else understands what you go through.

Bill feels that his bout with hypothyroidism has given him added insight:

> *Does it bother me to be a victim of what is known as a woman's disease? Not at all! Women have been an integral*

part of my life for many years. Having personally experienced the disease, I have a great deal of empathy for "The Sisterhood of the Shattered Butterfly" with all of its unpleasant aspects.

I urge men to join more support groups, or get online and become involved in the online support groups for thyroid disease, where there are many men who participate regularly. You'll be able to share information on some of the unique aspects of hypothyroidism for men, and realize that you are absolutely *not* alone.

■ Living Well Tip #16: Women—Be Prepared for Pregnancy and Menopause

When we were little girls, before we had our first period, our mothers and teachers typically sat down with us and went over one of those cryptic little books about the menstrual cycle and women's anatomy. Often, this was the first and *last* time we actually studied and learned about our hormonal cycles—and it's not enough, particularly to get you through pregnancy and menopause.

Pregnancy and menopause can cause hormonal fluctuations for women with hypothyroidism. The shifting hormones can wreak extra havoc on an already unstable endocrine system. To help ride out the ups and downs, I have several key suggestions.

First, get several must-read books. I consider these the absolute basics in any woman's "hormonal library":

• *Listening to Your Hormones*, by Gillian Ford—Ford, a specialist in women's hormonal issues, outlines how hormones affect our well-being, and discusses the most common hormonal problems. Ford examines the full range of hormone therapies, as well as a host of natural alternatives.

• *Taking Charge of Your Fertility*, by Toni Wechsler—Not just a book for people interested in fertility, this presents a comprehensive overview of nearly everything about the menstrual cycle and hormones.

Two, prior to pregnancy and as you start approaching the age of menopause (keep in mind, you're often likely to go into menopause at about the same time your mother did), be sure to keep detailed records of all your various hormonal levels. It's useful to have handy baseline levels of estrogen, progesterone, testosterone, and thyroid hormone levels, reflecting a period when you're feeling well. This way, you'll have a target number to work with when you are pregnant or postpartum, and as you become perimenopausal and, ultimately, menopausal. Ask for copies of all bloodwork, and keep charts and copies yourself.

Finally, be sure you're working with a doctor who truly understands women's hormonal medicine. You may need to switch around to find the right doctor. For example, a doctor who doesn't know that pregnant hypothyroid women often need more thyroid hormone is not particularly knowledgeable. The right doctor may be a family-practice osteopath, or an ob-gyn who understands hormonal issues, an endocrinologist, or a practitioner of the newer field of "women's medicine." Whoever it is, make sure he or she is passionate about understanding and staying up-to-date on all facets of women's hormonal issues, and is open to the full range of options in treating hormonal deficiencies or fluctuations.

■ Living Well Tip #17:
Maintain a Positive Attitude and Outlook

I'm the first person to admit that maintaining a positive attitude isn't always easy. And don't let anyone else tell you it is, either. Take a person who used to be in perfect health, make them exhausted all the time, add forty extra pounds, and toss in some fistfuls of hair falling out in big wads, and then show me how many of *them* can maintain a positive attitude! When you add the various health complaints of hypothyroidism, *plus* a tendency toward depression, it's a wonder anyone with hypothyroidism can maintain a positive attitude. But *we* can—and do.

Research published in the *Journal of Personality and Social Psychology* in 2001 found that a positive emotional state can actually help ward off disease and even prolong life. The experts theorized that the more optimistic a person is, the less stress put on the body over time. When there is little stress, the body thrives, is able to better ward off infection, and has more resources to devote to healing.

How you stay positive is unique to you. Some people believe in support groups, whether in person or online. Others find prayer useful. Yet others find aerobic exercise or more mind-body energy exercise, such as yoga or T'ai Chi, to be the keys to a sense of well-being and positive feelings.

Dr. Brian Sheen expresses it well. He believes that living well and staying positive is a spiritual quest:

> *Learn to live a peaceful life filled with forgiveness that shares your essential spiritual nature with an open loving heart and expresses itself in a creative and empowering fashion.*

Some days, being positive just means putting one foot in front of the other and moving forward, however you can. Sue has this philosophy when she's not feeling up to par:

> *I just put a small goal in front every day and try by the end of the day to get it done . . . even if you start out dusting off three things . . . the next day I try to dust two rooms. . . . I can now run the vacuum cleaner and dust! (Laugh!) I don't let myself get into too much. I expect help and get it . . . if you can't do it, well, let it go.*

Patient advocate and writer Kim Carmichael Cox says that when she first started treatment for her illness she thought she would take a pill and everything would be okay:

> I have since come to understand that there is a complex interplay within the body and all the hormonal systems. I have realized that there is no pill that can precisely alleviate every symptom of a disease process. While my health has improved from when I first became ill, there are many days when I still struggle with fatigue and a feeling of depression or "brain fog." The biggest challenges for anyone dealing with a chronic illness are managing lingering symptoms and trying to live fulfilling, productive lives. What has kept me going physically, mentally, and spiritually is the belief that no matter how bad things may be there will be better days ahead.

Being positive also means being fair about what you expect from yourself. Part of Sue's recovery has been in learning how to move forward positively but realistically:

> My husband, a doctor, understood. He lived with me and had to deal with my lack of energy, fuzziness in concentrating and seeing firsthand how it affected me. He has realized that there is something to this disease. He lets me sleep when I need to and understands the energy spurts and the recovery days. It has impacted my whole family. Maybe replacement is getting back to normal for some people, it wasn't for me. Maybe my doctor thought I was a whiner when all I wanted was to be like I was before. It has been a big adjustment for me and hard to accept that "normal" was going to have to have a different definition for me than it did before. I'm more accepting of my limitations. I'm healthy, and live a pretty full,

busy life, but I can tell the difference. Pacing *has become my "word of the day."*

Joyce, a quilt artist with hypothyroidism, has found a new philosophy of hope and openness to help her deal with her illness:

Nothing stays constant in life; life is about change and how you handle it. My promise is never to take myself too seriously, to laugh myself through anything and everything, to love, to live every day as though it is my last and to be kind and nonjudgmental. I know as I age, new discoveries will emerge about my disease and perhaps one day, I'll be totally symptom free! For now, I am grateful that I can put a few words together that actually make sense and that I no longer need a padded floor for unscheduled naptime landings. My creativity as a quilt artist has not only returned, it seriously threatens taking over my whole life. I suspect my family and friends are thankful to have the person they vaguely remember back, the one who lives life to the fullest, laughs herself silly, and falls to sleep each night with a smile on her face.

The first time I read Joyce's predictions and hope for the future was actually the first time I personally had considered the possibility of a real cure. Every day, it seems, new developments and cures for various diseases are announced, and new medicines or therapies—conventional and alternative—are launched. It's entirely possible that in our lifetimes, we *will* see dramatic improvements in the way hypothyroidism is treated, especially if we patients work together to insist on this progress. And pondering those thoughts *definitely* gives me a positive attitude.

■ Living Well Tip #18: Aim to Truly Live Well

Ultimately, living well with hypothyroidism means deciding that you are going to be a person who voyages through life, rising above the hypothyroidism. You may ultimately learn to live with it, work around it, even reverse or cure it, but somehow you will live well. Susan has found her own answer to living well:

> I had obvious thyroid symptoms for years but "normal" TSH that kept creeping up: 2.5, 3.5, 5.2, etc. I was the one who did the research and insisted on an antibody test when my throat felt swollen in the thyroid area. This was with the horrible primary doc who used to just shrug and dismiss all my inquiries. I have new docs for myself now who are much more respectful. My new primary started me on thyroid hormone replacement when I asked to be retested at her lab and my TSH was 7.2 and antibodies sky high. She set me up with a decent endo who also listens pretty well. I'm hanging in at 2.5 TSH, and although I may be able to do better, I feel pretty good in comparison to before, and am down 14 pounds!

Pam is excited finally to be back on track with her life and health:

> Right now, I feel that I am feeling the best I have for twenty years. My ability to think, concentrate, and express myself has much improved, due to thyroid meds and hormone replacement therapy. You have to advocate for yourself (or be lucky enough to find a doctor who really understands thyroid). Low thyroid is so subtle in the way it takes away your life—slowly, slowly, slowly taking away your health, your thinking abilities and, due to tiredness, your relationships, your recreational activities. It's amazing to me to wake up out of this fog, and now to have so far to go to catch up and gain

my life back. For the first time in years, I feel good enough to
want to exercise!

Suzanne has had to redefine somewhat her expectations and, in
doing so, has learned how to live well:

> *I feel great actually, lots of energy most of the time. Now*
> *and then a few symptoms will be noticeable, but I don't let*
> *them keep me down. I'm not sure about other thyroid suffer-*
> *ers, endos, or doctors, but to be told that you are now in your*
> *forties and things are just the way they are and get used to it—*
> *I don't agree. Sure, some things aren't going to be quite the*
> *same, but other things can be dealt with and between the doc-*
> *tor and the patient a happy medium should be able to be met.*

I feel that part of living well is also being realistic. Even if you
can't be cured, you can strive to be *healed.* I know that most of us
are on a mission to find the cure, the drug, herb, or combination of
alternatives that will return us to the way we used to feel: well, slim,
energetic, with thick hair, normal periods, and limbs that don't tin-
gle and ache. We read, we visit practitioners, we share with other
patients. We talk to everyone from top endocrinologists to the local
herbalist, from infectious disease experts to T'ai Chi instructors,
looking for answers. We talk to everyone, try everything, certain
that the cure is out there. That search for the "cure" is what spurred
me to start my Web site, to write this book and become a thyroid
patient advocate.

But there's a question we ultimately need to ask ourselves, and often don't: What if we can't be cured? What if, as much as we want to
be cured, and work toward it, we can't find all the answers. What if
we can't ever go back? What if the only way we can move is forward?

Asking yourself this question, and being able to live with the answer, is in my mind the difference between being healed and being
cured. For me, being healed means:

- Accepting myself as I am, even loving myself as I am, with whatever limitations I currently have, without giving up hope that I can improve—in both mind and body
- Refusing to live in the past, and refusing to worry about the future, but instead living for now, enjoying this time, now
- Learning how to value myself for what's really important, my spirit, my kindness, how I live my life, instead of focusing on superficialities such as weight changes, thinning hair, a missing thyroid, not having enough energy to be everything to everyone, and other imperfections
- And, above all, finding within the cloud of disease, the silver lining, the positive effects that thyroid disease has had on my life. If you think about it, there have to be some good things that have come from it. Dear friends you've made in support groups, finally starting to exercise, eating better and caring for your health, or perhaps learning how to stick up for yourself and your family with doctors. Or perhaps taking time to slow down a bit and take more time for yourself.

In my life, having thyroid disease has introduced me to so many fascinating and pioneering practitioners: I've also made lifelong friends of many amazing and caring fellow thyroid patients, and I've learned how to treasure the days and weeks and months when I *do* feel well, and how never to take my health or the health of others for granted.

Ups and downs in health may always be there for those of us with lifelong hypothyroidism, but there's one thing that no pill or endocrinologist or herb can change, and that's how we choose to live our lives, and whether our health controls us or vice versa.

You have the power within you to live well. I wish you success, and good health, as you continue your journey.

19

Looking Toward the Future

The best way to predict the future is to invent it.
— ALAN KAY

During the first half of the twentieth century, hypothyroidism was diagnosed by a variety of different tests and criteria. It was treated with natural thyroid hormone. The second half of the twentieth century will be remembered for the rise—and subsequent dominance—of the TSH test and the synthetic drug levothyroxine.

What can we look forward to in terms of hypothyroidism treatment? Hopefully, books like this one are helping to educate and empower patients so they can have a greater voice in their thyroid diagnosis and treatment. And educated, empowered, and properly treated patients can mobilize to speak out about the need for long-overdue research and breakthroughs in hypothyroidism diagnosis and treatment. At the same time, we need to energize the nearly nonexistent search for ways to prevent, reverse, or even cure some forms of hypothyroidism.

Now, during the early part of the twenty-first century, you—whether you are a thyroid patient, friend, family member of a thyroid patient, or health care practitioner—have a *critical* role in ensuring that diagnosis and treatment for hypothyroidism does not remain static for the next fifty or hundred years. Start by speaking out and taking an active role in some of the following important issues of hypothyroidism and thyroid care that we face in the twenty-first century.

■ Improve the Quality and Availability of Existing Drugs

Sometimes, it seems as if a week doesn't go by without an announcement of another recall of a thyroid drug. In the past few years, we've seen recall after recall of various thyroid drugs, especially levothyroxine drugs, cited for problems with potency, stability, and consistency. The inexplicable thing is, that this isn't supposed to be happening. All the levothyroxine drugs recently went through a lengthy and often bitter struggle to obtain FDA approval. This process started in 1997, when the FDA decided that levothyroxine drugs were to be officially classified as "new" drugs and would need to go through the new drug application (NDA) process. This decision was due to a long history of stability and potency problems with levothyroxine products. According to the FDA, many levothyroxine sodium tablets were not remaining potent through their expiration dates, and tables of the same dosage strength from the same manufacturer varied substantially in potency from lot to lot. At the time, it was published in the *Federal Register* that "no currently marketed orally administered levothyroxine sodium product has been shown to demonstrate consistent potency and stability . . ."

Why was levothyroxine not "FDA-approved"? Synthroid, the first levothyroxine product on the market, never went through any formal testing or approval process when it was introduced back in the 1950s. It was "grandfathered in," at the time positioned as *equivalent* to natural thyroid hormone products. At the same time, marketers wasted no time in making claims that synthetic thyroid drugs were far superior to the natural drugs. Along the way, because levothyroxine was not formally FDA approved, there was little formal collection of information on side effects, both minor and serious.

In order to pass the NDA process, several of the manufacturers had to revise their formulations and scramble to produce a levothyroxine that would pass approval. While one of the lesser-known products, Unithroid, made by Jerome Stevens Pharmaceuticals, was able to meet the FDA's initial deadline and was approved in August 2000, it wasn't until two years past the initial deadline, in July 2002, that top-selling Synthroid managed to get approved. Eventually, with numerous delays and extensions, a number of products were finally approved. Unfortunately, the problems with consistency, potency, and stability continue.

It was thought that the rigors of the approval process would result in products that were more consistent. But this does not appear to be the case. What can be done?

• Thyroid drugs are highly profitable, and the drug manufacturers need to use less of those profits on marketing, and more on improving quality control in manufacturing so they can produce more stable, reliable products.

• While they're at it, manufacturers should put some of those profits toward research into new technologies that could produce more stable, consistently potent products.

• The professional and patient organizations should have allegiance first and foremost to patients and patient care—not to the pharmaceutical companies whose funding they solicit. That means holding these companies to a higher standard, and demanding more reliable, stable products.

• Finally, the FDA, which has been particularly lax in enforcing problems with thyroid drugs, needs to crack down on manufacturers who consistently produce subpar products, no matter how big the companies are or how much influence they wield over Washington lawmakers.

■ Research and Develop New Drugs

Another important issue is the need for research and development of new, more innovative thyroid drugs.

There's evidence that some new drugs may be on the horizon. For example, Belcher Pharmaceuticals, a subsidiary of Innovative Companies, has filed a patent on a new way to stabilize levothyroxine. The company believes they can substantially improve the stability of levothyroxine through their new production technology. The company is filing an abbreviated new drug application (ANDA) drug with the FDA that would permit Belcher to manufacture and sell levothyroxine for human use, but no time frame is set. Another company, Lotus Biochemical Corporation, is reportedly developing a combination T4/T3 time-released formula thyroid drug. This drug has supposedly been in development for years, but no further news or release dates are pending.

Thyroid patients desperately need more options when it comes to thyroid drugs. For example:

• If T1 and T2, the ingredients in natural thyroid, have a biological action on the thyroid, researchers should be studying ways to create synthetic combination drugs that include all active and relevant thyroid hormones.

• Based on understandings of optimal T4 and T3 levels, different combination drugs should be developed that include different levels of T4 and T3, based on patient needs.

• More research and development efforts should go into creating thyroid drugs that mimic the action of the thyroid itself, ideally releasing more hormone when the body needs it and cutting back as needs are reduced.

- The usefulness and effectiveness of other delivery formats should be investigated, including patches, creams, and implants.
- The possible need for co-factors, such as selenium, may warrant creation of new thyroid drugs that also include additional vitamins or minerals.

Again, some of the vast profits earned by the pharmaceutical manufacturers who make thyroid drugs should be reinvested into research into new treatment options for thyroid patients.

■ Research Thyroid-Related Medical Issues

When it comes to thyroid disease and hypothyroidism, practical, unbiased patient-oriented research is desperately needed. So much of the research, while valuable, focuses on issues that don't have any near-term practical application for patient quality of life. The government, pharmaceutical companies that make thyroid drugs, the universities that conduct research, the corporations doing research, the patient and professional organizations—they all need to make it a priority to support, fund, and facilitate *practical*, unbiased patient-oriented research. We need more scientific evidence, but the kind of evidence that practitioners—both conventional and alternative—can get behind and trust. As Dr. Sanford Siegal pointed out:

> *Scientific evidence is wonderful. Would you happen to know where I can find some? Is scientific evidence the kind that is funded by grants from vested interests?*

When pharmaceutical companies are the primary sources of funding, the results often get skewed, as many independent studies have shown. The government, professional groups, and patient organizations need to step up to the responsibility of taking a more active part in thyroid research on a number of key topics.

Normal TSH Levels

We need much more of an understanding of "normal" TSH range than the current laboratory reference range. While the clinical endocrinology community believes that the normal reference range for TSH should be 0.3 to 3.0, many labs and doctors are still working with the outdated 0.5 to 5.5 level. Even the newer, narrower range may not be accurate. Studies need to be conducted to look at this issue comprehensively, evaluating the true normal range for a population of individuals who have *no thyroid antibodies* and who do not *ever* go on to develop thyroid disease in their lifetimes.

In addition to looking at new definitions of the normal range, quality of life research needs to be conducted that defines narrower-target TSH ranges where symptoms are minimized or eliminated, without serious long-term health dangers. This *must* take into account patients' reports of symptoms, quality of life, energy, fatigue, weight gain, and all the other symptoms that frequently continue in "treated" hypothyroidism. It's not enough to determine one target range for all adults of all ages. These ranges must look at optimal TSH levels that are specific to a variety of different population groups and circumstances, including infants; adolescent boys; adult men; senior men; adolescents, premenstrual girls; women in different hormonal states, i.e., menstruating, pregnant, perimenopausal, menopausal, and postmenopausal. Other questions need to be studied, including:

- How thyroid hormone requirements in a woman change during the menstrual cycle, how this can be reproduced with a better form of thyroid hormone delivery, i.e., a patch or a daily pill with changing dosage based on the menstrual cycle
- How TSH fluctuates during the day, and whether it warrants administering thyroid hormone by other means, such as different dosages split throughout the day, or via time-released pills, for optimum results and reduction of symptoms

- More in-depth understanding of how to prescribe thyroid hormone based on the seasonal fluctuations that are known to occur in TSH levels and the body's inhibited ability to convert T4 to T3 during cold weather
- If and how major physical stress, disease, surgery, pregnancy, and breast-feeding warrant specific or planned modifications in dosage to meet the body's thyroid hormone requirements, and what the implications are for optimal treatment

Patient Quality of Life Issues

We need a much better idea of the quality of life faced by people with hypothyroidism. From late 2001 to 2002, I conducted a survey among my site and newsletter readers. This survey, based on a tally of 907 respondents, was the first large-scale quality of life survey of thyroid patients, and the first to look at critical patient concerns, such as unrelieved symptoms, weight problems, attitudes toward patient organizations, smoking behavior, and effective treatments and solutions. (Since the survey was conducted among those who volunteered to submit information, it is considered informational and not statistical.)

Of the 907 people surveyed, more than 70 percent were hypothyroid. And among them, when asked if they were satisfied with the treatment they were receiving, more than half indicated that they were not satisfied. Many patients reported that they still suffered from symptoms despite treatment. Among those responding to this question:

- Almost 92 percent feel fatigued, exhausted more than normal.
- 65 percent are unable to lose weight with proper diet/exercise.
- 62 percent feel run down, sluggish, lethargic.
- 60 percent have difficulty concentrating.
- 58 percent have no sex drive, or a reduced sex drive.
- 51 percent have pains, aches and stiffness in various joints.
- 45 percent feel depressed.

- 43 percent are experiencing hair loss.
- 38 percent have eyes that are light sensitive, gritty or dry-feeling.
- 38 percent have strange feelings in neck or throat.

When asked about their worst symptom, 794 respondents answered, and fatigue was the symptom most often cited, followed by weight gain/inability to lose weight, depression, brain fog/loss of concentration, and muscle/joint pain.

Why are the majority of *treated* hypothyroidism patients *not satisfied* with their treatment? Why are people who are being treated—in most cases they are considered *fully* treated by their practitioners—continuing to suffer unusually high rates of fatigue, exhaustion, weight problems, cognitive difficulties, libido problems, muscle and joint pain, depression, hair loss, and other symptoms?

We need more information about the quality of life of people with hypothyroidism, and we need more answers to these important questions. It's not enough for physicians to run a TSH test, give thyroid hormone replacement until the TSH is "normal," and then send the patient away to come back again next year for another TSH test. This is not good doctoring, this is not good medicine, and it's not acceptable. People with hypothyroidism deserve far better.

The Need for T3

Once and for all, the question of whether some, or maybe all, people with hypothyroidism would have improvements in health with the addition of T3 to their thyroid hormone treatment must be decided. And it needs to be studied and decided in a way that will satisfy even the most conventional doctors.

There's no question that T3 is a critical part of adequate thyroid hormone replacement for some people. But the use of T3 is, for the most part, still relegated to "alternative" treatment and is not part of thyroid replacement therapy for most hypothyroid patients in the United States. With conflicting research findings, the issue is even more muddied than ever before.

Most of the conventional medical authorities advocate the use of brand-name levothyroxine/synthetic T4 alone as treatment for hypothyroidism. These doctors do not recommend the addition of T3 to the regimen, whether it comes from synthetic T3 drugs like Cytomel, or from the combination synthetic T4/T3 drug Thyrolar, or from the natural thyroid hormone replacement drugs like Armour.

There are a number of studies that have demonstrated a clear physical, cognitive, and psychological benefit to most patients taking some T3 along with their T4 drug. At the same time, other studies have found that the addition of T3 did not provide any particular improvements.

All of the T3 studies done to date have had small patient populations, have studied patients who became hypothyroid in different ways, used different amounts of T3 and T4, and monitored patient blood levels and evaluated improvements in different ways. Some practitioners feel that all the studies—pro or con—are in the end meaningless because they simply do not use T3 in the forms and amounts that knowledgeable practitioners typically prescribe it.

When used properly, thyroid drugs with T3 are safe, effective, and FDA approved. And their usefulness needs to be more intensively researched. Questions need to be answered, such as: How much T3 does the body need? What problems or conditions might impede T4 to T3 transformation? Are there certain situations or conditions where patients would *definitely* do better with the addition of T3?

More research is also needed on the role of Reverse T3. Reverse T3 refers to the process by which the body converts T4, not to T3, but to an inactive form, Reverse T3, during times of physical stress. A 1977 report in the *Journal of Clinical Endocrinology and Metabolism* found that both pregnancy and estrogen administration were associated with increases in Reverse T3 concentrations, for example. Does this increase in Reverse T3 during periods of hormonal upheaval explain why women with hypothyroidism tend to suffer greater fluctuations and worsening of symptoms after pregnancy, or during menopause, or after starting the Pill or hormone replacement therapy? This is something that deserves serious study by impartial researchers.

When it comes to the T3 issue, there may be conflicting journal research for and against its use, but there is a wealth of evidence from patients and practitioners that T3 can be a helpful addition to the options available for thyroid treatment. It is time to explore fully the role of T3 in proper thyroid treatment.

Effectiveness of Natural Thyroid

Research also needs to revisit the role of natural desiccated thyroid. While this drug has been around for a century, very little research has looked closely at the drug, particularly in comparison to its synthetic counterparts.

We need to answer three key questions: (1) Are there cases or conditions where natural thyroid is superior to levothyroxine or to a synthetic T4/T3 drug like Thyrolar? (2) Do the additional hormones beyond T4 and T3 have a specific action that we don't understand yet? And (3) does natural thyroid demonstrate a stability and potency equal to or better than its synthetic counterparts?

In the case of natural, desiccated thyroid hormone like Armour, we're talking about a product that was safely used exclusively the entire first half of the twentieth century. And its safe use continued through the second half of the century.

Dozens of seniors have contacted me saying that their doctors took them off Armour after twenty or thirty years or more, and only *then* did symptoms begin to plague them after years of good health on Armour. Many of the old-time doctors *still* prefer Armour, because they simply can't get satisfying results with levothyroxine alone. And some practitioners treat all hypothyroid patients with Armour as a matter of course. Only if patients *don't* respond to Armour do they then prescribe a synthetic product.

It's time to really study natural thyroid and assess its role in thyroid treatment.

The Autoimmune Connection

The autoimmune element of thyroid disease is an area ripe for further study. As practitioners begin to understand the common pathways to autoimmunity, there's a good chance that they will better understand the linkages and triggers. For example, one known connection—that untreated celiac disease/gluten intolerance can cause autoimmune thyroid disease—is rarely mentioned by most practitioners and in most literature. Yet a gluten-free diet can in some patients *eliminate* thyroid antibodies and actually *cure* their hypothyroidism.

Here there's a clear action point for patients. Join the American Autoimmune Related Diseases Association, known as AARDA. AARDA is one of the most reputable and effective patient-oriented organizations I have encountered in my work as a patient advocate, and I am always impressed by their effectiveness at putting autoimmune disease on the research map.

AARDA is supporting research efforts to pinpoint better the risks, triggers, causes, and mechanisms behind autoimmune disease, and ultimately to find ways to prevent it, cure it, or fully treat it, rather than simply "manage" it, as is the case in many conditions, including Hashimoto's and Graves' diseases—the diseases that ultimately result in most cases of hypothyroidism.

AARDA founder, president and executive Virginia Ladd, a lupus patient herself, has built an effective organization that has made tremendous strides in its efforts to advance the understanding and treatment of autoimmune disease, and has spearheaded the development of an Office on Autoimmunity at the National Institutes of Health, as well as a nationwide series of "Centers on Autoimmunity." AARDA publishes a helpful quarterly newsletter, and sponsors various research efforts and functions. Annual membership for an individual is very affordable, and your support and research dollars go toward the only national organization dedicated toward studying and eradicating autoimmune disease.

To join, contact the American Autoimmune Related Diseases Association/National Office, 22100 Gratiot Avenue E., Detroit, MI

48021, 810-776-3900, or visit their Web site, http://www.aarda. org.

Other Causes and Triggers of Thyroid Disease

The study of bacteria as a cause of chronic diseases is also just gaining momentum, but these sorts of investigations certainly should include thyroid disease. Just as scientists now know that ulcers and certain forms of heart disease can result from bacterial exposure, there is growing evidence that some autoimmune diseases have a bacterial component. We know, for example, that infection with the food-borne bacterium Yersinia can trigger autoimmune thyroid disease, and that antibiotic treatment can actually *eliminate* the underlying thyroid condition.

Imagine if other forms of thyroid disease could be cured with an antibiotic or even prevented by a vaccine? It would be a revolutionary finding for many millions of people. This research needs to be a priority.

At the same time, throughout this book, we've discussed the anecdotal link between the Epstein-Barr/mononucleosis virus and the development of autoimmune hypothyroidism. While research has yet to document a clear and obvious link between the Epstein-Barr virus and thyroid problems, this is an area that deserves extensive study. In addition, the search for other viral causes and links, and possible antiviral agents or vaccines, should also be a research priority.

Finally, the issue of toxic chemicals and their ability to affect thyroid and endocrine function negatively is also an area that needs far more in-depth study and research. While I touched upon some of the chemical exposure "risk factors" in Chapter 2, many people don't realize how pervasive these concerns are and how many of us probably suffer from thyroid problems that stem from toxic environmental exposures.

Perchlorate, for example, a chemical used in rocket fuel and fireworks production, is a far greater concern than officials typically reveal. Perchlorate was manufactured near Henderson, Nevada.

Specifically, there is concern that there is perchlorate-contaminated groundwater feeding the Las Vegas Wash, Lake Mead, and into the Colorado River system. There is now evidence that perchlorate has reached the Central Arizona Project canal, which carries water from the California line to Phoenix and Tucson. Recently, perchlorate-contaminated drinking water has been discovered in dozens of communities around the country, not just in the Southwest, raising the concern even further. In some areas where perchlorate concentrations are high, the rates of congenital hypothyroidism are substantially higher than normal, indicating that perchlorate-contaminated water may even be having an effect in utero.

The understanding of how long-term exposure to various chemicals affects the thyroid is really just beginning. Scientists are just now documenting the ability of certain chemicals to affect our endocrine glands and the thyroid gland in particular. But there's definite evidence that exposure to certain chemicals increases the risk of developing thyroid disease.

Endocrine disrupters are man-made chemicals that mimic thyroid, estrogen, testosterone, and other hormones and, thus, affect the endocrine system, including the thyroid gland and its function. They also cause birth defects, cancer, infertility, and other serious health problems. The Endocrine Disrupter Screening and Testing Advisory Committee (EDSTAC) of the U.S. Environmental Protection Agency says that about *fifteen thousand different chemicals* that are included in common products like pesticides, cosmetics, and plastics should be analyzed to see if they act as endocrine disrupters. Internationally known health researcher and author Dr. Theodora Colborn, author of *Our Stolen Future*, believes that exposure to even low doses of endocrine disrupters can be harmful to our health. Coburn says:

> They're in lipstick, in the cosmetics you put on, in the solvents you clean house with, in fire retardants. These things are everywhere, and we know nothing about them.

Some researchers are now speculating that consistent postwar exposure to many synthetic chemicals that are foreign to our bodies may be causing a variety of toxic health affects, including thyroid problems, reproductive difficulties, and other increasingly common diseases and cancers.

Pesticides and dioxins are known to affect the thyroid. Frighteningly, even commercial nonorganic baby foods are known to contain what some deem unacceptable levels of dioxins. Another problem is methyl tertiary butyl ether, known as MTBE. MTBE is added to gasoline in high concentrations to increase octane levels, enhance combustion, and improve air quality. The Environmental Protection Agency classifies MTBE, which can contaminate water supplies, as a possible human carcinogen because laboratory animals exposed to it have developed thyroid tumors, among other problems.

Scientists are still in the process of researching and documenting the specific relationships between chemical exposure and various illnesses, as well as the levels of exposure and time involved in order for exposures to be considered dangerous. But these are not just issues for scientists and environmental activists. We all need to make these concerns a priority. Environmental exposure may be at the root of our thyroid problems, and the environment may pose an even greater danger to the thyroid and endocrine function of our children as well. Find out what sorts of chemicals are being released into your neighborhood, and take a look at what types of health effects they have. You can find out more at the Chemical Scorecard Web site, http://www.scorecard.org.

Ultimately, we need to focus on the causes of hypothyroidism and thyroid disease because understanding the causes is the first step toward prevention and, ultimately, a cure.

■ Reduce the Domination of Synthroid

There's no question that the influence of big drug companies is the proverbial double-edged sword for patients. On the plus side, these companies have the power and resources to study new drugs, develop them, and bring them to market. On the minus side, these companies have inordinate power and influence over doctors and regulators, take an inappropriately large role in educating and influencing physicians, and exert control over professional and patient organizations, using funding as leverage.

This is a particular concern when it comes to the drug Synthroid. Synthroid is the top-selling thyroid drug, and regularly ends up in the list of top five–selling drugs in the United States. For most of the 1990s, Synthroid, the top-selling brand of levothyroxine, was the *third most prescribed medicine in the United States*. Synthroid is estimated to control 85 percent of the total market for levothyroxine. It is a huge and profitable moneymaker in the United States and around the world.

The name "Synthroid" is so ubiquitous that many physicians and patients even incorrectly use the brand name "Synthroid" as a generic term for all thyroid medication, reflecting this particular drug's predominance in the thyroid hormone market. This predominance is the result of half a century of marketing, along with many millions of dollars spent annually to fund professional and patient groups, lobbying various lawmakers and regulatory officials, and financing extensive marketing and advertising efforts. Over the years, everything from patient brochures, to golf tournaments, to cocktail parties at scientific meetings, to prescription pads and pens have been paid for by the makers of Synthroid.

While the various companies that have manufactured Synthroid—currently, the drug is made by Abbott Laboratories—do make some positive contributions to thyroid awareness, there has been a culture of arrogance that surrounds the drug and seems to move with it even as it has been sold from one big drug company to another. This culture doesn't consider the best interest of patients a priority.

To help consolidate its marketing position in the 1980s, Boots Pharmaceuticals, Synthroid's manufacturer at that time, commissioned and funded a study to demonstrate that Synthroid was superior to its competitors. They were hoping to justify the company's practice of charging up to twice the price of competitive products. Unfortunately, study results did not prove that Synthroid was superior. They found that Synthroid was bioequivalent to other brand names of levothyroxine. Instead of publishing the research, the company challenged the research they themselves commissioned and, over the author's objections, stopped publication. After seven years, in April 1997, the study was finally published, over the company's objections, in *the Journal of the American Medical Association.*

In May 1997, an $8.5 billion class-action lawsuit was filed against the manufacturer of Synthroid, which at that time was Knoll Pharmaceuticals, a division of parent company BASF. The lawsuit charged that patients should be compensated for overpaying for Synthroid for up to seven years—the period between when the study was completed and when the study was published. The lawsuit claimed that because the product was not superior to its competitors, and the research demonstrating that was not being released, consumers were being unfairly overcharged.

In August 1997, just several months later, Knoll agreed to a proposed settlement of the class-action lawsuit. By all estimates, the announcement of a settlement seemed a lightning-fast resolution of a process that typically takes years. It also seemed to benefit primarily the manufacturer, as under the proposed program, each patient would receive an average of less than $19. This $19 was just a fraction of the estimated overpayment in the range of $40 to $60 per year—or $264 to $408—for each patient who was on Synthroid during the full six and a half years that results were not published.

That spring and summer of 1997, I contacted the main organization for thyroid patients in the United States, the Thyroid Foundation of America. In addition, I contacted the American Medical Women's Association, sponsors of the major "GlandCentral" thyroid awareness advertising and outreach campaign, which was funded by Synthroid's manufacturer at the time. I asked these organizations to comment publicly on what appeared to be a rush to settlement that did not benefit thyroid patients or compensate them in any way for the amount of money overpaid for Synthroid. In particular, I expected the Thyroid Foundation of America to be appalled that patients—*their paying members*—had overpaid in the hundreds of dollars and were being mistreated by such a paltry settlement. Unfortunately, neither organization—with their claims to educate, support, and serve as an advocate for thyroid patients—said they felt it was their role to address this concern publicly.

In December 1998, the judge certified the class action and approved the settlement, but additional challenges kept the payments on hold for several years, until they were finally shipped out in January 2004. The outcome? Those on Synthroid since 1990 were supposed to receive $106, and those on Synthroid since 1995 were supposed to receive $71, little reimbursement for the years of vast overpayment most patients endured. To compound the insult, many patients who had spent decades on Synthroid have reported that they only received checks for the smaller $71 amount, in error, and have been unable to obtain the additional $35 owed them.

Synthroid also earned a less than stellar reputation as it went through the FDA's new drug application process. The company filed Freedom of Information Act (FOIA) requests with the FDA, asking for documents related to levothyroxine, and bogging down the approvals process to such an extent that they asked for, and received several deadline extensions. The company then attempted to bypass the requirement entirely by claiming that it shouldn't have to provide testing data and product information, but rather deserved to be grandfathered in under a special "Generally Recognized as Safe and Effective" (GRAS/E) provision.

In what was a fairly scathing response, the FDA officially denied the request, meaning that Synthroid needed to apply for a new drug application in order to remain legally on the market. Said the FDA:

> *Synthroid cannot be generally recognized as safe and effective because it is of no fixed composition . . . the difficulties in finding Synthroid to be GRAS/E are compounded by the fact that its formula has been changed numerous times throughout its marketing history. . . . Synthroid has a long history of manufacturing problems. . . . In August of 1989, Knoll initiated a recall of 21 lots of Synthroid tablets . . . because of a decrease in potency during stability studies.*

The letter went on to outline recalls in February 1991 affecting twenty-six lots of subpotent Synthroid, and a recall of lots of subpotent Synthroid in June 1991. An April 1991 inspection of Synthroid's manufacturing facility resulted in the firm being cited for two deviations from good manufacturing practices. Another manufacturing review in December 1992 uncovered nine separate incidents of failure to follow good manufacturing practices. As the FDA letter indicates, the problems continued. "FDA also found that the firm had continued to manufacture and distribute low dosage Synthroid tablets during 1990, 1991 and 1992." Said the FDA:

> *The history of potency failures . . . indicates that Synthroid has not been reliably potent and stable. Furthermore, Knoll's use of an overage that has not remained consistent over the years suggests that Synthroid has stability, potency and consistency problems. Although you claim that Synthroid has been carefully manufactured, the violations of current good manufacturing practices discussed above indicate that Knoll has not always manufactured Synthroid in accordance with current standards for pharmaceutical manufacturing.*

The FDA letter also said that "patients need a precise dose of levothyroxine," and went on to summarize all the dangers of inconsistent dosing for hypothyroid patients. In particular, they stated:

> . . . *patients using Synthroid have experienced significant, unintended variations in their doses of levothyroxine sodium . . . these variations are not conducive to proper control of hypothyroidism.*

Surprisingly, despite the clear concerns the FDA had about the quality, stability, potency, and safety of Synthroid, the American Thyroid Association, The Endocrine Society, and ThyCa: The Thyroid Cancer Survivors' Association all joined forces to mount a public-relations effort in support of Synthroid, issuing press releases and writing letters to the editor of major newspapers, all defending the product and calling on the FDA to ensure availability of Synthroid brand levothyroxine. Dr. Rhoda Cobin, who was president of the American Association of Clinical Endocrinologists, wrote to the *Wall Street Journal*:

> *While the American Association of Clinical Endocrinologists does not endorse specific products, the 3,700 physicians in our organization, all specialists in thyroid disease, have found that Synthroid has a long record of safety, efficacy, reliability and consistency. . . .*

If this isn't endorsing a specific product, I'm not sure what would be. It's no surprise, however, that these groups jumped so quickly to the defense of Synthroid. They all receive high levels of support, funding, and resources from Synthroid's manufacturer, and had a selfish interest in defending the product, even if that defense was not in the best interest of patients.

At the same time as all of these application problems were taking place, Abbott was also being investigated by the U.S. Justice Department as part of a pricing investigation, because Synthroid was identified as one of the drugs that had the biggest price jumps in 2000.

Synthroid failed to meet official FDA deadlines, and got a softball penalty from the FDA, which threatened to ramp down production and sales of Synthroid if it didn't file for and receive approval by yet another extended deadline. There were more supportive calls to keep Synthroid available from the various organizations and associations receiving funding from the manufacturer.

Despite the change in ownership from Knoll to Abbott, Abbott has kept up Synthroid's reputation for aggressively attempting to squelch competition. In 2001, the company mounted a massive lawsuit against Unithroid's distributor, claiming that they were engaging in unfair marketing practice by advertising that Unithroid was the only FDA-approved levothyroxine (which was, at that time, true). Synthroid actually won, forcing their competitor, a small company, to change its marketing practices.

While the FDA's call for new drug applications was issued in 1997, and gave companies three years to file for and receive approval, the only drug that made the deadline was Unithroid. This drug, made by a tiny family-owned pharmaceutical company, was able to file for and receive FDA approval by the original August 2000 deadline. Synthroid, however, received approval in July 2002, almost a full two years after the original deadline, and after missing its first extended deadline.

The story of Synthroid is one that patients need to know. In addition to all of the issues mentioned, patients need to be aware that:

• Most of your endocrinologists and physicians have probably met with a drug representative and received free product samples promoting Synthroid—most of them many times. Very few have met with a company representative for any other thyroid drug—simply because these companies are much smaller and don't have the marketing staff and budgets.

- Most endocrinologists belong to groups that receive extensive funding from Synthroid's manufacturer.
- When your doctor was a hospital intern, it's likely that he or she enjoyed catered lunches, dinners, and coffee breaks—possibly many meals—that were paid for by Synthroid, where Synthroid drug reps mingled and handed out informational literature promoting their drug.
- Most endocrinologists attend professional meetings that are sponsored by Synthroid. At many of the conferences and events, meals and functions are also sponsored by Synthroid.
- Many endocrinologists have patient brochures, handouts and materials, prescription pads, informational posters, pens, and other paraphernalia provided by Synthroid.
- A substantial amount of thyroid research is funded by Synthroid's manufacturer.
- Most of the researchers doing research regarding hypothyroidism benefit—either indirectly or directly—from funding by Synthroid.
- The makers of Synthroid have a highly paid, high-powered team of lobbyists whose sole job it is to ensure that their products enjoy unfettered market access with minimal oversight.

Is it any wonder that practitioners, professional organizations, and patient groups act as if they are nearly brainwashed when it comes to Synthroid?

The Impact on Patients

The fact that Synthroid is so lucrative and influential has many downsides for you as a thyroid patient. First, most of the patient "educational" pamphlets handed out by your doctor are produced by Synthroid. These "educational" pamphlets are often thinly disguised marketing brochures, provided free to doctors by the pharmaceutical companies that manufacture levothyroxine. There is no real incentive to include in these brochures any infor-

mation about alternatives to levothyroxine, much less Synthroid—
options that might, in fact, be better able to help resolve your symptoms.

Second, maintaining, and even gaining, market share is a key
mission of Synthroid's maker, along with its fellow pharmaceutical
manufacturers. To that end, a tremendous amount of time and
money is spent conducting aggressive marketing and sales efforts to
introduce even first-year medical students to their drugs. There are
also ongoing marketing efforts designed to steer practicing doctors
away from products sold by competitors, even though those competitors may sell similar or alternative drugs that are equally effective, safe, and FDA approved. This heavy marketing also means that
the primary, and sometimes sole, source of information about thyroid drugs for many doctors may be the drug reps in and out of their
offices. And those drug reps don't have your best interests at heart—
they are there to earn commissions selling drugs.

Third, so many professional endocrinological organizations rely
on pharmaceutical company funding, and their members benefit
from a variety of private and institutional research grant funding,
particularly from Synthroid. These organizations and their members, therefore, are far less likely to do or say anything that isn't in
the interests of those companies who are fattening their wallets.
There is a self-perpetuating insularity and a built-in resistance to
anything new or to alternatives that challenge the dominance of the
predominant thyroid drugs, the ones who hold the purse strings.

Fourth, much like the professional organizations, most of the
major patient service organizations, also primarily run by doctors,
rely on pharmaceutical company funding. These organizations publicly claim to represent patients, but are noticeably absent on key
patient issues that might criticize drug companies. Yet they are often
the first ones to jump to the defense of companies—particularly
Synthroid. This conflict of interest has serious and long-term implications for patients and our wellness. The American Thyroid Association has recently joined forces with some of the patient

organizations, including the Thyroid Foundation of America, ThyCA: Thyroid Cancer Survivors' Association, and the National Graves' Disease Foundation, to form what they call the "ATA Alliance for Patient Education." It's likely that this group will conduct activities designed to provide outreach to patients. While this is, in general, a positive goal, it's a major concern that all of these groups are heavily funded by pharmaceutical companies, Synthroid in particular, and are all heavily mired in the narrow endocrinology dogma regarding hypothyroidism diagnosis and treatment. While efforts to raise general awareness among the undiagnosed are much needed, this new combination effort isn't likely to sponsor any sessions or materials that present anything other than the official party line of conservative endocrinology and thyroid treatment.

Fifth, since a substantial part of research into thyroid disease is funded by Synthroid's manufacturer and, to a lesser extent by the other major thyroid drug manufacturers, it is not likely that any meaningful research will be conducted that could truly *improve the quality of life* of people with hypothyroidism. Manufacturers are not likely to fund research into prevention of hypothyroidism or search for real cures for hypothyroidism. Why would they? If anyone prevented or cured hypothyroidism, their sales would drop. And since alternative drugs or therapies don't result in highly profitable patented medicines, very little research is likely in that arena. This is an important point.

There is no incentive for manufacturers to research prevention, cures, or alternatives because there is no reason to fund research that might result in reduced sales of levothyroxine.

Nearly all mainstream research on drugs involves the manufacturers in some way. According to an investigation by the *New England Journal of Medicine*, 96 percent of the doctors, scientists, and researchers who write articles supporting particular drugs or therapies receive some financial benefit from the pharmaceutical companies that make the drugs.

This influence makes it all the more important for patients to take it upon themselves to get more information about their hypo-thyroidism. You can't assume that you will get complete, balanced, and unbiased information from patient brochures, pharmaceutical company-sponsored informational sessions, or doctors who may be biased due to sponsorships, research funding, or their medical education.

What Can You Do?

First, educate yourself, but be sure that your information is from sources that are *not* beholden to the pharmaceutical companies. You simply are not going to get patient-oriented information if a Web site, organization, brochure, or physician is heavily funded or supported by the drug companies.

Second, join the Thyroid Foundation of America, pay your dues, and speak up loud and often, but *insist* that they represent you, *not* the pharmaceutical company interests that provide financial support. They at least had the good sense not to publicly defend Synthroid in the debacle over quality and FDA approval. However, keep asking them the questions that no one wants to answer, and keep insisting that they answer them if they want to keep you as a member.

Third, consider participating in grassroots efforts at patient education that are not sponsored by the pharmaceutical-funded patient organizations. Attend local health fairs, put up flyers on your office bulletin board, participate in Internet support groups, urge your library to get copies of this book—anything to help get the word out in a way that is untainted by the pharmaceutical company influence and message.

Fourth, ask your doctor if he or she is receiving funding, research grants, freebies, perks, honorarium funds, lunches, weekly cookie deliveries, or anything else of material value from Synthroid's maker, or any other pharmaceutical manufacturers. If the doctor is on the receiving end of drug company largesse, ask if he or she can honestly be impartial about drugs prescribed for you.

Your doctors, the nation's researchers, and *our* patient organizations cannot serve two masters—the patient *and* the pharmaceutical companies. Right now, there appear to be serious questions about who is being served. If we want this to change, every single one of us needs to speak up about the big business of hypothyroidism, or we're putting our health and lives in the hands of companies and doctors who don't see us as patients but, instead, as dollar signs.

Each thyroid patient spends—either directly or via medical coverage—several hundred dollars a year at least on thyroid hormone replacement, plus additional costs for periodic blood tests and doctor visits related to the hypothyroidism. Thyroid disease and its treatment, therefore, represent a highly profitable arena for some drug manufacturers, laboratories, and doctors. It's absolutely essential that thyroid patients—as well as lawmakers and the media— become far more aware of the negative influence that the "profitability" of hypothyroidism has on our current health, the state of thyroid research, and the implications for the health and welfare of our children and future generations.

■ Need for Price Consistency

Before you fill a prescription, it's important to know that the brand of thyroid hormone your doctor prescribes can mean a difference of hundreds of dollars a year, even though there is no difference in the drugs themselves. The brand-name levothyroxine drugs—such as Levoxyl, Levothroid, and Synthroid—are considered bioequivalent, meaning they are considered interchangeable. So a 50-mcg tablet of Synthroid is basically the same as a 50-mcg tablet of Levoxyl, and so on. The brand you're prescribed has to do with your doctor's preferences and susceptibility to the marketing of manufacturers, not the quality or consistency of the prescribed drug.

Before you have a prescription filled, you might want to check with the pharmacy to compare prices of the top thyroid drugs. Synthroid, for example, is often twice the cost of Levoxyl per month. In a February 2004 survey of online drugstore costs, for example, an average monthly cost for Synthroid (112-mcg dose) was $17.25 ($207/year), versus $13.29 ($159.48/year) for Levoxyl, $10.49/month ($125.88/year) for Unithroid, and $10.86 ($130.28/year) for Armour. The difference between Synthroid and Levoxyl, for example, works out to more than $80 per year.

When the consumer is paying, the price of Synthroid is still substantially more than its competitors at most drugstores. A 1999 House Government Reform and Oversight Committee found that the monthly retail cost of Synthroid for seniors paying out of pocket for the drug was $27.05, an astounding *1,446 percent* more than the $1.75 paid by favored group purchasers such as HMOs.

You can fight back. If your doctor prescribes Synthroid, you could ask him or her about one of the less expensive—but equally effective, safe, and reliable—brand-name products. Is there a reason to pay a high price when less expensive brands will work just as well?

■ Need for More Study and Knowledge About Alternative and Complementary Approaches

Conventional medicine is wedded to the treatment of the end condition—giving drugs to replace the missing thyroid hormone. But for people who still have a thyroid capable of functioning, alternative medicine offers the tantalizing possibility of returning the thyroid to normal, or even the potential to prevent, slow, stop, and even reverse some forms of hypothyroidism and thyroid disease. And barring complete "cures," alternative medicine also offers potentially effective options for treatment of unresolved symptoms, such as fatigue and weight gain.

It is clear that some of the therapies for hypothyroidism—such as Chinese medicine, acupuncture, osteopathy, herbs, nutrition/

supplements, and yoga among other treatments—may be able to help hypothyroidism and its symptoms. Unfortunately, each effective alternative treatment rarely comes with a definitive medical journal article proving its effectiveness or an easy-to-follow treatment protocol. Instead, most of what is known and practiced is literally in the heads of individual practitioners, or is part of an alternative system's accepted body of knowledge, as in traditional Chinese medicine.

Unfortunately, there is strong resistance to alternative medicine and therapies. This resistance stems from the mainstream health care industry's economic interest to prevent consumer health dollars from flowing to alternative practitioners and remedies. At the same time, the resistance also stems from the rigid adherence to mainstream-style, peer-reviewed "research" that drives conventional medical knowledge.

Since few companies are likely to profit from rigorous testing of products like guggul or from using selenium to lower antibody levels, and since the profile for hypothyroidism is not high, the kind of research that satisfies the mainstream medical establishment isn't likely to occur. It's inexplicable, for example, that among all the alternative research projects currently funded by the National Institutes of Health, something as common as hypothyroidism is not well represented.

We patients need to continue to ask that this sort of research take a higher priority with patient organizations and federally funded programs.

■ More Education Needed About Thyroid Disease Among Doctors and Practitioners

Many doctors, including some who position themselves as national health advocates or media experts, are misinformed when it comes to thyroid disease. As a patient advocate, I am constantly being sent e-mails about newspaper articles, television interviews, or radio shows in which one doctor or another issues unclear—or outright incorrect—information about thyroid disease and hypothyroidism. Many doctors are apparently willing to go "on the record" with *wrong* information!

In April 2000, in an article titled, "Could It Be Your Thyroid?" Dr. Isadore Rosenfeld, the health editor for *Parade* magazine, said:

> *All you need to do to treat your hypothyroidism is replace the missing hormone. It's easy—just a pill a day.*

In 2002, Hossein Gharib, M.D., F.A.C.E. who at the time was president of the American Association of Clinical Endocrinologists (AACE), pronounced:

> *The prevalence of undiagnosed thyroid disease in the United States is shockingly high—particularly since it is a condition that is easy to diagnose and treat.*

In May 2003, the Ralph Nader–founded group Public Citizen's *Worst Pills, Best Pills* newsletter—published by Public Citizen's Health Research Group, and edited by the group's director, Dr. Sidney Wolfe—issued a poorly researched condemnation of Armour thyroid, claiming that the drug should be on the publication's "Do Not Prescribe" list due to a variety of perceived concerns. Among their concerns were that Armour was mostly a "niche market for unscrupulous . . . practitioners." This, despite two million prescriptions written for Armour in 2002.

I wrote a detailed, fully referenced response to the opinions expressed in this article, and received a short response that did not address the medical issues and journal research I brought up in my letter. At the same time, patients contacted Public Citizen to express their concern over the article. Public Citizen responded with e-mails and letters defending their decision, stating erroneously:

> *There are many levels of treating people who do not have the ability to write prescriptions and recommend Armour Thyroid instead which does not need a prescription. . . .*

While I was able to extract a retraction from the organization on the statement that Armour Thyroid was a nonprescription drug, they refused to clarify their original article, revisit the condemnation, or respond to a point-by-point assessment of their concerns. Other than their form letter, they failed to respond to the concerns of the other thyroid patients who contacted them with correct information about Armour and levothyroxine drugs. Clearly, Public Citizen had not done its homework regarding Armour thyroid or thyroid treatment in general, because first they had issued a poorly researched condemnation and then compounded it by backed it up with egregious errors.

The extent of this error, and the organization's utter unwillingness to openly and publicly revisit their many errors, calls into question much of what Public Citizen and Dr. Sidney Wolfe recommend regarding health, drugs, and doctors, including their *Worst Pills, Best Pills* newsletter, and their *Questionable Doctors* reports. In my opinion, Dr. Sidney Wolfe should be on his own on the list of questionable doctors, given his apparent lack of basic information about thyroid disease, and his inability to correct even the most fundamental mistakes.

Dr. Peter Gott is a nationally syndicated columnist for United Media whose column appears in newspapers around the nation. In March 2004, he answered a question from a patient who took issue with his position that levothyroxine is the only appropriate thyroid drug, and Armour is unsatisfactory. Gott said he would not reconsider his position and defended his decision by saying:

> *Armour thyroid is extracted from the thyroid glands of cattle that are butchered. Several years ago, researchers discovered that there was considerable variation in potency from batch to batch—in short, a manufacturing quality issue. This*

was not found to be the case with synthetic thyroid supplements.

All three statements are, of course, completely wrong. Armour Thyroid comes from porcine (pig) thyroid. There have been no potency or manufacturing quality issues researched in recent years. And, in fact, it's the FDA itself that found that potency, stability, and quality *were* a problem with synthetic thyroid drugs.

These cases are just the tip of the iceberg, and point up the need for many doctors, including some of our nation's most prominent physicians and spokespeople, to go back to basics when it comes to their understanding of thyroid conditions. And clearly, while continuing education on thyroid disease—the kind that doesn't come from a pharmaceutical company representative—is apparently an urgent need for many practitioners, our medical schools also need more focus on thyroid disease.

■ More Awareness Among Those Specifically Treating Thyroid Disease

Many doctors, even specialists like endocrinologists, simply don't have the time to keep up with the latest developments and literature. But because thyroid disease is so common and so often missed, it's essential that physicians and endocrinologists stay informed about the latest developments. How many practitioners, for example, do not realize that the bastion of "medically acceptable" conservative thyroid treatment, the American Association of Clinical Endocrinologist (AACE), updated its Clinical Practice Guidelines for the Evaluation and Treatment of Hyperthyroidism and Hypothyroidism in 2002.

Some key recommendations, according to the AACE:

1. AACE uses an upper limit of normal for TSH of 30.mIU/L established in a population of patients carefully screened for thyroid disease by the National Academy of Biochemistry in 2002.

2. AACE feels that thyroid antibodies should be measured in patients having subclinical hypothyroidism and used as a clinical tool in deciding upon treatment.

3. AACE guidelines recommend treatment of patients with TSH>5mIU/L if the patient has a goiter or if thyroid antibodies are present. The presence of symptoms compatible with hypothyroidism, infertility, pregnancy or imminent pregnancy would also favor treatment.

4. AACE feels that the physician who has performed a comprehensive history and physical examination should decide on treatment of each individual patient.

The AACE believes that "integrating current best evidence with clinical expertise and experience, improves patient care. In our opinion, until adequate data are available, best practice combines clinical judgment with patient preferences."

Many doctors and endocrinologists are not following these guidelines, and would actually be surprised to know that these statements are the official treatment guidelines and position of the AACE.

■ More Public Awareness—of the Right Kind— Needed for Thyroid Disease

Every year, Oprah, the queen of all talk shows, features numerous programs on health issues. She's had Dr. Christiane Northrup talking about menopause. The sister-sister team of Jennifer Berman, M.D., and Laura Berman, Ph.D., talking about low sex drive. And, of course, a multipart series on weight loss, which featured her former contributor Dr. Phil McGraw, who now has his own popular show. Time and again, these programs have shown women describing symptoms such as fatigue, difficulty losing weight, depression, anxiety, and low sex drive. And yet thyroid was *never* mentioned, except in one statement from Dr. Phil, in response to a woman who said that she had been diagnosed with hypothyroidism after she gained quite a bit of weight, and he said something along the lines of "You're not overweight because of your thyroid. That's just an excuse."

Some of Oprah's programs have actually offered detailed lists of symptoms related to a program's subject matter. For example, one list of "early warning signs" for a show she did on stress and its effects on the body listed cold hands and feet, hair loss, muscle aches, low sex drive, and low energy as signs that "your lifestyle is ruining your health." Obviously, to anyone familiar with thyroid disease, this list of symptoms reads like an Endocrinology 101 textbook list of *common hypothyroidism symptoms*. Yet thyroid disease was *never mentioned once* in the entire hourlong program, despite the fact that millions of people have undiagnosed hypothyroidism, and the symptoms match up *exactly* to this list.

While Oprah's done an admirable effort to offer the public greater information about so many important, life-changing issues, it's totally inexplicable that she and her producers have overlooked hypothyroidism so completely and consistently, over so many years.

And Oprah is the tip of the iceberg. Now that he has his own show and diet empire, Dr. Phil goes on about weight loss, yet almost never touches on the thyroid, except to dismiss it as a lazy excuse. Thyroid patient and humorist Celisa Dyan has some tough words for McGraw:

> *My prayer is that when medical science does catch up to the Hell we thyroid patients live daily, you'll go back on*

Oprah to eat healthy servings of crow pie: I'd gladly bake a few dozen to donate, myself. I do not need for you to "pat my back" and say it's ok to be fat because I am thyroid-challenged as you so outrageously implied. . . .

Other talk shows, morning news shows, women's issues shows, the Discovery Health channel—why aren't they talking about hypothyroidism in a meaningful way? Why are they quicker to talk about surgical treatments for carpal tunnel syndrome, when the condition that may be causing it is ignored? Why is obesity one of the main topics on news and talk shows, but it's rarely mentioned that undiagnosed hypothyroidism may be a key contributing factor for millions of Americans?

When thyroid disease is covered, there are also many inaccuracies. The NBC *Today* show contributor Judith Reichman, M.D., for example, said that natural thyroid came from cows (it comes from pigs), and that "once you settle on the right dose, it generally doesn't change." (Age, diet, weight, hormonal status, and fluctuating potency are all factors that cause frequent dosage change needs in many patients.)

Thyroid problems also take a beating with advertisers, who use "thyroid disease" as a safe code word for "fat" in ads. This way, they think they won't offend the 60 percent of the population that is obese, but can still make their points about how inconvenient and annoying fat people are.

Marriott promoted their hotels in a series of radio spots, talking about how uncomfortable business travel can be, citing that it's particularly bad "being stuck on a plane next to someone with a thyroid condition." The ad was suggesting that a thyroid patient was likely to be obese and use up too much space on a plane. After an outcry from thyroid patients, I contacted Marriott's vice president of advertising, and negotiated with them to agree not to run the ad anymore because it was offensive.

Dairy Queen and Grey Worldwide Advertising teamed up to produce a television ad in which an obese man returns several times to a Dairy Queen counter, requesting a particular ice cream treat. At one point, he shows up in a ballet outfit, trying to pretend that he is a twin sister of a girl he is with, and when the counter clerk looks at him strangely, he says he has a "thyroid problem." The insinuation is, of course, that the reason he is so overweight and not slim and attractive like his "twin" is his thyroid. After hearing from a number of thyroid patients who found the ad insulting, I contacted the president and executive vice president of Dairy Queen, to share with them the concerns of the thyroid patient community. After I led patients in a grassroots communications effort, the company agreed to pull the ad.

Media celebrities, news outlets, and celebrity doctors have in their hands the life-saving opportunity to educate and change the health of millions of Americans. We need more coverage of hypothyroidism, we need media outlets to bring in hypothyroidism when it's appropriate, and the coverage needs to be accurate and patient oriented.

■ Regular Screening Needed

The issue of whether or not there should be universal screening for thyroid disease is an area of major controversy. In June 2000, the American Thyroid Association (ATA) issued guidelines regarding thyroid screening, which were published in the *Archives of Internal Medicine*. According to the ATA, everyone should receive regular TSH screening for thyroid problems beginning at age thirty-five, and every five years thereafter. According to the ATA, the rationale for screening is particularly justified in women. They also indicated that those with symptoms, signs, and risk factors may require more frequent TSH testing.

This announcement was the first formal call for universal screening, and the guidelines stemmed from recent research findings demonstrating the health risks and increased prevalence of undiagnosed thyroid disease.

According to the Colorado Thyroid Disease Prevalence Study, published in February 2000 in the *Archives of Internal Medicine*, thyroid disease is far more prevalent than previously thought: As many as thirteen million people in the United States may have undiagnosed thyroid conditions. A study presented at the 1997 annual meeting of the American Thyroid Association reported that 11.7 percent of the study participants had abnormal thyroid function, yet only 1 percent of the total population was receiving treatment.

Why are so many millions of people undiagnosed and untreated? As we've seen before, some of them don't even mention their symptoms to doctors, and aren't aware that what they're going through isn't simply aging, or fatigue, or the results of weight gain, or other excuses. Others have discussed their symptoms, but are ignored or patronized by physicians who can't be bothered to run a TSH test and who aren't enough familiar with the symptoms of hypothyroidism to suspect the problem.

The American Academy of Clinical Endocrinologists (AACE), in its 2004 Thyroid Awareness Month campaign, backed up the ATA's position, and issued a press release calling for thyroid testing. Says the AACE release:

> *If you are exhibiting symptoms . . . or are over age 35, ask your doctor to perform a Thyroid Stimulating Hormone (TSH) blood test to check your thyroid function.*

At the same time these various calls for screening have gone out, the American Association of Clinical Endocrinologists, the American Thyroid Association, and the Endocrine Society (TES), cosponsored a Consensus Development Conference in September 2002. That group reported:

There is insufficient evidence to support population-based screening. Aggressive case finding is appropriate in pregnant women, women older than 60 years, and others at high risk for thyroid dysfunction.

But a separate team of endocrinologists from the AACE came back with an additional response, contradicting the consensus panel they participated in, saying that the panel's advice against both routine testing and routine treatment of subclinical disease is:

a position at variance with what several medical organizations including AACE and ATA had previously published. It is clear from several published studies that subclinical hypothyroidism can result in clinical symptoms, hyperlipidemia and cardiac dysfunction.

Apparently, even "the experts" can't even agree among themselves.

The doctors need to get it together on the issue of screening for thyroid disease and treatment for subclinical conditions. This back and forth is taking precious time away from the important business of actually practicing medicine.

Doctors also need to become vastly more aware of the prevalence of thyroid disease. They need to learn to recognize the many possible symptoms and know to test for thyroid problems when any one of the common symptoms appears, and who is most at risk for developing the condition. Cameron, a woman in her twenties, wrote to me and said that she'd had to go to a second doctor for diagnosis, after she asked for a thyroid test and was told by her gynecologist that hypothyroidism "didn't affect younger women, only women after menopause." This is, of course, completely wrong.

A February 2004 article in the *American Medical News* shows how complicated the issue of screening really is for the so-called experts. In the article, Paul Ladenson, M.D., Professor and Director of

Endocrinology and Metabolism at Johns Hopkins, shows his stripes by pronouncing that:

> it isn't easy to decide who to screen. . . . The only hard part about making the diagnosis of an underactive or overactive thyroid gland is thinking about the possibility.

Leaving out the issue that Ladenson thinks treatment is a breeze, why does one of the most prominent endocrinologists in the United States think it's not easy to decide who to screen? The vast majority of thyroid patients are women. Women should be tested. Women who are trying to get pregnant and can't get pregnant should be tested. Women having persistent miscarriage should be tested. Women having menstrual disruptions or a difficult menopause should be tested. Women and men complaining of fatigue should be tested. Women and men with high cholesterol levels should be tested. Women and men complaining of unexpected hair loss should be tested. Women and men complaining of unexplained weight changes should be tested. Women and men complaining of anxiety or depression should be tested. All diabetics should be tested. Every man over thirty-five should be tested every five years, at minimum, and every year after sixty. Every woman should be tested annually after thirty-five. Everyone being prescribed an antidepressant should have a thyroid test. How complicated *is* this, Dr. Ladenson? Sounds pretty basic to me.

■ Toward the Future . . .

Until now, hypothyroidism has never been a disease that garnered much attention from the media or even from patients. Until recently, thyroid patients who did not feel well on the standard treatment suffered in silence, unaware that they were not the only ones who were still plagued by a list of symptoms and health problems despite normal TSH values and treatment with levothyroxine. Now the rise of the Internet, online support groups, bulletin boards, e-mail, and newsletters has allowed for the dissemination of information not developed or funded by pharmaceutical companies and their related doctor and patient groups. And this revolution in information is reaching out beyond the Internet, by a variety of means—such as in books like this one, newsletters, and other informational materials—that help patients learn more about their condition, connect with others, and stay up-to-date on the latest news and information.

The result is that a hypothyroid person today may actually know *more* than his or her doctor about hypothyroidism and the treatment options, better understand proper management of TSH levels, and have a much greater knowledge of the various tests beyond the TSH level to diagnose and evaluate thyroid function.

The power that knowledge and information offer to us as patients is a power we must exercise, if anything is to change. We must continue to speak out, make others aware, insist on representation from our legislators and patient groups, fight against overcharging by drug manufacturers, and keep asking for the research and answers we deserve.

Patients need to keep speaking up. Write the Thyroid Foundation of America, keep asking your doctor questions, write your legislators and the National Institutes of Health and ask them why more research isn't being conducted on thyroid disease, write your HMO, your local newspapers, Oprah, anyone who can help get the word out.

Patients need to expect more, demand more, and insist on proper treatment and further research. It's the only way that many of us, and future generations, will ever move beyond the limitations imposed on our health and our lives by hypothyroidism and get on with the most important business of living well.

I encourage you to write me anytime with thoughts, ideas, comments about the book, or if you want to share your personal story or experiences with hypothyroidism. You can reach me by e-mail at mshomon@thyroid-info.com, or by regular mail P.O. Box 565, Kensington, MD, 20895-0565.

Our education about thyroid disease doesn't stop here. This book is just one effort in what should be an ongoing search for answers, information, and new developments to help diagnose, treat, and even potentially cure hypothyroidism. Every day, I review medical journals, news sources, Web sites, and conventional and alternative health resources, looking for information that can be of help to people with thyroid disease. Each month brings new developments in the search for conventional and alternative solutions for thyroid patients, information that can help you continue your efforts to live well with thyroid disease. I feature links to the best of this new information on the Web, and summarize important information at my Web site, http://www.thyroid-info.com.

I also publish key information and news in my monthly newsletter, *Sticking Out Our Necks*. Each issue of *Sticking Out Our Necks* features the kind of advice you've found in this book—knowledge you won't find assembled in one place anywhere else. You'll read about the newest thyroid-related ideas in complementary and alternative medicine. You'll discover exciting new ideas for better diagnosis, treatment, symptom relief, overall health, and empowerment for people with thyroid problems. You'll find more tips on the latest information that will help you effectively lose weight, stop hair loss, improve fertility, minimize allergies, and much more. Reader questions, stories, and letters will make you feel less alone in your journey on the road to living well with thyroid disease.

To order your subscription to *Sticking Out Our Necks*, write P.O. Box 0385, Palm Harbor, FL 34682, or call toll-free at 1-888-810-9471 (order processing only). Or visit http://www.thyroid-info.com for more information.

Appendix

RESOURCES

I felt that an essential mission of this book was to assemble a list of useful resources to help you find the information and support you need regarding your hypothyroidism, thyroid disease, and health.

Resource sections are by their very nature subject to change. You may, therefore, run into a phone number or Web address that has changed since publication. If you come across out-of-date information and would like an update, please visit my Web site, http://www.thyroid-info.com. At the site, you'll find current listings for organizations and their contact information, current Web site addresses, links to online sources where you can get more information about any books that are mentioned, and other helpful resources.

New resources of interest to thyroid patients are also featured regularly in my patient newsletter, *Sticking Out Our Necks*.

■ *Sticking Out Our Necks*—The Thyroid Patient Newsletter

Sticking Out Our Necks is my newsletter, designed to keep thyroid patients up-to-date on important thyroid-related and health news— both conventional and alternative—that affects your ability to live well. I scour the health wires, medical journals, and alternative medicine sources—in the United States and around the world—looking for information that promises better diagnosis, treatment, and symptom relief for people with thyroid problems. Special articles look at the latest information on weight loss with hypothyroidism or up-to-the-minute news on the thyroid drugs and their manufacturers, your inspiring letters and testimonials about the solutions you are finding that help you live well, in-depth looks at linkages between thyroid and allergies, thyroid and fertility, and much more. A unique feature of *Sticking Out Our Necks* is the regular reporting on new developments in complementary and alternative medicine that have promise in dealing with all facets of thyroid disease, as well as treatment for unresolved thyroid symptoms. Finally, unlike other patient-oriented newsletters, *Sticking Out Our Necks* has no affiliations with any pharmaceutical companies or patient groups. This leaves me free to be honest and up front, telling it like it is about thyroid drugs and treatments and pharmaceutical company politics that have an impact on *your* quality of life. Each issue features eight pages packed full of news and information similar to what you've found in this book, information that helps you live well. Free news highlights from *Sticking Out Our Necks* are available via e-mail and online. Visit my book and newsletter Web site, http://www.thyroid-info.com, for more information.

■ Mary Shomon's Health Information

Mary Shomon's "Thyroid-Info" Web Site
http://www.thyroid-info.com
A comprehensive site, featuring news, articles, interviews and information on all facets of thyroid disease, including both conventional and alternative approaches to diagnosis and treatment. Not sponsored by any pharmaceutical companies, so you get thousands of pages of unbiased, patient-oriented information from the nation's leading thy-

roid patient advocate. Find chats, support groups, online forums, and more to help you in your effort to live well with thyroid disease.

Thyroid Top Doctors Directory
http://www.thyroid-info.com/topdrs
A directory of patient-recommended top thyroid practitioners, from around the country and the world, organized by state and country.

Thyroid Site at About.com
http://thyroid.about.com
Founded and managed by Mary Shomon, the Thyroid Site at About.com features hundreds of links to top sites on the net, a weekly newsletter, support community, and more.

Sticking Out Our Necks Print Newsletter
http://www.thyroid-info.com/subscribe.htm
A bimonthly, 12-page print newsletter mailed directly to you that features key thyroid-related conventional and alternative information in an unbiased, patient-oriented format. Order online, or write or call:
Sticking Out Our Necks/Thyroid-Info
P.O. Box 565, Kensington, MD 20895-0565
Phone: 1-888-810-9471

Sticking Out Our Necks E-mail Newsletter
http://www.thyroid-info.com/newsletters.htm
A monthly e-mail newsletter, featuring key thyroid-related news, developments, links, interviews, and more. To subscribe, visit the Web site or e-mail: thyroidnews@thyroid-info.com

Thyroid Guide to Fertility, Pregnancy and Breast-feeding Success
http://www.thyroid-info.com/pregnancyguide.htm
A 40-page guide that covers the critical relationship between the

thyroid gland—our master gland of metabolism—and nearly every aspect of childbearing. Reviews how undiagnosed thyroid problems can cause infertility or recurrent miscarriage, making it difficult or impossible to get or stay pregnant. Covers thyroid problems and how they can complicate pregnancy; worsen pregnancy symptoms, such as morning sickness, fatigue, hair loss, and depression; and increase the risk of miscarriage, intrauterine growth retardation, preterm labor, stillbirth, and cognitive problems/mental retardation in your child. Also discusses postpartum thyroid problems, and breast-feeding difficulties with thyroid disease and solutions. Order online, or write or call:

Sticking Out Our Necks/Thyroid-Info

P.O. Box 565, Kensington, MD, 20895-0565

Phone: 1-888-810-9471

The Thyroid Diet / "A Weight Off My Mind" Newsletter

http://www.GoodMetabolism.com

Information on my book *The Thyroid Diet*, the first book to tackle the critical connection between weight gain and thyroid disease, offering a conventional and alternative plan for lasting weight loss. An undiagnosed thyroid condition may contribute to weight gain, or doom diets to failure for as many as 20 million Americans with metabolic slowdown due to a malfunctioning thyroid gland. *The Thyroid Diet* helps many previously unsuccessful dieters get diagnosed and treated—and proper thyroid treatment may be all that's needed to successfully lose weight. Even after optimal treatment, however, weight problems plague many thyroid patients. For those patients, *The Thyroid Diet* identifies the many frustrating impediments to weight loss, and offers solutions—both conventional and alternative—to help. It discusses optimal dietary changes, including how a thyroid sufferer should focus on a low-glycemic, high-fiber, lower-calorie diet; optimal timing of meals for maximum hormonal impact; thyroid-damaging foods to avoid; helpful herbs and supplements; and more. It contains several different eating plans, food lists, and a set of delicious and healthy gourmet recipes. With handy worksheets to use in weight-loss tracking, and a special resources section featuring Web sites, books, and support groups, here is vital help for the millions of thyroid patients dealing with weight problems. The GoodMetabolism.com Web site features the latest diet and weight-loss news of interest to thyroid and autoimmune disease patients, including developments, links, interviews, and more. "A Weight Off My Mind," free e-mail newsletter features the latest news and developments to help you lose weight.

Living Well with Autoimmune Disease: What Your Doctor Doesn't Tell You . . . That You Need to Know
Mary J. Shomon
HarperCollins, 2002
http://www.autoimmunebook.com
After numerous printings, *Living Well with Autoimmune Disease* has established itself as the definitive guide to understanding mysterious and often difficult-to pinpoint autoimmune disorders like thyroid disease, Hashimoto's thyroiditis, Graves' disease, multiple sclerosis, rheumatoid arthritis, Sjögren's syndrome, lupus, alopecia, irritable bowel syndrome, psoriasis, Raynaud's, and many others— and offers a road map to finding both conventional and alternative diagnosis, treatment, recovery . . . and in some cases, even prevention or cure! *Alternative Medicine* magazine has said, "*Living Well with Autoimmune Disease* should not only prove inspirational for those afflicted with these mysterious conditions, but also offers solid, practical advice for getting your health back on track."

Autoimmune Site / The Autoimmune Report E-mail Newsletter
http://www.autoimmunebook.com
A Web site and monthly e-mail newsletter that review the latest conventional and alternative medical journals to bring you breaking in-

formation on autoimmune disease treatments, including new drugs, diet, and supplements.

Living Well with Chronic Fatigue Syndrome and Fibromyalgia: What Your Doctor Doesn't Tell You . . . That You Need to Know
Mary J. Shomon
HarperCollins, 2004
http://www.cfsfibromyalgia.com
The book and Web site feature an integrative approach to diagnosis and treatment of chronic fatigue syndrome and fibromyalgia, two conditions that are more common in thyroid patients, and that share similar symptoms. While most books promote one particular theory and treatment approach, *Living Well with Chronic Fatigue Syndrome and Fibromyalgia* looks at the bigger picture, by exploring a myriad of theories and treatment options—from conventional therapies, such as medication and vitamins, to alternative approaches, including yoga and massage. The book and site feature descriptions of risk factors and symptoms, and a detailed checklist you can use to aid in self-evaluation and diagnosis with your physician. *Living Well with Chronic Fatigue Syndrome and Fibromyalgia* is the first book to provide a comprehensive, personalized plan for those suffering with CFS and fibromyalgia.

■ Patient Organizations and Advocacy Groups— North America

Broda Barnes Research Foundation
P.O. Box 110098, Trumbull, CT 06611
Phone: 203-261-2101; fax: 203-261-3017
E-mail: info@BrodaBanes.org
Web site: http://www.brodabarnes.org
This organization was founded to advance the theories and approaches begun by Dr. Broda Barnes during his career. If you're in-

terested in finding a doctor who applies the Barnes Basal Metabolism Approach to diagnosing thyroid disease, or who works with natural thyroid treatment, you might want to contact this group. Some people have reported finding excellent, open-minded doctors through this organization. For a small fee, they'll send you a package of informational articles and materials, and information on doctors who practice using their approaches.

The Thyroid Foundation of America

One Longfellow Place, Suite 1518, Boston, MA 02114
Phone: 800-832-8321; fax: 617-534-1515
E-mail: info@allthyroid.org
Web sites: http://www.allthyroid.org, http://www.tsh.org/
This is the main U.S. organization involved in thyroid education and outreach Primarily run by doctors and medical interests, and funded in part by pharmaceutical companies, this organization stays fairly close to the official party line, but does offer decent conventional introductory information on thyroid disease and hypothroidism.

The MAGIC Foundation

6645 W. North Ave., Oak Park, IL 60302
Phone: 708-383-0808; fax: 708-383-0899
E-mail: mary@magicfoundation.org
Web sites: http://www.magicfoundation.org/clinhypo.html
The MAGIC (Major Aspects of Growth in Children) Foundation provides support and education regarding growth disorders in children—including thyroid disease—and related adult disorders. MAGIC offers educational brochures, national networking for parents, an annual national convention, and a quarterly newsletter.

American Foundation of Thyroid Patients
4322 Douglas Ave., Midland, TX 79703
Phone: 432-694-9966
E-mail: thyroid@flash.net
Web site: http://www.thyroidfoundation.org/
A patient founded this thyroid organization, which offers a newsletter and other support.

American Thyroid Patients
Web sites: http://www.geocities.com/americanthyroidpatients
http//www.health.groups.yahoo.com/group/americanthyroidpatients/
National clearinghouse for support groups, and burgeoning advocacy group for patients.

Thyroid Foundation of Canada/La Foundation canadienne de la Thyroide
797 Princess St. Suite 304, Kingston, ON K7L 1G1
Phone: 613-544-8364, 1-800-267-8822 (IN CANADA);
fax: 613-544-9731
E-mail: thyroid@limestone.kosone.com
Web site: http://www.thyroid.ca/
Canada's thyroid education-related organization for patients.

American Autoimmune-Related Diseases Association
22100 Gratiot Ave., E. Detroit, MI 48021
Phone: 810-776-3900
E-mail: aarda@aol.com
Web site: http://www.aarda.org/
Information about more than 50 different autoimmune disorders, including Hashimoto's disease and Graves' disease. This Web site and organization provide general information about autoimmune disorders and profiles of specific diseases.

■ Professional Thyroid Disease and Endocrinology Organizations

The Endocrine Society
8401 Connecticut Ave., Suite 900, Chevy Chase, MD 20815-6817
Phone: 301-941-0200; fax: 301-941-0259
E-mail: endostaff@endo-society.org
Web site: http://www.endo-society.org/
Professional organization focusing on endocrine diseases, including thyroid disease, that primarily serves practitioners, but also provides information to thyroid patients.

American Association of Clinical Endocrinologists
1000 Riverside Ave.; Suite 205, Jacksonville, FL 32204
Phone: 904-353-7878; fax: 904-353-8185
Web site: http://www.aace.com
The American Association of Clinical Endocrinologists (AACE) is a professional medical organization devoted to clinical endocrinology. At their Web site they sponsor an online "Specialist Search Page," at http://www.aace.com/directory, which allows you to identify AACE members by geographic location, including international options. A unique feature is the ability to select by subspecialty. Again, as a mainstream organization of endocrinologists, expect conventional approaches from these referrals.

Hormone Foundation
8401 Connecticut Ave., Suite 900, Chevy Chase, MD 20815-5817
Phone: 1-800-HORMONE
Web site: http://www.hormone.org
Facts sheets and information about hormones and hormonal conditions, including thyroid disease

American Thyroid Association
6066 Leesburg Pike, Suite 650, Falls Church, VA 22041
Phone: 703-998-8890; fax: 703-998-8893
Patient information: 1-800-THYROID
E-mail: admin@thyroid.org
Web site: http://www.thyroid.org
Professional organization for practitioners that also provides information to thyroid patients

■ Organizations and Advocacy Groups—United Kingdom

ThyroidUK
32 Darcy Road, St. Osyth, Clacton-on-Sea, Essex, CO16 8QF, UK
Web site: http://www.thyroiduk.org/

British Thyroid Foundation
P.O. Box 97, Clifford, Wetherby, West Yorkshire LS23 6XD UK
Phone: 0113-392-4600
Web site: http://www.btf-thyroid.org

British Thyroid Association
http://www.british-thyroid-association.org/

Diana Holmes
1, The Pastures, Perton, Wolverhampton, WV6 7UJ, UK
E-mail: dianaholmes@tiscali.co.uk
Web site: http://www.thyroidtears.co.uk
In her book *Tears Behind Closed Doors*, published in England, thyroid sufferer, author, and patient advocate Diana Holmes tells her compelling account of years of misdiagnosis. Diana now provides support and advocacy to other U.K. thyroid sufferers.

Thyroid Eye Disease (TED)
Solstice, Sea Road, Winchelsea Beach, East Sussex, TN36 4LH UK
Phone: 01797 222 338
E-mail: tedassn@eclipse.co.uk
Web site: http://www.thyroid-fed.org/members/TED.html

■ Organizations and Advocacy Groups—Other

European Thyroid Association
E-mail: euro-thyroid-assoc@rh.dk
Web site: http://www.eurothyroid.com

Thyroid Australia
P.O. Box 2575, Fitzroy Delivery Centre, Victoria 3065, Australia
Phone: +61-3-9561 2483; fax: +61-3-9561 4798
E-mail: support@thyroid.org.au
Web site: http://www.thyroid.org.au/

Australian Thyroid Foundation
P.O. Box 186, Westmead NSW 2145, Australia
Phone: +61-2-9890 6962 (answering service);
fax: +61-2-9845 7287
E-mail: thyroid@icpmr.wsahs.nsw.gov.au
Web site: http://www.thyroidfoundation.com.au/

Thyreoidea Landsforeningen
Lis Larsen, Strandkrogen 4 A, 3630 Jægerspris, Denmark
Phone: 47 53 03 70
E-mail: lis_1@get2net.dk
Web site: http://www.thyreoidea.dk/

Schilddrüsen Liga Deutschland e.V.
Postfach 800 740
65907 Frankfurt
Germany
Phone: +49-69-31 40 53 76; fax: +49-69-31 40 53 16
Web site: http://www.thyrolink.com/sf-liga

Associazione Italiana Basedowiani e Tiroidei
c/o Centro Minerva, 7 Via Mazzini, 43100 Parma, Italy
Phone: +39-521-207771; fax: +39-521-207771

Schildklierstichting Nederland
Stationsplein 6, 3818 LE Amersfoort, The Netherlands
Phone: 0900-899 88 66; fax: 073-656 50 64
Web site: http://www.schildklier.nl/

Vastsvenska Patientforeningen for Skoldkortelsjaka
Mejerivalen 8, 439 36 Onsala, Sweden
Phone: +46-30-06 39 12; fax: +46-30-06 39 12

■ Thyroid Cancer-Specific Advocacy and Information

Thyroid Cancer Survivors' Association
P.O. Box 1545, New York, NY 10159-1545
Phone: 877-588-7904 (toll-free); fax: 630-604-6078
E-mail: thyca@thyca.org
Web site: http://www.thyca.org
Known as ThyCa, this patient-founded-and focused organization provides information and support to survivors of thyroid cancer and their families. They hold an annual conference and sponsor a popular patient-support listerv. Also have a free online low-iodine cookbook for cancer patients "going hypo."

Light of Life Foundation
32 Marc Drive, Englishtown, NJ 07726
Phone: 732-972-0461; fax: 732-536-4824
E-mail: info@lightoflifefoundation.org
Web site: http://www.lightoflifefoundation.org
The group, founded in 1997, works on quality of life and education
for thyroid cancer patients.

Thyroid-Cancer.net (Johns Hopkins Thyroid Tumor Center)
http://www.thyroid-cancer.net

■ Thyroid Support Groups

Master List of Thyroid Patient Support Groups and Forums
http://www.thyroid-info.com/support
A listing of various support groups and forums, including my own
various forums for thyroid patients, weight loss, hormones, and
more, plus others. Because information changes so frequently for
the various boards, groups, and chats, this will have the latest list of
support groups.

Thyroid Support Groups—USA
Web site: http://health.groups.yahoo.com/group/Thyroid_Support_
GroupsUSA/
A place to sign up for local and regional online support groups, and
to find out about in-person support groups in your area.

Alt.support.thyroid
Usernet: alt.support.thyroid
Web site: http://www.altsupportthyroid.org/
The Usernet bulletin board for thyroid patients

■ Thyroid Self-Testing/Order Your Own Thyroid Tests

Biosafe

Web site: http://www.thyroid-info.com/tshtest.htm

Phone: 1-800-768-8446, ext. 123

Biosafe offers an FDA-approved self-test for TSH that you can do at home. Order it (by mail), use the easy self-test kit to get a finger-prick of blood, and mail the kit back to get results. In addition to TSH, Biosafe offers home test kits for prostate PSA, diabetes, and cholesterol.

HealthCheckUSA

Web sites: http://www.thyroid-info.com/tshtest.htm;
http://www.healthcheckusa.com/livingwell

Phone: 1-800-929-2044

HealthCheckUSA offers a full range of thyroid tests, including thyroid antibodies testing. You order your own tests, and then get the bloodwork done at a local HealthCheckUSA–affiliated lab. Results are sent to you. In addition to various thyroid tests, HealthCheckUSA offers a large number of other tests, including heart disease testing, hormone panels, allergy testing, cholesterol tests, diabetes, and blood sugar tests.

■ Finding Thyroid and Other Doctors, Verifying Credentials

Thyroid Top Doctors Directory

Web site: http://www.thyroid-info.com/topdrs

A free state-by-state and international listing of top doctors for thyroid disease, founded by Mary Shomon in 1997. Doctors are recommended by thyroid patients, and listings often feature detailed information on why the particular doctor was recommended. Many open-minded holistic doctors and doctors who work with innovative therapies such as Armour, T3, etc. are included. There are some truly excellent doctors on this list, and many of the practitioners featured in this book were found via the *Thyroid Top Doctors Directory.*

Armour Thyroid/Thyrolar—Find a Prescribing Physician Database
Web site: http://www.armourthyroid.com/locate.html
A database of doctors who are open to prescribing Armour and/or Thyrolar

Broda Barnes—Informational Packet
P.O. Box 110098, Trumbull, CT 06611
Phone: 203-261-2101; fax: 203-261-3017
E-mail: info@BrodaBarnes.org
Web site: http://www.brodabarnes.org/educational_packets.htm
Their informational package includes a listing of holistic referral physicians in your state.

American Association of Clinical Endocrinologists—
Find an Endocrinologist Database
Web site: http://www.aace.com/memsearch.php
A source for conventional endocrinologists who are AACE members.

American Thyroid Associations Find a Thyroid Specialist Database
Web site: http://www.thyroid.org/patients/specialists.php3
A source for conventional thyroid doctors who are AACE members

Thyroid-Cancer.net's Locate a Thyroid Cancer Specialist
Web site: http://www.thyroid-cancer.net/resources/findaspec.php3
A source for conventional thyroid cancer specialists

Endocrine Surgeons/Membership List
Web site: http://www.endocrinesurgeons.org/members/members.html
A source for endocrine surgeons

NY Thyroid Center—Surgeon Referrals
Phone: 212-305-0442; fax: 212-305-0445
E-mail: surgery@columbia.edu
A source for finding conventional thyroid surgeons and specialists

HealthyNet Find a Practitioner
Web site: http://www.healthy.net/scr/center.asp?centerid=53
Excellent resource for finding alternative, complementary, holistic, and herbal practitioners

American Osteopathic Association
142 E. Ontario St., Chicago, IL 60611
Phone: 800-621-1773, 312-202-8000; fax: 312-202-8200
E-mail: info@aoa-net.org
Web site: http://www.aoa-net.org/
The American Osteopathic Association has state referral lists for osteopaths in all 50 states.

American Board of Medical Specialties "Certified Doctor" Service
Phone: 800-776-2378
Web site: http://www.certifieddoctor.org
This is an online service that allows you to browse for conventional doctors by specialty and locale and get certification info on specific docs.

American Medical Association (AMA) "Physician Select"
Web site: http://www.ama-assn.org/aps/amahg.htm
The AMA's "Physician Select" program allows you to browse their database for AMA member doctors, almost always conventional doctors. It lists medical school and year graduated, residency training, primary practice, secondary practice, major professional activity, and board certification for all doctors who are licensed physicians.

AIM—Administrators in Medicine "DocFinder" Service

Web site: http://www.docboard.org/docfinder.html

American Holistic Health Association

P.O. Box 17400, Anaheim, CA 92817-7400 USA

Phone: 714-779-6152

E-mail: mail@ahha.org

Web site: http://www.ahha.org

The American Holistic Health Association offers an online referral to its members—holistic doctors.

American Holistic Medical Association

12101 Menaul Blvd., N.E., Suite C, Albuquerque, NM 87112

Phone: 505-292-7788; fax: 505-293-7582

Web site: http://www.holisticmedicine.org/

The American Holistic Medical Association publishes a Referral Directory of member M.D.s and D.O.s.

1-800-DOCTORS and Similar Services

Many areas have telephone-based doctor referral services. For example, 1-800-DOCTORS allows you to call up and obtain information on doctors in your area. You can also find out which conventional doctors in their system match up to your health care program. 1-800-DOCTORS operates in a number of major markets, including Chicago; Washington, DC; Dallas/Fort Worth; Denver; Houston; Milwaukee; and Philadelphia; and many cities have similar services. Check your yellow pages.

Hospital Referrals

If a hospital in your area has a referral service, this can be a decent source of information and referrals to doctors. If the hospital's reputation is good, the doctors typically are going to be of a better caliber. Some of the more sophisticated hospital referral services will offer educational and practice style information about doctors in their databases.

Doctor Ratings

Find out if any of your local magazines rate doctors. *Washingtonian* magazine, for example, periodically asks physicians to pick those other Washington, DC/Maryland/Virginia area doctors they'd most recommend in particular specialties, and publishes the results. It's always a comfort to me to see a doctor I've been referred to appear on this list, although it doesn't always guarantee I'll *like* that doctor!

Best Doctors

Phone: 1-888-DOCTORS
Web site: http://www.bestdoctors.com
Best Doctors has a Family Doc-Finder at their Web site, where, for a small fee, you can find recommended primary-care physicians in your area. You'll find only conventional doctors via this service. Best Doctors also conducts specialized physician searches for rare, catastrophic, or serious illnesses. The specialized search costs $1,500, only called for in the direst situations, but it's worth knowing about if you find yourself seriously in need of a specialist or expert.

Medical Board Charges or Actions

You can also find out if disciplinary action has even been taken with your doctor or if charges are pending against him or her, by calling your state medical board. A good list of all medical boards is found at http://www.fsmb.org/members.htm.

■ Communicating with Your Doctor

The Savard Health Record—Health Information Binder

Marie Savard, M.D.
Web site: http://www.drsavard.com/

■ Drug Information

RxList
Web site: http://www.rxlist.com
A professional site, featuring in-depth information on various drugs

WebMD Drug Checker
Web site: http://my.webmd.com/medical_information/drug_and_
herb
Consumer-oriented information on drugs and herbs

■ Thyroid Drug Manufacturers and Web Sites

Levoxyl and Cytomel
Jones Pharma, Subsidiary of King Pharmaceuticals, Inc.
501 Fifth St., Bristol, TN 37620
Phone: 888-840-5370; fax: 866-990-0545
Corporate Web site: http://www.kingpharm.com
Levoxyl phone info: 1-866-LEVOXYL (538-6995)
Levoxyl Web site: http://www.levoxyl.com
Levoxyl is a levothyroxine product. Cytomel is liothyronine, the
synthetic form of triiodothyronine (T3).

Armour Thyroid, Thyrolar, Levothroid
Forest Pharmaceuticals
Professional Affairs Department
13600 Shoreline Drive, St. Louis, MO 63045
Phone: 1-800-678-1605, ext. 7301; fax: 314-493-7457
E-mail: info @forestpharm.com
Corporate Web site: http://www.forestpharm.com/
Armour site: http://www.armourthyroid.com
Thyrolar site: http://www.thyrolar.com
Levothroid site: http://www.levothroid.com

Armour Thyroid is a natural thyroid hormone replacement product. Thyrolar is the brand name for liotrix, synthetic T4/T3 levothyroxine/liothyronine combination drug. Levothroid is a levothyroxine drug. (Note: Currently, Armour Thyroid and Thyrolar are not readily available outside the United States. If you are interested in these products in Canada or other countries, start by contacting the Broda Barnes Foundation.)

Unithroid
Made by Jerome Stevens Pharmaceuticals
Distributed by Lannett Pharmaceuticals
Phone: 1-800-325-9994, ext. 4
Unithroid was the first levothyroxine drug approved by the FDA.

Westhroid/Naturethroid
Western Research Laboratories
21602 N. 21st Ave., Phoenix, AZ 85027
Phones: (toll-free) Phone: 877-797-7997
Administrative phone: 623-879-8537; fax: 623-879-8683
Web site: http://www.westernresearchlaboratories.com/
Westhroid is a cornstarch-bound, natural thyroid hormone product, made from desiccated pig thyroid gland. Naturethroid is also made from desiccated pig thyroid gland, but as it is bound with microcrystalline cellulose, it is hypoallergenic. Patients can get a list of doctors in their areas who use these products by contacting the company directly.

Synthroid
Abbott Laboratories
100 Abbott Park Rd., Abbott Park, IL 60064-3500
Phone: 800-255-5162
E-mail form: https://abott.com/contact.cfm
Corporate Web site: http://abbott.com

Synthroid Web site: http://synthroid.com
Synthroid is the top-selling levothyroxine drug.

Thyrogen
Genzyme Therapeutics
500 Kendall St., Cambridge, MA 02142
Phone: 800-745-4447; fax: 617-768-9000
Corporate Web site: http://www.genzyme.com/
Thyrogen Web site: http://www.thyrogen.com
Thyrogen is a synthetic thyroid-stimulating hormone for use in preventing hypothyroidism symptoms in thyroid cancer patients undergoing scans to detect cancer recurrence.

■ Compounding Pharmacies

Some compounding pharmacies that will service mail-order prescriptions and have expertise in preparing thyroid drugs, including time-released T3, are listed here.

Village Green
5415 Cedar Lane, Bethesda, MD 20814
Phone: 1-800-869-9159
Web site: http://www.the-apothecary.com

The Compounder Pharmacy
575 West Illinois Ave., Aurora, IL 60506-2956
Phone: 630-859-0333; fax: 630-859-0114
E-mail: info@theCompounder.com
Web site: http://www.theCompounder.com

■ Some Helpful Thyroid-Related Web Sites

Thyroid-Info/Thyroid Information Central—http://www. thyroid-info.com
Home page for this book, and for my monthly news report. *Sticking Out Our Necks*. You'll find thyroid news and information, personal thyroid stories, and more. The site has hundreds of comprehensive, up-to-date links to the Web's best resources on hypothyroidism, thyroid disease, and health information.

Thyroid Disease at About.com—http://thyroid.about.com
This is my Thyroid Disease Web site at About.com (formerly the Mining Company), where you'll find dozens of feature articles related to all facets of thyroid disease, in-depth annotated links to hundreds of the Web's best thyroid disease sites, and my popular thyroid bulletin boards and twenty-four-hour-a-day chatroom, where you can exchange information and support with other people with thyroid disease.

Thyroid History—http://www.thyroidhistory.net
Edna Kyrie's well-researched, comprehensive site features many articles covering thyroid disease and thyroid research, going back to the 1900s.

Endocrineweb—http://www.endocrineweb.com
A large site developed by doctors with more in-depth information on thyroid disease. Conventional focus but good depth of information, especially on thyroid surgery.

Thyroid Disease Manager—http://www.thyroidmanager.org
Full-length book offering detailed, highly conventional thyroid information with a medical tone and focus, primarily for doctors

Jacob Teitelbaum's Web Site—http://www.endfatigue.com
Discusses chronic fatigue syndrome, fibromyalgia, and the connection to thyroid problems.

Alt.support.thyroid—http: sh/www.altsuppportthyroid.org/
Patient-oriented information on the full range of thyroid issues

Broda Barnes Research Foundation—http://www.brodabarnes.org
Features information on thyroid and adrenal conditions

Hormone Foundation—http://www.hormone.org
Good conventional overview information on thyroid and other hormone problems

American Thyroid Association—http://www.thyroid.org
Good conventional overview information on thyroid and other hormone problems

Dr. Bruce Rind—http://www.drrind.com
Good resource for information on thyroid and adrenal problems

■ Thyroid-related Books

There are a number of conventional thyroid books written by doctors and health writers, and frankly I'm not even going to list them here. I find them sometimes condescending, too similar to each other, and consistent in presenting a narrow, conventional, doctor-oriented—instead of patient-oriented—view. Following is a list of books that I do recommend that can be of help in covering certain aspects of thyroid disease or hypothyroidism.

Overview Books

Overcoming Thyroid Disorders
David Brownstein, M.D.
Medical Alternatives Press, 2002
Good information on holistic and hormonal approaches to thyroid treatment.

The Thyroid Solution: A Mind-Body Program for Beating
Depression and Regaining Your Emotional and Physical Health
Ridha Arem, M.D.
Strongest in its discussion of "brain fog," depression, loss of libido, weight gain, anxiety, and the need for T3. Interesting information on the relationship of thyroid disease to brain chemistry, and resulting depression, anxiety disorders, mood disorders, and other mental and emotional effects of hypothyroidism.

Thyroid Balance
Glenn Rothfeld, M.D.
Valuable book covering the various issues that cause the thyroid to go out of balance, including some alternative focus

Thyroid for Dummies
Alan L. Rubin, M.D.
If you need a detailed conventional overview book on thyroid disease, this comprehensive book is the one. Note, however, that it is *very* conventional, and does not discuss alternative, holistic, or complementary ways of diagnosing and treating thyroid conditions.

Books About Hypothyroidism

Hypothyroidism: The Unsuspected Illness
Broda Otto Barnes, M.D.
This book, published back in 1982, was written by the now-deceased Dr. Broda Barnes. It is considered the bible for alternative thyroid information and use of basal body temperature in diagnosis.

The book is still in print, but is not likely to be stocked in bookstores. It is, however, available by special order, or at the Web's online bookstores. The book contains a fair amount of out-of-date information, but it is the first to truly acknowledge the wide-ranging impact the thyroid has on nearly every facet of health. Also, it doesn't talk down to patients or dismiss various health concerns.

What Your Doctor May Not Tell You About Hypothyroidism
Kenneth Blanchard, M.D.
Published in 2004, this interesting and helpful book is by popular Boston-area thyroid expert Kenneth Blanchard, who documents his innovative approach to treating hypothyroidism using a specific combination of T4 and T3 drugs.

Solved: The Riddle of Illness
Stephen Langer, M.D., and James F. Scheer
Langer, a follower of Broda Barnes's theories, has written what he calls the follow-up to Barnes's book. It looks at some nutritional and vitamin approaches for hypothyroidism. It still feels like a doctor telling the patient what to do and doesn't address in any depth the problems of getting a diagnosis, dealing with doctors, and dealing with depression. The book is at its best discussing supplements and nutritional approaches that might help hypothyroidism.

ThyroidPower: Ten Steps to Total Health
Richard Shames, M.D., and Karilee Halo Shames, R.N., Ph.D.
Puts some basics of hypothyroidism's causes, test, diagnosis, and treatment into a 10-step program of information that can help patients get properly diagnosed and treated. Also extra focus on autoimmune disease.

Tears Behind Closed Doors
Diana Holmes
This book, originally published in England in 1998, is one woman's account that would sound very familiar to many people. Diana was misdiagnosed six different times with everything from celiac disease to myasthenia gravis and, ultimately, was found to have hypothyroidism, despite TSH levels in the "normal range." Diana tells her own moving and empowering account in the hope that her story will help others. For more information, see http://www.thyroidtears .co.uk.

■ Graves'/Hyperthyroidism

Graves' Disease: A Practical Guide
Elaine Moore and Lisa Moore
Excellent, comprehensive, and well-researched overview of Graves' disease and hyperthyroidism that offers conventional and alternative information on diagnosis and treatment

Other Thyroid and Hormone Books
The Thyroid Diet: Manage Your Metabolism for Lasting Weight Loss
Mary J. Shomon
Information on how undiagnosed thyroid disease may cause weight problems, how to maximize the ability to lose weight in a thyroid patient, and effective weight-loss approaches, including recommended supplements and recipes for effective weight loss

The Great Thyroid Scandal
Barry Durrant-Peatfield, M.D.
Published in the U.K., discusses some of the holistic approaches used by popular thyroid expert Barry Durrant-Peatfield, M.D., be-

fore he stopped his active practice. Interesting discussion on adrenal support. Hones in on problems in U.K. health care system.

Your Guide to Metabolic Health
Drs. Gina Honeyman-Lowe and John C. Lowe
Excellent overview of hypometabolism, including hypothyroidism, and an integrative approach to help treat this multidisciplinary problem

Thyroid Eye Disease: Understanding Graves' Ophthalmopathy
Elaine Moore
Excellent book covering the details of thyroid eye disease (TED) and Graves' ophthalmopathy, conditions that can affect some hypothyroid patients

Iodine: Why You Need It. Why You Can't Live Without It
David Brownstein, M.D.
Information on the role of iodine in thyroid disease and other health concerns

Is Your Thyroid Making You Fat?
Sanford Siegal, D.O.
Dr. Siegal, primarily a weight-loss expert, explains a controversial but interesting method to assess metabolism and thyroid function using a low-calorie monthlong diet as a test.

The Hormone Heresy: What Women MUST Know About Their Hormones
Dr. Sherrill Sellman
Helpful overview of hormones and the controversies surrounding use of estrogen

Sara Rosenthal's Books

Health writer Sara Rosenthal has several books and self-published guides that provide overview information on thyroid topics, from a conventional health perspective. Books include *The Thyroid Cancer Book*, *The Thyroid Sourcebook*, and *The Thyroid Sourcebook for Women*.

■ Controversies/Issues

Wilson's Syndrome

- Wilson's Syndrome Site—http://www.wilsonssyndrome.com/

Soy

- Weston A. Price Foundation/Soy Alert—http://www.weston aprice.org/soy
- Soy Online Service—http://www.soyonlineservice.co.nz
- Soy Info Online—http://www.soyinfo.com/

Coconut Oil

- *The Healing Miracles of Coconut Oil*, Third Edition, by Bruce Fife
- *Eat Fat, Look Thin*, by Bruce Fife
- Coconut Oil Info Guide—http://www.coconutoil-online.com*
- Tropical Traditions—http://www.tropicaltraditions.com*
- Coconut Information—http://www.coconut-info.com*
- Weston A. Price Foundation/Coconut Oil—http://www.weston aprice.org/know_your_fats/coconut_oil.html

*Note—these sites are product promotional sites, but do have quite a bit of information about coconut oil amid the marketing information.

Fluoride

- Fluoride Action Network—http://www.fluoridealert.org
- Parents of Fluoride Poisoned Children—http://www.bruha.com/pfpc/
- ZeroWaste America—http://www.zerowasteamerica.org/Fluoride.htm

Perchlorate

- Perchlorate.org—http://www.perchlorate.org
- EPA Perchlorate Site—http://www.epa.gov/safewater/ccl/perchlorate/perchlorate.html
- Environmental Working Group—http://www.ewg.org/issues/perchlorate/index.php

■ Complementary and Alternative Resources

Acupuncture

American Association of Oriental Medicine
5530 Wisconsin Ave., Suite 1210, Chevy Chase, MD 20815
Phones: 301-941-1064, toll-free: 888-500-7999;
fax: 301-986-9313
E-mail: info@aaom.org
Web site: http://www.aaom.org/
AAOM provides referrals to practitioners who are state-licensed or certified by various respected certifying organizations. They also have an online state-by-state referral search for TCM and acupuncture practitioners at http://www.aaom.org/referral.html.

National Certification Commission for Acupuncture and Oriental Medicine
11 Canal Center Plaza, Suite 300, Alexandria, VA 22314
Phone: 703-548-9004; fax: 703-548-9079
E-mail: info@nccaom.org

Web site:http://www.nccaom.org/
NCCAOM awards the title Dipl.Ac. to acupuncture practitioners who pass its certification requirements. You can get a list of Diplomates of Acupuncture in your state for a small fee.

American Academy of Medical Acupuncture
4929 Wilshire Blvd., Suite 428, Los Angeles, CA 90010
Phone: 323-937-5514
E-mail: JDOWDEN@prodigy.net
The AAMA, which provides referrals, requires that its members—who are all physicians—undergo at least 220 hours of continuing medical education in acupuncture.

Accreditation Commission for Acupuncture and Oriental Medicine
Maryland Trade Center #3, 7501 Greenway Center Drive, Suite 820, Greenbelt, MD 20770
Phone: 301-313-0855; fax: 301-313-0912
This organization can verify which American schools of acupuncture and Oriental medicine have reliable reputations.

Acupuncture.com
Web site: http://www.acupuncture.com
Acupuncture.com offers a list of licensed acupuncturists by state.

Ayurveda
The Maharishi Ayurveda Medical Center
Phones: 800-248-9050, 800-255-8332; fax: 719-260-7400
Provides information on Ayurveda as well as referrals to Ayurvedic practitioners.

Herbal Medicine
It doesn't hurt to start with a good overview of herbal medicine. I highly recommend *Herbal Defense*, by Robyn Landis, with Karta Purkh Singh Khalsa, published in 1997. Landis has a Web site lo-

cated at http://www.bodyfueling.com with a variety of herbal information. Khalsa's site is located at http://www.kpkhalsa.com.

Herb Research Foundation
4140 15th St., Boulder, CO 80304
Phone: 303-449-2265 (office); voice mail: 800-748-2617;
fax: 303-449-7849
E-mail: rmccaleb@herbs.org
Web site: http://www.herbs.org/
More information on herbal support, specifically for thyroid func-
tion, is available, along with memberships in the group.

Nutritional and Vitamin Therapy
Many people read up on the various vitamin therapies and treat
themselves using vitamins and minerals. This is a very common
form of self-care. If you choose to self-treat, I'd urge you to get a
copy of two key books:

Prescription for Nutritional Healing
James F. Balch, M.D., and Phyllis A. Balch
I consider this book the ultimate reference source for information
on various natural approaches to disease and health problems. Part
One reviews nutrients, food supplements, and herbal supplements.
Part Two reviews various disorders and recommended nutritional
treatments. Part Three covers other remedies and therapies. Before
you buy another vitamin or herb, get a copy of this book.

8 Weeks to Optimum Health
Andrew Weil, M.D.
This book is by Andrew Weil, alternative medicine's current guru
and spokesperson. It outlines an excellent 8-week, step-by-step
guide to building up and nourishing the mind, body, and spirit, and
restoring energy and resilience to the immune system. His recommendations range from adding various supplements to your diet to

going on a "news fast" periodically. Dr. Weil's suggestions are practical, doable, and surprisingly effective.

You can also see Dr. Weil's Web site, http://www.drweil.com, for an excellent vitamin adviser and database.

American Dietetic Association's Nationwide Nutrition Network
Phone: 800-366-1655
Web database: http://www.eatright.org/Public/index_7684.cfm
This organization offers referrals to registered dietitians and a searchable online database of registered dietitians.

Naturopathy
The American Association of Naturopathic Physicians
3201 New Mexico Ave. N.W., Suite 350, Washington, DC 20016
Phones: toll-free: 1-866-538-2267; local: 202-895-1392;
fax: 202-274-1992
E-mail: member.service@Naturopathic.org.
Web site: http://www.naturopathic.org/
This group offers a referral line, directory, and brochures that explain naturopathic medicine. A small fee is charged for their directory.

Manual Healing and Bodywork
National Certification Board for Therapeutic Massage and Bodywork
8201 Greensboro Drive, Suite 300, McLean, VA 22102
Phones:1-800-296-0664; 703-610-9015; fax: 703-610-9005
Web site: http://www.ncbtmb.com/
This organization provides names of bodywork therapists certified by the board.

American Massage Therapy Association
820 Davis St., Suite 100, Evanston, IL 60201-4444
Phone: 847-864-0123; fax: 847-864-1178

Web site: http://www.amtamassage.org
This group offers only information on massage therapy and referrals to therapist who are members of AMTA.

Associated Bodywork & Massage Professionals
1271 Sugarbush Drive, Evergreen, CO 80439-9766
Phones: 800-458-2267, 303-674-8478; fax: 800-667-8260
E-mail: expectmore@abmp.com
Web site: http://www.abmp.com

Osteopathic Manipulation

American Osteopathic Association
142 East Ontario St. Chicago, IL 60611
Phones: 800-621-1773, 312-202-8000; fax: 312-202-8200
E-mail: info@aoa-net.org
Web site: http://www.aoa-net.org/
The association has state referral lists for all 50 states and can provide additional information on osteopathic medicine.

Mind-Body Therapy

There are so many places you can look for mind-body practitioners, everything from psychotherapists to ministers to yogis to art therapists. Ask friends, check bulletin boards, or publications at your local health food store, even local alternative health or alternative newsweeklies, for ideas on how to find a good mind-body therapist. For traditional mental health support, such as a psychologist, a counselor, or general support groups, contact:

National Mental Health Association
2001 N. Beauregard St., 12th floor, Alexandria, VA 22311
Main switchboard: 703-684-7722; toll free: 800-969-NMHA (6642); TTY: 800-433-5959; fax: 703-684-5968
Web site: http://www.nmha.org/

Provides referrals to state and regional mental health associations and resources

National Mental Health Consumers Self-Help Clearinghouse
1211 Chestnut St., Suite 1207, Philadelphia, PA 19107
Phones: 1-800-553-4KEY (-4539) or 215-751-1810;
fax: 215-636-6312
E-mail: info @mhselfhelp.org
Web site: http://www.mhselfhelp.org/
Offers articles and books on consumer-oriented and mental health issues; and a reference file on relevant groups, organizations, and agencies.

Canadian Mental Health Association
8 King St. E., Suite 810, Toronto ON M5C 1B5
Phone: 416-484-7750; fax: 416-484-4617
E-mail: national@cmha.ca
Web site: http://webmaster@cmha.ca
Provides referrals to regional mental health associations and resources

For other types of referrals, some of these organizations can help:

Center for Mind/Body Medicine
5225 Connecticut Ave., N.W., Suite 414, Washington, DC 20015
Phone: 202-966-7338
E-mail: center@cmbm.org
Web site: http://www.cmbm.org
A nonprofit educational organization dedicated to reviving the spirit and transforming the practice of medicine

American Chronic Pain Association
P.O. Box 850, Rocklin, CA 95677
Phone: 1-800-533-3231; fax: 916-632-3208

E-mail: ACPA@pacbell.net

Web site: http://www.theacpa.org

This group manages a list of over 500 support groups internationally and publishes workbooks and a newsletter.

Center for Attitudinal Healing

33 Buchanan Drive, Sausalito, CA 94965

Phone: 415-331-6161; fax: 415-331-4545

E-mail: Home123@aol.com

Web sites: http://www.healingcenter.org;

http://www.attitudinalhealing.org

Support groups throughout the nation for people with chronic or serious illness

Wellness Community

919 18th St., N.W., Suite 54, Washington, DC 20006

Phones: 1-800-793-WELL, 202-659-9709; fax: 202-659-9301

E-mail: help@thewellnesscommunity.org

Web site: http://www/thewellnesscommunity.org

Chapters throughout the nation offer support groups for people with chronic or serious illness.

Phylameana lila Désy—Reiki/Healing Expert

Web sites: http://www.spiralvision.com;

http://www.healing.about.com

Excellent resource for information or all facts of mind-body healing and wellness, including Reiki

The Everything Reiki Book

Phylameana lila Désy

This book offers an excellent and reader-friendly overview of Reiki, and is appropriate at any level of Reiki interest and knowledge.

Yoga

Yoga in Daily Life Center/US
2402 Mt. Vernon Ave., Alexandria, VA 22301
Phone: 703-299-8946; fax: 703-299-9051
E-mail: alexandria@yoga-in-daily-life-usa.com
Web site: http://www.yoga-in-daily-life-usa.com
Offers yoga information and an extensive online book, video/audio, and supplies store. I highly recommend their "Yoga Nidra" relaxation tapes, and I practice yoga at home using their beginner video.

Yoga Journal
2054 University Ave., Berkeley, CA 94704
Phones: 1-800-I-DO-YOGA, 510-841-9200; fax: 510-644-3101
Web site: http://www.yogajournal.com/
This bimonthly magazine also publishes a directory of yoga teachers and organizations. Their Web site features an online directory of teachers.

Yoga Class
Web site: http://yogaclass.com/
Yoga class offers free online yoga, relaxation, and breathing classes, presented in "RealPlayer" video/audio format.

YogaSite's Directory of Yoga Teachers
Web site: http://www.yogasite.com/teachers.html
This is a decent online directory of yoga teachers.

General Alternative Medicine Referral Sources

The following are multidisciplinary national referrals to alternative medicine practitioners:

American College for Advancement in Medicine
Web site: http://www.acam.org

This nonprofit medical society, dedicated to educating physicians on the latest findings in complementary/alternative medicine, has a searchable listing of ACAM physicians at their Web site.

HealthWorld Online's Professional Referral Network
Web site: http://www.healthy.net/clinic/refer/index.html
Offers referrals to practitioners of alternative and complementary medicine and integrative health care. Searchable referral databases for a variety of alternative modalities

Dr. Andrew Weil's Practitioner Database
Web site:
http://cgi.pathfinder.com.drweil/practitioner/search/index.html
Excellent database of more than 10,000 alternative practitioners, searchable by state, zip code, or area code

American Holistic Health Association
Web site: http://www.ahha.org/
This organization offers referrals to a variety of certified holistic practitioners. Go to "Resource and Referral Lists" from the home page

Well Mind Association
Phone: 301-774-6617
Offers national referrals to over 700 alternative practitioners

Alternative Medicine Content Web Sites
Dr. Weil—http://www.drweil.coin
A searchable alternative medicine database, interactive vitamin adviser, and alternative practitioner index make this one of the Web's premier alternative medicine resources.

**Alternative Medicine Magazine—
http://www.alternativemedicine.com**

Full-text archive of this popular, well-done alternative medicine magazine. Features several excellent articles on alternative treatment for hypothyroidism.

HealthWorld Online—http://www.healthy.net/

Home page for extensive information on complementary and alternative medicine options in health care, including excellent database of articles related to hypothyroidism.

Healthy Ideas—http://www.prevention.com

Web site home page for *Prevention* magazine uses the magazine's vitamin, nutrition, exercise, and self-care focus

■ Losing Weight with Thyroid Disease

Some recommended weight-loss sites and products include:

- Good Metabolism/Thyroid Diet—http://www.goodmetabolism.com
- Ediets Online—http://www.ediets.com
- Physique Transformation—http://www.physiquetransformation.com
- Weight Watchers—http://www.weightwatchers.com/
- WebMD—http://my.webmd.com/health_and_wellness/food_nutrition
- iVillage Fitness—http://www.ivillage.com/topics/fitness/0,,165513,00.html
- MEDLINEPlus Weight Loss—http://www.nlm.nih.gov/medlineplus/weightlossdieting.html
- Weight Loss at About.com—http://weightloss.about.com

- Glycemic Index—http://diabetes.about.com/library/mendosagi/ngilists.htm
- Crani Yums—http://www.craniyums.com

Selected books and their Web sites include:

- *The Thyroid Diet*—http://www.GoodMetabolism.com
- *Mastering Leptin*—http://www.masteringleptin.com
- *Fat and Furious*/Loree Taylor Jordan—http://www.loreetaylorjordan.com
- *The Atkins Diet*—http://atkins.com
- *The Zone Diet*—http://www.zoneperfect.com/Site/Content/index.asp
- *The No-Grain Diet*—http://www.mercola.com/nograindiet
- *The Fat Flush Diet*—http://www.fatflush.com
- *The South Beach Diet*—http://www.southbeachdiet.com
- *Sugar Busters*—http://www.sugarbusters.com
- *8 Minutes in the Morning*—http://www.jorgecruise.com
- *Fat Tracker Daily Diary*—http://www.thefattracker.com

For a detailed list of resources, support groups, diet systems, books and Web sites, see *The Thyroid Diet: Managing Your Metabolism for Lasting Weight Loss*, by Mary J. Shomon, and visit the book's Web site, http://www.GoodMetabolism.com

■ Depression and Hypothyroidism

These organizations can provide more information, referrals, and support groups for depression:

National Alliance for the Mentally III
Colonial Place Three, 2107 Wilson Blvd., Suite 300, Arlington, VA 22201-3042
Phone: 703-524-7600; fax: 703-524-9094; TDD: 703-516-7227; member services: 800-950-NAMI
Web site: http://www.nami.org/

National Depressive and Manic Depressive Association
730 North Franklin St. Suite 501, Chicago, IL 60610
Phone: 1-800-826-DMDA (-3632)
Web site: http://www.ndmda.org/

National Mental Health Association
2001 N. Beauregard St., 12th Floor, Alexandria, VA 22311
Phones: 703-684-7722; toll-free: 800-969-NMHA (-6642); TTY: 800-433-5959; fax: 703-684-5968
Web site: http://www.nmha.org

American Psychological Association (APA) Consumer Help Center
Phone: 1-800-964-2000
Web site: http://helping.apa.org

■ Pregnancy, Infertility, and Hypothyroidism

Thyroid Guide to Fertility, Pregnancy and Breastfeeding Success
Mary J. Shomon
Web site: http://www.thyroid-info.com/pregnancyguide.htm
A 40-page guide that covers the critical relationship between the thyroid gland—our master gland of metabolism—and nearly every aspect of childbearing. Order online, or write or call:
Sticking Out Our Necks/Thyroid-Info,
P.O. Box 565, Kensington, MD, 20895-0565
Phone: 1-888-810-9471

Taking Charge of *Your* Fertility: The Definitive Guide to Natural
Birth Control and Pregnancy Achievement
Toni Wechsler, M.P.H.
I consider this book the bible for understanding the menstrual cycle,
fertility, and the hormonal fluctuations each woman experiences
monthly and throughout her life. This is the book we all *should*
have been handed before we had our first periods.

Sher-Brody Institute for Reproductive Medicine (SBI), Geoffrey
Sher, M.D.
6719 Alvarado Rd., Suite 108, San Diego, CA 92120
Phone: 619-265-1800: fax: 619-265-4055
E-mail: sbronymd@cts.com
Drs. Sher and Brody are pioneers in the field of infertility in the
United States. Sher is author of *In Vitro Fertilization, The A.R.T. of
Making Babies*. He has expertise in working with heparin and IVIG
treatments for infertility in patients with antithyroid antibodies.

Web Sites:
- Pregnancy at About.com—http://pregnancy.about.com
- The InterNational Council on Infertility Information Dissemination, Inc.—http://www.inciid.org/
- Immunology/Pregnancy Loss—
  http://www.inciid.org/immune.html
- Fertility Plus—http://www.fertilityplus.org/

■ General Conventional Health Information—
Central Web Sites

WebMD—http://my.webmd.com
Well-organized, informative general medical site, including conventional and some alternative information

Intellihealth—http://www.intellihealth.com
High-quality, overall medical site sponsored by Johns Hopkins

Mayo Health O@sis—http://www.mayohealth.org
High-quality, overall medical/health site sponsored by the Mayo Clinic

Sympatico Healthy Way—http://www.nt.sympatico.ca/heathyway
Top-notch Canadian site offering medical information, community, and support on a variety of conditions

About.com Health—http://home.about.com/health
Collection of personal expert guide-managed sites on a variety of health topics and medical conditions

■ Health/Medical News Web Sites

Medical Breakthroughs
http://www.ivanhoe.com

ScienceDaily: Health & Medicine News
http://www.sciencedaily.com/news/health_medicine.htm

HealthScout
http://www.healthscout.com

Google Health News
http://news.google.com/news/en/us/health.html

Yahoo Health News
http://news.yahoo.com/news?tmpl=index&cid=751

■ Medical Research Web Sites

National Library of Medicine's PubMed—
http://www.ncbi.nhn.nih.gov/PubMed
This is the Web's premier medical research source, offering an easy searchable database of abstracts and journal references from major medical journals for more than 30 years.

Medscape—http://www.med.scape.com
While primarily for health professionals, Medscape offers in-depth articles that explore the medical aspects of various issues, usually written in English consumers can understand.

Journal of the American Medical Association (JAMA)—
httpaVwww.ama.assn.org/public/journals/jama/jamahome.htm
Key medical journal in the U.S.

New England Journal of Medicine (NEJM)—
http://www.nejm.org
Key medical journal in the U.S.

British Medical Journal—http://www.bmj.com
Key medical journal in the U.K., features full text of many articles. Extensive coverage of hypothyroidism

■ Health Magazines and Newsletters

Some of the best health magazines and newsletters for conventional and alternative health news include: Dr. Andrew Weil's *Self-Healing* newsletter; *Alternative Medicine* magazine; *Prevention* magazine; *Dr. Julian Whittaker's Newsletter; Townsend Letter; Health* magazine; *Natural Health*; and *Men's Health*.

■ Updates

Please note: If you have new resources you'd like to recommend for future updates, or if you know of updates to the information in this section, please drop me a line by e-mail, mshomon@thyroid-info.com, or regular mail, at P.O. Box 0385, Palm Harbor, FL 34682.

■ Doctors and Practitioners Who Contributed to This Book

I've listed many of the practitioners who contributed to this book and how you can contact them:

Kenneth R. Blanchard, Ph.D., M.D.
2000 Washington St., Newton, MA 02462
Phone: 617-527-1810; fax 617-965-5524

David Brownstein, M.D.
4173 Fieldbrook, West Bloomfield, MI 48323
Phone: 248-851-3372
E-mail: info@drbrownstein.com
Web site: http://www.drbrownstein.com

Hyla Cass, M.D.
1608 Michael Lane, Pacific Palisades, CA, 90272
Phone: 310-459-9866; fax: 310-459-9466
E-mail: thyroid@cassmd.com
Web site: http://www.cassmd.com

Manelle Fernando, M.D.
Manelle Fernando Medical Clinic
15 W. Milwaukee St., Janesville, WI 63540
Phone: 608-756-0791

Theodore Friedman, M.D.
4727 Wilshire Blvd., Suite 100, Los Angeles, CA 90010
Phone: 310-335-0327
Web site: http://www.goodhormonehealth.com

Dr. Dale Guyer, M.D.
Advanced Medical Center
836 East 86th St., Indianapolis, IN 46240
Phone: 317-580-9355
E-mail: patientcare@daleguyermd.com
Web site: http://www.daleguyermd.com

Kent Holtorf, M.D.
Hormone and Longevity Medical Center/Fibromyalgia and Fatigue
Center of Los Angeles
23441 Madison Ave, Suite 215, Torrance, CA 90505
Phone: 1-310-375-2705; fax: 310-375-2701
E-mail: drholty@usa.net
Web sites: http://www.fibroandfatigue.com,
http://www.chronicfatigue.about.com,
http://www.hormoneandlongevitycenter.com

Dana Godbout Laake, M.S., R.D.H., L.N.
11140 Rockville Pike, Suite 600, Rockville, MD 20852
Phone: 301-998-6575; fax: 301-984-6559
E-mail: danalaake@erols.com
Web site: http://www.danalaake.com/

Dr. Gina Honeyman-Lowe
Center for Metabolic Health
1007 Pearl St., Suite 280, Boulder, CO 80302
Phone/Fax: 303-413-9100
E-mail: MetabolicHealth@aol.com
Web site: http://www.drlowe.com

Donna Hurlock, M.D.
205 S. Whiting St., Suite 303, Alexandria, VA 22304
Phone: 703-823-1533; fax: 703-823-5873
Web site: http://www.dhurlock.yourmd.com/
(Note: Dr. Hurlock is a gynecologist and a certified menopause
clinician who also treats hypothyroidism.)

Joseph J. Lamb, M.D.
The Integrative Medicine Works
5249 Duke St., #309, Alexandria, VA 22304
Phone: 703-823-8206; fax: 703-823-1189
E-mail: DrJJLamb@aol.com
Web site: http://www.theintegrativemedicineworks.meta-ehealth.com

Stephen Langer, M.D.
General Preventive Medicine & Clinical Nutrition
3031 Telegraph Ave., Suite 230, Berkeley, CA 94705
Phone: 510-548-7384

Kate Lemmerman, M.D.
Kaplan Clinic
5275 Lee Highway, Suite 200, Arlington, VA 22207
Phone: 703-532-4892
Web site: http://www.kaplanclinic.com

Sandra Levy, M.S., C.M.T.
Alexandria Myotherapy
333 North Fairfax St., Suite 303, Alexandria, VA 22314
Phone: 703-548-2270
Web site: http://www.alexmyo.com

John C. Lowe, M.A., D.C.
Board Certified: American Academy of Pain Management
Director, Fibromyalgia Research Foundation

C/O Center for Metabolic Health
1007 Pearl St., Suite 280, Boulder, CO 80302
Phone: 303-413-9100, fax: 303-604-0773
E-mail: DrLowe@drlowe.com
Web site: http://www.drlowe.com

Ron Manzanero, M.D.
4412 Spicewood Springs Rd., Suite 1007, Austin, TX 78759
Phone: 512-343-6223; fax: 512-343-0727

Michael McNett, M.D.
The Paragon Clinic
4332 N. Elston Ave., Chicago, IL 60641
Phone: 773-604-5321; fax: 773-604-5231
E-mail: mmcnett@paragonclinic.com
Web site: http://www.paragonclinic.com

Joseph Mercola, D.O.
Optimal Wellness Center
1443 W. Schaumburg Rd., Schaumburg IL 60194
Phone: 847-985-1777
Web site: http://www.mercola.com

Donald Michael, M.D., P.C.
328 N. Michigan St., B3, South Bend, IN 46601
Phone: 574-2387-6010; fax: 574-287-6651
E-mail: Dmichaelmd@aol.com

Roby Mitchell, M.D. ("Dr. Fitt")
3501 Soncy #110, Amarillo, TX 79119
Web site: http://www.drfitt.com

Viana Muller, Ph.D.
Whole World Botanicals

P.O. Box 322074, Ft. Wash. Station, New York, NY 10032
Phones: 888-757-6026, 212-781-6026; fax: 212-781-0440
E-mail: postmaster@wholeworldbotanicals.com
Web site: http://www.wholeworldbotanicals.com/

Richard Podell, M.D., M.P.H.
Clinical Professor, Dept. of Family Medicine
UMDNJ—Robert Wood Johnson Medical School
105 Morris Ave., Springfield, NJ 07081;
53 Kossuth St., Somerset, NJ 08873
Phone: 973-218-9191; fax: 973-218-1199
Web site: http://www.DrPodell.org

Bruce Rind, M.D.
5225 Wisconsin Ave., N.W., Washington, DC 20015
Phone: 202-237-7000, ext. 5; fax: 202-237-0017
E-mail: drrind@aol.com
Web site: http://www.drrind.com

Carol Roberts, M.D.
Wellness Works
1209 Lakeside Drive, Brandon, FL 33510
Phone: 813-661-3662
Web site: http://www.wellnessworks.us/

Glenn Rothfeld, M.D.
180 Massachusetts Ave. Suite 303, Arlington, MA 02474
Phone: 781-641-1901; fax: 781-641-3963
E-mail: info@WholeHealthNE.com
Web site: http://www.wholehealthne.com

Richard Shames, M.D., and Karilee Shames, Ph.D., R.N.
Preventive Medicine Center of Marin
25 Mitchell Blvd., Suite 8, San Rafael, CA 94903

Phone: 866-468-4979; fax: 415-472-7636
E-mail: ThyroidPower@aol.com
Web site: http://www.ThyroidPower.com

Dr. Brian Sheen—Executive Director
Quantum Healing, Yoga and Meditation Center
12 N.E. 5th Ave., Delray Beach, FL 33483
Phone: 561-272-3733
Web site: http://www.spiritgrowth.com

Robban A. Sica, M.D.
Center for the Healing Arts
370 Post Rd., Orange, CT 06477
Phone: 203-799-7733; fax: 203-799-3560
E-mail: support@centerhealingarts.com
Web site: http://www.centerhealingarts.com

Sanford Siegal, D.O.
Siegal Medical Group, Inc.
10661 N. Kendall Drive, Suite 108, Miami, FL 33176
Phone: 305-595-6113; fax: 305-595-4571
Web site: http://www.drsiegal.com
(Note: Practice specializes in obesity and weight loss, with thyroid
as a subset of those patients.)

Robert G. Saieg, M.D.
Gynecology, Hormonal, Preventative/Nutritional Medicine
44199 Dequindre, Suite 408, Troy, MI 48085
Phone: 248-828-8484

Sherrill Sellman, N.D.
E-mail: golight@earthlink.net
Web site: http://www.ssellman.com

Jacob E. Teitelbaum, M.D.
Annapolis Center for Effective CFS/Fibromyalgia Therapies
466 Forelands Rd., Annapolis, MD 21401
Phone: 410-573-5389; fax: 410-266-6104
Web sites: http://www.vitality101.com; http://www.endfatigue.com

Cynthia White
Aerobic Instructor/Personal Trainer
Denton, TX
Phone: 940-440-9130

Kenneth N. Woliner, M.D., A.B.F.P.
Holistic Family Medicine, L.L.C.
2499 Glades Rd., #106A, Boca Raton, FL 33431
Phone: 561-620-7779; fax: 561-367-9509
Web site: knw6@cornell.edu

GLOSSARY

Alt.support.thyroid: Internet-based newsgroup for patients interested in sharing support and information about thyroid disease

Amiodarone: A heart drug that contains iodine and can trigger thyroid problems

Antidepressant: A medication used to treat depression

Antiperoxidase (antimicrosomal) antibody: An antibody against peroxidase, which is a protein within the thyroid

Antithyroid antibodies (ATA): Antibodies directed against the thyroid gland

Antithyroid drugs: Medications that slow or stop the thyroid gland's ability to produce and synthesize thyroid hormone

Armour Thyroid: Brand name for a nonsynthetic thyroid hormone replacement drug, produced using the desiccated thyroid gland of pigs

ATA: *See* Antithyroid antibodies

Autoimmune: Refers to a condition in which the immune system reacts against one's own tissues or organs, causing disease

Basal body temperature: Body temperature taken immediately after waking, before any movement.

Bioequivalent: Term used to refer to a drug that has the same strength and similar availability to the body and organs when provided in the same dosage and form as another drug

Bladderwrack: An herb that contains iodine

Bugleweed: An herb that contains iodine

Carbohydrates: Compounds within foods that include monosaccharides (simple sugars) like glucose, and polysaccharides (complex sugars, complex carbohydrates) like starch or cellulose

Carpal Tunnel Syndrome (CTS): A condition in which compression of the median nerve in the wrist causes weakness, numbness, and pain in the hand, wrist, or fingers

CFS: *See* chronic fatigue syndrome

Chernobyl: Ukrainian site of the 1986 nuclear accident that released radiation throughout the former Soviet Union and Europe

Chronic fatigue syndrome (CFS): An illness of undetermined cause that is often characterized by unexplained fatigue, weakness, muscle pain, and swollen lymph nodes

Cold nodule: A nonfunctioning thyroid nodule/lump that does not concentrate radioactive isotopes in a thyroid scan and may be indicative of malignancy

Congenital hypothyroidism: Hypothyroidism at or before birth, due to missing or defective thyroid gland, or dysfunction of thyroid hormone secretion and processing

CTS: *See* Carpal tunnel syndrome

Cytomel: Brand name of liothyronine (synthetic triiodothyronine) drug sold in the U.S. and Canada.

D.O.: Doctor of Osteopathy

Desiccated thyroid: Term used to refer to nonsynthetic thyroid hormone replacement drug produced using the thyroid gland of pigs

Eltroxin: Canadian brand of levothyroxine

Endocrine disrupters: Chemicals in the environment that have the ability to mimic hormones or disrupt the endocrine glands

Endocrine glands: Glands that secrete hormonal and metabolic substances inside the body

Endocrinologist: A doctor who specializes in treating patients with endocrine problems, including thyroid disease

Epstein-Barr virus: A virus in the herpes family that causes infectious mononucleosis

Estrogen: The generic term for the various female sex hormones

Euthyroid: Refers to the condition in which the thyroid-stimulating hormone (TSH) test values are in the normal range, and the thyroid is neither hyperthyroid nor hypothyroid by test standards

Exophthalmos: An abnormal protrusion of the eyeball from the eye socket (orbit), which can be associated with Graves' disease

Fallout: Airborne radioactive material that falls to the ground after a nuclear accident and contaminates food and water supplies, creating potential health dangers

Fibromyalgia: A condition characterized by pain in muscles, sleep disturbance, stiffness, and fatigue

Follicular cancer: Second most common form of thyroid cancer

Gland: A soft body made up of a large number of vessels that produce, store, and release—or "secrete"—some substance, often hormones

Goiter: An enlargement of the thyroid. A goiter can be either diffuse, meaning that it is generally enlarged, or it can be nodular, asymmetrically enlarged.

Goitrogen: Referring to a substance or product that may cause thyroid enlargement and formation of a goiter

Graves' disease: Named after Dr. Robert Graves, this is an autoimmune form of hyperthyroidism.

Graves' ophthalmopathy: An autoimmune disease, more common in Graves' disease patients, that affects the eyes

Hashimoto's disease/thyroiditis: An autoimmune inflammation of the thyroid gland, named for Dr. Hashimoto. Can result in a goiter and often causes hypothyroidism.

HMO: Health maintenance organization

Hormones: Internal secretions carried in the blood to various organs

Hot nodule: A lump or mass on or in the thyroid gland that is often associated with hyperthyroidism

Hyperinsulinemia: The condition in which the body produces increasing amounts of insulin in order to maintain normal blood sugar levels, causing insulin to remain in the bloodstream in higher concentrations

Hyperthyroidism: Excess production of thyroid hormone, due to abnormal thyroid gland function, nodules, or excessive thyroid hormone replacement

Hypothalamus: A part of the brain that has a key role in endocrine function. It conducts thyroid hormone conversion.

Hypothermia: The condition of low body temperature

Hypothyroidism: Insufficient production of thyroid hormone due to abnormal thyroid gland function, absence of all or part of the thyroid gland, or insufficient thyroid hormone replacement

Insulin: Hormone released by the pancreas that helps process sugar in the blood

Iodine: An element—found in seafood and added to supplements and salt—that is the most essential component for the body's ability to manufacture thyroid hormone

Iodine-131: A form of iodine that, when released in sufficient quantities due to nuclear accidents or nuclear releases, can cause thyroid disease. Also used as a form of treatment for some overactive thyroid conditions

Isthmus: The area connecting the two lobes of the thyroid gland

Kelp: A form of seaweed containing high amounts of iodine

Levothroid: A brand of synthetic thyroxine (levothyroxine) sold in the U.S.

Levothyroxine, levothyroxine sodium: The generic name for synthetic thyroxine, also known as T4, a thyroid hormone replacement drug. Brand names in the U.S. and Canada include Synthroid, Levothroid, Levoxyl, Eltroxin, and PMS-Levothyroxine.

Levoxyl: A brand of levothyroxine sold in the U.S.

Libido: Sex drive

Liothyronine: The generic name for the drug that is a synthetic version of triiodothyronine, T3

Liotrix: A synthetic drug combining levothyroxine and liothyronine (synthetic T4 plus synthetic T3)

Lithium: A drug used to treat manic depression known to cause thyroid disease in some patients

Lobes: A term that refers to the two sides of the thyroid gland

Medullary cancer: The third most common form of thyroid cancer involving a specialized thyroid cell—the C cell—that manufactures calcitonin

Metabolism: The process by which oxygen and calories are converted to energy for use by cells and organs

Methimazole: An antithyroid medication used to treat hyperthyroidism

Mitral valve prolapse (MVP): A heart condition in which improper closure of one of the heart valves creates slight regurgitation, often accompanied by an audible "murmur."

Mono-deiodination: The conversion process by which one iodine molecule is removed from thyroxine (T4) converting it to tri-iodothyronine (T3); also known as T4 to T3 conversion

Mononucleosis: A condition of the lymph glands caused by infection with Epstein-Barr virus

Multinodular goiter: A condition in which the thyroid is enlarged and has two or more nodules

Myxedema: A condition characterized by swelling of skin and other tissues, particularly with puffiness around the eyes and cheeks, caused by hypothyroidism

Myxedemic coma: Severe myxedema, often accompanied with hypothermia, resulting in unconsciousness

Natural thyroid: Nonsynthetic thyroid hormone replacement drug produced using the desiccated thyroid gland of pigs

Naturethroid: Brand name for a hypoallergenic natural thyroid hormone replacement drug produced using the desiccated thyroid gland of pigs, sold in the U.S.

Naturopathy: Holistic medical practice based on a balance of physical, emotional, mental, and spiritual aspects, and the body's innate ability to heal itself

Nodular goiter: An enlargement of the thyroid gland characterized by one or more nodules

Nodule: A lump or abnormal growth of tissue on or within the thyroid

Osteopathy: A form of medicine that, in addition to medication and nutrition, relies on osteopathic manipulation, the process of working with the imbalances and misalignment in the body's musculoskeletal system as a way to treat illness

Osteoporosis: A condition in which calcium lost from the bones makes bones brittle and more easily broken. Most common in older women and men

Palpitation: The condition of feeling the heart beating, whether due to rapid heartbeat, irregular or missed beats, or just strong, forceful beating

Papillary cancer: The most common form of thyroid cancer, often caused by radiation exposure

Parathyroid glands: Small, paired endocrine glands located behind the thyroid that secrete parathyroid hormone and control calcium and bone metabolism

Perchlorate: A chemical used in the manufacture of rockets and fireworks that, when contaminating the water supply, can adversely affect the thyroid

Phytoestrogen: A plant product that acts like an estrogen and has an effect on the endocrine system, e.g., soy.

Pituitary gland: A small, peanut-sized gland located behind the eyes at the base of the brain. It secretes hormones that control other endocrine glands, and specifically secretes thyroid-stimulating hormone.

PMS-Levothyroxine: The Canadian brand of levothyroxine

Polycystic ovary syndrome (PCOS): A syndrome characterized by heavy or absent periods, lack of ovulation, and cysts on the ovaries

Postpartum: Refers to the period after pregnancy

Postpartum thyroiditis: A temporary inflammation of the thyroid, occurring after pregnancy, that can result in transient hypothyroidism

Potassium iodide: A drug used to treat certain thyroid disorders that can also be taken after nuclear accidents to protect the thyroid from damage by blocking the gland's uptake of radioactive-iodine isotopes

Premenstrual syndrome (PMS): Emotional, physical, psychological, and mood-related symptoms that take place in the menstrual cycle after ovulation and just prior to menstruation

Progesterone: A hormone produced in the corpus luteum of the ovary

Propylthiouracil (PTU): An antithyroid medication used for hyperthyroidism that blocks thyroid cells from producing thyroid hormone

PTU: *See* Propylthiouracil

Radioactive iodine (RAI): A radioactive form of iodine that is used to diagnose and treat thyroid problems

Resistance to thyroid hormone (RTH): Insufficient cellular response to thyroid hormone that can result in hypothyroidism

Reverse T3: A form of inactive triiodothyronine (T3) that is formed during periods of stress on the body

Subclinical hypothyroidism: Mild hypothyroidism that does not necessarily have associated symptoms

Suppression: The process of providing enough thyroid hormone replacement to thyroid cancer survivors to "suppress" TSH to low or barely detectable levels, in order to prevent thyroid cancer recurrence

Synthroid: The brand of levothyroxine sold in the U.S. and Canada.

T3: Shorthand for triiodothyronine, the more potent of the two key hormones produced by the thyroid gland. Triiodothyronine is also produced from the conversion of thyroxine (T4) in tissue and cells.

T4: Shorthand for thyroxine, the primary hormone produced by the thyroid gland

T4 to T3 conversion: The conversion process by which one iodine molecule is removed from thyroxine (T4), converting it to triiodothyronine (T3). Also known as mono-deiodination

Tapazole: The brand name of an antithyroid drug

TBG: *See* Thyroid binding globulin

Testosterone: A male sex hormone present in both men and women

TG: *See* Thyroglobulin

Thiocyanate: A chemical found in cigarettes and some foods that can cause thyroid dysfunction

Thyrogen: A drug that is administered to some thyroid cancer survivors prior to diagnostic scans that allows for scanning without withdrawal from thyroid hormone and resulting hypothyroidism

Thyroglobulin (TG): A protein in the thyroid gland that can be used as a marker for thyroid disease and thyroid cancer

Thyroid binding globulin (TBG): A protein in the bloodstream that binds with thyroxine

Thyroid eye disease: Autoimmune-related eye condition that accompanies autoimmune thyroid disease

Thyroid gland: Butterfly-shaped gland located in the lower part of the neck, in front of the windpipe, that secretes hormones that regulate metabolism

Thyroid-stimulating hormone (TSH, Thyrotropin): A hormone produced by the pituitary gland that stimulates the thyroid gland. Measurement of the levels of this drug is considered a primary way to assess hypothyroidism and hyperthyroidism.

Thyroidectomy: The surgical removal of all or part of the thyroid gland

Thyroiditis: An inflammation of the thyroid gland

Thyrolar: Brand name for the synthetic drug combining levothyroxine and liothyronine (synthetic T4 plus synthetic T3)

Thyrotropin-releasing hormone (TRH): A hormone released by the hypothalamus that communicates with the pituitary gland and stimulates release of thyroid-stimulating hormone

Thyrotropin-releasing hormone (TRH) test: A highly sensitive test that detects abnormal thyroid function

Thyrotropin: *See* Thyroid-stimulating hormone

Thyroxine (T4): The primary hormone produced by the thyroid gland

Toxic goiter: An enlarged thyroid gland that is causing hyperthyroidism

TRH: *See* Thyrotropin-releasing hormone

Triiodothyronine (T3): The more potent of the two key hormones produced by the thyroid gland. Triiodothyronine is also produced from the conversion of thyroxine (T4) in tissue and cells.

TSH: *See* Thyroid-stimulating hormone

Tyrosine: An amino acid necessary for the production of thyroid hormone

Westhroid: The brand name for a nonsynthetic thyroid hormone replacement drug produced using the desiccated thyroid gland of pigs

Wilson's Syndrome: Self-named syndrome identified by a former M.D. who believes that stress on the body causes chronic low body temperature and Reverse T3 production.

REFERENCES

Aarflot, T. "Association between chronic widespread musculoskeletal complaints and thyroid autoimmunity. Results from a community survey." *Scandinavian Journal of Primary Health Care* 14 (2) (1996): 111–25.

Adlin, Victor, M.D. "Subclinical Hypothyroidism: Deciding When to Treat." *American Family Physician Magazine*, 15 February 1998 [online edition]. http://www.aafp.org/afp/980215ap/adlin.html

American Association of Clinical Endocrinologists (AACE) press release, "January is Thyroid Awareness Month: 2003 Campaign Encourages Awareness of Mild Thyroid Failure, Importance of Routine Testing," January 2003, http://www.aace.com/pub/tam2003/press.php

American Association of Clinical Endocrinologists. Web site information. http://www.aace.com

American Medical Women's Association. "Facts about thyroid disease." Health Topics, http://www.amwa-doc.org/healthtopics/thyroid.html#Overview

American Thyroid Association. "Thyroid Disease in the Elderly." [Online patient brochure] http://www.thyToid.org/patient/brochur2.htm

American Association of Clinical Endocrinologists. "Symptoms List." http://www.aace.com/pub/spec/tam98/symptoms.html

American Tinnitus Association. Web site, http://www.ata.org

American Diabetes Association. Web site, http://www.diabetes.org

Anisman, H., et al. "Neuroimmune mechanisms in health and disease." *Canadian Medical Association Journal* 155(8) (Oct 1998): 1075–82.

Archives of Internal Medicine, Vol. 160, No. 11, June 12, 2000, "American Thyroid Association Guidelines for Detection of Thyroid Dysfunction."

Arem, Ridha, M.D. *Thyroid Solution*. New York: Ballantine Books, 2000.

Arizona Republic. "Pollutant Likely Migrated Via Canal." 27 August 1998.

Arnot, Robert, M.D.*Dr. Bob Arnot's Revolutionary Weight Control Program*. Boston: Little Brown & Company, 1998.

Aronne, Louis J., M.D. *Weigh Less, Live Longer: Dr. Lou Aronne's "Getting Healthy" Plan for Permanent Weight Control*. New York: John Wiley & Sons, 1996.

Atcheson, Steven G., M.D. "Concurrent Medical Disease in Work-Related Carpal Tunnel Syndrome." *Arch Intern Med*, July 27, 1998 et al., 158(1998):1506–12. http://Avww.ama-assn.org/sci-pubs/journals/archive/inte/vol_158/no_14/ioi70670.htm

Balch, James F., M.D., and Phyllis Balch. *Prescription for Nutritional Healing: A Practical A–Z Reference to Drug-Free Remedies Using Vitamins, Minerals, Herbs & Food Supplements*. Garden City Park, NY: Avery, 1996.

Barnes, Broda O., M.D., and Lawrence Galton. *Hypothyroidism: The Unsuspected Illness*. New York: Harper & Row, 1976.

Bell, David S. *The Doctor's Guide to Chronic Fatigue Syndrome: Understanding, Treating, and Living with CFIDS*. Cambridge, MA: Perseus Books, 1995.

Berger, M. M., et al. "Relations between the selenium status and the low T3 syndrome after major trauma." *Intensive Care Medicine* 22 (6) (Jun 1996):575–81.

Berkow, Robert, M.D. *The Merck Manual of Diagnosis and Therapy*. Rahway, NJ: Merck & Company, 1999.

Bhatia, P.L., O.P. Gupta, M.K. Agrawal, and S.K. Mishr. "Audiological and vestibular function tests in hypothyroidism." *Laryngoscope* 87(12) (Dec 1977):2082–89.

Blanchard, Kenneth, M.D. *What Your Doctor May Not Tell You About Hypothyroidism*. New York: Warner Books, 2004.

Blanchard, Kenneth, M.D. Telephone interviews with Mary Shomon, October 1998.

Boschert, Sherry. "T3 Plus T4 'Unproven' for Hypothyroidism." *Internal Medicine News*, 1 May 1999.

Brauman, A., et al. "Prevalence of mitral valve prolapse in chronic lymphocytic thyroiditis and nongoitrous hypothyroidism." *Cardiology* 75(4)(1998):269–73.

Brownstein, David, M.D. *Overcoming Thyroid Disorders*. West Bloomfield, MI. Medical Alternatives Press. 2002.

Brownstein, David, M.D. *The Miracle of Natural Hormones*. 3rd ed. West Bloomfield, MI. Medical Alternatives Press. 2003.

Buffalo News. "Researcher Warns of Potential Global Health Crisis." 7 October 1998.

Bunevicius, Robertas, et al. "Effects of Thyroxine as Compared with Thyroxine plus Triiodothyronine in Patients with Hypothyroidism." *New Eng J Med* 340 (1999):424–29, 469–70.

Bunevicius, R., and A.J. Prange. "Mental improvement after replacement therapy with thyroxine plus triiodothyronine: relationship to cause of hypothyroidism." *Int J Neuropsychopharmacol.* 2000 (Jun);3(2):167–74.

Bunevicius, R., et al. "Thyroxine vs. thyroxine plus triiodothyronine in treatment of hypothyroidism after thyroidectomy for Graves' disease." *Endocrine* 2002 Jul;18(2):129–33.

Burman, K.D., et al. "A radioimmunoassay for 3,3',5'-L-triiodothyronine (reverse T3): assessment of thyroid gland content and serum measurements in conditions of normal and altered thyroidal economy and following administration of thyrotropin releasing hormone (TRH) and thyrotropin (TSH)." *J Clin Endocrinol Metab* 44 (4) (Apr 1977): 660–72.

Canaris, Gay J., M.D., et al. "The Colorado Thyroid Disease Prevalence Study." *Arch Intern Med.* 2000;160:526–34. Vol. 160, No. 4, February 28, 2000.

Canaris, G. J., N. Manowitz, G. Mayor, and E. C. Ridgway. "Prevalence of Abnormal Lipid Abnormalities and Symptoms of Thyroid Disease in a Large Observational Cohort." Paper presented to the 70th Annual Meeting of the American Thyroid Association, Sunday, 19 October 1997.

Capen. C. C. "TI: Mechanistic data and risk assessment of selected toxic end points of the thyroid gland." *Toxicologic Pathology* 25 (1) (Jan–Feb 1997):39–48.

Cassidy, A., et al. "Biological effects of a diet of soy protein rich in isoflavones on the menstrual cycle of premenopausal women." *Am J Clin Nutr* 60(1994):333–40.

Cassio, A., E. Cacciari, A. Cicgnani, et al.: "Treatment of congenital hypothyroidism: thyroxine alone or thyroxine plus triiodothyronine." *Pediatrics* 111(5) (2003):1055–60.

Centers for Disease Control. *CDC's Diabetes and Public Health Resource.* http://www.cdc.gov/diabetes/

Chapin, R. E., et al. "Endocrine modulation of reproduction." *Fund Appl Toxical.* 29 (1996):1–17.

Cherkes, Kelly. E-mail and telephone interviews with Mary Shomon, October 1998.

Chorazy, P. A., et al. "Persistent hypothyroidism in an infant receiving a soy formula: case report and review of the literature." *Pediatrics* (1995):148–50.

Clarkson, T. B., et al. "Estrogenic soybean isoflavones and chronic disease. Risks and benefits." *Trends Endocrinol Metab* 6 (1995): 11–16.

Clyde, Patrick W., et al. "Combined Levothyroxine Plus Liothyronine Compared With Levothyroxine Alone in Primary Hypothyroidism: A Randomized Controlled Trial." *JAMA* 2003:290:2952–58.

Colborn, Theodora, et al. Our *Stolen Future*. London: Little Brown & Company, 1996.

College of Agriculture and Life Sciences, Cornell University, Comstock Hall, Ithaca, New York 14853–0901: Hawaii Department of Agriculture, Division of Plant Industry, Honolulu, Hawaii 96814.

Colquhoun, J. "Child Dental Health Differences in New Zealand." Community Healthy Services, XI 85–90, 1987.

Cruz, M. L., et al. "Effects of infant nutrition on cholesterol synthesis rates." *Ped Res* 35 (1994): 135–40.

Cudd, T. A., et al. "Fetal and Maternal Thyroid Hormone Responses to Ethanol Exposure During the Third Trimester Equivalent of Gestation in Sheep." *Alcohol Clin Exp Res.* 2002 Jan;26(1):53–8.

Danforth, E., Jr., and A. Burger. "The role of thyroid hormones in the control of energy expenditure." *Clinics in Endocrinology and Metabolism* 13 (3) (Nov 1984): 581–95.

Davidoff, Frank. "Shame: the elephant in the room: Managing shame is important for improving health care." *BMJ* 2002;324:623–24.

De Rosa, G., et al. "A slightly suppressive dose of L-thyroxine does not affect bone turnover and bone mineral density in pre- and postmenopausal women with nontoxic goitre." *Hormone Metabolic Research*. Italy 27(11) (Nov 1995):503–7.

Demers, Laurence, Ph.D., F.A.C.B., et al. "Laboratory Medicine Practice Guidelines: Laboratory Support for the Diagnosis and Monitoring of Thyroid Disease." National Academy of Clinical Biochemistry, November 2002.

Divi, R. L. and D. R. Doerge. "Inhibition of thyroid peroxidase by dietary flavonoids." *Chemical Research in Toxicology* 9 (1) (Jan–Feb 1996): 16–23.

Divi, R. L., et al. "Anti-thyroid isoflavones from the soybean." *Biochem Pharmacol* 54(1997):1087–96.

Doerge, D. R. "Goitrogenic and estrogenic activity of soy isoflavones." *Environ Health Perspect* 2002 Jun;110 Suppl 3:349–53.

Drane, H. M., et al. "Oestrogenic activity of soya-bean products." *Fd Cosmet-Technol* 18 (1980):425–27.

Durrant-Peatfield, Barry. *The Great Thyroid Scandal and How to Survive It*. London, UK Barons Down Publishing, 2002.

Dzurec, L. C. "Experiences of fatigue and depression before and after low-dose 1-thyroxine supplementation in essentially euthyroid individuals." *Research in Nursing and Health* 20 (5) (Oct 1997): 389–98.

Elfstrom, David. "How to Talk to Doctors." http://www.sunnybrook .utoronto.ca./~elfstrom/arthritis/articles/appointments.html

Ezrin, Calvin, M.D. *The Type II Diabetes Diet Book*. Los Angeles: Lowell House Publishers, 1999.

Fitzpatrick, Dr. Mike, and Sue Dibb. "Soya Infant Formula: the Health Concerns." *Food Commission Briefing Paper* (October 1998), London, U.K.

Flatt, J. P., E. Ravussin, K. J. Acheson, and E. Jequier. "Effects of dietary fat on postprandial substrate oxidation and on carbohydrate and fat balances." *J Clin Investig* (1985) 76: 1019–24.

Florkovvski, C. M., et al. "Bone mineral density in patients receiving suppressive doses of thyroxine for thyroid carcinoma." *New Zealand Medical Journal* 106(966) (Oct 1993):443–44.

Fontanarosa, Phil B., M.D., and George D. Lundberg, M.D. "Alternative Medicine Meets Science—Editorial." *JAMA* 280(18) (Nov 1998).

Fort, P., et al. "Breast feeding and insulin-dependent diabetes mellitus in children." *J Am Coll Nutr* 5 (Feb 1986): 439–41.

Fort, P., et al. "Breast and soy-formula feedings in early infancy and the prevalence of autoimmune thyroid disease in children." *J Am Coll Nutr* 9 (April 1990): 164–67.

Fowler, P. B., J. McIvor, L. Sykes, and K. D. Macrae. "The effect of long-term thyroxine on bone mineral density and serum cholesterol." *Journal of the Royal College of Physicians of London* 30 (6) (1996):527–32.

Fukata, S., et al. "Relationship between cigarette smoking and hypothyroidism in patients with Hashimoto's thyroiditis." *J Endocrinol Invest* 19(9) (Oct 1996):607–12.

Glinoer, Daniel, "Thyroid Regulation and Dysfunction in the Pregnant Patient," *Thyroid Manager* 2003, http://www.thyroid manager.org/Chapter14/14-text.htm

Glinoer, D., et al. "Risk of subclinical hypothyroidism in pregnant women with asymptomatic autoimmune thyroid disorders." *J Clin Endocrinol Metab* 79(1) (July 1994):197–204.

Grant, D. J., et al. "Suppressed TSH levels secondary to thyroxine replacement therapy are not associated with osteoporosis." *Clin Endocrinol* (Oxford) 39(5) (Nov 1993):529–33.

Greene, Loren Wissner, M.D., F.A.C.P., F.A.C.E. "The Thyroid and Reproductive System, Disorders of Menstruation, Fertility and Pregnancy." *The Bridge.* [Thyroid Foundation of America newsletter] 10(1). http:// www.clark.net/pub/tfa/bridge/bridge .vol10.no1.html

Haddow, James E., et al. "Maternal Thyroid Deficiency During Pregnancy and Subsequent Neuropsychological Development of the Child." *New Eng J Med* 341(8) (Aug 1999).

Hanford Health Information Network. An *Overview of Hanford Health and Radiation Effects.* http://www.doh.wa.gov/ hanford/publications/overview/overview.html

Hilgers, A. "Chronic fatigue syndrome: immune dysfunction, role of pathogens and toxic agents and neurological and cardiac changes." *Wien Med Wochenschr* 144(16) (1994): 399–406.

Hill, J. O., J. C. Peters, D. Yang, T. Sharp, M. Kaler, N. N. Abum-rad, and H. L. Greene. "Thermogenesis in humans during overfeeding with medium-chain triglycerides." *Metabolism* (1989) 38:641–48.

Hollowell, J. G., et al. "Iodine nutrition in the United States. Trends and public health implications: iodine excretion data from National Health and Nutrition Examination Surveys I and III (1971–1974 and 1988–1994)." *J Clin Endocrinol Metab* 83(10) (Oct 1998):3401–8.

Holmes, Diana. *Tears Behind Closed Doors.* 2nd ed. Wolverhampton, UK: Normandi Publishing Ltd., 2002.

Honeyman-Lowe, Gina, and John C. Lowe. *Your Guide to Metabolic Health.* Lafayette, CO: McDowell Health-Science Books, 2003.

Hotz, C. S., et al. "Dietary iodine and selenium interact to affect thyroid hormone metabolism of rats." *Journal of Nutrition* 127 (6) (Jun 1997):1214–18.

Hsiung, Robert, M.D. "Dr. Bob's Psychopharmcology Tips." http://uhs.bsd.uchicago.edu/dr-bob/tips;tips.html

Hydovitz, J. D. "Occurrence of goiter in an infants on a soy diet." *New Eng J Med* 262 (1960): 351–53.

Iacovides, P., et al. "Thyroid Function in Clinical Subtypes of Major Depression. K. Fountoulakis," *ABMC Psychiatry* 2004, 4:6.

Iijima, Takashi. *Obstetrics and Gynecology* 90 (Sept 1997):364–69.

Infant and Dietetic Foods Association. "Phytoestrogens in Soya Infant Formula." Letter to the Food Commission, 24 September 1998.

Information Dissemination, Inc. Web site, http://www.inciid.org, 1999

Irvine, C. H. G., et al. "Phytoestrogens in soy-based infant foods: concentrations, daily intake, and possible biological effects." *PSEBM* 217 (1998):247–53.

Ishizuki, Y., et al. "The effects on the thyroid gland of soybeans administered experimentally in healthy subjects." *Nippon Naibunpi gakkai Zasshi* 67 (1991): 622–29.

Jabbar, M.A., et al. "Abnormal thyroid function tests in infants with congenital hypothyroidism: the influence of soy-based formula." *J Am Coll Nutr.* 16 (1997): 280–82.

Jones P.J.H., and M.P. St-Onge. "Physiological effects of medium-chain triglycerides: potential agents in the prevention of obesity." *Journal of Nutrition* (2002) 132; 329–32.

Journal of Clinical Endocrinology and Metabolism 82 (August 1997):2455–57.

Kaplan, M.M. "Management of thyroxine therapy during pregnancy." *Endocrinol Pract,* (1996): 281–86.

Kellman, Rafael, M.D. "Energizing Chronic Fatigue." *Alternative Medicine,* Issue 19 (September 1997).

King, Ralph, Jr. "Judge Blocks Proposed Synthroid Pact, Criticizing the Level of Attorneys' Fees." *Wall Street Journal,* 2 September 1998.

Knoll Pharmaceuticals. *Knoll Settles Thyroid Medication Class Action Lawsuit.* Press release, 4 August 1997.

Konno, N., et al. "Seasonal variation of serum thyrotropin concentration and thyrotropin response to thyrotropin-releasing hormone in patients with primary hypothyroidism on constant replacement dosage of thyroxine." *J Clini Endocrinol Metab* 54 (6) (1982):1118–24.

Konstantinov, K., et al. "Autoantibodies to nuclear envelope antigens in chronic fatigue syndrome." *Journal of Clinical Investigation.* 98(8) (Oct 15 1996): 1888–96.

Lakshmy, R., et al. "Iodine metabolism in response to goitrogen induced altered thyroid status under conditions of moderate and high intake of iodine." *Hormone and Metabolic Research* 27 (10) (Oct 1995):450–4.

Landis, Robyn. *Herbal Defense.* New York: Warner Books, 1997.

Langer, Stephen, M.D., and James Scheer. *Solved: The Riddle of Illness*. New York: McGraw-Hill/Contemporary Books, 2000.

Las Vegas Review-Journal. "Rocket fuel chemical found in Arizona water." 28 August 1998.

Lasser, R. A., and R. J. Baldessarini. "Thyroid hormones in depressive disorders: a reappraisal of clinical utility." *Harv Rev Psychiatry* 4(6) (Mar–Apr 1997):291–305.

Laumann, Edward O., Ph.D., et al. "Sexual Dysfunction in the United States, Prevalence and Predictors." *JAMA* 281(6) (10 February 1999).

Leslie, P. J., and A. D. Toft. "The replacement therapy problem in hypothyroidism." *Baillieres Clinical Endocrinology and Metabolism 2* (3) (Aug 1998):653–69.

Leviton, Richard. "Reviving the Thyroid." *Alternative Medicine*. Issue 22 (February/March 1998).

Lowe, John C., et al. "Mutations in the c-erbA beta 1 gene: do they underlie euthyroid fibromyalgia?" *Medical Hypotheses* 48 (2) (1997):125–35.

Lowe, John C. "Thyroid status of 38 fibromyalgia patients: Implications for the etiology of fibromyalgia." *Clinical Bulletin of Myofascial Therapy* 2 (1997): 47–64.

Lowe, John C., D.C. Telephone and e-mail interviews with Mary Shomon, October 1998.

Lowe, John, DC, and Honeyman-Lowe, Gina, DC. *Your Guide to Metabolic Health*. Lafayette, CO: McDowell Publishing Co., 2003.

Maes, M., et al. "Components of biological variation, including seasonality, in blood concentrations of TSH, TT3, FT4, PRL, cortisol and testosterone." *Clinical Endocrinology* 46 (5) (May 1997):587–98.

Mandel, Susan J. "Thyroiditis After Pregnancy Loss." *J Clin Endocrinol Metab* 82(8) (Aug 1997):2455–57.

McCowen, K. C., et al. "Elevated serum thyrotropin in thyroxine-treated patients with hypothyroidism given sertraline." *N Eng J Med* 2;337(14) (Oct 1997): 1010–11.

McGaffee, J., et al. "Psychiatric presentations of hypothyroidism." *American Family Physician* 23 (5) (May 1981):129–33.

Mercado, G., et al. "Hypothyroidism: a Frequent Event After Radiotherapy and After Radiotherapy with Chemotherapy for Patients with Head and Neck carcinoma." *Cancer*. 2001 Dec 1;92(11):2892–7.

Mestman, Jorge H., M.D. "Perinatal Thyroid Dysfunction: Prenatal Diagnosis and Treatment." *Medscape Women's Health eJournal* 2(4), 1997.

Murphy, P. A., et al. "Isoflavones in Soy-Based Infant Formulas." *J Agric Food Chem* 45(1997): 4635–38.

National Cancer Institute. "Exposure of The American People To I-131 From Nevada Atmospheric Bomb Tests." *Technical Summary TS.5. Estimation of the Thyroid Doses from U-131* (1997). http://rex.nci.nih.gov/massmedia/repo rttofc.html

National Institute of Mental Health. Web site, http://www.nimh.nih.gov

National Institutes of Health, National Heart, Lung, and Blood Institute. "Facts About High Blood Pressure." http://www.nih.gov/health/htp-hbp/3.htrn

National Institutes of Health. *Complementary and Alternative Medicine Newsletter* V(1) (Jan 1998).

National Sleep Foundation. Web site, http://www.sleepfoundation.org

Nemeroff, Charles B. "The Neurobiology of Depression." *Scientific American* (June 1998). http://www.sciam.com/1998/0698issue/0698nemeroff.html

Newton, Gail, D., Ph.D., R.Ph. "Hasimoto's Thyroiditis." U.S. *Pharmacist: The Journal for Pharmacists' Education* (December 1998).

Nicolau, G. Y., et al. "Chronobiology of pituitary-thyroid functions." *Romanian Journal of Endocrinology* 30 (3–4) (1992): 125–48.

Nishi, I., et al. "Intra-individual and seasonal variations of thyroid function tests in healthy subjects." *Rinsho Byori. Japanese Journal of Clinical Pathology.* 44 (2) (1996):159–62.

Obstetrics and Gynecology 90(1997):364–69.

Obstetrics and Gynecology 92 (1998):206–11.

Ostrum, Janus L. "Tolerance of soy formulas with reduced phytate/phytoestrogens fed to healthy term children." Presentation at the Second International Symposium on the Role of Soy in Preventing and Treating Chronic Disease, Brussels, September 16–19, 1996.

Padberg, S., et al. "One-Year Prophylactic Treatment of Euthyroid Hashimoto's Thyroiditis Patients with Levothyroxine: Is There a Benefit?" *Thyroid.* 2001 Mar; 11(3):249–55.

Peat, Ray, Ph.D. "Thyroid: Misconceptions." *Townsend Letter for Doctors* (November 1993).

Pies, Ron, M.D. "The Diagnosis and Treatment of Subclinical Hypothyroid States in Depressed Patients." *General Hospital Psychiatry* 19 (1997):344–54.

Pies, Ron, M.D. "Mental Health Infosource." *Psychiatric Times,* http://www.mhsource.com/expert/expl092396h.html

Pinchera, A., et al. "Thyroid refractoriness in an athyreotic cretin fed soybean formula." *New Eng J Med.* 273(1965): 83–87.

"Practice Guidelines: Laboratory Support for the Diagnosis and Monitoring of Thyroid Disease." National Academy of Clinical Biochemistry. November 2002.

Reed, H.L. "Circannual changes in thyroid hormone physiology: the role of cold environmental temperatures." *Arctic Medical Research* 54 Suppl 2 (1995):9–15.

Rennie, Drummond, M.D. "Thyroid Storm." Editorial, *JAMA* (April 1997).

Ripp, J. A. "Soybean induced goiter." *Am J Dis Child* 102 (1961): 136–39.

Ross, D. S. "Hyperthyroidism, thyroid hormone therapy, and bone." *Thyroid* 4 (3) (Fall 1994):319–26.

Ross, Douglas S., M.D. "Ask the Doctor." *The Bridge* 13(2) (Summer 1998).

Rothfeld, Glenn, M.D. *Thyroid Balance*. Avon, MA: Adams Media Corporation; 2002. Rxlist.com. http://www.rxlist.com/

Ryan. P. J. "The Effects of Thyroxine Therapy on Bone Mineral Density." *Journal of Clinical Densitometry* 1(2)(1998): 173–77.

Santi, R., et al. "Phytoestrogens: potential endocrine disruptors in males." *Tox Ind Health* 14 (1998):223–37.

Saravanan, P., W. F., Chau, N. Roberts, et al.: "Psychological well-being in patients on 'adequate' doses of l-thyroxine: results of a large, controlled community-based questionnaire study." *Clin Endocrinol* (Oxford) 57(5)(2002): 577–85.

Sawka, A., et al. "Does a Combination Regimen of Thyroxine (T4) and 3,5,3'-Triiodothyronine Improve Depressive Symptoms Better Than T4 Alone in Patients with Hypothyroidism? Results of a Double-Blind, Randomized, Controlled Trial." *Clini Endocrinol Metab* 88(10)(2003): 455–55.

Schneider, R. "The effect of levothyroxine therapy on bone mineral density: a systematic review of the literature." *Exp Clin Endocrinol Diabetes* 2003.

Schneyer, Christine R., M.D. "Letters—March 11, 1998 Calcium Carbonate and Reduction of Levothyroxine Efficacy." *JAMA* 279 (11 March 1998): 750.

Sehnert, K. W., et al. "Basal metabolic temperature vs. laboratory assessment in 'posttraumatic hypothyroidism,'" *Manipulative Physiol Ther* 19(1) (Jan 1996): 6–12.

Setchell, K.D.R., et al. "Exposure of infants to phytoestrogens from soy-based infant formula." *Lancet* 350 (1997): 23–27.

Shames, Richard, M.D., and Karilee H. Shames, R. N. Ph.D. *ThyroidPower: Ten Steps to Total Health*. New York: HarperResource, 2002.

Sheeham, D. M. "Isoflavone content of breast milk and soy formulas: benefits and risks (letter)." *Clin Chem* 43(1997): 850.

Sherrill, Robert. "A Year in Corporate Crime." *The Nation* (1997). http://www.thenation.com:80/issue/970407/0407sher.htm

Shomon, Mary. *Living Well with Autoimmune Disease: What Your Doctors Don't Tell You . . . That You Need to Know*. New York: HarperResource, 2002.

Shomon, Mary. *Living Well with Chronic Fatigue Syndrome and Fibromyalgia: What Your Doctors Don't Tell You . . . That You Need to Know*. New York: Harper Resource, 2004.

Siafakas, X. M., et al. "Respiratory muscle strength in hypothyroidism." *Chest* 102(1) (Jul 1992): 189–94.

Sica, Robban, M.D. (ed.) Consensus Development Conference on the Clinical Management of Hypothyroidism. *Proceedings of the International College of Integrative Medicine*, Houston, TX, March 2003.

Siegal, Sanford, M.D. *Is Your Thyroid Making You Fat?* New York: Warner Books; 2001

Sinaii, N, et al., "High rates of autoimmune and endocrine disorders, fibromyalgia, chronic fatigue syndrome and atopic disease among women with endometriosis: a survey analysis." *Hum Reprod* 2002 Oct; 17(10): 2715–24.

Singh, N, et al. "The acute effect of calcium carbonate on the intestinal absorption of levothyroxine." *Thyroid* 2001 Oct; 11(10): 967–71.

Singh. A., Z. N. Dantas, S. C. Stone, and R. H. Asch. "Presence of thyroid antibodies in early reproductive failure: biochemical versus clinical pregnancies." *Fertility and Sterility* 63 (2) (Feb 1995): 277–81.

Stubbs, R. J., and C. G. Harbron. "Covert manipulation of the ration of medium- to long-chain triglycerides in isoenergetically dense diets: effect on food intake in ad libitum feeding men." *Int J. Obes* 1996 (20): 435–444.

Surks, M. I., et al. "Subclinical thyroid disease: scientific review and guidelines for diagnosis and management," *JAMA* 2004 (Jan 14): 291(2): 228–38.

Synthroid Lawsuit Claims. Web site, http://www.syndjroidclaims.com

Tamaki, H., et al. "Thyroxine requirement during pregnancy for therapy of hypothyroidism." *Obstetrics and Gynecology* 76 (2) (Aug 1990): 230–33.

The Tennessean. Nuclear Plant Health Series, 29 September 1998.

Thyrogen Product Information. Genzyme Web site, http://www.genzyme.com

"Thyroid Dysfunction in Patients With Type 1 Diabetes: A longitudinal study." *Diabetes Care* 2003;26:4:1181–85.

Thyroid Foundation of America. "Childhood Head and Neck Irradiation." http://www.clark.net/pub/tfa/brochure/brochure-irrad.html

Thyroid Foundation of America. *Hypothyroidism*. Thyroid Topics Brochures, 1995 [online version]. http://www.clark.net/pub/tfa/brocure/brochure-

Thyroid Foundation of America. "Is Your Thyroid Making You Fat." Boston, MA: 25 June 1996.

Tigas, S., J. Idiculla, G. Beckett, and A. Toft. "Is excessive weight gain after ablative treatment of hyperthyroidism due to inadequate thyroid hormone therapy?" *Thyroid* 2000, 10(12): 1107–11.

Toft, Anthony D., M.D. "Thyroid Hormone Replacement—One Hormone or Two?" *N Engl J Med* 340(6) (1999).

Tripathi. Yamini B., et al. "Thyroid Stimulating Action of Z-Guggulsterone Obtained from Commiphora mukul." *Planta Medica* (1) (Feb 1984): 78–80.

University of California at Davis. *MTBE Research*, http://tsrtp.uc-davis.edu/mtbe/

UPI. "Testing urged for thousands of chemicals." 5 October 1998.

Utiger, Robert D., M.D. "Cigarette Smoking and the Thyroid." *N Engl J Med* 333(15) (12 October 1995).

Van Wymelbeke, V., A. Himaya, J. Louis-Sylvestre, and M. Fantino, "Influence of medium-chain and long-chain triacylglycerols on the control of food intake in men." *Am J Clin Nutr* (1998) 68:226–34.

Van Wyk, et al. "The effects of a soybean product on thyroid function in humans." *Pediatrics* 24 (1959): 752–60.

Vliet, Elizabeth Lee, M.D. *Screaming to Be Heard: Hormonal Connections Women Suspect . . . and Doctors Ignore.* New York: M. Evans & Company, 1995.

Walsh, J.P., et al. "Combined Thyroxine/Liothyronine Treatment Does Not Improve Well-Being, Quality of Life, or Cognitive Function Compared to Thyroxine Alone," *J Clin Endocrinol Metabol* 2003 88 (10), 4543–50.

Wang, H., and P.A. Murphy. "Isoflavone content in commercial soybean foods." *J Agric Food Chem.* 42(1994): 1666–73.

Waylonis, G.W., and N.W. Heck. "Fibromyalgia syndrome. New associations." *J Phys Med Rehabil* 71(6) (Dec 1992): 343–48.

Wechsler, Toni. *Taking Charge of Your Fertility: The Definitive Guide to Natural Birth Control, Pregnancy Achievement, and Reproductive Health (Revised Edition).* New York: Quill, 2001.

Weetman, A.P. "Clinical review: Fortnightly review: Hypothyroidism: screening and subclinical disease." *British Medical Journal* 314 (19 April 1997): 1175.

Weil, Andrew. VI.D. *Natural Health, Natural Medicine.* New York: Houghton Mifflin Company, 1990.

Wilson's Syndrome Foundation. Web site, http://www.wilsons syndrome.com

Wolf, J. "Perchlorate and the thyroid gland." *Pharmacol Rev* 50(1) (Mar 1998): 89–105.

Xu, M., et al. "Effect of Chinese herbs on the circadian rhythm of body temperature." *Chung-Kuo Chung Yao Tsa Chih China Journal of Chinese Materia Medica* 4 (21 April 1996): 247–49.

Yiamouyiannis, J. A. "Water Fluoridation and Tooth Decay: Results from the 1986–87 National Survey of U.S. Schoolchildren." *Fluoride* 23, (1990):55–67.

Zha, L. L. "Relation of hypothyroidism and deficiency of kidney yang." *Chung-Kuo Chung Yao Tsa Chih China Journal of Chinese Materia Medica* 13 (4) (1993):202–4.

Zhang, J. Q. "Effects of yin-tonics and yang-tonics on serum thyroid hormone levels." *Chung-Kuo Chung Yao Tsa Chih China Journal of Chinese Materia Medica* II(2) (February 1991).

INDEX

LEARN HOW TO LIVE WELL WITH MARY J. SHOMON

THE THYROID DIET
Manage Your Metabolism for Lasting Weight Loss
ISBN 0-06-052444-8 (paperback)
An estimated 10 million Americans have been diagnosed with thyroid disease, and for the majority of them, losing weight is mentioned time and time again as a primary concern and chief frustration—a challenge made more difficult due to the metabolic slowdown of a malfunctioning thyroid gland. Here, Shomon identifies the factors that inhibit a thyroid patient's ability to lose weight and offers solutions—both conventional and alternative—to help.

LIVING WELL WITH AUTOIMMUNE DISEASE
What Your Doctor Doesn't Tell You . . .
That You Need to Know
ISBN 0-06-093819-6 (paperback)
Containing first-person accounts from patients, doctors, and holistic practioners, as well as check-lists, quizzes, and a proposed recovery plan, Shomon describes in detail the most common autoimmune conditions, what factors make us likely to develop them, how to know the key symptoms, procedures, and treatments, and how to find the right doctors to help you stall and even reverse your condition.

LIVING WELL WITH
CHRONIC FATIGUE SYNDROME AND FIBROMYALGIA
What Your Doctor Doesn't Tell You . . .
That You Need to Know
ISBN 0-06-052125-2 (paperback)
Highlighting the pros and cons of the antibiotic, metabolic/endocrine, hormonal, musculoskeletal, and many other approaches to treatment, Shomon explores the fads and viable alternatives—both conventional and alternative—and provides helpful, clear solutions to help sufferers of fibromyalgia and chronic fatigue syndrome.